# The ART® of Trading

## Trading

*A 7-Step Approach for Traders
and Investors
in the Financial Markets*

SECOND EDITION

Bennett A. McDowell

**WILEY**

Published by John Wiley & Sons, Inc., Hoboken, New Jersey.
Published simultaneously in Canada.

For general information on our other products and services or for technical support, please contact our Customer Care Department within the United States at (800) 762-2974, outside the United States at (317) 572-3993 or fax (317) 572-4002.

Wiley also publishes its books in a variety of electronic formats. Some content that appears in print may not be available in electronic formats. For more information about Wiley products, visit our web site at www.wiley.com.

*Library of Congress Cataloging-in-Publication Data is Available:*

ISBN 9781394171743 (Cloth)
ISBN 9781394171767 (ePDF)
ISBN 9781394171750 (ePub)

Cover Design: Wiley
Cover Image: © Billion Photos/Shutterstock
Author Photo: © Jean McDowell
SKY10091333_112024

*For my wife Jean and
our children, Heather Frances and Brady Bennett,
with love and affection.*

# Contents

# Introduction

It's been 15 years since the first edition of *The ART® of Trading* was released, and all I can say is ". . .time flies when you are having fun!" My philosophy has always been to make work (and trading) fun. When you love what you do, you never work a day in your life.

With that said, of course, the goal in trading and investing is to be successful. At www.TradersCoach.com, we've got a darn good track record in helping traders do just that since 1998. This second edition contains so much brand-new content that we've developed since the first edition, and it is designed to help you be more successful.

My use of multiple time frame analysis, for one, has developed significantly since the first edition and is included in this second edition. And thanks to my terrific coaching students that have helped me discover what works best for them in learning new trading and investing concepts. This new edition includes material they've inspired me to create for you.

My students have made me a better teacher, and I'm grateful.

So, whether you are just discovering us now for the first time, or you are already one of the family, welcome to this adventure we like to call *The ART® of Trading!*

## Revolutionary Learning Experience

You are about to embark on a revolutionary learning experience that will simplify the financial markets for you and very well may simplify how you live your life. This experience will help you focus on reality and is built around these major concepts:

- To be a successful trader and investor, you must look at the *current* market reality as it *is happening* and not get married to opinions, theories, or fantasies about what *will happen.*
- Successful trading and investing is based on *probabilities*—not on *absolutes.* Success comes to those that master how to find and then assess which are the highest probability trades.
- The market will tell you exactly how to trade and invest, if you *know how to listen* to what it is saying.
- Money management is essential; without it you will fail. You must know your risk *before* taking any trade.
- It is essential that you test your rules to ensure that you have a *proven edge* in the market prior to risking real money. Skipping this step leads to lack of confidence and eventual failure.
- Staying *honest* with consistent recordkeeping and tracking of your losses and wins is difficult for new traders. You will find the only way to be profitable for the long term is to maintain honest records on every trade every day.
- Obtaining the *trader's mindset* is a prerequisite for trading and investing with any approach or system to be successful.
- Developing the confidence to *think like a winner* and behave accordingly is an important part of developing the trader's mindset.

- Successful trading and investing requires that you align your *unique personality* with your chosen system.
- Finally, you must have the *perseverance* to become consistently successful.

*The ART of Trading* will show you how to use these concepts to help improve your performance. Have an open mind as you process the material. Some concepts may challenge the inner core of your belief system. While you read this book, try to be receptive so you can fully explore the infinite possibilities available to you.

You may discover that you've developed bad habits that are holding you back. Recognizing these bad habits is the first step. Unlearning these bad habits is the more difficult next step.

> *You must unlearn what you have learned.*
> —Master Yoda, Star Wars

Most important of all is that you embrace the process, and if you stumble and fall on occasion, be sure to get back up. Perseverance is probably the most important trait of any successful person because successful people never quit. See Figure I.1.

## 🎯 It's All About Reality

In 2003, I released trading software called *Applied Reality Trading®*, also known as *ART®*, to the public.

Notice that smack in the middle of the name of this software is the word *reality*, right? That's because to be consistently profitable as traders and investors, we must focus on reality . . . and not get distracted by emotions, illusions, or other people's opinions.

Part of doing that requires that you consciously separate fact from fiction. Which at times, if we have not trained our brains to do so, can be difficult. It is so tempting to give in to a fictional fantasy of getting rich quick with no effort and no risk. Who wouldn't love for that to be reality!

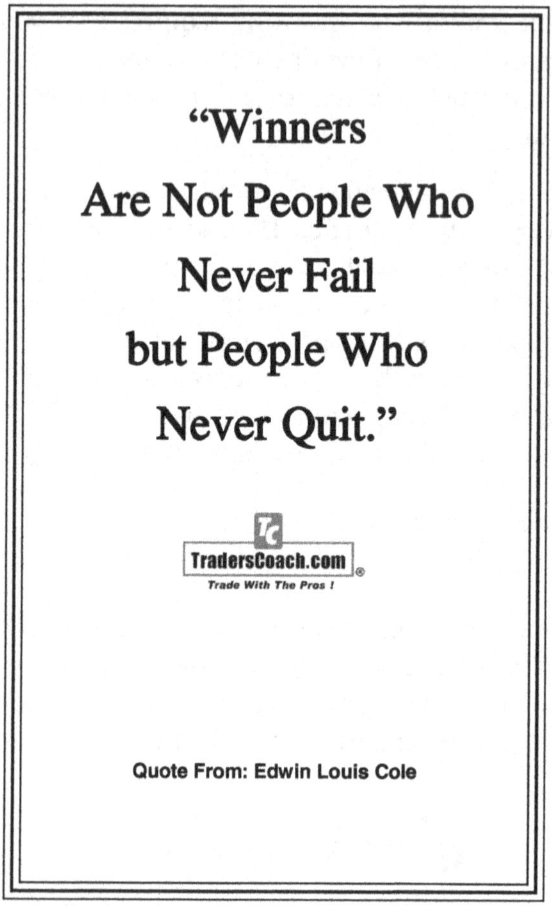

> "Winners
> Are Not People Who
> Never Fail
> but People Who
> Never Quit."
>
> **TradersCoach.com**
> *Trade With The Pros !*
>
> **Quote From: Edwin Louis Cole**

**Figure I.1** MINI POSTER—NEVER QUIT—Being successful at anything, trading and investing included, requires perseverance. This quote is one of my favorites. Quote from Edwin Louis Cole.

Of course, given any deep thought, we all know that succeeding in anything requires taking on some level of risk plus putting in the effort and persistence and pure grit to get there.

Lucky for you, the book in your hands will help you discover how to be successful by focusing on reality using a few simple steps that put you right on track toward reaching your goals.

## The Art Pie

You'll need to develop trading and investing skills in four major areas. Think of an apple pie cut into four slices and call this your ART pie. To be successful, you will need to master every piece of the pie; Figure I.2 illustrates the four major slices.

### The ART pie consists of four major slices:

1. Trading rules
2. Risk management
3. Trader's mindset
4. Debrief your trade

This is where so many fail, by not understanding and mastering all slices of the entire pie. It is a process, one that requires patience and focus. A novice must first become aware and understand that these different skills are all needed to create a consistently successful approach.

No single one piece of the pie will ensure lasting success. Sure, an occasional big win might be attained, but consistency over time is the primary goal. As more experience is gained, the seasoned trader and investor will hone their skills. When consistent positive cash flow over time is acquired, that is the true test of having mastered all pieces of the ART Pie.

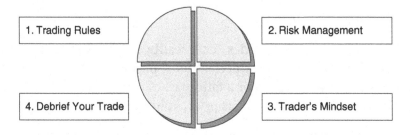

**Figure I.2** The ART pie illustrates that the four major areas of trading and investing are all equally important.

You might be surprised at how many traders in the markets don't have any trading rules to follow. And many of the traders that do have a set of rules, choose to ignore them on a regular basis. But the one area that I find my coaching students resist the most is debriefing the trade and recordkeeping.

Your goal is to become proficient in every slice of the trading pie, and I'm here to help you do just that.

## Layout of this Book

You will find that there are seven sections, or *seven steps to success*, in this book so that you can quickly find the right information as you travel along the path of *The ART of Trading*.

## Step 1: Focus on Reality

Start off by going back to square one. Forget just about everything you may have learned about trading and investing and build a new foundation from the ground up that is based on reality.

Begin by discarding any illusions or bad habits you may have picked up along the way and focus on reality going forward. Use your critical thinking to ask, "Does this make sense to me now?" and then move on from there. If it doesn't make sense to you now, then set it aside.

### Essential Reality Tips

1. You will have losing trades. This reality can be particularly difficult for traders who are perfectionist prone.
2. A trade is not a success or a failure until it is closed.
3. The only thing that is true is price, volume, and momentum.

Keep an open mind as we move forward, and again use your critical thinking to ask, "Does this make sense to me now?"

You may find that your thoughts and beliefs about trading may change as you rebuild and reevaluate your foundation.

## Step 2: Develop the Trader's Mindset

When I first began trading, the term *trading psychology* was thrown around, and my first reaction was "What on earth is that?" Being from New York City, where everyone has a psychotherapist on speed dial, it's not that the idea is foreign to me; it just didn't seem relevant to trading.

Until . . . it hit me, and the lightbulb went off.

After some personal losses and stress and sleepless nights, the idea of thinking about my psychology and how it related to my trading performance made perfect sense. The self-introspection is incredibly useful in determining what causes trading errors and lapses in judgment. I realized that I needed to turn the tables on fear and greed. Instead of letting them rule me, I learned how to rule them.

On the surface you'd think that finance and trading the markets is only about math and numbers and strategies, right? Yes, it is, but there's much more beneath the surface. Many traders would say that 90% of your success is due to your mindset.

In fact, you can give a tested, proven winning set of trading rules to 100 different traders, and they will all have different results based on their trading mindset. Successful traders trade in alignment with themselves and their mindset and not against it.

### Essential Trading Mindset Tips

1. Fear and greed can poison any trader's results, experienced and novice alike, when not detected and confronted head on.
2. Be aware of compulsive trading behavior and the need for an adrenaline rush during the trading day. This may indicate a gambling mindset. Good profitable trading is generally adrenaline free.
3. When you acquire the trader's mindset, you will have a sense of calmness during the trading day and the ability to focus on the present reality.

Generally, the trader's mindset is a "work in progress" since our life journey is constantly presenting new challenges. You've probably heard the saying "past performance does not guarantee future results." Even if you attained the trader's mindset in the past, new events might set you back. In which case it is good to take a break from live trading until you get your *mojo* back.

Any number of events can upset the apple cart and throw you off balance: health issues, family issues, world issues, or even a change in market cycle that gives you an unexpected loss. Not to worry, you can get your trader's mindset back, but until you do, it is important to take care of you first.

## Step 3: Implement Risk Management

Anyone that knows me has heard me say a million times, "Without risk there is no opportunity." Which is why I'm so passionate about risk control. Because once you master risk control, you can truly benefit from the massive opportunity every day in the financial markets.

When you think about it, this applies to trading and life. In life we accept risk every time we get into an automobile, either as a passenger or a driver. To control that risk, we take precautions such as wearing a seat belt, using safety air bags, following speed limits and traffic laws, carrying automobile insurance for both liability and collision, and making sure that the driver's judgment is not impaired by alcohol and the like. These precautions are designed to reduce, not eliminate, risk.

And in this example, the opportunity is that we can drive anywhere we like, cross country and beyond. Think about the freedom that allows us. It is certainly worth the risk, agreed?

It's no different for traders and investors. We understand the risks in the financial markets and to control that risk we take precautions that are designed to reduce, not eliminate, risk. But the opportunity is infinite, so the risk is worth the reward. Stay tuned for a complete strategy to manage your risk in the coming chapters.

**Essential Risk Management Tips**

1. You must respect and believe you need risk management to implement it effectively. Sometimes this respect only comes after a large loss.
2. The best way to think of risk control is to think about getting into a car and speeding at 70 miles an hour *without* a seat belt. You wouldn't think of doing that since statistically you know it means certain death if you were to get in an accident. When trading, always use risk control just as you would always use a seat belt. Then, you will be able to walk away from most accidents to drive (or trade) again.
3. Not every trade will be a winner. Use stop loss exits to help keep your losing trades small so you can let your winning trades ride.

When it comes to risk management, if you do not have any plan in place, it is important to implement one immediately. This step is important in terms of reducing stress and anxiety and avoiding the risk of ruin.

# Step 4: Design Your Trading Rules

Here is where you get to be the captain of your ship and the master of your destiny. Designing your trading rules is a very personal affair because they must serve you and no one else.

Only you know what will work for you. Consider your tolerance for risk, your preferences in markets, your need for speed or not. And remember that rules that might work for another trader may not work for you. Hence you can see the need for testing your rules in a simulated environment prior to trading with your hard-earned cash right off the bat.

There are lots of questions: (a) what market; (b) what size account; (c) what speed, are you a day-trader or investor or somewhere in between; (d) how to identify your entry, exit, and target zone; and (e) how you will manage your risk. The questions are endless, but these give you a head start.

### Essential Trading Rules Tips

1. Keep it simple. Start off slow with the KISS method with your trading rules. The key is to write your rules down on paper and to be sure that your rules include risk control.
2. Test your rules first in a simulated paper trading environment. The temptation is of course to go in with real money ASAP, but I'm all about reality. The cold hard reality is that if you can't be profitable with your rules in a simulated environment, you will do even worse with real money on the line.
3. Practice, practice, practice. Repetition is your friend. Prove to yourself that you can in fact follow your rules, with no cheating, and don't think about the "wins and losses." By just following your rules perfectly, you are winning.

This step in your trading journey is crucial. Some students lack the patience to test and develop their trading rules. Or they jump from one set of rules to another set of rules too quickly, which prevents them from gaining confidence and giving the rules a valid test. Always test new ideas before implementing them with real money.

Be patient with yourself and your set of rules.

## Step 5: Scan For the Best Opportunities

There are countless *trading pick* services, and some of them are good at giving you a starting point to finding the needle in the haystack.

One problem for people using someone else's picks can be that if they don't understand the strategy behind the pick, they are unable to execute the trade effectively. Furthermore, if the service gives you 10 picks and you only take two of them, you run the risk of taking the two losers out of the 10 and missing out on the possible winners. To match the results of the pick provider, you typically must take all their picks.

Which is why you need to develop your own approach to finding trades that work for you with your own strategy. This may come from testing and trial and error, but it must come from you.

Don't blindly rely on picks that you have not personally cleared for takeoff. Trust and then verify. It's the only way you can manage a trade confidently without second guessing the plan. Take ownership and make every trade you pull the trigger on your own.

### Essential Best Scanning Tips

1. Keep a running *watch list* of trade opportunities that you are not quite ready to take but are close to being ready. This is your go-to list for high probability trades that you closely monitor.
2. When the criteria for your set up to take a trade is met, always make sure the risk-to-reward is at least two to one. This means for every $1 at risk the potential reward is $2. This is done by calculating what your trade's *profit target zone* is at the time you are ready to pull the trigger.
3. Develop your scanning skills and learn different approaches to finding the best opportunities. Depending on your trading style, you will choose scanning strategies that complement that. Some popular scans are (a) bracketed market for a trend trade breakout; (b) Elliott wave scans to catch a wave 3 or wave 5 trade; and (c) trend exhaustion scans to catch a new trend in the opposite direction.

Finding the best opportunities in the current market is a developed skill. Depending on what market cycle the overall market is in, you may need to change up your approach. What you will find is that scanning strategies are going to be different depending on whether you are in an overall trending, channeling, or choppy market cycle.

And once you come up with a list of candidates, you will want to filter them down to the highest probability trades.

## Step 6: Manage Your Trade

After pulling the trigger on a trade, complete with the carefully chosen trade size and initial protective stop loss exit in place, you then get to see how it will progress. The right side of the chart is always an unknown. And like a good book or motion picture, no one knows how it will end, which is the magic of it all.

Remember the concept of a "work in progress" that we touched on when talking about the trader's mindset? As you manage every trade, you get to exercise those mindset muscles and build up confidence in yourself and your plan. If you find yourself feeling stress and doubt during the process of managing your trade, make a note of it to review later. But continue to follow your rules.

Your written list of trading rules must map out how you will manage your trade. And your trading mindset will determine how well you will follow your rules and execute the plan. This is where the rubber meets the road.

### Essential Manage Your Trade Tips

1. Always follow your rules when managing your trade, even if you are having anxiety or doubt. Accept and manage your emotions; this will strengthen your trader's mindset.
2. Using a *scaling out* strategy can assist you with managing anxiety when a trade has gone in your favor, it is a way to lock in profit. The only time to use this strategy is when your rules state that you can. For example, "if the trade profit has increased by at least 10%, you can scale out a third of your position" might be put into your rules.
3. When a trade goes against you and hits your stop loss exit, exit the trade immediately. Sounds obvious, but emotions might tempt you to stay in the trade.

Managing trade, after trade, after trade is how you build up the confidence in your trading rules. The repetition of mechanically following the rules like a robot will help you to take the emotion out of the equation.

Emotion can blur your vision and create trading errors that can cost you your trading account. Manage each trade like a pilot navigates his aircraft. There are protocols in place for virtually every scenario, and you must follow them without fail. Practice makes perfect.

# Step 7: Debrief Your Trade

Okay that's a wrap!

The trade is closed, and it's time to debrief. You'll need a checklist of items to review that include but are not limited to (a) profit, loss, or break even; (b) did you follow your rules; (c) were there any trading errors; (d) was there an unexpected market gap up or down; and (e) what could have made the trade better.

To facilitate an effective debrief, you'll need to keep thorough records so that you can look at the current trades and compare them to historical performance in your account. Basically, you want to review your trading from a *micro level* up to a *macro level*.

Which means you will have records of (a) each individual trade on a trade posting card; (b) summary of all trades for each day on a daily ledger; (c) summary of all trades for each week on a weekly ledger; (d) summary of all trades for each month on a monthly ledger; and (e) summary of all trades for each year on an annual ledger.

As you build up a good historical sample size, you can then graph your equity curve, which is essential to evaluate how consistent your performance is over time. Remember, you will have losing trades, and you will also have periods of drawdown, which is normal.

### Essential Debriefing Tips

1. Keep thorough trading records on every trade from a *micro level* to a *macro level*. Log in your records every day and don't let it get behind.
2. Always know your current trading statistics of win ratio and payoff ratio. These numbers are the same as the vitals that a doctor

takes from a patient. Your temperature, blood pressure, oxygen level, etc., are clues that help determine if there is something that needs to be treated. It's the same with your trading vital statistics.

3. The only time you should change your trading rules is after you have enough trades, *a sufficient sample size*, that indicate a change is needed. Never change or break your rules during a live trade. Debriefing enables you to hone your rules and make them better.

By consistently performing your debrief after every trade, you will be able to grow from a novice trader to a master trader. You are encouraged to embrace the debrief so that you can systematically improve your trading every single day.

In trading as in life, there will always be traders who are more successful than you are and ones that will be less successful than you are. Don't get distracted by other traders in trading rooms or elsewhere that make claims of or that have huge wins.

It's best to compete only with yourself; that is where you will make the quickest progress. Go for the little victories, build on those, and keep growing. And remember, account drawdowns and setbacks are not the end of the world. View them as a learning opportunity.

## How Do I Personally Determine Exact Entries and Exits for Each Trade?

Every successful trader has their own unique approach to determining exact entries and exits. All traders must develop their own edge in the markets through trial and error and testing, to find out what works for them.

There is no shortcut and no one-size-fits-all approach. Traders are each unique and will find success when they are able to find the approach that matches their trading personality.

My personal approach to entries and exits is based on a suite of software tools that I developed based on the realities of the market, which are price, volume, and momentum. As mentioned earlier, my software Applied Reality Trading, also known as ART, was released in 2003.

Interestingly enough, prior to creating the ART software, I used to draw all my charts by hand when I managed money for my brokerage clients. My clients asked me how I was able to make money for them in the markets, and that is when I created software, to make it easier for them to see.

The software ended up being a time saver and a life saver and made my job much easier. But the software is nothing more than my manual strategies put into an easier to use format.

So that's the answer to how I personally determine exact entries and exits for each of my trades daily.

## You Don't Have to Use My Software to Benefit from This Book

The examples and charts in this book may be created using my software, but the patterns and lessons are timeless and universal.

You don't have to use my software to be successful in the markets or to benefit from this book. You may already have an entry and exit plan that you are using now. Or you may be searching for a clear reproducible strategy for your entries and exits.

Either way, this book is designed to help you become consistently profitable. You can use the knowledge in this book to either improve the results of your existing approach or to create a brand-new approach from scratch.

Remember, it doesn't matter how you get there, it just matters that you get there. By following the seven steps and sections that follow, you'll be on your way to greater prosperity, more confidence, and less stress in your trading and investing.

I'm excited to begin our journey together.

# Sign-Up For Free Access to "The Art of Trading" Companion TradersCoach.com Website Portal

As a benefit of your book purchase, you are entitled to a companion website access that has supplemental material that will enable you to improve your trading and investing.

This website will be kept up to date with new material so you will always have the current information you need. Use the link here to access this material:

https://www.traderscoach.com/book/

If you need help with access to this portal contact us via email at support@traderscoach.com, and we will supply you with access.

## We're Here For You!

If you'd like more help in your journey to becoming a successful trader and investor, we are here for you every step of the way.

**The following resources may be helpful:**

1. Visit the TradersCoach.com YouTube page for videos that will help you improve: https://www.youtube.com/traderscoach

2. Check out McDowells' books on Amazon.com: https://www.amazon.com/Bennett-McDowell/e/B001JS8NWY

3. Email our support team with any trading or investing questions: support@traderscoach.com

Just know that we are here 24/7, and you can count on us to help you succeed throughout your trading and investing journey. Don't hesitate to reach out.

# Acknowledgments

Thank you to Kevin Harreld at John Wiley & Sons for orchestrating the Second Edition of *The ART® of Trading;* you are a pleasure to work with and we couldn't have done it without you. Also, a shout out to Susan Cerra, senior managing editor: You made the manuscript ready for prime time and your expertise is greatly appreciated. And a special thank you to Richard Samson and Premkumar Narayanan for your patience and attention to detail, and for keeping us on track. This team work made our dream work, deep gratitude to you all!

## Thank You!

So many folks have helped us at *TradersCoach.com®* along the way, and I'd like to send a special thank you to our many wonderful students who have helped to shape the educational content we've developed since 1998. You all know who you are, and we consider you family and enjoy the journey with you past, present, and future.

Much inspiration was given to me by my mother and father, Frances McDowell and Robert McDowell, and I am so grateful to them for their support. Though my father is sadly no longer with us, my mother is still going strong at 103 years old. She is living proof that having a positive attitude in life can work wonders, and I do my best to follow her example.

Last, but most certainly not least, thanks to my wife, Jean McDowell, for your love, for taking care of our family, and for being my best friend and a great partner all wrapped in one.

My deepest thanks go to all of you for making this adventure a fun and exciting one!

Bennett A. McDowell,
December 2024

Thank you to our students around the world who have inspired us since 1998 to create the content in this new edition of *The ART of Trading*; we cherish and appreciate you all!

# Disclaimer

The information in *The ART® of Trading,* Second Edition, is intended for educational purposes only. Readers are strongly advised to do their own research and testing to determine the validity of any trading idea or system. We recommend you consult with your personal advisor(s) such as your accountant, attorney, or money manager prior to implementing any of the information contained in this book.

## Past Performance Does Not Guarantee Future Results

Trading in the financial markets involves substantial risk and TradersCoach.com®, Bennett A. McDowell, or affiliates assume no responsibility for your success or failure in trading or investing in the markets. For this reason, you should only use money you can afford to risk.

Past performance does not guarantee future results, and even if you were successful with your trading and investing in the past, you may not be successful in the future. TradersCoach.com® and Bennett McDowell make no performance guarantee of any kind, and you are encouraged to engage in numerous practice "paper" or "simulated" trades prior to risking any actual money.

Hypothetical or simulated performance results have certain inherent limitations. Unlike an actual performance record, simulated results do not represent actual trading. Since trades have not actually been executed, results may have under- or overcompensated for the impact, if any, of certain market factors, such as lack of liquidity.

No representation is being made that any account will, or is likely to, achieve results like those discussed in this book.

# Epigraph

*"All our dreams can come true, if we have the courage to pursue them."*

—Walt Disney

Walt Disney is an inspirational American film producer who transformed the animation and the entertainment industry. Faced with challenges along the way, he managed to succeed in making his dreams come true. This publicity photograph of Walt Disney was taken on October 23, 1956.
SOURCE: Anonymous Unknown author, Public domain, via Wikimedia Commons

# Step I

# Focus On Reality

# Chapter 1
# Reality Check

*T*he *ART of Trading* is all about reality. The basis of this approach is built on the realities of the market—price, volume, and momentum—and the entire philosophy is centered on facing the truth about your money and the markets. It is also about facing the truth and reality of you.

We live in a world that has evolved with technology to the point where reality can be distorted and concealed. With the stroke of a brush in Adobe Photoshop, images can be retouched and altered, and yet you would never know it. Audio recordings can be fabricated to have your voice say anything.

It's fantastic and frightening all at the same time. All that this means is that we must, more than ever, focus on finding reality.

*We live in a fantasy world, a world of illusion. The great task in life is to find reality*
　　　　　　　　　—Iris Murdoch, philosopher and novelist.

The great task in life, and in trading then, is to find reality. So, now's the time for a *reality check* where you will build a solid foundation from the ground up completely based on the realities of the market and the realities of you. You've got an opportunity to filter out any illusions and replace them with the strength of unshakable truth and solid bedrock.

## Reality-Based Trading and Investing

Reality can be an elusive thing. Our illusions can get in the way and cloud what deep down we know to be true. This is why it's important to focus on finding the truth and the reality of every situation, market, and methodology.

We may be seduced by illusions and fantasies. As humans, it's hard to resist a charming and convincing offer of ". . . an easy profession that takes little to no investment of capital but rewards you with big profits instantly. . . ."

You've seen the infomercials on television. The images of expensive cars, yachts, and luxurious swimming pools are all yours if you sign up for the *offer du jour.* Sounds good enough, don't you think?

But you know deep down, it probably is too good to be true. And it can be a tough pill to swallow when you realize that the fantasy you believed in may be unobtainable.

## Make Your Dreams Come True

Let's take a different approach. Instead of chasing fantasies (that with common sense we know are not true), how about if we follow our dreams and make them come true and make them into reality?

The distinction is that a dream is a genuine goal with realistic opportunity. It might require work and perseverance, but it is well worth the investment once you create the reality toward which you are working.

That is what this book is all about.

We want you to realize your financial goals and dreams and make them into realities by using an approach that is based on reality. You will discover ways to implement money management, risk control, and trading psychology so that every step of the way you are on solid ground with an intelligent plan—designed by you specifically for your personal needs.

## Your Thoughts Create Your Reality

You will not develop the trader's mind-set, which is the *Holy Grail* to trading and investing until you master your mind and your thoughts.

> *Whether you think you can or think you can't, you're right.*
> —Henry Ford, Founder Ford Motor Company

Entrepreneurs, inventors, and visionaries like Henry Ford all need to master their thoughts to achieve greatness. There are obstacles at every turn and to overcome them you must be focused and driven to succeed. As a trader, you are just like Henry Ford. You are creating your reality with your thoughts. And that reality is successful trading.

## Don't Take Thoughts of Failure Lightly

Our thoughts shape our beliefs, which create our reality. In trading, this has profound implications. If we think that we may fail, then we create the seed that shapes our beliefs and manifests failure, all because we just think it.

High achievers maintain a philosophy that failure is not an option and that it pays to be a winner. They think of positive outcomes and envision themselves as being successful. See Figure 1.1.

Traders and investors who experience thoughts of failure should not take them lightly. Instead, they must find out what is causing these thoughts and take action to understand them and then to eliminate them. Traders who fear failure will ultimately fail.

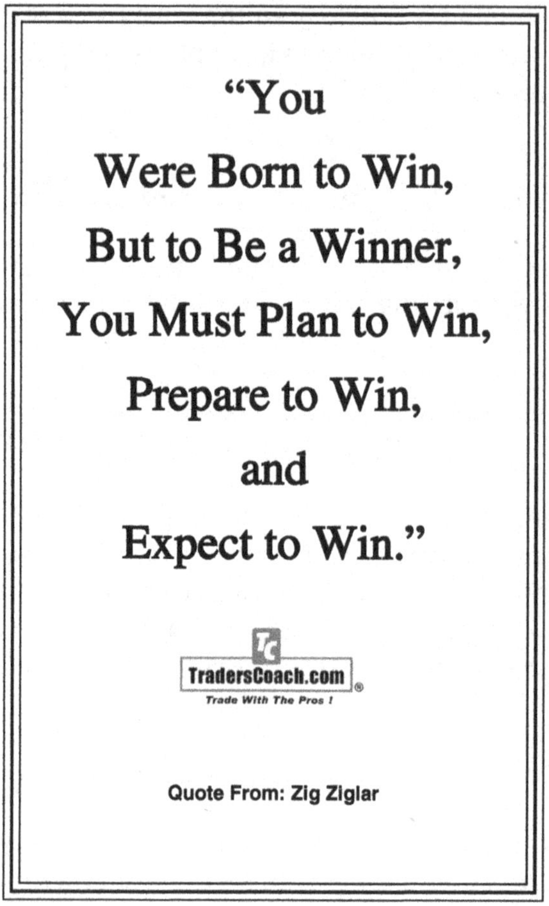

> ## "You
> ## Were Born to Win,
> ## But to Be a Winner,
> ## You Must Plan to Win,
> ## Prepare to Win,
> ## and
> ## Expect to Win."
>
> **TradersCoach.com**
> *Trade With The Pros !*
>
> **Quote From: Zig Ziglar**

**Figure 1.1** MINI POSTER—EXPECT TO WIN—It is not enough to want to win and to be successful. As this quote states, you must plan to win, prepare to win, and most of all, expect to win. Quote from Zig Ziglar.

If you have these thoughts, don't trade until these thoughts are dealt with and you are able to control them. You must confront them and remove their power, so they don't occupy your mind.

If not, they will sabotage you until your worst fear becomes a reality.

## Choose and Protect Your Thoughts Carefully

Your life literally depends on it. If this concept is new to you, keep an open mind to the power of your thoughts. The quality of your life truly depends on your ability to choose and protect your thoughts.

- You may not even be aware that you have thousands of thoughts daily.
- Your thoughts shape your beliefs.
- These beliefs create emotions such as fear and greed.
- Fear and greed drive markets and life itself.
- Ultimately, you live your beliefs, which create your reality.
- What's important to understand is that the thoughts you energize the most will shape your reality more than those that you don't energize.
- It is possible to change your thoughts consciously, which in turn can change your beliefs, change your reality, and change your trading results.
- Trading is a vehicle that will reveal your core beliefs.
- Financial markets have an uncanny knack for ferreting out your weaknesses and your destructive thoughts.
- So choose and protect your thoughts carefully and only energize the ones that will create the reality you desire.

This one concept, about how to choose and protect your thoughts, is so powerful that it alone it could change your trading and investing for the better.

## The Good News

There are effective strategies to rewire your brain and change your thoughts, and I will share them with you in the fitness chapter. These strategies can help improve your trader's mindset and your results.

*Progress is impossible without change; and those who cannot change their minds and their thoughts cannot change anything.*
        —George Bernard Shaw, playwright and novelist

For now, just know that once you are more aware of your thoughts, you will be able to work on eliminating the negative ones and building up the positive ones. And once you find the positive thoughts that work for you, be sure to protect them.

You'll also find that some of the fear and lack of confidence you may have now will naturally dissipate by creating a solid plan that is designed for you and by you. When you start to see small victories along the way, you will become energized to raise the bar and go for bigger victories.

That was then and this is now. Whatever challenges you may have had before can stay in the past. Trade and invest in this present moment, just as you can live your life in the present moment. The future and the past have no bearing on the now.

Again, remember to always trade in the present moment and the present reality.

# Chapter 2
# Perception Versus Reality

There is perception, and there is reality, and sometimes it's hard to distinguish between the two. Our eyes, our minds, and our emotions can deceive us with illusions, and it is important to be mindful of this possibility. Traders and investors who stray from reality and are overcome with false perceptions are likely to lose money in the markets.

We must be forever diligent in seeking out reality to succeed over time in the financial markets. It is not always an easy road, it is one that requires effort, but the payoff is well worth it.

## William James Was the Father of American Psychology

This guy was a rock star in his time. Born in 1842 at the Astor House in New York City to a rather wealthy family, he was destined to make his mark on American psychology.

His work delving into the mind and how it works changed the face of medicine. Countless quotes are attributed to him with exceptional insights into human emotions and the power of our thoughts, perception, and reality. One such quote is quite relevant in that as traders and investors if we change our thoughts, we can change our reality. See Figure 2.1.

Our psychology has a profound effect on our results, and if we are willing to change our thoughts and respect the intense power of them, it is possible to change our reality.

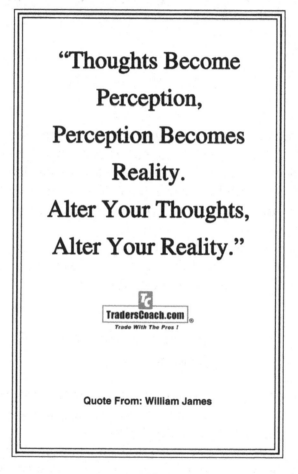

**Figure 2.1**   MINI POSTER—THOUGHTS, PERCEPTION, AND REALITY—Psychologist William James circa 1900 sums up the importance of how your thoughts create your reality. Which in turn determines your chances of success in trading and investing. Quote from William James.

## Perception Can Be Determined
## by Perspective

Perceptions can be different between people simply because of their *perspective* and *where they are standing* . . . literally. In this case, it is not a matter of false perceptions; it is a matter of different points of view that are both correct but opposite.

Figure 2.2 illustrates how two individuals can see the same data and stimuli and process the data differently because they are standing in different places that allow them to see only their version of the truth and the reality.

**Figure 2.2**   This illustration is of two individuals looking at the same information (a number laying on the ground). Each person sees something different; one sees a number 6 and the other sees a number 9. They are both correct. You can see that based on *where you are standing* and what your *perspective* is, you may see the same trading signals differently than another trader.

# Seeing Reality Clearly Helps Our Bottom Line

As traders, seeing reality clearly will help our bottom line. You are going to see how our unique perceptions can sometimes cloud our understanding of the current reality. These perceptions may even be false. This inhibits our ability to effectively respond. In turn, our response when we rely on false perceptions can dramatically alter our outcomes in a negative way.

There are ways to sharpen our awareness of the current reality. One way is first to be aware that our personal perceptions even exist at all. They can throw us off course without us even realizing it. Another way is to change our thought processes to rewire our brain to create more positive and accurate perceptions.

Let's look at a few of the different ways our unique perceptions can be influenced.

# Three Factors That Influence Your Trading

Figure 2.2 begins to help us understand the complexity of perception versus reality. When trading, the quality of your data and your interpretation of that data creates a make-or-break situation. Which is why you always want to start with the best signals to tell you when to get in or out of the market.

The next question is, even with the best signals, how will you and your unique perspectives and biases process these signals? The answer depends on three different factors that play a huge role in your trading performance:

1. **Visual Perception:** How do your eyes and your brain process the visual data they are receiving?
2. **Emotional Perception:** How does your emotional state impact the data you are receiving?
3. **Environmental Perception:** How do your past and present environment create perspectives that may influence the data you are receiving?

**The power of perceptions and perspectives may surprise you.**

And it may be these unique aspects of each trader that make it near impossible for any two traders to trade the same system and get the same results. Each trader's perceptions of the market and their relationship to fear and greed is different. This will determine the outcome of their trades and investments, even with the same tools and approach.

# 1. Visual Perception

This topic is fun, and it always entertains me to look at the visual examples that show how our eyes can in fact play tricks on us. Look at Figures 2.3, 2.4, 2.5, and 2.6, which illustrate how our brains process visual information and can create illusions. As always, a picture is worth a thousand words.

These optical illusions occur because of the way the neurons in our brain interact. The way our minds perceive stimuli both visually and intellectually is not always reality. We must be conscious of

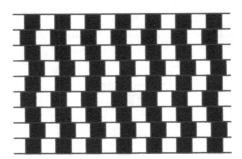

**Figure 2.3** Café Wall Illusion—Get your ruler out because those seemingly wavy, bent lines are in fact perfectly straight. This phenomenon was first described in 1973 by Richard Gregory, a professor of neuropsychology at the University of Bristol.

**Figure 2.4**   Scintillating Grid Illusion—Discovered by E. Lingelbach in 1994, this illusion is considered a variation of the Hermann grid illusion that was reported by Ludimar Hermann in 1870. Try to count the black dots. You will find that there really aren't any black dots, even though your brain may think otherwise.

**Figure 2.5**   Chubb Illusion—This illusion was observed by Chubb and colleagues in 1989. Fold the page of this book to lay the two inner squares of this image next to each other. You will find they are exactly the same shade, even though the right inner square seems lighter than the left inner square.

**Figure 2.6**   Figure Ground Perception—There is a tendency of our visual system to simplify a scene into the main object that we are looking at (the figure) and everything else that forms the background (or ground). This classic example of the "faces or vases" illusion, also known as the Rubin vase, is like Figure 2.1 in that whether you see the *face* or the *vase*, you are correct. It's a bit like the psychological "ink blot" tests. What did you see first, the face or the vase?

this fact to guard against misinterpreting market information and losing money by reacting to an illusion as opposed to seeing and understanding the market reality for what it is.

Now look at Figures 2.7 and 2.8 to see how these optical illusions can relate to your trading. Our sensory perception of the same information can deliver quite different emotions.

The daily chart in Figure 2.7 seems to show a calm sideways market with not much action to speak of. In contrast, Figure 2.8 shows a dramatic break to the downside with a gap down; it seems like a completely different chart.

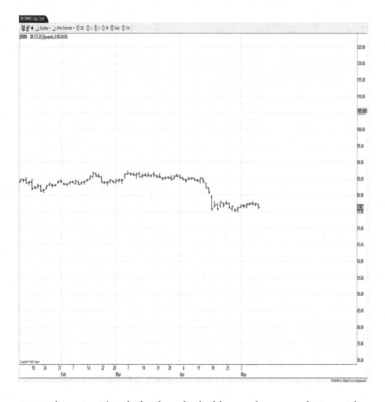

**Figure 2.7**  Chart A—This daily chart looks like a calm, meandering, sideways market.

SOURCE: eSignal. Published by eSignal (www.esignal.com).

**Figure 2.8**   Chart B—This daily chart looks like a dramatic gap to the downside.
SOURCE: eSignal. Published by eSignal (www.esignal.com).

**The reality is that Figure 2.7 and Figure 2.8 are the same chart.**

Both contain the same information; they are just sized differently. The same time frame, same market, same everything. Lesson here is to use caution when sizing your charts, since this can have a dramatic impact on how you perceive market information, which in turn can determine how you enter and exit the market.

## 2. Emotional Perception

Just as visual perception can cloud our judgment with optical illusions, emotional perception can cloud our judgment as well. Becoming aware is the best way to combat the tendency to stray from reality. It's helpful to be introspective enough to understand our own personal emotional perceptions.

We've all got good days and bad days. The emotions we feel during these days will color our emotional perceptions from rosy on good days to not so rosy on bad days. It stands to reason that our trading will be influenced by the emotions we are feeling on any given day.

Be conscious of days you feel strong negative emotions of anger, fear, and hopelessness. These emotions will cloud your judgment and will lead to poor trading.

### Emotional Perception Exercise for Traders

Without thinking, write down what animal the financial market signifies to you . . . super-fast . . . just write it down on a piece of paper . . . or write it down here in this book. Don't read any further until you write down what animal you think of when you think of the financial markets.

### What animal does the market signify to you?

Did you make a note of the animal that you think of when you think of the financial markets? YES? Okay, now you can continue reading.

### Your answer will tell you a lot about your beliefs about the market.

First, think about the animal you chose and then write down how you feel about your animal and your answers to the questions in this list:

- How do you feel about this animal?
- What is the most important characteristic of this animal?
- Is it a friend or a foe or somewhere in between?
- Do you respect this animal?
- Is it smart or not so smart?
- Are you afraid of this animal?
- Is it a fast or a slow animal?

- Can this animal deceive you or hurt you?
- Is the animal predictable or unpredictable?

The animal you chose is not the most important part of this exercise. What is important is *how you feel* about the animal. Because that is how you will know what your emotional relationship to the financial market is. See Table 2.1 to see what your animal tells you.

For example, sometimes people will select a bear. To some folks a bear is the most frightening and dangerous animal on the planet. And to others a bear is a cuddly, friendly strong animal. Others might select a dog, and they might be terrified of dogs, or they might have a favorite pet that is a dog that is loyal and loving. Then there are sneaky animals like snakes, and fast animals like cheetahs.

You can see that the clues are not found in the animal you chose but instead in what you think of that animal. Whichever characteristics you associate with the animal you chose are the characteristics you associate with the financial markets.

## Fear of the Market

When your animal is dangerous and can hurt or deceive you, the likelihood is your underlying emotion is that you are afraid of the financial markets. If you feel the market is threatening or tricky or hostile, you will continue to trade from a fearful mindset until you can resolve these feelings. This negative fear of the markets can present itself by causing inappropriate trading responses. Usually, fearful traders exit the market too quickly or cannot "pull the trigger" at the right time to get in the market. This fear causes them to lose money.

Table 2.1  Look at this table to determine what your emotional relationship is to the financial markets. Are you: fearful of the market, respectful of the market, or have no fear of the market?

| Fear of the Market | Respect of the Market | No Fear of the Market |
|---|---|---|
| Your animal is dangerous and can hurt you or deceive you. | Your animal is smart and powerful, but you are not afraid of it. | Your animal is a cuddly sweet pet that wouldn't hurt a fly. |

## Respect the Market

If your animal is smart and powerful, but you are not afraid of it, you have a healthy balance of caution and confidence that you can handle anything the market throws at you. Your emotional relationship with the market is one of respect. This is the ideal outcome to this exercise.

## No Fear of the Market

Now, if your animal is so cuddly and nonthreatening that it wouldn't hurt a fly, chances are you have a dangerous lack of respect for the power of the markets. Taken to the extreme, this will lead to a lackadaisical unstructured trading approach leading to poor risk control and eventual loss. This may come from inexperience, and it is important to develop a healthier respect for the markets before any active trading in the markets.

## What Now?

The purpose of this exercise is to find out where you are right now in terms of your relationship with the markets. You may need to work on where you are by either reducing your fear of the markets or by increasing your respect of the markets.

Your first step is being aware of your emotional perceptions of the market and how these perceptions can influence your trading performance.

# 3. Environmental Perception

Everyone comes from a unique environment and background. Your current and past environment will influence your belief system and the direction you take in life. A lot of what we believe can be achieved comes from what we have learned from our families, school, heroes, and our environment. Observation of cause and effect plays a big part as well.

For example, if we have seen that our parents went to college and the effect of that was a good paying job we may choose that path. Or maybe we learned that our hero Steve Jobs chose to skip college and went on to become one of the most wealthy and influential men in history, then that path may be more appealing to us.

Depending on which cause and effect our environment has conditioned us to appreciate, we will have a different perception of data and information that is provided to us. And we will adapt our behavior and our path accordingly.

The goal is to overcome any negative environmental perceptions we may have, just like Jack Canfield, author and motivational speaker, did with his *Chicken Soup for the Soul* book series.

## Jack Canfield, Gives an Example of Negative Environmental Perception He Overcame

Jack Canfield is a motivational speaker best known as the cocreator of the *Chicken Soup for the Soul* book series (along with coauthor Mark Victor Hansen).

**Here's is Jack Canfield's story about overcoming his environmental perceptions in his own words:**

*I grew up with a very negative father who thought that rich people were people that had ripped everyone off and thought that anyone that had money must have deceived somebody.*

*So, I grew up with a lot of beliefs about money; that if you had it, it made you bad, only evil people have money, and money doesn't grow on trees. "Who do you think I am, Rockefeller?" That was one of his favorite phrases.*

(continued on next page...)

*(...continued from previous page)*

*It was only when I met W. Clement Stone that I began to shift my life. When I was working with Stone he said, "I want you to set a goal that's so big that if you achieved it, it would blow your mind, and you would know it's only because of what I've taught you that you would have achieved this goal."*

*At the time I was making about eight thousand dollars a year, so I said, "I want to make a hundred thousand dollars in a year." Now, I had no idea how I could do that. I saw no strategy, but I just said, "I'm going to declare that I'm going to believe it, I'm going to act as if it's true." So, I did that.*

*About four weeks after that, I had a hundred-thousand-dollar idea. It just came right into my head. I had a book I had written, and I said, "If I can sell four hundred thousand copies of my book at a quarter each, that'd be a hundred thousand dollars."*

*About six weeks later I gave a talk at Hunter College in New York to six hundred teachers, and afterward a woman approached me and said, "That was a great talk. I want to interview you." That article came out and our book sales started to take off.*

*To make a long story short, I did not make a hundred thousand dollars that year. We made ninety-two thousand three hundred and twenty-seven dollars.*

**The Moral of the Story:** Is that if you can overcome negative environmental perceptions, like Canfield did, there's no telling what you can accomplish.

Source: This Jack Canfield excerpt is from a book entitled *The Secret*, by Rhonda Byrne, Atria Books, 2006, starting on page 95.

# Ask Yourself, "Is the Glass Half Full or Is it Half Empty?"

Considering all that we have covered in this chapter, ask yourself, "Am I a glass half full person, or am I a glass half empty person?" Your trading results may in fact be affected by your answer to this question without you even realizing it.

If you answered that you are a glass half full person, then your optimism and positive thoughts may help you in finding opportunity where other traders fail to find anything of value. And you may be able to find solutions where others find only more problems. Cautious optimism is a beneficial quality for traders.

On the other hand, if you currently see yourself as a glass-half-empty person, your pessimism and negative thoughts may cause you to find problems and threats where none exists. This state of mind is dangerous for traders. See Figure 2.9.

### Pessimism Versus Optimism

Do you have a tendency toward either pessimism or optimism? While pessimists expect the worst outcome, optimists expect the best outcome. Some research suggests that the left brain drives optimism, and the right brain drives pessimism. See Table 2.2.

Table 2.2   This table outlines some of the possible characteristics associated with both optimism and pessimism.

| Optimism | Pessimism |
| --- | --- |
| Left brain driven | Right brain driven |
| Dominant side | Nondominant side |
| Focus on the positive | Focus on the negative |
| Bright attitude | Gloomy attitude |
| Masters of their destiny | Slaves to good or bad luck |
| Glass half full | Glass half empty |
| Power | Weakness |

**Figure 2.9**    One measure of what your visual, emotional, and environmental perceptions are, is to ask yourself, "Am I a glass-half-full person, or am I a glass-half-empty person?" Your trading results may in fact be affected by your answer to this question.
SOURCE: Photo 29005303 @ Andreykuzmin Dreamstime.com

Whether you are a pessimist or optimist can play a role in your perceptions when trading. Negative thoughts created by pessimism can lead to a self-fulfilling prophecy. For example, if your thoughts are consumed with "I will never be successful at this . . . ," you may create your own reality with your thoughts of failure.

Conversely, an optimist's positive thoughts when energized can lead to more successful outcomes when trading.

*Pessimism leads to weakness. Optimism leads to power.*
        —William James, Father of American psychology

It may not be possible to change from a pessimist into an optimist overnight. And yet, the idea of changing your thoughts from negative to more positive may be a good one in terms of improving your psychological perceptions when trading.

**Remember, your thoughts create your reality.**

## ◎ Which Thoughts Do You Energize?

At the end of the day, thoughts and perceptions are fleeting. They only take on more meaning when you *energize* them.

That is an important word, *energize*, because it is the thoughts that you give the most attention to or maybe even obsess over that become very powerful beliefs. And these beliefs have the power to ultimately change your reality.

### Which Do You Energize More, Your Wins or Your Losses?

Successful traders typically win about 60% of the time. No trader ever wins every trade. Which means you will have losing trades; it is a cost of doing business. You know your system has an edge and that over time on average you will be profitable.

So if you have a losing trade, or a series of losing trades, do you energize that more than you energize your wins? The reason for this question is that it is a dangerous habit to over-energize your losses.

Yes, you want to debrief and determine if the loss was due to a trading error or was it just part of a normal drawdown. After that, let it go and move on. To over-energize your losses will lead to more losses. Simple as that.

# Chapter 3
# Too Good to Be True?

**M**any trading and investing tools and services are available to you today. Some will boast fabulous returns and provide examples. They may even claim that you can "get rich quick" with little or no effort. How disappointing for you to find that even when you use that system or stock picking service, those fabulous returns are usually unobtainable when you implement them yourself.

So, use your critical thinking and ask yourself with every new approach, ". . . does this make sense, or does it sound too good to be true?"

## System Rates of Return Are Meaningless

Just about every system can work profitably over an isolated period. It is consistency that counts. That can be misleading too.

Why?

Because every trader and investor will implement the same system differently based on their own unique trading personality and as a result will produce different results. So even if the creator of a system generates consistent success, you may not.

We will focus on customizing a system to your unique trading personality with the approach you are now discovering in this book. It will include a foundation of solid money management, trading psychology, and tested trading rules. We want you to concentrate on developing your skills so you can see how your own performance has the unlimited potential to improve.

While *The ART of Trading* will teach you how to trade and invest using the realities of the market, one of the most important aspects of it lies in its flexibility. It can be tailored specifically to you and to the realities of you.

And you will ultimately design *your own* approach, which can be a powerful force.

## The Art of Trading Approach Is Not a Black Box System

The reality is there is no such thing as a black box system. They fall under the umbrella of "too good to be true."

Some folks may tell you that their system or approach can offer you a 100% mechanical solution that requires no discretionary decisions. The truth and reality is that these black box systems don't work well over time because they can't adapt to ever-changing market cycles.

What you want to do is become a "master trader and investor," blending your beliefs with your trading tools to produce a unique financial approach that you can implement in any market condition or cycle.

Master traders and investors use trading tools to help them make financial decisions. Trading and investing is not simplistic—there are far too many market variables for trading tools alone to make all your decisions for you.

And the most important trading tool you have is the one between your ears. Your brain is the best tool you have because you can train it to see things that a black box system would never see.

The most successful traders have developed the necessary trading skills that encompass risk control, trading psychology, ability to manage their response to fear and greed, discipline, and identifying the different types of market cycles and knowing how to adapt to them.

By the time you complete *The ART of Trading* program, you will have firsthand experience in how to integrate your belief system into your discretionary decisions to adapt to a variety of market conditions.

## Identifying Market Cycles Is Essential

Markets move in cycles, and each time frame (even in the same market) can experience a different cycle as well.

**The primary market cycles are:**

- trending
- consolidating
- breaking out of a consolidation
- corrective

Different cycles warrant different trading approaches. This is why The *ART of Trading* approach is not a black box system—you need to adjust your style and adapt as the market changes. You need to adapt to changing market cycles. The key to being consistently profitable is to master your trading skills in different market cycles.

Markets can also experience volatility changes. Certain market cycles are accompanied by changes in volatility. A change in volatility can also be caused by traders on other time frames dominating that market. This can cause unexplained volatility on the time frame you are trading and may cause you to experience losses.

You will need to learn how to trade in a variety of market cycles and in relation to your own style.

# Why Do 90% of All Traders Lose Money?

Don't let this 90% statistic intimidate you because the reality is that in most professions, only about 10% of the people make it to the top anyway. It is quite normal.

### Traders fail for several reasons:

- No structured trading rules
- Risk control not used
- Unable or unwilling to do the work that is needed
- Don't know what they don't know
- Never attain the traders mindset
- Set in their ways, unable to break bad habits
- Lack perseverance and grit to work through problems

You may even be able to add some reasons to the list you may have experienced along the way. At the end of the day, trading the financial markets is rewarding, but it is also hard work. See Figure 3.1.

Every trader must believe that failure is not an option to reach the winner's circle. Only those with a winning attitude and perseverance will survive the financial markets and come out on top.

# Practice Makes Perfect

Take, for example, the person who wants to play the piano. The first step is to buy a piano, take lessons, and practice.

Many who start may not realize the commitment it will take to play well. In fact, when they find out how much time and practice and the number of lessons they will need, many give up. It is just too much work for them. Also, some may not have a musical ear or the ability or aptitude to master the piano.

**Figure 3.1** MINI POSTER—DRESSED IN OVERALLS—There is an infinite amount of opportunity in the financial markets. Finding it though requires effort on the part of the trader or investor. Quote from Thomas Edison.

This is a good analogy for learning to trade because the commitment, ability, and aptitude to master trading is like that of learning to play the piano.

Playing music is the ability to integrate yourself with your musical instrument to create your own unique expression. Trading is no different. Master traders or investors integrate their beliefs with their system or approach to create desired results.

Just as with learning to master the piano, trading involves developing your skills to a level where you are profitable on a consistent basis which will take time and a lot of practice.

## 🎯 There Are No "Minor League" Trading Markets

The minute you place a live trade with real money in any financial market, you are most definitely playing in the "major leagues." You are up against the most experienced and talented players.

Unlike certain sports where you are paired up with players who have similar skills, in trading there is only one game in town. You can't work your way from "little" league to "minor" league to "major" league.

To win consistently in the "major leagues" of trading, you must become a major league player. You can do this by implementing structured trading rules with risk management along with the discipline to adhere to these rules. Understand though that you will be playing with the best of the best every day. You must be ready for that.

# Chapter 4
# Price, Volume, and Momentum

T here are no greater realities in trading than price, volume, and momentum. Based on actual, live, real-time data coming from the exchanges, they are not opinions, and they cannot be distorted or misrepresented.

Price patterns represent the history of where price has travelled, and the momentum represents how fast price has travelled over time. Together, they are the footprint of the market.

As you continue reading, you'll begin to appreciate that price, volume, and momentum are your most reliable and trustworthy tools in reading the market. See Figure 4.1.

## Definition of Price, Volume, and Momentum

Technical traders and investors look at price, volume, and momentum on charts to see what patterns are occurring in the markets. These current patterns can give us clues as to what the market is likely to do in the future based on historical patterns from past market activity.

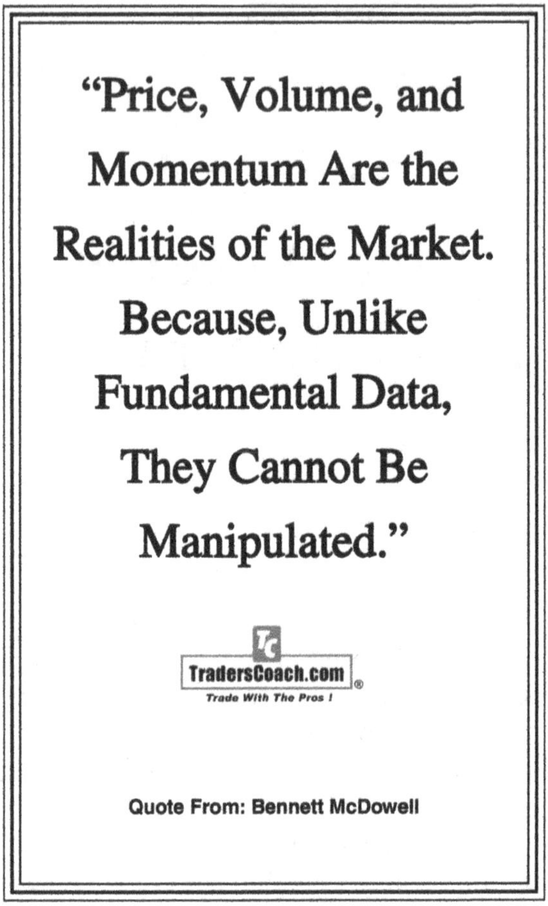

**Figure 4.1** MINI POSTER—PRICE, VOLUME, AND MOMENTUM — Fundamental data can be distorted and misrepresented by the companies reporting the data. Case in point is the Enron scandal, where in 2001 the company went bankrupt due to illegally hiding mountains of debt from its investors and submitting falsified accounting reports. Quote from Bennett McDowell.

### Definitions to give you a better under standing:

- **Price:** This refers to the last traded price which may be higher, lower or the same as the previous price during a given period.
- **Volume:** The total number of shares or contracts traded during a given period.
- **Momentum:** It is how fast price moves over time and it occurs on both low and high volume. Depending on whether price is

changing quickly or slowly during a given period, will indicate either fast or slow momentum.

For example, price, volume, and momentum can be measured based on how much they changed during the following periods:

- 15 seconds
- 1 minute
- 5 minutes
- 10 minutes
- 60 minutes
- Daily
- Weekly
- Monthly
- Yearly

These time frames are just a small sample of periods that are available to traders and investors. It is important to select very specific time frames based on your strategies. Through testing you will determine which works best for you.

### Note About Tick Charts

Many futures and forex traders use tick charts. These charts are different from fixed time-based intervals like the 1-minute or 60-minute chart. With tick charts instead of a time interval, each bar is created when a specific/given number of transactions are executed or the price moves.

Some feel that tick charts help in reducing the amount of noise on the chart as opposed to time-based charts.

## ◎ Why Are Price, Volume, and Momentum Reality?

When there is no interpretation or manipulation of data, then it can be relied on as real. Therefore, price, volume, and momentum data that you receive directly from the exchanges are the best realities of the market you will ever find.

The closer you are to the origin of the data, the more it can be relied on. For example, when reviewing fundamental data on corporate earnings and such, there is always a possibility that the data may have been manipulated. Or when listening to a financial news network, you cannot know for sure if you are hearing a newscaster's opinion or hearing facts.

The beauty of price, volume, and momentum data is that there is no middleman or interpreter (other than your data provider) that will distort the information you are relying on. You are getting the information directly from the horse's mouth.

This is why price, volume, and momentum are your best friends when trading and investing in the financial markets. These are market truths, which are the realities of the market. Your trading tools should incorporate the use of these truths in making your trading decisions.

Figure 4.2 shows how price, volume, and momentum data give you a picture of the market. Just as with this chart, a picture is worth a thousand words. On this chart you can clearly see the 2008 crash

**Figure 4.2** This chart of the DJIA, Dow Jones Industrial Average, illustrates how price, volume, and momentum will look on a chart when it is plotted on the TIME and PRICE axis. You can see the patterns created tell the story of where the market has been. The right side of the chart is always an unknown and will only reveal itself by telling you where the market is going, after the fact.
SOURCE: NinjaTrader. www.ninjatrader.com

where the market experienced the biggest single day drop in history up to that point. And then of course you can see the COVID-19 crash of 2020 clear as a bell.

## Live Market Data

To implement the strategies in *The ART of Trading*, you will need to obtain a live market data feed that comes directly from the exchanges. You may already have this, but if not, refer to the back of this book for references to good live market data providers.

**There are several types of live streaming data feeds that you can sign up for including:**

- **Real time data:** Delivered by the minute during the trading day. Generally, data providers charge more money for real-time data because it is more labor intensive to provide. Real-time data are used by day traders. With this type of data, you can use any type of chart from tick, minute, 5-minute, etc.
- **Delayed data:** Typically, there is a 10-minute to 20-minute delay on the data. There is always a danger in day trading with delayed data because you will get the information later than other traders. Sometimes you might not know you are receiving delayed data if the data are throttled or slowed down due to a variety of issues.
- **End of day data:** Is provided at the end of the day and gives you final price and volume information for the markets each day. This type of data is less expensive than real-time data. End of day data are used primarily by investors and position traders. Charts will be limited to daily, weekly, monthly, etc.

Depending on which market(s) you are interested in trading, separate data feed packages may be needed. Each market varies in cost, since the costs from the *exchange fees* that are charged by each individual market exchange varies.

Many traders and investors receive a data feed and charting platform included with their brokerage account free of charge. The reason brokers can absorb the cost of providing the data and charting platform is that they make money on commissions.

## Charting Platform

To implement the strategies in *The ART of Trading*, you will need to obtain a charting platform. You may already have this, but if not, refer to the back of this book for references to good charting platforms, some of which are free of charge.

**Your charting platform, depending on how robust it is, can provide you with several things including but not limited to the following:**

- Charting that plots price, volume, and momentum movement
- A *trading simulator* for paper trading and testing
- Market scanning tools
- Fibonacci and Elliott wave tools
- Market depth tools
- Order flow VWAP tools
- Volume profile tools
- Options tools
- Seasonality tools
- News feeds
- Videos and education to master the platform

Many traders and investors receive a data feed and charting platform included in their brokerage account free of charge.

You may decide that all you need is your brokerage account data and charting platform. Although, when looking for specific features and benefits, it sometimes makes sense to purchase an additional add on package.

## Dangerous Opinions

Strive to create an environment without opinions. That means avoid reading financial newspapers, watching financial TV, or listening to financial news in any form while trading.

News programs form opinions, and market analysts form opinions. We do not know how the markets will react to news and financial recommendations. If we think we do, then we are forming an opinion about the news.

How many times have companies come out with great earnings and sold off right after the announcement. And when the market does sell off, the news commentator comes out and says "... the stock had run up already in expectation of the good numbers and then sold off. ..." If instead the stock continued upward, the news commentator would say, "... good earnings drove the market upward. ..." News commentators operate on 20/20 hindsight. We do not have this luxury.

Listen to what the market is saying through price action, volume, and momentum.

## Supply = Demand

When supply equals demand, both the seller and the buyer disagree on value, but agree on price. This is important.

It is a truth in the marketplace when this happens. The amount of supply and demand occurring in the market at any time is represented by *volume*. That also is a truth. Both price and volume are absolute and are truths of the market because they are not distorted.

## Overbought and Oversold Conditions

Markets work to bring price in line with supply and demand. Markets are perfectly efficient. If supply always equals demand, then how can a market be overbought or oversold? It may be expensive, but *expensive* can be a relative term.

### The Market Itself Is Never Overbought or Oversold—Think About It

For example, suppose you purchased a painting by a currently unknown artist/painter for $1,000. The next week your artist/

painter gets reviewed in a famous magazine and his work is now nationally recognized, so your painting increases in value to $1,500. Some say that your painting is too expensive or that prices are now overbought because it went up in value too quickly in just one week.

What if the next week a famous collector buys a similar painting by the same artist/painter for $4,000, and now the value of your painting increases to $3,000?

All the indicators said that it was overbought at $1,500 because the price went up too high in a short period. The reality is that because of supply and demand, prices are exactly where they should be—regardless of the reasons.

I will say it again, when supply equals demand, both the seller and the buyer disagree on value, but agree on price. There is no such thing in an efficient market as overbought and oversold. Prices are where they are because that is where they are supposed to be.

# Chapter 5

# Get Down to Business

Y ou are building a real business; make sure your mindset reflects that. Just like a restaurateur has accounting to do, food that spoils, profitable and not so profitable periods, overhead to pay, and funding needs, you will face similar business challenges.

Food that spoils is like being stopped out of trades, money gone. Overhead to pay is like having to buy computers, internet access, trading software, data feed services, brokerage fees, and maybe an office. You'll have profitable periods and then periods of draw down, and you'll need to keep an eye on your cash flow.

Also, when you approach this as a business, your psychology will change to that of a professional. It will be easier to succeed if you approach your trading and investing as a business rather than a hobby.

## You Are an Entrepreneur Now

They, the entrepreneurs that is, can decide at a moment's notice to just take off on Tuesday or just take off all next week, because they are the boss. They have the freedom to call the shots and make their

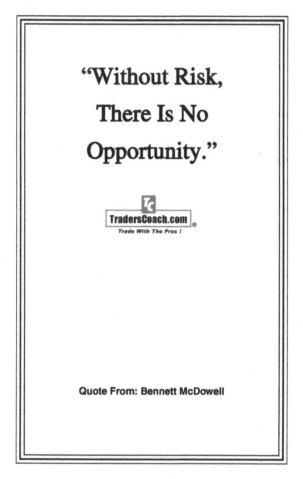

**Figure 5.1**  MINI POSTER—OPPORTUNITY—Entrepreneurs are rewarded for taking on risk, only when they succeed. Remember, without risk there is no opportunity. Quote from Bennett McDowell.

own hours and come in late every day if they want to. And no one tells them what to do. It's just a life of leisure, right?

Well, not really. It's not all glamour and glitz. Yes, there is someone to answer to, and that would be their bank account. That is because, if they are not making a profit, the party is over, and the business shuts down. And let's face it, that's not fun.

The truth about being an entrepreneur is that it is a lot of hard work, a lot of taking on risk, and a lot of not giving up when the going gets tough. These are things that most people don't know until they dive in and start their own business. See Figure 5.1.

But when the business throws its first curve ball at you, what are you going to do? The answer is that if you already have a business plan and a contract for success in place, you know what you are going to do when the going gets tough.

*An idiot with a plan can beat a genius without a plan.*
—Warren Buffett, American business magnate and investor

## Your Business Plan

*Objective:* Get profitable. Design a business plan for your trading and investing business. This is an essential step. Every great company has a business plan. You are no different. Your business plan should be very specific. Will this be a part-time business or full-time business? Following are seven issues and topics to address:

1. **Capital, equity drawdown, and margin.** Plan out how you will fund this new business. Be sure to allow for all living expenses necessary to maintain your current lifestyle while trading. Itemize both personal expenses and business operating expenses in detail to determine your estimated monthly overhead.

   Determine what dollar amount you will start off with in your active trading account. Also, will you use margin, and if so, how will you limit your risk? Establish how much equity drawdown (trading losses) will be acceptable before you stop trading and reevaluate your approach to the market.

2. **Business and office setup.** Outline exactly what you want your business to look like. List everything you will need, from computers to chairs. Then calculate what the cost of all these items will be and allocate a portion of your start-up capital for that purpose.

Where will you conduct business? Is this going to be a home-based venture, or will you be operating from an outside office? What will your office space cost, and will you be operating on a full-time or part-time basis? Plus, have you decided what markets you will trade and what brokerage house you will use to execute your trades? Determine in advance what the commission cost of your trades will be.

And, most importantly, develop a set of trading rules that you feel comfortable with and truly believe in. Your rules and approach should be tested thoroughly and should suit your psychological approach and your personality.

3. **Legal and financial concerns.** If you are going to be a full-time trader, will you incorporate or be a limited partnership or sole proprietor? Will you open a separate bank account for this purpose? If you are managing your own investments, to which accounts will you be giving your attention, some of them or all of them? About taxes, be familiar with any tax laws that relate to your trading and investing. Who will prepare your tax returns, and can they counsel you on how to structure your business? Be prepared for an Internal Revenue tax audit since random audits are always a possibility.

4. **Education.** Plan to test your trading rules and approach by paper-trading until you know the system inside and out. Decide how long to paper-trade before going live.

Once you've started trading real dollars with your system, be true to this system and follow it to the letter. During periods of equity drawdown, do not be quick to abandon your chosen system. It's like a marriage. Use great caution before switching from one approach to another. If it's genuinely suited to you, stick with it.

Next, how will you develop the skills to become consistently profitable? Can you obtain training and education to speed you along on the path of profitability by developing the proper trading skills you will need for your selected trading system?

Then, find a mentor to whom you can look for support, guidance, and direction. This should be someone that you respect and admire and that you feel has in the past and will in the future continue to teach you what is important about trading and/or life.

Finally, you may need periodic coaching to help you stay on track with your trading approach and business plan. Try to set up some coaching support in advance for those times when you feel that you are not achieving the goals set out in your business plan.

5. **Goals and expectations.** Ask yourself: "What do I hope to accomplish by setting up this new business?" Ask yourself "What is my WHY?"

Financial freedom? An independent and entrepreneurial work environment? Maybe it's as simple as being able to do what you love to do. Or do you just want to be in the driver's seat when it comes to your investments, instead of relying on a broker. The important thing is for you to look inside yourself and to find out what your answer to this question is. It will be revealing and will help you determine if you are pursuing this road for the right reasons.

### Following are other important questions to ask:

- Where do I want my trading and investing to be in 6 months, 1 year, and 5 years from now?
- How much net revenue do I expect to generate on a monthly and yearly basis?
- Do I anticipate continuing with this business indefinitely if it is everything I am hoping it will be, or is this a short-term steppingstone to something else?
- If this is a short-term steppingstone, what is the next step after a successful trading and investing business?
- If I am trading on a part-time basis, do I plan to leave my current employment and, if so, when?

By clarifying your goals on paper, you are more likely to make them into a successful reality. You can also see in black and white if your goals and expectations are realistic and can plan more effectively to overcome any obstacles that might present themselves when you start to sketch in the details.

6. **Record keeping and measuring progress.** Essential to your success is thorough and accurate recordkeeping. Be sure to record each trade's activity on a trade posting card to determine profitability.

It is important to have your trades on paper to prevent confusion should your computer system go down. A handwritten card system also enables you to quickly jot down any feelings or thoughts that occur during the trading day. This will help you to work on your trading psychology.

Then maintain a running trade ledger of all trades to evaluate your profitability on a daily, weekly, monthly, and annual basis. Look for any strengths or weaknesses that appear to correspond to the time of day, week, or year or the type of trade being executed. Where are you most profitable, and where are you least profitable?

It is beneficial to have your tested trading rules in place before you begin to make live trades. Trading is a fast-paced business, and your recordkeeping can easily get away from you if it is not considered a priority.

7. **Your new trading and investing job.** Consider yourself an employee of this new company and map out what your new job will be like. It can be part time, or it can be full time.

Specify how many days a week you will work, how many hours per day, whether you will take a vacation, how you will manage sick days, and what kind of performance reviews there will be, and when they will take place. How will you create accountability? Finally, are there retirement benefits and health care benefits in place?

*A peak performance trader is totally committed to being the best and doing whatever it takes to be the best. He feels totally responsible for whatever happens and thus can learn from mistakes. These people typically have a working business plan for trading because they treat trading as a business.*

—Van K. Tharp, trader

Don't neglect doing a business plan. If you don't do one or feel it is not necessary, think again. It is vital. Another added benefit to this exercise is that you are instilling within yourself the discipline needed to succeed, much like the discipline and preparation needed before making a trade. It is all connected.

## Do Not Disturb!

This can be a somewhat delicate topic—keeping well-meaning coworkers, family members, and phone solicitors "out of your hair." Trading and financial investing success cannot be attained without your undivided attention and concentration. Here's a plan of action:

1. Find a room in your house or office with a door that you can close and make that your "work room."
2. Communicate to your family or coworkers that you are under no circumstances to be interrupted while you are working (or studying).
3. Hang a "Do Not Disturb" door sign while trading and studying.
4. Do not answer the phone while working on your trading and investing. Use an answering machine or answering service. Get caller ID so you can screen out unnecessary calls.

## Small Businesses Are the Backbone of the Economy

According to the Small Business Administration (SBA), small businesses are the backbone of the economy. The SBA website provides the following facts about small businesses in the United States:

- Represent 99.9% of all employer firms
- Employ more than half of all private sector employees
- Are 50% percent home-based
- Have owners who do not have a college degree

Real innovation and creativity comes from the entrepreneurial sector. That's where the new ideas are. You as a private trader and investor are in good company with many other entrepreneurs.

**Here are just a few of your fellow entrepreneurs:**

- Steve Jobs and Steve Wozniak started Apple in a garage.
- Mark Zuckerberg started Facebook in his dorm room at Harvard.
- Larry Page and Sergey Brin started Google while at Stanford.

Entrepreneurs are often misunderstood and don't always fit in. They think out of the box, try things that other people think are crazy, and generally take on more risk than the average person would ever consider. But they love what they do and wouldn't trade it for anything else; that's what makes them special.

Because if they beat the odds and succeed at doing what they love, there is no better job in the world. To be able to create something, a company, out of nothing is nothing short of a miracle. Yes, miracles do happen, but you must make them happen. They don't just fall in your lap.

Granted, the life of an entrepreneur is not for everyone, and the true test is in the launching and maintaining of a business. You will never know until you try.

## ◎ Circumstance Reveals Me

Some people say when the going gets tough, the tough get going. And that is so true. To be sure there will be obstacles just like in any business, but you can pivot and solve problems that arise.

> *Circumstance does not make me; it reveals me.*
> —William James, Father of American psychology

How you respond to challenging circumstances can be thought of as making a person who they are. But as this quote from William James illustrates, the way you respond to circumstances and pressure reveals who you truly are.

Here's another quote that sums up perfectly how the exact same circumstance can render two completely different results:

*The same boiling water that softens the potato hardens the egg. It's what you're made of. Not the circumstances.* —Unknown

Be sure to take responsibility for everything in your trading and investing, regardless of the circumstances. And refrain from excuses, they will weaken you. Instead, when things go badly, learn from that, and grow.

## Adapt or Die; Don't End Up Like Blockbuster

When market cycles change, when problems arise, pay attention. If you don't adapt to a constantly evolving environment, you will die. Case in point is Blockbuster the video rental company that was booming from 1985 to 2010, when it went out of business. See Figure 5.2.

**Figure 5.2**   Be sure you always have your eye on the ball and don't end up like the company Blockbuster. They completely missed the opportunity to become Netflix, and as a result went bankrupt. As the biggest video rental company on the planet from 1985 through the 2000s, they were perfectly positioned to jump into the live streaming video market had they adapted to new technologies. But they failed to adapt, and as a result, they died.
SOURCE: ID 126457248 @ Mkopka Dreamstime.com

Many say that their decline was attributed to poor leadership and many view Blockbuster as a main example of failing to change with the times.

> *Blockbuster, if it isn't already, is going to go into the Harvard Business Review for how not to run a business, or how to run a business into the ground.*
> —Ken Tisher, former Blockbuster franchise owner

As an entrepreneur, business owner, and trader, what happened to Blockbuster can happen to you if you aren't paying attention. Be alert and mindful that past performance does not guarantee future results. Learn to adapt to changing market cycles and pivot when there is a problem. Solving problems is going to be one of your most valuable skills.

# Step II

# Develop the Trader's Mindset

# Chapter 6

# Your Mindset

Developing the trader's mindset is a must for trading (and investing) success, and this can take some time. It is not an area where you can just flip a switch and have it turn on. It can be developed only by trading and investing, either simulated or real, and from the experience you will gain.

By trading and investing you will become aware of how your mindset affects your performance, and as you become more aware of that, you can give more attention to your psychology.

In this chapter, we will help guide you toward developing your unique personal mindset into one with a winning attitude, confidence, and the ability to be resilient. We'll also help you manage the emotions associated with account drawdowns, losses, and profits (yes, profits and winning can cause stress).

*The biggest asset in the world is your mind-set.*
                    —Gary Vaynerchuk, motivational speaker

Having a healthy and motivated mindset can be the asset that gets you to the finish line. Never underestimate the power of you and your mind.

## It's Okay to Think Differently

The community of active traders and investors is a small one. And everyone in this community to one degree or another is an entrepreneur and a risk taker. Our friends and family might not understand or even appreciate what we do; they might even think we are a little bit different, for lack of a better word.

For this reason, it is important for you to know that it is okay to think differently. See Figure 6.1, which is a classic quote from an advertising campaign that Apple did in 1997.

> *Here's to the crazy ones. The misfits. The rebels. The troublemakers. The round pegs in the square holes. The ones who see things differently. They're not fond of rules. And they have no respect for the status quo. You can quote them, disagree with them, glorify, or vilify them. About the only thing you can't do is ignore them. Because they change things. They push the human race forward. And while some may see them as the crazy ones, we see genius. Because the people who are crazy enough to think they can change the world, are the ones who do.*
> —Rob Siltanen
> Creative Director, Chiat Day Advertising Agency

This quote is often attributed to Steve Jobs, but in fact it was written by Rob Siltanen, creative director of the Chiat Day Advertising firm. It's an excerpt from a television spot created for Apple Computer's "Think Different" campaign in 1997.

My point in sharing this with you is that it's okay to be different and to think differently. Matter of fact, by being true to yourself you can change the world, even if it's only your world. So have confidence in your pursuit of trading and investing success and make that confidence part of your mindset.

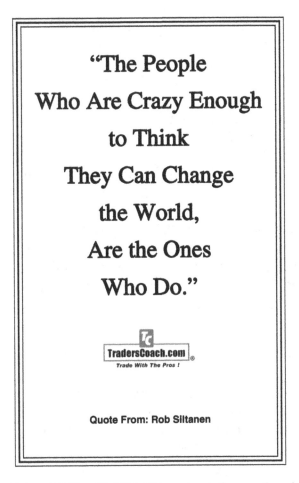

**Figure 6.1**   MINI POSTER—CRAZY—This quote is often attributed to Steve Jobs, but in fact was written by Rob Siltanen, creative director of the Chiat Day Advertising. It's an excerpt from a television spot created for Apple Computer's "Think Different" campaign in 1997. Quote from Rob Siltanen.

## Develop an Enthusiastic Mindset

You can call it passion, drive, or enthusiasm, but you need to possess either one or all of these to reach the winner's circle. Success comes only to those who can face failure with the enthusiasm to overcome.

Winston Churchill was prime minister of the United Kingdom from 1940 to 1945, during the Second World War. The Allies were fighting against Nazi Germany led by Adolf Hitler and had their fair share of failures and defeat. The most famous of their losses was during the Blitz Bombing of London, where England was under constant attack from German air raids. Much of the city was reduced to rubble.

> *Success is going from failure to failure without losing enthusiasm.*
> —Winston Churchill, prime minister of the United Kingdom

Churchill knew firsthand that to succeed in getting through this dark period in history, enthusiasm would need to be in plentiful supply. And that comes from one's mindset. Accept that you may fail at times along the way, and you will have defeats, but focus on maintaining your enthusiastic mindset and you can succeed in the end.

## One Hundred Traders and Investors—Each Is Unique

If you show the same successful financial approach to 100 different people, no two of them will use it in the same way. Why? Because everyone has a unique belief system and mindset, and this will determine his or her personal style.

Simply put, everyone is predisposed to certain preferences. Some are prone to be trend traders, some scalp traders, and then others are countertrend traders. It you attempt to trade a set of rules that are not aligned with your predisposed preferences and personality, you are likely to fail.

Then even with a profitable and proven approach and rules that are aligned with their preferences, many traders and investors will fail. If they do not have the proper winning belief system, they will lose.

In other words, they lack the trader's mindset.

## Self-Awareness of Your Current Mindset

When you encounter a psychological issue, it is best to recognize the issue and not to deny it. To eliminate psychological obstacles, you must first become aware of the obstacles and the issues causing them. This requires self-awareness.

In psychoanalysis, a psychotherapist helps a patient see a problem. The reason this process can take so long, perhaps even years, is that individuals will have varying levels of denial. Often denial is born out of a defense, or coping, mechanism.

And in the past, it may have been useful to rely on a defense mechanism to avoid anxiety. The defense may have been to ignore, or deny, the reality of a situation if it was too painful. Which enables one to function on some level at least, instead of shutting down completely. And often the defense can be carried out unconsciously.

When it comes to financial markets, there is no room for defense mechanisms or denial. The markets will uncover them quickly. In a way, the market can be an effective psychotherapist; it will take your money and wipe your account out if you are not living in reality. That kind of wakeup call either kills you or makes you stronger, as a trader or investor.

Do an inventory of your current self-awareness. The first step is accepting when you have a mindset problem. Once you accept it and take ownership of it, you can fix it.

## Fifteen Common Destructive Psychological Trading Issues and Their Causes

To strengthen your trader's mindset, look at your trading emotions and behaviors in the same way a medical doctor examines a patient. First identify your symptoms and then make a trading diagnosis based on those trading symptoms.

### Here are 15 common symptoms and their causes:

1. *Fear of being stopped out or of taking a loss.* The usual reason for this is that the trader fears failure and feels like he or she cannot take another loss. The trader's ego is at stake.

2. *Getting out of trades too early.* The trader relieves anxiety by closing a position. Has a fear of the position reversing. Has a need for instant gratification.

3. *Wishing and hoping.* The trader does not want to take control or take responsibility for the trade or has an inability to accept the present reality of the marketplace. The trader is unwilling to honor the stop loss exit or has no stop loss exit in place.

4. *Anger after a losing trade.* The trader has the feeling of being a victim of the markets, unrealistic expectations, or caring too much about a specific trade. Self-worth is tied to success in the markets, or the trader needs approval from the markets.

5. *Trading with money the trader cannot afford to lose or trading with borrowed money.* The trader feels that this is the last hope at success and is trying to be successful at something. Trader has a fear of losing chance at opportunity. Exhibits no discipline, combined with greed or desperation.

6. *Adding on to a losing position (doubling down).* The trader does not want to admit the trade is wrong and is hoping it will come back. The trader's ego is at stake.

7. *Compulsive trading.* The trader is drawn to the excitement and adrenaline of the markets. Addiction and gambling issues are present. Needs to feel always in the game and has difficulty when not trading, such as on weekends. Obsessed with trading.

8. *Excessive joy after a winning trade.* The trader ties his or her self-worth to the markets, feeling unrealistically "in control" of the markets.

9. *Stagnant or poor trading account profits—limiting profits.* The trader feels that he or she doesn't deserve to be successful, and doesn't deserve money or profits. There are usually psychological issues, such as poor self-esteem.

10. *Not following the trading system.* The trader doesn't believe it really works. Did not test it well. The system does not match his or her personality. Wants more excitement in trading. Doesn't trust his or her own ability to choose a successful system.

11. *Overthinking the trade, second-guessing trading.* The trader has a fear of loss or being wrong. Has a perfectionist personality, wanting a sure thing where sure things don't exist. Does not understand that loss is part of trading, and the outcome of each trade is unknown. Does not accept that there is risk in trading and does not accept the unknown. Afraid to pull the trigger.

12. *Not trading the correct trade size.* The trader is dreaming that the trade will be only profitable and not fully recognizing the risk or understanding the importance of money management. Refuses to take responsibility for managing risk or is too lazy to calculate proper trade size.

13. *Trading too much.* The trader has a need to conquer the market. Greed. Trying to get even with the market for a previous loss. Revenge trading. The excitement of trading (like Number 7, compulsive trading).

14. *Afraid to trade.* The trader has no trading system in place. The trader is not comfortable with risk and the unknown and has a fear of total loss, fear of ridicule, need for control, and no confidence in self or the trading system.

15. *Irritable after the trading day.* The trader is on an emotional roller coaster due to anger, fear, and greed, putting too much attention on results only, and not enough attention to the process and learning the skill of trading. Focusing on the money too much and having unrealistic expectations.

These are by no means all the psychological issues but some of the most common. They usually center on the fact that, for one reason or another, the trader is not following his or her chosen trading approach or system.

Your goal is to maintain an even keel. And to get off the roller coaster and let go of the adrenaline rush. See Figure 6.2. Your

**Figure 6.2**   Maintain an even keel and strengthen your mindset so that you don't have massive emotional highs and lows. Take yourself off the roller coaster and focus on the process of trading and investing. Focus on developing a proven and tested edge in the financial markets.
SOURCE: Photo 19793875 @ Brett Critchley Dreamstime.com

winning trades and losing trades should not affect you. Obviously, you are trading better when you are winning, but emotionally, you should strive to maintain an even balance regarding wins and losses.

It will happen when it happens. It cannot be forced. When you achieve this level of mental ability, it will come after working long and hard on your weaknesses. It usually happens when you least expect it.

## Here Is What You'll Feel After Acquiring the Trader's Mindset

In answer to "what is the trader's mindset," the following list helps you to understand what you will feel after you have acquired it. In short, the trader's mindset is a state of mind where you are confident, unafraid, and not disabled by losses or draw down. You will know when you have a proven edge and will approach trading as a business.

**Here are 20 traits of traders who have developed the trader's mindset:**

1. Not caring about the money
2. Acceptance of the risk in trading and investing
3. Winning and losing trades accepted equally from an emotional standpoint
4. Enjoyment of the process
5. No feeling of being victimized by the markets
6. Always looking to improve skills
7. Trading and investing account profits now accumulating and flowing in as skills improve
8. Opened-minded, keeping opinions to a minimum
9. No anger, just flowing with the market
10. Learning from every trade or position
11. Using one chosen approach or system and not being influenced by the market or other traders
12. No need to conquer or control the "market"
13. Feeling confident and feeling in control
14. A sense of not forcing the markets
15. Trading with money you can afford to risk
16. Taking full responsibility for all trading results
17. Sense of calmness when trading
18. Ability to focus on the present reality
19. Not caring which way the market breaks or moves
20. Aligning trades in the direction of the market

When you can read the trader's mindset list and genuinely say "that's me," you have arrived.

One important key in acquiring the trader's mindset is to create a sense of balance. Each of us can reduce stress in different ways, and you will need to find what works best for you. By reducing stress daily, you are one step closer to the trader's mindset.

## Are You a Winner?

It's all about your mindset; if you have a winning attitude, your brain is going to make it easier for you to follow a path that leads to success. Of course, your attitude is determined by your thoughts and that is where you must start.

> *Every day stand guard at the door of your mind, and you alone decide what thoughts and beliefs you let into your life. For they will shape whether you feel rich or poor, cursed or blessed.*
> —Tony Robbins, motivational speaker

To develop a winning attitude, be careful of what thoughts and beliefs you let in. Be mindful of only allowing thoughts that enable you to feel that you are rich, blessed, intelligent, successful, worthy, and that you are a winner.

# Chapter 7

# Brain Power

The human brain is like a supercharged computer with feelings. It is an impressive supervisory center of the nervous system that serves as the site for all human emotions, memory, self-awareness, and thought. It weighs only 3 pounds, and yet it controls every action we take.

> *Wasting brain power ruminating about things you can't control drains mental energy quickly. The more you think about problems you can't solve, the less energy you'll have leftover for more productive endeavors.*
> —Amy Morin, author of *13 Things Mentally Strong People Don't Do*

Our brains consist of some 10 billion interconnected nerve cells with innumerable extensions. This interlacing of nerve fibers and their junctions allows a nerve impulse to follow any of a virtually unlimited number of pathways.

The result gives us a seemingly infinite variety of responses to sensory input. In this chapter you will see how using your brain and understanding your brain can enable you to create greater financial success.

61

## Five Factors that Affect How Trading Input is Processed in Your Brain

The pathway a brain chooses for a sensory impulse depends on many factors:

1. A particular brain's unique physical characteristics
2. Temporary physical conditions such as fatigue or malnourishment
3. Information previously implanted by experience and learning
4. Intensity of the stimulus producing the impulse
5. Current emotional states such as anger, fear, greed, happiness, or sadness

## Anatomy of the Brain

The cerebrum, occupying the topmost portion of the skull, is by far the largest sector of the brain. Split vertically into left and right hemispheres, it appears deeply fissured and grooved. Its upper surface, the cerebral cortex, contains most of the master controls of the body. The left half of the cerebrum controls the right side of the body; the right half controls the left side of the body.

The brain is working during both sleep and consciousness for our entire life. The ceaseless electrochemical activity in the brain generates brain waves that can be electronically detected and recorded. The adult human brain consumes 25% of the energy used by the body, while the developing brain of an infant consumes around 60%.

## Left Brain and Right Brain

Our brain is made up of two halves, a left brain and a right brain. A big fold goes from front to back in our brain, essentially dividing it into two distinct and separate parts—well, almost separate.

They are connected to each other by a thick cable of nerves at the base of each brain. This sole link between the two giant processors is called the corpus callosum. Think of it as an Ethernet cable or network connection between two incredibly fast and immensely powerful computer processors, each running different programs from the same sensory input.

## Left Brain, Right Brain Characteristics

| Left Brain (Scientific) | Right Brain (Artistic) |
| --- | --- |
| Dominant side of the brain | Nondominant side of the brain |
| Controls the right side of the body | Controls the left side of the body |
| Controls optimism | Controls pessimism |
| Uses logic and planning | Uses feelings and emotions |
| Follows rules | Follows impulses |
| Uses words | Uses pictures |
| Identifies words | Identifies patterns |
| Factual and analytical | Conceptual and intuitive |
| Analyzes | Synthesizes |
| Detail oriented | Big picture oriented |
| System dominates | Imagination dominates |
| Science and math strength | Art and creativity strength |
| Reality based | Fantasy based |
| Looks at what is | Looks at what could be |
| Linear | Nonlinear |
| Orderly and methodical | Random and spontaneous |

Scientists are learning more about the nature of the left and right brains every day. They have learned that each side of the brain has strengths in certain areas (see left brain, right brain table), although the fact is that mental abilities are not entirely separated into the left and right cerebral hemispheres. Speech and language tend to be localized to specific areas in one hemisphere, but if one hemisphere is damaged at an early age, these functions can often be recovered in part or even in full by the other hemisphere.

*There appears teo be two modes of thinking, verbal and nonverbal, represented rather separately in left and right hemispheres respectively and that our education system, as well as science in general, tends to neglect the nonverbal form of intellect. What it comes down to is that modern society discriminates against the right hemisphere of the brain.*
—Roger Wolcott Sperry, Psychologist and Nobel Prize winner

As Sperry's quote states, modern society may very well discriminate against the right hemisphere of the brain. The artists and dreamers are not encouraged in academia as much as the scientists and logical thinkers are.

Then there is the question: are you left-handed or right-handed? Only 10% of the population is left-handed, so they are rare. Since the left hand is controlled by the right brain, there is a theory that left-handed people are more artistic and creative.

But as you will see in the next section, Albert Einstein believed both science and art are equally important to achieve greatness in science. One might argue that both science and art are equally important to achieve greatness in anything at all.

Trading the financial markets is included.

## Whole Brain Thinking

Ideally, our success in anything, including the financial markets, requires that we become "whole brain" thinkers.

*After a certain high level of technical skill is achieved, science and art tend to coalesce in esthetics, plasticity, and form. The greatest scientists are always artists as well.*
—Albert Einstein, theoretical physicist and Nobel Prize winner

We must do our best to develop both sides of our brain and use them together to become masters of our own minds. As nature decides, it seems that we each are born with a unique given set of attributes. Some of us are more "left brain" thinkers, and some of us are more "right brain" thinkers.

Then there are the lucky ones among us that are already born as "whole brain" thinkers.

# Neuroplasticity

They say you can't teach old dogs new tricks, which is in fact not true. It just takes a little longer to get the old dogs to create change. The brain has far greater plasticity when we are young, and it gets progressively "hardwired" as we age.

The good news is that recent scientific research has confirmed that the brain maintains significant plasticity even into old age. The key is to constantly work the brain, using repetition and behavior modification to manipulate that malleable plasticity in a way that creates your desired results.

Remember, if you don't use it, you lose it.

## Neurons and Neuronets

The brain is made up of approximately 100 billion tiny nerve cells called neurons. Each neuron has between 1,000 and 10,000 synapses, or places where they connect with other neurons. These neurons use the connections to form networks among themselves.

These integrated or connected nerve cells form what are called neural networks or neuronets. A simple way to think about this is that every neuronet represents a thought, a memory, a skill, a piece of information, and so on.

Everyone has their own collection of experiences and skills represented in the neuronets in their brains. All those experiences shape, neurologically, the fabric of what's taking place in our perception and in our world.

## Chemicals and Neurotransmitters in the Brain

When we receive certain stimuli from our environment, aspects of our neuronets will kick in and create chemical changes in our brain. These chemical changes in turn produce emotional reactions we have to the people and events in our lives.

In addition to that, a complex process occurs whenever we experience a thought or a feeling. First, an electrical signal in a neuron travels through the axon where molecules bind to receptor sites. A second neuron either accepts or rejects the signal. The first molecule can sometimes take back some of the remaining molecules, a process known as *reuptake*. Basically, messages are being sent back and forth between neurons via neurotransmitters.

The result of this complex process is what can make us experience a host of emotions such as happiness, sadness, gratitude, revenge, enthusiasm, anger, joy, regret, fear, or greed. There are an infinite number of emotions and feelings, but these chemicals and neurotransmitters determine which feelings we are more likely to experience.

All of this relates directly to you and your trader's mindset.

### Happiness Chemicals

Four main brain chemicals—dopamine, serotonin, oxytocin, and endorphins—all play a role in how you experience happiness.

- **Dopamine:** Pleasure neurotransmitter—Produced by the hypo-thalamus, this helps feelings of pleasure and also addiction, movement, and motivation. Dopamine release is increased by setting goals, seeing the finish line, completing tasks, and by being kind to others. People repeat behaviors that lead to dopamine release.
- **Serotonin:** Mood neurotransmitter—Contributes to feelings of well-being, satisfaction, importance, and happiness. Helps sleep cycles and digestive system regulation. Serotonin release is increased by exercise, meditation, confidence, thoughts of believing in yourself, being kind to others, and sunlight exposure. Many anti-depressant medications are selective serotonin *reuptake* inhibitors (SSRI) that help boost levels of serotonin.
- **Oxytocin:** Love hormone—Produced by the hypothalamus and released by the pituitary gland that produces feeling of love and connection. Oxytocin release is boosted when you are kind and give compliments, when you communicate with other people, when you are in love, during sex, and during maternal behavior such as childbirth or breastfeeding.
- **Endorphins:** Euphoria neurotransmitter—These are opioid peptides produced by the hypothalamus and pituitary glands. Endorphin release is increased during exercise, laughing, doing something you enjoy, excitement, and sex. The positive euphoric feeling endorphins produce give a feeling of well-being and help mask and reduce pain. Their ability to stimulate pain relief creates the same reaction that occurs chemically when taking prescriptions opioids such as morphine.

As you can see, our brains have the seemingly magical ability to naturally generate chemicals that help make us happy. Of course, at times the synapses are not firing correctly, which causes the serotonin levels to be reduced, resulting in symptoms of depression.

Some people do experience problems, or imbalances, with their brain chemicals. As many as one in four adults have a diagnosable mental health disorder. If you have concerns about this, it is worth talking to your doctor about whether you would benefit from medications or talk therapy. Of course, that is a personal decision to be made with you and your medical doctor.

The upside though, to understanding the happy chemicals in our brain, is that we can naturally generate these positive chemicals with the following activities: exercise, laughing, completing tasks (no matter how small), being outside in the sunshine, thoughts of believing in yourself, being in love, and sexual activity. Another way to naturally create happy chemicals in our bodies is through a healthy diet.

With some thought and focus, you may be able to increase these happy chemicals naturally, and possibly avoid or reduce the use of pharmaceuticals.

## Other Chemicals

Many other chemicals are produced by the brain in addition to the happy chemicals. They each have important functions. Here are a few important ones to be aware of.

- **Glutamate:** Memory neurotransmitter—Most common brain neurotransmitter. Responsible for maintenance of neural communication in the brain. Involved in learning and memory. Physical exercise increases the glutamate levels in your brain.
- **Cortisol:** Steroid hormone—Its release is increased in response to stress and low blood sugar. It functions to increase blood sugar, and it can weaken the activity of the immune system. Too much of it for too long can cause memory loss.
- **Adrenaline:** Fight or flight neurotransmitter—Produced in stressful or exciting situations. Increases heart rate and blood flow, leading to a physical boost and heightened awareness.
- **GABA:** Calming neurotransmitter—Calms firing nerves in the central nervous system. High levels improve focus and the ability to be relaxed; low levels cause anxiety, ADHD, and memory

issues. Also contributes to motor control and vision. Yoga and meditation increase your GABA levels.

- **Noradrenaline:** Concentration neurotransmitter (also known as norepinephrine)—Primary role is a part of the body's stress response. It works with adrenaline in our body to create the fight or flight feeling. Its release is lowest during sleep, rises during wakefulness, and reaches much higher levels during situations of stress or danger. Affects attention and responding actions in the brain. Contracts blood vessels, increasing blood flow.
- **Acetylcholine:** Learning neurotransmitter—Involved in thought, learning, attention, focus, and memory. Activates muscle action in the body. A deficit in this chemical can contribute to PTSD, bipolar disorder, and schizophrenia. Nicotine mimics acetylcholine. Drinking caffeinated coffee or tea will increase the release of acetylcholine.

So, you can see a lot is going on behind the scenes in our brains. Typically stress, fear, panic, rage, and despair can release chemicals that can be harmful over time.

> *It is well known that panic, despair, depression, hate, rage exasperation, frustration all produce negative biochemical changes in the body.*
> —Norman Cousins, author of *Anatomy of an Illness*

With more awareness, you can increase your happy chemicals, which in turn will reduce the negative effects of stress and fear. It can go a long way in helping you attain the trader's mindset.

## ◎ Use Muscle Memory to Rewire Your Brain Along With Your Trading and Investing

We have the power and ability to change the neuronets in our brains if we consciously set out to do so. By using repetition and thought modification, we can literally reprogram the system. Creating a new go-to reflex. Just like muscle memory.

It is possible to rewire a negative thought process into a positive thought process by consciously changing that thought process. Eventually, the neuronets will rewire and the positive thought process will become "hardwired." See Figure 7.1.

This quote is a good way to look at how to fix problems:

> *I do not fix problems. I fix my thinking. Then problems fix themselves.*
> —Louise Hay, author of *You Can Heal Your Life*

The expression of "mind over matter" is when a person is so focused that they can achieve the seemingly impossible. Again, you can use this approach to rewire your brain to be so focused that it can relentlessly solve problems and puzzles at will.

Another example of rewiring your brain is when you conduct paper trading, or simulated trading. The repetition of repeatedly using a set of specific rules will literally program your brain to do the right thing during real trading with real money. It reduces anxiety and stress. Which means, with muscle memory you almost don't need to think, instead you just do.

Be conscious of this and you will see results.

**Figure 7.1**    You can rewire your brain if you set your mind to do so. It is possible to rewire a negative thought process into a positive thought process by consciously changing that thought process. Eventually, the neuronets will rewire and the positive thought process will become "hardwired."

SOURCE: Photo 3621629 Brain © Cammeraydave Dreamstime.com

## The Computer Between Your Ears

As we've covered in this chapter your brain has enormous abilities and literally never sleeps. Factor in the beautifully designed two hemisphere functionality, where we can tap into both our left brain and our right brain, and you can't help but be impressed.

Which is why I often say, "The best computer on the planet is the one between your ears." Traders must master their right brain and their left brain. And once they can do that, the sky is the limit.

Matter of fact, once mastering both hemispheres of the brain in your trading, you'll be able to look at a chart and your brain will automatically assess exactly what to do in a short amount of time. See Figure 7.2.

## Keep an Open Mind

Just keep an open mind with the information in this chapter because your mind and your brain are enormously powerful and can enable you to achieve great success.

**Figure 7.2**   MINI POSTER—BEST COMPUTER—Never underestimate the power and capabilities of your brain and your mind. Quote from Bennett McDowell.

# Chapter 8
# Stress Reduction

Stress in trading and investing can be disastrous. In excess, it can lead to operator errors, poor psychology, and losses. Make no mistake, if you have excessive stress and are in denial about it, you need to bring it to the forefront and work on how to eliminate or reduce it.

An added bonus of reducing stress is that you will be healthier overall. When you are relaxed, your happiness brain chemicals are increased, and your heart rate and blood pressure are lowered.

## Eliminate Negative Thinking and Negative Beliefs

Easier said than done, for sure. But since we've been talking about our thoughts and how powerful they are, it makes sense that negative thoughts can create stress. Sometimes it's a matter of replacing the negative thoughts with something else before they will go away.

Positive thinking alone will not make you successful. But it can help. And one way to implement positive thinking is through affirmations. Louise Hay was a pioneer in this field of replacing negative thoughts with positive ones. See Figure 8.1.

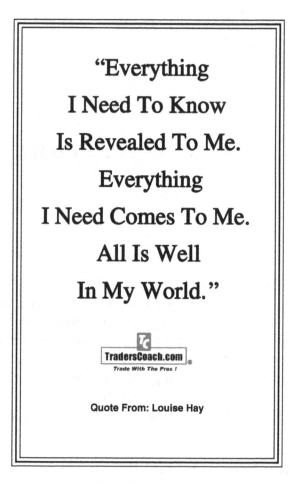

**Figure 8.1** MINI POSTER—ALL IS WELL—Affirmations can help in reducing negative thoughts. They can work in the same way as meditation does. Louise Hay was a pioneer in the field of *new thought*. Quote from Louise Hay.

We will cover more on this kind of *cognitive restructuring* in the fitness chapter. For affirmations to work, the idea is to say the words either out loud or to yourself silently as if they were a *mantra*.

The repetition of repeating the mantra over and over can in fact rewire your brain. When there is no energy given to feed the negative thoughts, they will disappear. It is then easier to make room for the positive and more productive thoughts.

> *The greatest weapon against stress is the ability to choose one thought over another.*
> —William James, Father of American psychology

This technique of affirmations and positive thinking may not be your cup of tea. But if you've never tried it, give it a chance, and see if there is something to it. What have you got to lose?

## Deep Breathing and Meditation Exercises

Deep breathing and meditation are both popular techniques for reducing stress. They increase the oxygen in your blood and can significantly lower your resting heart rate, which is a good thing. They also boost your natural production of *serotonin* in your brain which contributes to feelings of well-being and happiness.

> *Meditation is not a way of making your mind quiet. It is a way of entering into the quiet that is already there, buried under the 50,000 thoughts the average person thinks every day.*
> —Deepak Chopra, alternative medicine advocate

If you search the internet, you can even find "guided breathing and meditation" exercises where you can listen to a calming voice that guides your breathing and relaxation. Sometimes they include ocean sounds and other relaxing audio. See Figure 8.2.

**Here's a basic breathing and meditation exercise:**

1. **Breathe In:** Slowly take in a deep breath through your nose, so that your stomach expands and think about taking in positive energy.

**Figure 8.2**    Deep breathing and meditation exercises are effective tools in reducing stress. Do an internet search for "guided breathing and meditation" exercises; there are lots to choose from on YouTube. Find ones that appeal to you. Start small with a 2-minute or 6-minute exercise and then you can increase the length of time as desired.

SOURCE: Photo 56996585 @ Inara Prusakova Dreamstime.com

2. **Breathe Out:** Slowly exhale completely through your mouth, thinking about expelling any negative energy.
3. **Repeat:** Do 10 repetitions of this exercise or at least a minimum of 2 minutes.

If you do this exercise two or three times a day, there will be a noticeable difference in your stress level and in your resting heart rate.

## 🎯 Too Much Information Leads to Information Overload

Eliminate the extra noise created by the media and created by too much information. Seek the truth of the markets to become successful. Avoid information overload.

You don't know how the market will respond to news, earnings reports, world events, economic events, Federal Open Market Committee meetings, and so on. In fact, at times you won't know if the earnings numbers are even the truth. Some major companies have altered their numbers in the past, such as Enron, and who's to say it isn't happening now; there is no way to know.

Then there are the news commentators who love to tell their listeners stories about why this stock dropped and another went up. Sometimes they are right, and sometimes they are not. And when they are right, it is usually in hindsight when the market has already moved, which has no value for you after the fact.

Be mindful of how much information and media you bombard yourself with and you will find that less can be more.

## Simplify and Flow with the Market

Strive to keep things simple. Follow and flow with the markets. Don't try to figure out why they are moving; instead, move along with them. You can do this if you focus on the present reality.

*That's been one of my mantras—focus and simplicity. Simple can be harder than complex. You have to work hard to get your thinking clean to make it simple. But it's worth it in the end because once you get there, you can move mountains.*
—Steve Jobs, co-founder Apple Computer

The *ART of Trading* approach will help you get in this focused zone where everything is in harmony. With each chapter in this book, step by step, you are learning how to simplify and flow with the market.

## Guidelines to Simplify Your Trading and Investing

Let's set up some ground rules to simplify your trading. You may already be doing some of these but maybe there are a few ideas you can add to your simplicity plan.

**This list is what I have found works for me:**

1. Don't rely solely on your broker for trading advice; look at the charts to confirm with the technicals.
2. Remember, trading and investing is a skill—be patient.
3. Continually practice the art of focusing on the present moment (it's hard to do). Don't think about yesterday or tomorrow—focus on the now.
4. Manually keep excellent records of all your transactions.
5. Eliminate negative distractions while trading.
6. Enjoy the process.
7. Don't listen to financial news during business hours.
8. Use one trading and financial approach and follow it consistently.
9. Don't have lofty and unrealistic expectations. Ambition is good for you as long as it is not blind.
10. Focus on your skills when you are not meeting your performance expectations.
11. Don't solely rely on newspapers or trading news or pick services for trading decisions; look at the charts to trust and verify.
12. If you feel sick, don't trade until you feel better.
13. If you feel emotionally upset, don't trade until you are more stable.

**14.** If you have a specific problem that is distracting you, don't trade.
**15.** Resist the temptation to form opinions about each trade.
**16.** Eliminate any opinions you may have about the market.
**17.** Keep your mind clear and focused.

The goal is to create a clear mind, free of distractions and opinions. The markets are a living system, much like humans are, and as a result are unpredictable. The only way you can successfully profit in the markets is to stop trying to predict the unpredictable.

Like a tail on a dog, just follow the markets. When they go up, go with them. When they go down, go with them. When they are doing nothing, do nothing.

# Reducing Stress and Creating Balance In Your Trading

Here are some ideas to get you started in reducing stress and creating harmony and balance:

- Go to the gym; start an exercise program, get fit, and stay fit.
- Consider getting a dog (or bird, or cat, or fish or any pet).
- Go outside, away from the office, and get some fresh air.
- Do some gardening.
- Get a massage, manicure, or pedicure.
- Soak up some sunshine—lie in the sun or sit outside; if you live in a cloudy climate, visit a sunny destination.
- Go for a dip in the Jacuzzi or take a hot bath.
- Enjoy your favorite hobby or start a new hobby.
- Go on vacation, take a drive, change your scenery.

*(continued on next page ...)*

*(... continued from previous page)*

- Play your favorite game (e.g., checkers, chess, canasta, poker, solitaire, computer games).
- Start eating healthier.
- Go for a bicycle ride or jog on a new route you haven't tried before.
- Donate time or money to a favorite organization or cause.
- Do yoga or meditation or deep breathing exercises.
- Read a good book.
- Go out to a movie (instead of renting one at home).
- Call up an old friend; make a new friend.
- Enjoy the nature around you—watch an eagle flying overhead, the clouds, a sunset or a sunrise, the ocean waves, or a sandy beach.
- Stop to smell the roses.

Finding harmony and balance is a personal choice. It is crucial that you don't get obsessed with your trading and finances 24 hours a day, 7 days a week.

## Errors, Artistic Blocks, and Overcoming Them

Every artist is bound to encounter periods where they hit a "brick wall"—their creativity is blocked, and they just get stuck. Every professional athlete has "errors" on occasion. As traders and investors, we face the same challenges, and there are ways we can get back on track.

**Here are a few of the ways to get back on track:**

1. Take time off and relax; then, when you are fresh, try again.
2. Before sleeping, ask yourself a question regarding your "brick wall"; then, while you're sleeping, let your subconscious mind work on it.

3. Try focusing on your problem at different times of the day or evening.
4. Switch from trading your live cash account and go back to paper-trading and simulated trading to take the pressure off but still be in the game.

Humans are not designed to be perfect. You are human, and thankfully you are a living breathing person and not a robot. Frankly, sometimes mistakes can lead to the greatest discoveries, and you never know where they will lead you (if you let them). You might have a trading error that leads to you improving your entire approach. The key is to not let the errors disable you; work the problem and fix it.

# Positive and Negative Emotions in Trading and Investing

| Positive Emotions | Negative Emotions |
| --- | --- |
| Relaxed | Stressed, Anxious |
| Confident, Fearless | Doubt, Fear, Panic, Worry |
| Content, Satisfied | Regret |
| Calm, Peace, Bliss | Anger, Rage, Revenge |
| Pride | Shame |
| Joy | Sorrow |
| Grateful | Ungrateful |
| Enthusiastic | Apathetic |
| Feeling Like a Winner | Feeling Like a Failure |
| Energized | Exhausted |
| Generosity | Greed |
| Patience | Impatience |

## Stressful Emotions

One way to monitor your stress level is to be aware of your current emotions. Review the list here of positive and negative emotions in trading and investing. It's a starting point to see if any negative emotions have been triggered for you.

Practice the ability to tolerate emotional discomfort. There will be times when you are feeling emotions from the negative column, and when you do, it's a good idea to give yourself some self-care and focus on reducing your stress levels.

## Write in Your *Sunrise Trading Journal*

The *Sunrise Trading Journal* is a "long" journal approach where you will write three long pages every morning at sunrise or when you first wake, prior to your trading day.

Begin writing in your journal every day from this day forward, including weekends. The purpose of this is so that you can start to develop an understanding of your feelings and your psychology. You will also see how this can improve your investing and trading performance. In addition, the routine of the journal creates instant structure and discipline in your trading and finances.

Before you begin your day, when you first wake up, go to your *Sunrise Trading Journal,* and write down your feelings, thoughts, and ideas. They don't have to be trading or investing related and can basically ramble on as a stream of consciousness. The idea is to empty your mind of any distractions and do a "mind dump."

This will enable you to focus on the reality of the present moment and to work in the here and now. If you have no thoughts or emotions, just write down that you "have no thoughts or emotions."

The goal is to capture whatever unconscious information you can gather when you first wake up and then release it onto the handwritten page. Then you've transferred any distracting unconscious baggage into your journal before you start your workday. You will find it enlightening, and it will clear your mind.

After writing for 1 full month, review your journal and use a colored highlighter to mark any recurring words or themes you find. Look for patterns in your writing and in your thoughts as well as any changes from the time you first began writing in your journal.

Do you see any themes of anger, fear, or greed? Are your journal entries changing from negative themes to more positive ones? Reviewing in this way will lead you to discover clues about yourself and ways to improve your trading and investing.

Repeat this process every month. The link here gives you free access to a PDF file of the journal for you to use:

https://www.traderscoach.com/book/

If you need help with access to this portal, contact us via email at **support@traderscoach.com,** and we will supply you with access.

## Get a Personal Coach

Sometimes having an impartial sounding board can help you to relieve stress in your trading and in your life. For me, having a personal coach helped me get to the next level when I was starting out.

My trading coach was Bill Williams, that experience showed me firsthand what the benefits of having a mentor and trading coach could be. For one, it reduced the feeling of isolation and helped me to see an experienced trader in action. Prior to that, my trading was stressful. I discovered that you could be calm in the markets when you had a plan and approach to follow. That was a big turning point for me.

*Want what the market wants.*
—Bill Williams, author and trading coach

Now that I've been coaching students since 1998, I have to say it is a rewarding experience. Taking what I have learned and sharing it with other traders is exciting to see when they have lightbulb moments like I did.

It's worth looking into finding a coach that you connect with to see if having that support and experience might reduce stress in your day-to-day trading.

## In 100 Years, It Won't Matter

Back in 1997, Richard Carlson, psychotherapist and motivational speaker, wrote a *New York Times* bestseller entitled *Don't Sweat the Small Stuff*. The book immediately became a worldwide sensation. His niche was stress management, and this little book was designed to help people reduce their stress.

For traders, stress is public enemy number 1. Anything you can do to reduce or eliminate stress is highly recommended. I've listed some ideas in this chapter, "Reducing Stress and Creating Balance," that are a good starting point.

At the end of the day, "What are you worrying about?" When you answer that question, it will help you to put things in perspective. Maybe when you say the answer out loud, you'll realize that you are worrying about "small stuff" and that will reduce your stress right there.

When I look back 20 years and think about what I was worrying about then, it seems that it all worked out. And the few things that didn't work out, surprisingly, lead me to some people and things that I can't imagine my life without today. Sure, there were some painful moments, but the journey of life will never be completely without some of that.

Whatever you're worrying about, remember that in 100 years, it won't matter. Think about that for just a minute. And then, think about the fact that in 10 years it probably won't matter either. It is all about perspective.

My advice is to live each day to the fullest and decide right now how much energy your worries deserve. You may find that your energy is better spent on something more productive than worrying.

# Chapter 9

# Fitness

To achieve lasting success as a trader and investor and to develop the right mindset, you must first become fit and remain fit. There are many types of fitness, including physical, emotional, and mental, to name a few.

Just as when you fly on a commercial airplane, the flight attendant will explain to the adults that in the event of an emergency, they should put the oxygen mask on themselves first and only after securing their own masks help any children or anyone else having difficulties. Because if you are the adult in the room, you can't help anyone else unless you take care of yourself first.

Be the adult in the room when it comes to your trading and investing; take care of yourself and your fitness first. This chapter covers some areas to focus on.

## A Body in Motion Tends to Stay in Motion

The first rule of thumb is to keep moving. In the seventeenth century, a physicist, defined his universal laws of motion.

*An object at rest stays at rest and an object in motion stays in motion*
*with the same speed and in the same direction unless acted upon by*
*an unbalanced force.*

—Isaac Newton, seventeenth century physicist,
astronomer and mathematician

Newton was referring to the science of physics, yet this law is applicable to other areas of life including fitness and success. Generally, a *couch potato* at rest watching television will remain at rest. And an *entrepreneur in motion* (like you) who is innovating and solving problems will stay in motion. Who will be more successful? The answer is most likely the person in motion.

Newton's observations about inertia and objects at rest may spark a conversation about physical fitness. The lack of physical motion is something that current society has been battling since the onset of technological advances such as the automobile, computer, streaming videos, and Amazon.com delivery on demand.

Add to that the new culture of *work-at-home remote workstations* where many workers work from home via computer and don't have to leave the house or commute.

You will notice the graph in Figure 9.1, from the National Center for Health Statistics, shows that, since 1960, the number of people who are considered obese has increased dramatically.

In 1960 about 10% of the population was obese. This jumps to around 35% percent in 2010. The projection for the year 2030 is that a staggering 50% of Americans will be obese.

See Table 9.1 for the guidelines for BMI (body mass index) for the weight categories of underweight, normal weight, overweight, obese, and severely obese. And Table 9.2 provides a BMI calculator.

Why the huge increase? Maybe we're all ordering fast food and eating processed foods like potato chips and Twinkies. Or maybe since folks work at home remotely and sit behind a computer all day, there isn't much activity. Not to mention the fact that we can shop online and have Amazon.com deliver to our door, sometimes within a few hours. It's a lot different than it was in 1960.

We literally don't need to leave the house!

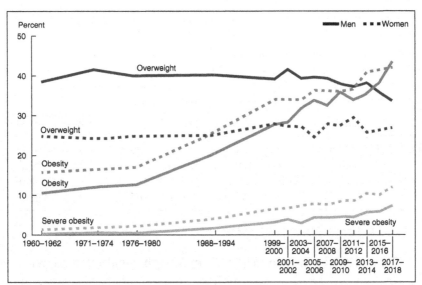

NOTES: Data are age adjusted by the direct method to U.S. Census 2000 estimates using age groups 20–39, 40–59, and 60–74. Overweight is body mass index (BMI) of 25.0–29.9 kg/m². Obesity is BMI at or above 30.0 kg/m². Severe obesity is BMI at or above 40.0 kg/m². Pregnant women are excluded from the analysis.
SOURCE: National Center for Health Statistics, National Health Examination Survey and National Health and Nutrition Examination Surveys.

**Figure 9.1**  This graph illustrates the dramatic increase in the percentage of obese Americans. In 1960, only about 10% of Americans were considered obese. In 2010, that number jumped up to around 35%. The projected number for the year 2030 is a staggering 50% percent.

SOURCE: CDC and the National Center for Health Statistics. https://www.cdc.gov/nchs/data/hestat/obesity-adult-17-18/obesity-adult.htm

**Table 9.1**  BMI Guidelines—This table outlines the definitions for each weight category: underweight, normal weight, overweight, obese, and severely obese. The BMI figures are calculated based on the relationship between body weight and height.

|       | Underweight | Normal Weight | Overweight | Obese    | Severely Obese |
|-------|-------------|---------------|------------|----------|----------------|
| BMI   | Under 18.4  | 18.5–24.9     | 25–29.9    | Above 30 | Above 40       |

SOURCE: National Center for Health Statistics.

**Table 9.2**  BMI Calculator—This table estimates what your BMI is based on your height and your weight. You can find calculators online that can determine a more precise BMI estimate like the one here: https://www.nhlbi.nih.gov/health/educational/lose_wt/BMI/bmicalc.htm Keep in mind that muscle weighs more than fat, so these BMI calculators don't take into account muscular athletes who have more muscle mass compared to non-athletes.

|  | 20 BMI | 25 BMI | 30 BMI | 35 BMI | 40 BMI | 45 BMI | 50 BMI |
|---|---|---|---|---|---|---|---|
| 60" height | 102 lbs. | 128 lbs. | 153 lbs. | 179 lbs. | 204 lbs. | 230 lbs. | 255 lbs. |
| 65" height | 120 lbs. | 150 lbs. | 180 lbs. | 210 lbs. | 240 lbs. | 270 lbs. | 300 lbs. |
| 70" height | 139 lbs. | 174 lbs. | 209 lbs. | 243 lbs. | 278 lbs. | 313 lbs. | 348 lbs. |
| 75" height | 160 lbs. | 200 lbs. | 240 lbs. | 279 lbs. | 319 lbs. | 359 lbs. | 399 lbs. |

SOURCE: U.S. Department of Health & Human Services.

The point is, we don't get as much physical exercise as previous generations did. So much so that it's become a phenomenon where we are encouraged to get 10,000 steps a day to stay healthy. We may even have a fitness tracker that counts our steps and our active minutes and reminds us of when we aren't being active enough.

The secret is to stay in motion, even if you don't have to. Go to the gym, or for a walk, ride a bicycle, just keep moving. Fight the obesity curve shown in Figure 9.1. Even a small change can make a big difference. Studies show that just getting up from your computer at least once an hour for 250 steps can do wonders.

It's really all about balance. You don't need to be an Olympic athlete; just balance your life with your fitness plan. And if you realize you need to be more active, start right away.

Einstein knows how to sum things up. It is so true; keep moving and you will find everything falls into place and your life becomes more balanced. See Figure 9.2.

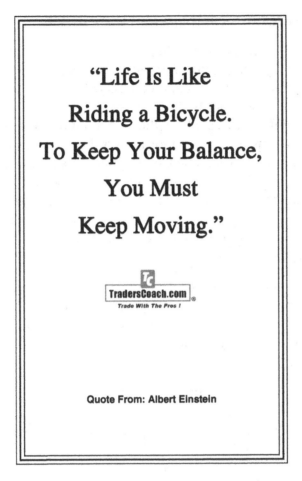

**Figure 9.2** MINI POSTER—BICYCLE—Just make sure you keep moving; it's the only way to stay balanced and to not fall over. Plus, you will be healthier. This quote is taken from a letter Einstein wrote to his son Edward on February 5, 1930. Quote from Albert Einstein.

## Three Areas of Fitness

Just as we strive to be whole-brain thinkers, we must become whole-body fitness enthusiasts. It's not about only going to the gym and getting physical exercise; we must strengthen our minds, hearts, and souls as well to be completely in the zone.

**These are the most important to focus on:**

1. **Physical Fitness:** Strengthens the heart, lungs, and muscles through physical activity. Interestingly, when you are physically fit, your emotional and mental fitness will improve as a result, so physical fitness benefits all three fitness areas.
2. **Emotional Fitness:** Strengthens our emotional response to adversity. This is a big area for traders, because emotions play a big part in how profitable we are. Emotions of anger, fear, and greed can derail even the most successful traders.
3. **Mental Fitness**: Strengthens the brain's ability to solve problems and process information. Again, this is a big area for traders since there are always changing market scenarios that need to be analyzed.

You can see that fitness is an all-encompassing endeavor. The rewards of taking care of yourself go much further than just becoming a better trader or investor. The rewards can enable you to be a healthier and more well-rounded person.

## 1. Physical Fitness

Keeping our bodies physically fit enables us to perform up to our full potential. Physical fitness involves strengthening the heart, lungs, and muscles of our bodies. Exercise can also influence both mental alertness and emotional stability, which is a bonus.

> *We can do nothing without the body, let us always take care that it is in the best condition to sustain us.*
> —Socrates, Greek Philosopher

Most of us recognize that taking care of our bodies is a priority. Which makes sense since every New Year the most common resolution is to exercise and get in shape. Hence, the world rushes out to sign up for a new gym membership. But did you know that according to the Fitness Industry Association, 80% of all new gym members quit or stop going to the gym after only 24 weeks?

That's disappointing, but common. The fantasy and dream of losing weight and getting those toned abs is present. What's lacking is the commitment to do the work and the patience to keep at it when the results don't appear instantly.

Believe me, been there, done that. I've had my battles with weight, and I'm here to tell you that you can win the battle, if that is something you struggle with. The secret is to have a heart-to-heart talk with yourself and make the commitment before you sign up for the gym.

Then do everything in your power to win the battle. Keep a regular routine that you adhere to. And work on your eating habits. A little further in this chapter, there's some helpful material on what to eat and how to eat. And don't get discouraged by setbacks because that is part of the process.

When my son was born in 1999 I weighed in at 228 pounds, with a BMI of around 37, which put me in the obese category according to Table 9.1. Having a family can shift the focus away from taking care of personal health, but I realized that wasn't a healthy path to follow. So with much effort and focus, my weight came back to a healthier number at 156 pounds.

That's 72 pounds lost and kept off. It didn't happen overnight, and it was a long 2-year process. There were times out with friends when I'd have to say, "No, can't have that pizza." But, in the end, a combination of being disciplined and going to the gym regularly four times a week, working with a trainer, and eating better worked for me.

But the reward is that I'm healthier and feel better than ever before. It's been more than 10 years that the weight has stayed off. On occasion I put on a few pounds, but overall, it's a happy ending.

Now that you know my story, let's talk about your story. You may already have a complete physical fitness routine in place and if so bravo! If you don't have one yet, it's important to tailor your program to your unique needs.

Even if you are thin and have absolutely no weight concerns, you still need to get exercise regularly. It's a matter of strengthening your heart and building endurance. You'll have more energy as a result. Case in point is my daughter, who recently joined a local gym. She is thin but wanted to get stronger. She goes three times a week, and what a huge difference it has made for her.

Be sure to take into consideration your age, current physical fitness condition, and any possible medical conditions you may have. You may even want to employ a trainer to help create a plan that is suited for you. And of course, consult with your physician before making any changes to your current exercise routine.

**A balanced physical fitness program strives to work on these primary areas:**

- **Aerobic and Cardio Endurance:** Delivers oxygen and nutrients to tissues and removes wastes, over sustained periods. Achieved with activities such as running, elliptical, bicycling, game sports such as tennis, etc.
- **Muscular Strength:** Builds up the strength and endurance of your muscles. Strength training can help you improve your muscular fitness. Achieved with free weights, a variety of exercise machines, etc.
- **Flexibility:** Helps to move joints and use muscles through their full range of motion. Flexibility can help improve circulation and posture, aid in stress relief, and enhance coordination. Achieved with stretching exercises.
- **Stability and Balance:** Building up your body's core muscle strength improves stability and balance. Working on the muscles in your lower back, pelvis, hips, and abdomen helps combat lower back pain and poor posture. Achieved with exercises focusing on the core muscles. The Pilates approach is known to focus on these areas.

Another important thing about physical fitness is that you must make it fun. Yeah, there's that saying, "no pain, no gain." And at first you might have muscle fatigue, but in the end it feels good. Plus, you will sleep better after some cardio and after you've stretched those muscles.

For me, the ways I've kept fit have varied over the years. It is easier to do something you enjoy, so if the gym isn't your thing, do something else. For example, as a kid sailing was my passion. Then when I was in the Navy running on the beach was a great workout. In New York City, my two favorites were karate and running in Central Park. Today my current love is mountain biking on the trails See Figure 9.3.

**Figure 9.3**    There are different ways to stay physically fit that don't require going to the gym. For me, I've done martial arts, running, and now my passion is mountain biking on the trails. Sometimes I go riding at night, and it's majestic. There is wildlife like deer and coyotes. Plus, it's nice to be outside in the fresh air. Find something that inspires you and not only will it keep your body fit but your mind and soul as well.

SOURCE: Photo 72910200 Bicycle Rider @ Bogdan Hoda Dreamstime.com

You can see there are lots of different ways to keep physically fit. Find the one that is fun for you and then stick with it. And be sure to be consistent with your program; make it part of your lifestyle. My success with fitness only came after it became an essential part of my life.

Every week I'm either riding the trails on my mountain bike, or if it's raining, I'm at the gym four times a week. You may start off with a different routine that is only two or three times a week. The trick is to not skip a workout day. Because that is a slippery slope; skipping one day turns into two, and so on. Again, consistency is the key.

## 2. Emotional Fitness

It's important for traders and investors to work on their emotional fitness because emotions play a big part in how profitable they are. Excessive emotions of anger, fear, or greed can take the wind out of your sails and impact your bottom line.

**Here are a couple of ways to build strong emotional muscles:**

- Cognitive restructuring
- Laughter therapy

By looking inward and taking the time to focus on our emotional fitness, we can strengthen our emotional muscles. When experiencing disrupting emotions in your trading, experiment with the following strategies to see which help you best.

### Cognitive Restructuring

This strategy helps to eliminate negative thinking. Thoughts when energized create emotions, so if we can change our thoughts, we can change our emotions. Basically, the goal is to eliminate negative self-talk that has developed into a *habit* that we may, or may not, be aware of. Generally, it is important to come up with a *replacement habit*, or positive self-talk to fill the void of the negative self-talk.

**Here's how it works:**

1. **Identify negative self-talk.** Listen to your self-talk, and write down what are the most common themes. Writing in your *Sunrise Trading Journal* will illuminate this negative self-talk for you. (Refer to Chapter 8 for more on the journal.) Following are examples of negative self-talk: "Nothing ever works out for me. No one likes me. I'm a loser. My future looks bleak."
2. **Replace the negative self-talk.** Once you can identify the negativity, the idea is to replace it with an opposite positive self-talk affirmation or mantra that you can say to yourself instead. Following are examples of positive self-talk: "Everything works out for me. Everyone likes me. I'm a winner. My future looks bright."
3. **Catch yourself in the act of negative self-talk.** Regularly concentrate on your thoughts, and when you do catch yourself with negative self-talk, consciously replace the negative thoughts with the positive thoughts. You will find that in time, the negative self-talk will go away.

Typically, in the world of affirmations, it is important to say the words either out loud, silently to yourself, or both. And it is crucial to say them as if they are true right now. At first, this will be uncomfortable, but over time the repetition makes it easier. Think of it as you are simply replacing your negative energy with positive energy; that is really all it is.

Affirmations and mantras are not a complete cure all, but they are effective at reducing negative energy and rewiring your brain. Remember, your thoughts do in fact create your reality.

## Laughter Therapy

Believe it or not, laughter therapy is a thing! For me all you really need is a healthy sense of humor. But the result of a good sense of humor is laughter, so the idea of *laughter therapy* is worth looking at.

Probably the first person to recognize the value of laughter in a big way is Norman Cousins who battled a life-threatening illness in the 1970s and was able to force it into remission with what he called *laughter therapy*.

*Laughter serves as a blocking agent. Like a bulletproof vest, it may help protect you against the ravages of negative emotions that can assault you in disease.*
        —Norman Cousins, author of *Anatomy of an Illness*

Some people have also called laughter the best medicine, with good reason, because it's been scientifically proven that laughter provides many amazing benefits.

### Laughter has natural physical benefits:

- Increased levels of happy brain chemicals such as serotonin, endorphins, oxytocin, and dopamine in the brain
- Reduced levels of cortisol, a stress hormone, by increasing the intake of oxygen and stimulating blood circulation
- Improved immune system, which assists in fighting infection and disease by increasing antibodies
- Lowered blood pressure
- Pain relieved by releasing endorphins, which are natural opiates and more effective than pharmaceuticals
- Combated insomnia because the cerebral cortex releases electrical impulses that block the passage of negative thoughts after laughter
- Increased emotional resilience

Did you know that laughter is 30 times more likely to occur in the company of others than when one is alone? Laughter is contagious. You are much more likely to laugh if you hear someone else laughing. So, part of the laughter therapy concept is to not isolate yourself, which is common among traders and investors who are glued to their computer screens all day.

I'm not suggesting that you to sign up for an in-depth laughter therapy retreat, but as you can see, laughter has benefits. When you have drawdowns and losses in your trading and investing, there is value in not taking them too seriously. You may find that being able to laugh at the situation, and maybe even laugh at yourself, will take the weight of the world off your shoulders.

It's a matter of exercising your sense of humor just like any other type of exercise program.

*Laughter is a form of internal jogging. It moves your internal organs around. It enhances respiration. It is an igniter for great expectations.*
   —Norman Cousins, author of Anatomy of an Illness

My prescription to you for more successful trading and investing, find humor every day and enjoy hearty laughter on a regular basis. Watch a funny movie, surround yourself with people who make you laugh, and avoid people that don't.

# 3. Mental Fitness

Mental fitness is different than physical or emotional fitness. It's the ability to keep our minds sharp, which is essential.

**Focus on the following areas to keep mentally fit:**

- Memory
- Processing speed
- Reaction speed
- Ability to learn
- Critical thinking
- Problem solving
- Ability to focus and concentrate

You may already have a well-rounded life that is keeping your mental fitness in tip-top shape. But if you don't, we've got a few ways to exercise those brain muscles, because if you don't lose it, you lose it!

**Improve your mental fitness the following ways:**

- Physical exercise
- Meditation
- Eat healthy nonprocessed foods

- Get a good night's sleep
- Playing games like chess, card games, doing crossword puzzles, jigsaw puzzles, etc.
- Learn something new
- Use your nondominant hand
- Socialize

Interestingly enough, physical exercise, meditation, healthy eating, and a good night's sleep are considered excellent ways to keep your mental capacities in peak condition. So, you get a triple benefit from them since they all keep you physically and emotionally fit as well.

## Annual Check-Ups

Of course, everyone has their own ideas regarding medical care and the like. I encourage you to follow your personal preferences. With that said, it is beneficial to have an annual check-up with your primary care physician to check you over once a year.

We can get busy with life and forget to do our annual check-ups, but keep in mind when you catch a problem early, it is easier to correct it. These days testing has gotten so efficient that a standard blood work panel and your physical exam can give you early detection of a variety of medical issues.

**An annual checkup can detect some health issues early:**

- Cancer
- Diabetes
- High blood pressure
- Vision
- High cholesterol
- Heart disease

I've known more than one person who could have prevented a fatal illness had they had an annual check-up with the recommended tests. Even if you are a young person, getting a routine check-up can save your life. None of us enjoy going to the doctor, but my friendly advice is to be proactive in this area.

## You Are What You Eat

Good food and nutrition help in all areas of fitness. Take note, the processed food revolution has filled our bodies with toxins, mostly from the preservatives that are used that can be damaging over the long term. Now more than ever, it's important to be mindful of what we put in our bodies.

The direct correlation between what you eat and your health is no big secret. You might be surprised though, or maybe not surprised, to know that there are many foods that can be used as remedies to common ailments. Matter of fact, many pharmaceuticals are derived from natural sources, not chemicals.

My favorite book on this kind of natural healing is *Prescription for Nutritional Healing* by Phyllis A. Balch, which is now in its fifth edition. It's a huge book with 883 pages jam packed with recipes and suggestions that can help you heal just about anything from A to Z.

The point is that food not only nourishes us with energy, but it can also heal us and keep us healthy.

**Here are some tips to healthy eating:**

- Avoid processed foods, saturated fat intake, and deep-fried foods.
- Thirty grams of unsaturated fat per day is recommended.
- Eat five portions of fruits and vegetables per day.
- Strive for variety in the whole foods you eat with the goal of 30 different types of whole-plant-based foods each week.
- Twenty-eight grams of fiber per day is recommended.
- Cut down on sugary sodas, candy, and treats.
- Limit the amount of salt you use.
- Be sure to include good protein in your diet.

- Limit your carbohydrate intake to 30% of your total calorie intake.
- The standard recommended number of calories per day is 2,000 calories, but any of the many calorie calculators online can give you more specific numbers.

When I was focused on losing weight, my routine was very strict. There were fasting days each week, and my carbohydrate and overall calorie intake was low. Now that my weight is normalized, it's more a matter of balance and quality of food.

Lots of materials online will assist you in customizing a healthy eating plan that will fit your needs. You might even enlist the help of a nutritionist if that is of interest. In the end, using common sense and balance is the best course of action.

## Night Night, Sleep Tight

Another important way to keep physically, emotionally, and mentally fit is by getting a deep night's sleep. You'll have clearer thinking, make fewer mistakes, and make better decisions. It also improves brain function allowing you to learn and remember more. Your reflexes will be faster, and your focus will be sharper.

**A good night's sleep provides many benefits:**

- Reduces stress
- Improves immune system
- Sharpens brain function allowing you to learn more
- Stimulates tissue repair and muscle growth
- Improves mood and minimizes irritability
- Affects appetite hormones in a positive way making it easier to keep weight off
- Repairs heart and blood vessels while you sleep

There are four stages of sleep: awake, light, deep, and REM (rapid eye movement). These stages are important because they allow the brain and body to recuperate and develop. Failure to obtain enough of both deep sleep and REM sleep may lead to health and emotional problems. Improving the quality of your sleep, can have profound effects.

**There are several ways to get a deeper sleep:**

- Get enough physical activity during the day.
- Increase daylight exposure, especially sunlight, which improves circadian rhythms.
- Cut down on evening caffeine intake.
- Set up a sleep routine with a fixed bedtime and wake-up time.
- Budget 30-minutes for winding down with music, reading a book, or light stretching.
- Test relaxation methods at bedtime, such as meditation, deep breathing, and mindfulness.

It's not about the quantity; it is more about the quality of your sleep. Be mindful of getting a good night's sleep when you are trading and investing; it can have a significant impact on your results.

## Motivation

So how do we get motivated to start, and then continue, our fitness program? We can all use a little extra motivation now and again. Many motivational speakers are out there to help give us that nudge in the right direction.

I can remember listening to Tony Robbins cassette tapes while driving around in my car in the 1980s. They did get me thinking about everything from eating right to having a positive mindset. I even went to see him in New York City in the 1990s. And frankly, he did get me motivated, which is a good thing.

You, on the other hand, may already be motivated and may not need any help with this. Although, if you are interested in tuning in to some of today's most popular motivators, here are a few to check out:

- **Tony Robbins:** Works on overcoming fears, strengthening communication, and staying fit and healthy. **Quote:** "Stop being afraid of what could go wrong, and start being excited about what could go right."
- **Deepak Chopra:** Works on healing, spirituality, personal development, and empowerment. **Quote:** "Negative emotions are like unwelcomed guests. Just because they show up on our doorstep doesn't mean they have a right to stay."
- **Gary Vaynerchuk:** Works on business strategies, content creation, and personal branding. **Quote:** "Look yourself in the mirror and ask yourself, 'What do I want to do every day for the rest of my life?' . . . then do that."

This is by no means a thorough list, but it's a start. There are motivational gurus that specialize in everything from losing weight to having a positive attitude to spiritual healing. Search online if you are interested in something specific, and you will surely find a variety to choose from.

Stay motivated and stay fit!

# Chapter 10
# Nothing to Fear

Arguably, fear can be the trader and investor's biggest challenge. To clarify, this is more often true for an inexperienced trader or investor. With financial market experience and success comes confidence, skill, and the absence of fear.

Fear is undeniably a powerful force and our strongest human survival mechanism. Yet, with its valuable qualities, unreasonable fear has sabotaged many traders and investors.

## We Have Nothing to Fear But Fear Itself

Certainly, during the Great Depression of the 1930s, fear was rampant in the United States with excessive unemployment as a result of the stock market crash of 1929.

> *This great Nation will endure as it has endured, will revive, and will prosper. So, first of all, let me assert my firm belief that the only thing we have to fear is fear itself—nameless, unreasoning, unjustified terror which paralyzes needed efforts to convert retreat into advance. Our greatest primary task is to put people to work. This is no unsolvable problem if we face it wisely and courageously.*
> —Franklin Delano Roosevelt, 32nd president of the
> United States from 1933 to 1945

103

Roosevelt's speech was a declaration of war on the economic hardship that 1929 brought upon the country. He referred to fear as a *". . . terror which paralyzes needed efforts to convert retreat into advance. . . ."*

One can't help but draw comparisons to fear in trading and investing with the kind of fear Roosevelt alluded to. If left unchecked, fear can become terror, which can paralyze efforts to convert losses into wins. When overcome with terror, it's impossible to think clearly.

Which is why Roosevelt continued in his address, *"The only thing we have to fear is fear itself."* See Figure 10.1. We can learn from this. In our trading and investing, the only thing we really have to fear is fear itself and the paralysis that accompanies it.

**Figure 10.1**    MINI POSTER—FEAR—This quote is from a presidential inaugural speech in 1933 during the Great Depression. For traders and investors, this quote is extremely useful. Quote from Franklin D. Roosevelt.

Another play to take from Roosevelt's playbook is to get to work and face problems with courage. Sitting idly by watching mounting losses in your account will not solve any problems. Courage and the action to attack a problem are what is needed. If you want to win the war on losses, you need courage and action.

## Name Your Fears

Taken to the extreme, a fear becomes a phobia. Doctors have identified hundreds of official phobias that each have specific treatment protocols.

**Here are 10 common phobias:**

- **Mysophobia—fear of germs or dirt**
- **Aerophobia—fear of flying**
- **Acrophobia—fear of heights**
- **Ophidiophobia—fear of snakes**
- **Arachnophobia—fear of spiders**
- **Nyctophobia—fear of the dark**
- **Cynophobia—fear of dogs**
- **Agoraphobia—fear of crowded places**
- **Claustrophobia—fear of small places**
- **Astraphobia—fear of thunder and lightning**

Some of these common fears or phobias might be on your list, but they probably won't make your trading and investing difficult. The fears that inhibit financial success are not as common, but just as challenging.

Many people believe that the most common fear for traders and investors is fear of failure, and you will see in my list of eight fears, that is number one on the list.

> *Don't fear failure. Not failure, but low aim, is the crime. In great attempts it is glorious to even fail.*
> —Bruce Lee, martial artist and actor

There is honor in failing when aiming high. And if you never give up, like Thomas Edison making 10,000 prototypes until the first lightbulb worked, you are victorious in the end. It's okay to lose the battle if you win the war. Okay, let's get back to naming fears and phobias.

**Here are eight fears and phobias that may be holding you back from being financially successful:**

1. **Atychiphobia—fear of failure.** This fear can be a self-fulfilling prophecy, focusing thoughts (even obsessing) on failure and therefore manifest failure by doing so. Must replace failure thoughts with success thoughts.

2. **Achievemephobia—fear of success.** Limits upside potential, environmental biases may be that successful people are bad, or that it's lonely at the top, fears of abandonment. Baby steps approach to become gradually comfortable with success with small victories, building up to larger ones. It is okay to be successful without guilt.

3. **Metathesiophobia—fear of change.** Humans are uncomfortable with change of any type. When taken to a phobic level, it requires courage to go from being a struggling (or break even) trader and investor to transform into a successful one. Baby steps are best with small victories, building up to larger ones.

4. **Atelophobia—fear of making mistakes.** Perfectionists can get stuck and not move forward for fear of making mistakes. Trading and investing inherently involves risk and mistakes are part of the cost of doing business. When losses occur, do positive thought work to overcome the fear.

5. **Ergophobia—fear of work.** Not necessarily lazy but concerned with putting effort in and the risk of not being rewarded. Concentrate on enjoying the process of trading and investing itself, regardless of the financial outcome.

6. **Peniaphobia—fear of becoming poor.** This phobia can afflict both wealthy and poor individuals alike. Risk tolerance is non-existent, making trading and investing difficult for this person. Concentrate on risk management to alleviate these fears.

7. **Enosiophobia—fear of criticism.** Ego is delicate to the extreme, which prevents learning from past failures. Denial is preventing constructive criticism (even self-criticism) from assisting in improving performance. Develop the courage to self-assess and take criticism without anger, resentment, or discomfort.

8. **Xenophobia—fear of the unknown.** Having this type of fear is related to not having control, not being able to anticipate, due to the nature of the unknown. Accept the adventure of the journey and the unknown. Let go of the need to control.

Each of these eight fears can have their own unique hold on our psyche. Which ones may afflict us can be revealing as to our financial psychology. No doubt we could debate as to which are the most common or most powerful fears.

*The oldest and strongest emotion of mankind is fear, and the oldest and strongest kind of fear is fear of the unknown.*
    —H. P. Lovecraft, author of *Supernatural Horror in Literature*

Lovecraft wrote horror novels in the 1920s that inspired the likes of current authors such as Stephen King. So, he knew a thing or two about how to generate fear. Interesting that he would say that the strongest fear is fear of the unknown.

*People have a hard time letting go of their suffering. Out of a fear of the unknown, they prefer suffering because it is familiar.*
    —Thich Nhat Hanh, Buddhist monk

While Lovecraft and Thich Nhat Hanh recognize the power of fear of the unknown, others like Napoleon Hill, author of *Think and Grow Rich*, lists the top six fears preventing success but does not include fear of the unknown.

**Six fears Napoleon Hill lists in his book *Think and Grow Rich*:**

- **Fear of poverty**
- **Fear of criticism**
- **Fear of ill health**
- **Fear of the loss of love**
- **Fear of old age**
- **Fear of death**

It was Hill's firm belief that one must learn how to outwit the six ghosts of fear by recognizing fear as a state of mind and replacing a fear with positive alternative thinking:

*Fears are nothing more than a state of mind.*
—Napolean Hill, author of *Think and Grow Rich*

One of the best ways to conquer fears is to name them. And then as Napoleon Hill suggests, replace them with positive alternative thinking. Look at our list of eight fears and phobias that can hold you back from financial success, including fear of the unknown, and see if any of them might ring true for you.

Once you've started to name your fears, you can begin to face them, manage them, and ultimately conquer them.

## Fear of Missing Out—FOMO

Have you ever had trouble finding a setup, where nothing is lining up with your strategy to give you a high probability entry? You are looking, scanning, waiting, and there's nothing. So, you start forcing setups where there are none. Just to get in the market, to be in the game, so you won't miss out.

Well, sometimes, no trade is the best trade. Meaning, staying out of the market doing nothing is better in the end than jumping in on a bad trade or investment and losing money. And yet, we've all been there; it's easy to get impatient.

There's a new term that has been coined: FOMO. The fear of missing out. It's so new that there is no official medical definition to diagnose and treat it although it can cause stress, anxiety, and depression.

First identified in 1996 by marketing strategist Dr. Dan Herman, it is so commonly used that you can look it up in Merriam-Webster's dictionary. Herman conducted extensive research on the subject and published the first academic paper on the topic in 2000.

His initial study was primarily focused on social media. Before the internet there was an old-fashioned related phenomenon known as "keeping up with the Joneses," similar to FOMO.

The condition involves a feeling of apprehension that one is missing out on information, events, experiences, or life decisions that could make one's life better. It can also create apprehension that one is not as good as the "Joneses," which triggers a competition reflex to keep up with the "Joneses" in one way or another.

Fear of this kind can lead to poor financial decisions as a result of perceived social pressure. It can also lead to an obsessive need to watch the markets constantly and to join as many financial online groups as possible, to be sure nothing is missed out on.

And it can lead to entering positions just to not miss out on the action, even if there is no good entry strategy. Again, sometimes no trade is the best trade.

Remember, worrying about how other traders and investors are doing and whether you are missing out will end in unneeded stress. Focus your energy on your method and your process and be skillfully patient.

## Fear of Pulling the Trigger

The opposite of FOMO is fear of pulling the trigger. This can happen even when all the stars are aligned and the setup is perfect. Maybe a previous trade or investment failed, and the fear is that this one will turn out the same way. Or you may be innately risk averse, which creates fear on every single position.

## Fear of Letting Go

A number of brokerage houses have revealed statistics from the aggregate from millions of trades placed by their traders. This is where the "90% of active traders lose money" figure comes from.

You might find another statistic interesting, which is supported by actual data. Traders are right more than 50% of the time. But they lose more money overall because they are losing a significantly more on the losing trades than they are winning on the winning trades.

Which brings us to our next fear.

The fear of letting go, or the fear of being wrong. The statistics suggest that it is more likely for a trader to hold onto a losing trade than to hold on to a winning trade.

Why?

The quick answer is ego. It's not easy to admit when we are wrong, but at what cost? The experienced traders have mastered the ability to let go of the losers and have no remorse or regret. Their ego is not at stake, whereas inexperienced traders will cling on to losing trades hoping that they will turn around.

Lesson learned: let your winners ride, cut your losers short, and leave your ego at the door.

## Is it Reasonable or Unreasonable Fear?

The causes of fear are varied and complex. Understanding our personal relationship with fear is the start to diffusing its power. Before we go any further though, we must determine if our fears are reasonable or unreasonable.

For example, a thousand-pound brown bear protecting her baby cubs may attack you in the woods; that is a real reason to be afraid. The fear is reasonable because the bear is a deadly threat. On the other hand, if a child is afraid of the dark and has a severe panic attack when the lights are turned out, that is not a real reason to be afraid; the fear is unreasonable.

To be sure, both are feeling real emotions of fear with all that it entails. First cortisol is released, then adrenaline starts pumping, pupils will dilate, breathing accelerates, heart rate and blood pressure rise, maybe there is a bit of that sweaty palm and dry mouth syndrome.

These symptoms are the amygdala (in the brain's cerebrum) at work, eliciting the fear response. The brain makes decisions about what will keep us safe, regardless of whether the threat is genuine or not.

The brain chooses between four different responses, which are fight, flight, freeze, or fawn response. We will go into that in just a bit, but for now, how do we determine if the fear is reasonable or unreasonable with our financial endeavors?

## Reasonable Fear

Our earlier example of the thousand-pound brown bear attacking you in the woods is a reasonable fear. That is a life and death situation, literally, and generates the same primal fear that a cave man would have felt back in the day, complete with adrenaline pumping and heart racing.

But today, literal life-and-death events are less common, so one has to ask what would cause that kind of fear now? Maybe financial life and death could generate the same response? I think so.

So, let's say someone is trading and investing in the financial markets, and he hasn't used any risk control, doesn't have a stop loss exit, and is using the money that was supposed to go toward next month's rent and food.

The position is going against him fast, really fast, his heart is racing, and he is scared of losing all his money on this one position. Yup, the rent and food money. In essence, that is the same as the thousand-pound bear attack. Because if there's no food to eat and no roof overhead, it is kind of like life and death.

In this case, the fear is reasonable.

The trading and investing approach is not reasonable. But the fear is reasonable. Not too much one can do about the fear in this example, except to not trade with rent and food money in the future. And be sure to use risk control and stop loss exits next time. Plus getting education prior to trading with real money is not a bad idea.

What is interesting about this example is that anyone in the financial markets using rent and food money (money they can't afford to risk) is prone to a gambling mindset. There is an attraction or addiction to the thrill and the adrenaline of the ups when winning and the downs when losing, much like a roller coaster ride.

If you are attracted to the adrenaline of winning and losing and enjoy the adrenaline rush of just being in the game, take a look at whether you are in the markets for the right reasons.

### Unreasonable Fear

With our other example earlier, a child is afraid of the dark and experiences a severe panic attack when the lights are turned out. That is not a real reason to be afraid. That is unreasonable fear.

An example of unreasonable fear for traders or investors is when they have money in the markets, are using money they can afford to risk, have a system that has a proven edge, and have a stop loss exit set to a level where the most they can lose is two percent on this position—and yet they have a severe panic attack. Or they exit the trade too soon and miss out on getting more profit.

In this case the fear is unreasonable.

Or consider this, you enter a position, and it immediately goes against you with a small pullback, which is quite typical. You suddenly feel that fearful twinge. Here's the thing, markets do not go in a straight line, they move in zig zag lines, and that is normal. So don't panic. Don't bail on the position unless it hits your stop. No need for fear in this case. Thankfully with experience, the fearful twinges will lessen.

The moral of this story is that when you've done everything right and still have excessive anxiety, fear, or panic, there is something going on that needs to be examined. That's when you must name your fear and work on managing it. See Figure 10.2.

### All-or-Nothing Fear

Another kind of fear that can disable you is "all-or-nothing" fear. It is the same as unreasonable fear, but with a twist. With this kind of fear, there is no gray area; in your mind, you are either winning

# **F**ALSE

# **E**VIDENCE

# **A**PPEARING

# **R**EAL

**Figure 10.2** *False evidence appearing real* creates the acronym FEAR. Sometimes the cause of unreasonable fear can be false evidence or distorted perceptions. Whenever you experience fear while in the financial markets, check to determine if the fear is reasonable or unreasonable, and then act accordingly.

big or losing big. You're living in a black-and-white world. The responses are heightened and exaggerated.

For example, you're in a position, and your stop gets hit. You exit at a loss. But it's a small loss. The problem is, when experiencing "all-or-nothing fear," there is no such thing as a small loss. Instead, emotionally, the small loss generates an exaggerated response, to the point of spiraling out of control. The fear is that everything is ruined, the account will go to zero, and you will go broke. The fear is that you are out of control and that you are gambling.

The reality is that it's a normal loss, a normal drawdown, one that has been managed due to your excellent risk control. And this kind of loss is part of the business and to be expected.

Keep an eye out for this, and if you experience it again name it, and work on managing it. Remember, it is not the end of the world; keep things in perspective.

## Four Responses to Fear

When we are afraid, we experience a number of symptoms that range from adrenaline pumping, heart rate and blood pressure rising, and accelerated breathing. The amygdala, in the brain's cerebrum, is at work generating the fear response. Basically, the brain is making decisions about what will keep us safe. There are four different responses:

1. **Fight response.** The brain attempts to have you ward off danger by defeating it. This can be a verbal or physical attack and is accompanied by intense anger. High energy.
2. **Flight response.** If our brain doesn't feel you can fight off danger, it may decide to have you run away or hide, triggering a flight response. High energy.
3. **Freeze response.** The brain decides to have you shut down, stay frozen, and quiet, like a deer in the headlights. Processing is slowed down, making it difficult to speak or make rational decisions. Theories suggest that this response is a primal strategy to make us *invisible* to the danger (a bear for example) until the danger passes. Low energy.
4. **Fawn response.** The brain decides to have you try and please whatever is triggering the fear response to prevent it from causing harm. Appease the threat, abandon one's own needs to serve another's needs. Low energy.

Typically, most people will refer to only the fight-or-flight response to fear. But if you think about it, the freeze and fawn response are also very common. You alone will know what your brain is telling you to do during fearful trading and investing episodes. Use a journal or trade posting card to document when these responses kick in.

## Are You Suffering From Financial Market PTSD?

If you had a significant loss already in the financial markets, it may have left an emotional imprint on you. If the loss was so big that it was traumatic, you may in effect be suffering from a type of PTSD (posttraumatic stress disorder) that you may not be aware of.

Once trading and investing becomes associated with a traumatic experience, the brain comes to expect losses and betrayal from the market on future positions. Small normal losses can trigger the same amount of fear that was experienced during the previous traumatic loss, even though the current losses are much smaller.

Because risk cannot be eliminated from trading, the inability to tolerate even small risk works against you. It makes you late in pulling the trigger or makes it impossible to stay in a good trade and let the winners run.

When you've got baggage like a traumatic loss in your past, you've got to reprogram your brain to reduce your fear. The first step is to be aware that your brain is influenced by the financial trauma you experienced in the past. Next try *cognitive restructuring,* which is covered in the Fitness chapter. Then start using the tips to reduce fear that are listed later in this chapter. It is possible to overcome your past trauma.

## Getting Stuck in Your Comfort Zone

At times we get stuck in our comfort zone because it is familiar. Just like that *fear of the unknown,* it takes courage to break out and try something you have never tried before. You may fear falling on your face, but then there's also the thrill of the opportunity of succeeding. See Figure 10.3.

Have the courage to go for it!

##  Tips to Reduce Fear

You got this. As Roosevelt said, ". . .there's nothing to fear but fear itself. . . ." You'll find that the more experienced you get, with small victories and then larger victories, your fear will wither away. In the meantime, a few tried and true strategies can help you manage any fear you might be experiencing now.

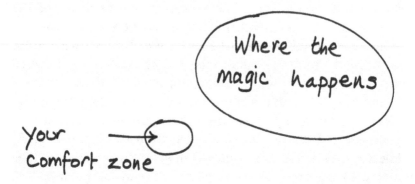

**Figure 10.3**    Fear can prevent us from leaving our comfort zone, but of course if we never leave our comfort zone, we will never grow. Playing it safe never helped anyone to achieve anything of real value. Have the courage to take risks, leave your comfort zone, and make your dreams come true.

My favorite tip is to stay productive and active, which is why it is first on the following list.

> *Inaction breeds doubt and fear. Action breeds confidence and courage. If you want to conquer fear, do not sit home, and think about it. Go out and get busy.*
> —Dale Carnegie, author of *How to Win Friends and Influence People*

Taking action can turn around fear in an instant. Sitting and worrying will only make the fear multiply. So, if you've got some fear, as Carnegie says, *get busy!*

**Following are some tips to reduce your fear:**

- Stay productive and active.
- Identify and name the fear(s) you have.
- Write in your *Sunrise Trading Journal* every day.
- Create a detailed plan with specific rules in writing.
- Identify one single strategy and master it.
- Paper-trade in a safe risk-free simulated environment.
- Debrief both your winning and losing positions.

- Build your confidence.
- Go smaller in your trade and investment size.
- Step away from the monitor when the fear is too much.
- Strive for small victories at first and build on them.
- Educate yourself.
- Stay in the present moment, avoid unreasonable fear of the future and unproductive guilt of the past.

When you feel fear, ask yourself, "Is it reasonable and in response to a real threat? Or is it unreasonable and in response to an imagined threat?" The fact that you feel fear may indicate you do not trust or believe in your trading and investing skills. In this case, you need to go back to testing your system in a simulated environment to gain confidence that you are ready.

Remember, this is an exciting journey you are on—embrace it. Think of any fears that come up as growing pains. And know that you are building skills that will last a lifetime.

## Be Courageous!

No doubt about it, facing fear takes courage. It's not a fun task. But the reward can be that you get the monkey off your back, or at least manage the monkey.

*Courage is resistance to fear, mastery of fear, not absence of fear.*
—Mark Twain, author of *The Adventures of Tom Sawyer*

You can resist your fear and ultimately master it. In the end not only will your trading and investing thrive, but you find greater freedom in all that you do.

## All You Need Is Love

If you experience fear when you are in the financial markets, there is something that is not right. Either you are reckless, which is causing justified fear, or you are inexperienced and haven't mastered your emotions yet. In the end, you need to like yourself, even when you make mistakes. As the song goes ". . .all you need is love. . . ."

> *Love, love, love. There's nothing you can do that can't be done. Nothing you can sing that can't be sung. Nothing you can make that can't be made. No one you can save that can't be saved. Nothing you can do, but you can learn how to be you in time. It's easy. All you need is love.*
> —Paul McCartney and John Lennon, The Beatles

It may sound corny, but it's true. Folks who beat themselves up for every financial loss, mistake, and stop out are the ones that don't really like themselves. And often fear comes out of excessive self-criticism, self-loathing, and doubt.

So, work on cutting yourself some slack, especially while you are learning. You'll find it can do wonders for your bottom line, the speed of your learning, and your enjoyment of the process.

# Step III

# Implement Risk Management

# Chapter 11
# Risk Management Essentials

Why do you need risk management?

Typically, experienced traders understand the life-and-death aspect of the financial markets. They know that there is, in fact, a risk of ruin. They know the answer to the question "Why?" and they deeply believe risk management is needed.

Maybe this is because they have lived it. Maybe it's because they've been knocked down and had to get up. Maybe the-eat-or-be-eaten reality of financial survival in the markets is familiar for them. Whatever the reason, professionals all use risk management on every trade without fail, and that is how they stay profitable for the long haul.

## ◎ The Question Is Why?

In contrast to professional traders, the inexperienced tend to jump into the markets with a naïve illusion that all one needs is a great entry into a great trade, end of story. They are searching for the magic bullet, the perfect system, the Holy Grail.

They aren't thinking about the potential downside; they are focusing only on the upside. And they're looking for a winning system that will be right all the time.

Ordinarily I would applaud this sense of optimism.

Sure, it would be nice to have the perfect winning system that operated like a printing press for creating cash every day, in all market cycles, no matter what. Just push a button and get rich quick.

But trading and investing in the financial markets is a different animal. No matter how good you get, you will always have losing trades and investments. And there is no perfect system. The good news is, you don't need a perfect system when you implement effective risk control.

### Question

Why do you need risk management?

### Answer

- It protects you when you are wrong, and you will be wrong.
- You can cut your losses short and let your winners ride.
- It reduces your stress level, which reduces costly trading errors.
- You get peace of mind, so you can sleep at night.
- You can run a real business with risk control as part of the plan.
- It changes your trading mindset from gambler to professional trader.
- The very real risks in trading and investing are controlled.

Feel free to add your own answers to this question, since we all have a unique take on this topic.

When you implement risk management, you have a far better chance at long-term profitability. Without risk management, you are basically gambling at a casino in Las Vegas, where the house always wins. Using risk control separates you from the rest of the pack and will put you on the road to success.

## Six Risks in Trading

There are different types of risk in trading and investing in the financial markets, much like life itself. And for each type of risk, we must implement a strategy to minimize the possible downside.

In life we accept risk every time we get into an automobile, either as a passenger or a driver. To control that risk we use precautions, such as seat belts, air bags, speed limits, and traffic laws, insurance for both liability and collision, and making sure that the driver's judgment is not impaired by alcohol and the like. These precautions are designed to reduce, not eliminate, risk.

It's the same with financial risks. Our money management plan is designed to reduce, not eliminate, the risk of losing some or all our capital.

**Here are six primary trading and investing risks:**

1. Trade risk
2. Market risk
3. Margin risk
4. Liquidity risk
5. Overnight risk
6. Volatility risk

Each of these six risks requires a different strategy. We'll cover the strategies needed later, but for now let's plant the seed in your mind. Keep an eye out for all risks and start thinking differently.

## Start Right Now!

Time is of the essence. If you don't have any risk management protocols in place, stop everything, and focus on getting them implemented right now. Not tomorrow, not next week, not when you have some extra time. Do it now.

If not, you may be only one trade away from financial ruin. The markets are swift and powerful and have a knack for finding our weaknesses.

Sometimes the worst thing that can happen to a newcomer in the financial markets is getting lucky with a couple of big wins in the beginning, before a risk control plan is in place, which gives the newcomer a false sense of security and confidence.

Often, what happens next is that the markets school the trader with an enormous, unexpected loss.

You may have already experienced a big loss. It's quite common. If you learn from the loss, that is a good thing. You can chalk it up to the school of hard knocks. In the end, what doesn't kill us makes us stronger.

## Twelve Risk-Management Essentials to Live By

Whether you are new to trading or a seasoned veteran, you must live by a few risk management essentials. All the time and without hesitation.

In coaching traders over the last 20 years, I've found that even some of the most experienced traders, folks who already know these money management essentials, get amnesia on occasion.

Typically, this amnesia occurs after a winning streak. Ego takes over. They don't need those pesky risk control rules because they are THAT good. You get the idea.

The reason for mentioning this is that no matter how new or how experienced you are, it is important to review the essentials from time to time, especially if you find yourself losing more than you are winning.

*Twelve Risk Management Essentials to Live By*

1. You have to BELIEVE you need risk management.
2. Write down your rules and stick to your rules, always.

3. Don't let a small loss (or mistake) turn into a gigantic loss.
4. Always set a stop-loss exit on EVERY position.
5. Set your stop-loss exit BEFORE you enter a position.
6. Once you are in a position and your stop-loss exit gets hit, get out immediately.
7. Calculate the optimal trade size on every position.
8. Keep meticulous DAILY records of your profit and loss (this keeps you honest).
9. Know your current win and payoff ratios at all times.
10. Paper trade until you have a profitable set of rules before trading with real money.
11. Accept that no matter how good you are, not every trade or investment will be a winner.
12. Strive for and attain the "Trader's Mindset" where you are in the zone with no stress or anxiety.

Now that you know what the 12 essentials are, the next step is to get up and running with your own custom system that works for you.

## A Penny Saved Is a Penny Earned

Benjamin Franklin is quoted as saying, "A penny saved is a penny earned."

*Fun Fact*

Although this is one of the adages most often attributed to him, he never actually said it. In his 1737 *Poor Richard's Almanac,* Franklin delivered the line: "A penny saved is two pence clear." And a century before Franklin's almanac was published, in 1640, the poet George Herbert wrote the following line in *Outlandish Proverbs*: "A penny spar'd is twice got." Meaning, if you don't spend a penny and save it instead, you're "up" a penny instead of "down" a penny. Thus, you are now twice as rich. The math isn't perfect, but you get the idea. See Figure 11.1.

**Figure 11.1**   It's not a new idea to focus on saving pennies because in the end, every penny you save (or every penny you don't lose in the financial markets) is a penny "twice got" as George Herbert wrote in *Outlandish Proverbs*, published in 1640.
SOURCE: File ID 12867454 © Vladimir Gladcov Dreamstime.com

It is paramount to focus on "not losing" capital (or saving a penny) as opposed to only thinking about "winning" more capital (or earning a penny). This is where novice traders get into trouble since logic suggests that there is nothing more important than "winning" or "earning" as many pennies as you can. See Figure 11.2, where legendary Paul Tudor Jones states just that.

### *The Reality Is in Trading; You Will Have Losing Trades . . . Period*

The following chapters in this book will show you how to manage those losing positions like a professional, resulting in greater profits at the end of the day. You'll discover how to cut the losers short and let the winners ride. And when your strategic plan is in place, you can sleep at night because you know your downside is protected.

Which brings me to an important story. In the beginning of my trading career, there was one AMAT trade that kept me up at night.

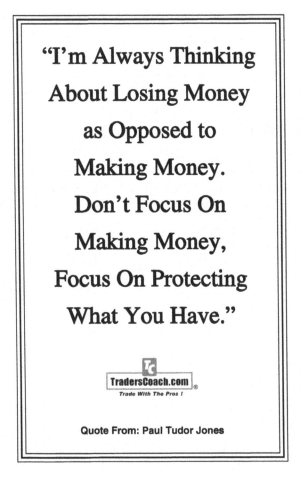

**Figure 11.2** MINI POSTER—PROTECTING WHAT YOU HAVE—This quote, from a legendary and successful trader, says it all. Focus on protecting what you have. Quote from Paul Tudor Jones.

Let's just say, it didn't end well. That painful trade drove me to focus like a laser beam on how to never experience that again. I picked up every risk control book I could get my hands on, no matter the cost. Every day was dedicated to studying the methods and formulas in these books, and the math was complicated to say the least.

Finally, what I needed to do became so crystal clear that I never looked back. Because I use the methods you'll discover here, that pain is a distant memory never to be repeated. So maybe that nightmare trade was a blessing in disguise.

My hope is that if you haven't yet experienced the pain of a losing trade gone out of control, maybe the next few chapters will save you from that kind of pain. And if you've already learned the hard way how powerful financial markets can be, you will discover some simple strategies to protect yourself going forward.

The moral of the story is that as traders we must learn to "save a penny" and control our downside, which in the end is just as important (if not more important) than learning how to "earn a penny." Let's get started saving those pennies!

# Chapter 12

# Win Ratio and Payoff Ratio

The foundation of your entire money management and risk control plan starts with knowing what your win and payoff ratios are. Knowing these ratios helps you decide how much to risk on each trade. These ratios tell you exactly what your current success and performance are at any given moment. If you are not currently tracking these numbers, now is the time to start.

On a very basic level, to calculate these ratios, you'll need to keep meticulous trading records. Chapter 15 of this book includes a comprehensive recordkeeping system that you can put into action immediately. Just print out the ledgers and posting cards, fill in the blanks, and you are good to go.

## Win Ratio Formula

Your win ratio is based on your percentage of wins and your probability of winning. For example, if your win ratio is 60%, you have 60% winning trades and 40% losing trades.

The more winning trades you have the better, although in trading you will never have 100% winning trades. This figure may fluctuate day to day, and it is important for you to constantly observe it to determine if there has been a market cycle change or if you're experiencing a normal drawdown.

### Win Ratio Formula

$$\frac{\text{Number of Winning Trades}}{\text{Number of Total Trades}} = \text{Win Ratio}$$

### Win Ratio Example

$$\frac{60}{100} = 0.60 = 60\% \text{ Winning Trades}$$

### Win Ratio Percentage Example

$0.60 \times 100 = 60\%$ winning trades to 40% losing trades
(To get a percentage, multiply the win ratio result by 100.)

## Payoff Ratio Formula

This ratio tells you how many dollars you earn for every dollar you lose. The higher your payoff ratio the better. If you are earning $3 for every $1 you lose (3 to 1), are doing well.

If you are earning $1 for every $1 you lose (1 to 1), you are breaking even and will need to determine how to improve this ratio. Sometimes, a comprehensive risk and money management system will enable you to fix a breakeven or losing trading system.

### Payoff Ratio Formula

$$\frac{\text{Average Winning Trade \$ Amount}}{\text{Average Losing Trade \$ Amount}} = \text{Payoff Ratio}$$

**Payoff Ratio Example**

$$\frac{\$300}{\$100} = 3 \text{ to } 1$$

# Risk of Ruin

Risk of ruin (ROR) is the probability that a trader is likely to lose so much capital that it would be impossible to recover the losses. The trader's account would be financially ruined.

It's why we use a risk management plan in the first place. Depending on how close we may have personally come to wiping out our own trading account, most of us understand the emotional and financial toll it takes when we lose a large sum of money.

Which brings us to the ROR tables. Table 12.1 is a portion of Balsara's 10% ROR table and shows how the relationship between the payoff and win ratios determines how likely a trader is to get wiped out.

TABLE 12.1  ROR probabilities with 10% of capital at risk.

| Risk of Ruin Probabilities with 10% Capital at Risk | Payoff Ratio 1 to 1 | Payoff Ratio 2 to 1 | Payoff Ratio 3 to 1 | Payoff Ratio 4 to 1 | Payoff Ratio 5 to 1 |
|---|---|---|---|---|---|
| Win Ratio 30% | 100.0% | 100.0% | 27.7% | 10.2% | 6.0% |
| Win Ratio 40% | 100.0% | 14.3% | 2.5% | 1.3% | 0.8% |
| Win Ratio 50% | 99.0% | 0.8% | 0.2% | 0.1% | 0.1% |
| Win Ratio 60% | 1.7% | 0.0% | 0.0% | 0.0% | 0.0% |

A 0.0% probability means the total loss of capital is unlikely, but not impossible.

SOURCE: The calculations on this table were prepared by Professor Nauzer Balsara. For additional calculations and reference tables on ROR, refer to his book, *Money Management Strategies for Futures Traders*, John Wiley & Sons, 1992, starting on page 18.

When you study Table 12.1 closely, it's easy to see that ROR is entirely dependent on your payoff and win ratios, combined with how much capital you are putting at risk.

## ROR Is a Clear and Present Danger for Traders and Investors

Next, Table 12.2 shows how you can go from a probability of 100% to 0% ROR just by changing your win ratio from 30% to 60% while keeping your payoff ratio and percentage of capital at risk the same.

Finally, in Table 12.3, notice that you can go from a probability of nearly 100% ROR to nearly 0% just by changing your payoff ratio from 1 to 1 to 5 to 1 while keeping your win ratio and percentage of capital at risk the same.

## Three Variables in the ROR Equation

Exploring the world of ROR, we find a lot of moving parts. By controlling what we can control, that being the percentage of capital we put at risk, we are closer to avoiding the risk-of-ruin.

TABLE 12.2    Relationship between win ratio and payoff ratio with 10% of capital at risk, changing the win ratio only.

| 100% Probability of risk-of-ruin | 0.0% Probability of risk-of-ruin |
|---|---|
| Win Ratio 30% with Payoff Ratio of 2 to 1 | Win Ratio 60% with Payoff Ratio of 2 to 1 |

A 0.0% probability means the total loss of capital is unlikely, but not impossible.

SOURCE: The calculations on this table were prepared by Professor Nauzer Balsara. For additional calculations and reference tables on ROR, refer to his book, *Money Management Strategies for Futures Traders*, John Wiley & Sons, 1992, starting on page 18.

**TABLE 12.3**   Relationship between win ratio and payoff ratio with 10% of capital at risk, changing the payoff ratio only.

| 99% Probability of ROR | 0.1% Probability of ROR |
| --- | --- |
| Win ratio 50%<br>  with payoff ratio of 1 to 1 | Win ratio 50%<br>  with payoff ratio of 5 to 1 |

**A 0.0% probability means the total loss of capital is unlikely, but not impossible.**

SOURCE: The calculations on this table were prepared by Professor Nauzer Balsara. For additional calculations and reference tables on ROR, refer to his book, *Money Management Strategies for Futures Traders*, John Wiley & Sons, 1992, starting on page 18.

### Three Variables in the ROR Equation

- **Win ratio**—constant fixed variable; you can't adjust this number.
- **Payoff ratio**—constant fixed variable; you can't adjust this number.
- **Percentage of capital at risk**—flexible variable; you can adjust this number.

After studying Balsara's and Vince's work, it's clear they are mathematical geniuses, and I'm happy to leave the heavy lifting on the actual ROR formulas, tables, and calculations to them. Rest assured, you can too.

All you need to do is grasp the big picture concepts that I'm simplifying here, and you can apply them to your money management quicker and benefit from controlling your risk right now.

## The Happy Couple

Your win and payoff ratios are not mutually exclusive; they are connected at the hip. Together they tell the whole story. Once you discover that your payoff and win ratios are married, it opens up a world of understanding. Be sure you respect the balance between your win and payoff ratios.

*Geraldine said, "What you see is what you get! (WYSIWYG)"*

What you see with your win and payoff ratios is what you get. You can't wave a magic wand and bend them to your will. The only way these variables ever change is when your skill or performance changes.

For example, if your skill improves, your payoff and win ratios are likely to improve. Or if a sudden market cycle change occurs and your current trading rules don't perform well in the new market cycle, your win and payoff ratios are likely to suffer.

Otherwise, they are always fixed and constant.

Flip Wilson coined the phrase, "What you see is what you get," when he performed as Geraldine, a favorite character on his 1970s comedy show. Geraldine's famous saying evolved into WYSIWYG, an acronym commonly used in computer programming.

Think of your payoff ratio and win ratio in WYSIWYG terms. You can't change them; they are what they are. What you see is what you get.

The amount of capital you choose to put at risk, on the other hand, is not a fixed variable. You can change the size of your trade and your capital at risk to suit your needs and your trading plan.

It's a powerful fact, because when you reduce your capital at risk, or trade size, you reduce your ROR. You have complete and total control over how much capital you put at risk on each trade. And that puts you in the driver's seat.

## ◎ That's When the Light Bulb Turns On

When we truly understand the importance of risk control and money management, that's when the light bulb turns on.

One of the first ways to manage your risk is to control your trade size and amount of capital at risk. It's so simple, and yet many traders miss this completely.

*Novice traders trade 5 to 10 times too big. They are taking 5 to 10% risk, on trades they should be taking 1 to 2% risk on.*
                    —Bruce Kovner, Original Market Wizard

Kovner is right on the mark with his observation. New traders and investors generally miss the mark on how important calculating optimum trade size is. They simply trade too big and don't even know it. Again, the only way to determine the correct amount of capital to put at risk is by always knowing what your current win and payoff ratio performance metrics are.

Time and time again, I've seen students experience that "aha" moment, when they see how much these truths affect their bottom line, the moment when they see how a previous big loss could have been avoided with a few simple tweaks to their trade size and their plan.

## Balsara's 10% Capital at Risk Is the Elephant in the Room

Before we go much further, let's address the "elephant in the room," that being the 10% capital at risk in Balsara's ROR (Table 12.1). Risking 10% of one's capital is a gutsy move and not for the faint of heart . . . or the novice trader. Some might consider 10% capital at risk downright reckless. See Figure 12.1.

Although Balsara's tables are extremely useful in illustrating the relationship between win ratio, payoff ratio, and capital at risk, keep in mind these tables were prepared for master traders.

A more conservative amount of capital to risk would be 1% or 2%. These amounts are more practical for the average trader.

## Optimal $f$ Formula

This formula calculates the optimal fraction $(f)$ of capital to be risked. The optimal $f$ formula was originally developed by John L.

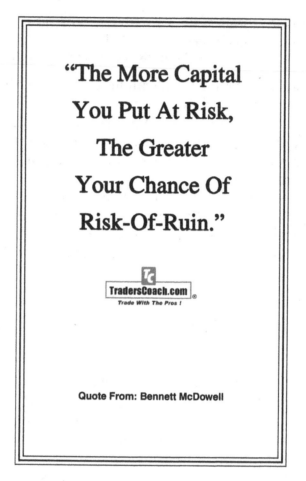

**Figure 12.1**   MINI POSTER—CAPITAL AT RISK—Be mindful of the danger in trading "too big." Control your trade size and capital at risk on every trade based on your current win and payoff ratios. Quote from Bennett McDowell.

Kelly, Jr., of Bell Labs in the early 1940s and is sometimes referred to as the *Kelly formula*. Edward O. Thorp, in *The Mathematics of Gambling*, modified the fixed-fraction formula to account for the average payoff ratio, $A$, in addition to the average probability of success, $p$.

In his book *Money Management Strategies for Futures Traders*, Balsara defined the formula for determining the optimal fraction, $f$, of capital to be risked on a trade, as shown next.

### Optimal *f* Formula

$$f = \frac{\left[(A+1)\times p\right]-1}{A}$$

### In this formula, the following definitions apply:

- *f* is the optimal fraction (percentage) to be risked on one trade.
- *A* is the average payoff ratio (dollars earned to $1 lost).
- *p* is the average win ratio (probability in percentage of success).

### Optimal *f* Example

- *f* is the unknown quantity (the optimal fraction percentage to be risked on one trade).
- *A* is the average payoff ratio of 2 to 1.
- *p* is the average win ratio of 35% winning trades.

$$f = \frac{\left[(2+1)\times 0.35\right]-1}{2} = \frac{1.05-1}{2} = \frac{0.05}{2} = 0.025 = 2.5\%$$

### Optimal *f* Percentage Example

This gives a value of 0.025 for *f*, or 2.5% is the optimal percentage of your trading account to risk on a trade based on this performance data and the optimal *f* formula. (To get a percentage, multiply the optimal *f* result by 100.)

# Comparing the Optimal *f* Formula Results to the ROR Tables

The amount of capital to risk on each trade can be calculated two ways based on your win and payoff ratios:

1. **ROR tables**
2. **Optimal *f* formula**

It's important to understand that these two methods yield different results. The optimal $f$ equation results give you a higher risk percentage than the ROR tables do when striving for a 0% likely chance of ruin.

**Let's look at the following example:**

- $f$ is the unknown quantity (the optimal fraction percentage to be risked on one trade).
- $A$ is the average payoff ratio of 2 to 1.
- $p$ is the average win ratio of 40% winning trades.

**The equation looks like this:**

$$f = \frac{\left[(2+1)\times 0.40\right]-1}{2} = \frac{1.2-1}{2} = \frac{0.2}{2} = 0.10 = 10\%$$

To get a percentage, multiply the optimal $f$ result by 100.

In this example, the optimal $f$ formula calculates that for a trader with a payoff ratio of 2 to 1 and a win ratio of 40% winning trades, the optimal amount of capital to risk is 10%.

When we refer to Table 12.1, we see Balsara's calculation for this scenario gives us an ROR probability of 14.3%, which is a small risk but not a zero probable risk. Table 12.4 will help you visualize how the optimal $f$ formula and the ROR table approaches compare.

In using the optimal $f$ formula, you should understand that it does not calculate a risk percentage that gives you a 0% probability of ruin. It is a more aggressive approach than when using the ROR tables.

**TABLE 12.4** The ROR tables and the optimal $f$ equation result in different probabilities for ROR when calculated with the same parameters.

| ROR Table 12.1 Results | Optimal $f$ Formula Results |
| --- | --- |
| 14.3% probability of risk-of-ruin | 0.0% Probability of risk-of-ruin |
| 10% capital at risk | 10% capital at risk |
| Win ratio 40% | Win ratio 40% |
| Payoff ratio of 2 to 1 | Payoff ratio of 2 to 1 |

A 0.0% probability means the total loss of capital is unlikely, but not impossible.

# Chapter 13
# Trade Size Matters

Calculating optimal trade or position size is often overlooked. Traders sometimes have an automatic knee-jerk reaction and choose a round number of shares or contracts on every trade, such as 100 shares or 10 shares and so on.

When coaching, if a trader tells me they always trade the same trade size, or it's a round number, that's a red flag. It means they are not calculating the optimal trade size for that exact trade entry, that exact initial stop loss, in addition to considering their current performance statistics.

Although we will cover stop-loss exits later, another red flag appears when traders set their stop-loss exit based on their pocketbook.

The market doesn't care what you can afford to lose. It's crucial to choose your stop-loss exit based on the current market dynamics of support and resistance. These dynamics are ever changing.

For example, don't set your stop-loss exit based on what you can afford to lose, such as when the trade goes against you $100. That is not a meaningful amount because it does not consider current market dynamics.

We'll cover more on how to set stop-loss exits in the next chapter.

# When Controlling Risk, You Can Plan To Control Three Variables

These three variables are all flexible; they are not fixed and constant. This means for every single trade you need a plan and a set of rules that determine how to calculate all three.

### Here are the three variables you can plan to control:

- Entry (where to get in)
- Stop-loss exit (where to get out)
- Size (how many shares or contracts)

Notice that we are going to plan to control these variables. We can completely control the trade entry, and we can completely control the trade size. The trade exit is something we can only plan to control, but due to factors such as market liquidity, our actual exit is at the mercy of the markets. Keep this in mind.

## 🎯 Trade Size and Getting It Just Right

As in Goldilocks and the three bears, we want our porridge not too hot, not too cold, but just right. With our trade size, we want it not too small, not too large, but just right.

A trade size that is too small will prevent us from fully profiting from a winning trade when we are right. On the flip side, we must be cautious of a trade size that is too large because it could wipe out our entire account when we are wrong. So how do we get it just right? The following examples will show you how.

**For the following formulas and examples, to get it just right, this trade information is needed:**

1. Entry
2. Initial stop-loss exit
3. Percentage of capital to risk
4. Commission cost
5. Account size

## What Is the Right Percent of Capital to Risk?

As a starting point, we will be using 2% capital at risk for the examples in this chapter. If you are more experienced, you may choose to risk a higher percentage. If you are less experienced, you may choose to risk a lower percentage.

To determine the exact percentage of capital to risk, refer to Chapter 12. Once you know your current payoff ratio and win ratio, use one of the following to calculate your percent of capital to risk:

- Risk of ruin (ROR) tables
- Optimal $f$ formula (also known as the Kelly formula)

Keep in mind that, even after you determine what percentage of capital to risk, you will want to test. This variable is not fixed and can be adjusted, depending on your risk tolerance. You may either increase or decrease it to compensate for your personal trading psychology.

## Dollar Risk Amount Formula

Step one in getting it just right is to determine how many dollars to risk on a trade. This is based on two factors: your account size and the percentage of capital at risk. In this example, we will be using a 2% capital-at-risk amount.

### Dollar Risk Amount Formula

Account Size × Percent of Capital at Risk = Dollar Risk Amount

### Dollar Risk Amount Example

$$\$25,000 \times 2\% = \$500$$

Not too difficult, right? Easy peasy. Now on to the next formula.

# Trade Size Formula—Not Using Leverage

Step two in getting it just right is to calculate how many shares or contracts to trade. This is based on four factors: dollar risk amount, commission cost, entry, and initial exit.

### Details of the Trade

- Account size: $25,000
- Two percent of capital at risk: $500 dollar amount risk
- MSFT trade entry value: $60 per share
- MSFT initial stop-loss exit: $58.50 per share
- Difference between entry and exit: $1.50
- Commission: $80 round trip
- Maximum trade size: 280 shares

### Trade Size Formula

$$\frac{\left[\text{Risk amount} - \text{Commission}\right]}{\text{Difference between entry and exit}} = \text{Trade size}$$

### Trade Size Not Using Leverage Example

$$\frac{\left[\$500 - \$80\right]}{\$1.50} = 280 \text{ shares}$$

# Trade Size Formula—Using Leverage

Using leverage increases risk and must be considered when calculating optimal trade size. This trade example will help clarify how to manage leverage and trade size together.

### Details of the Trade

- Account size: $50,000
- Amount of margin: 150%
- Trading account size (using margin): $75,000
- 2% of capital at risk (on $50,000): $1,000 risk amount
- IBM trade entry value: $91.49 per share

- IBM initial stop-loss exit: $90.23 per share
- Difference between entry and exit: $1.26
- Commission: $51.22 round trip
- Maximum trade size: 753 shares

### Trade Size Formula

$$\frac{\left[ \text{Risk amount} - \text{Commission} \right]}{\text{Difference between entry and exit}} = \text{Trade size}$$

### Trade Size Using Leverage Example

$$\frac{\left[ \$1,000 - \$51.22 \right]}{\$1.26} = 753 \text{ shares}$$

# The Distance Between Your Entry and Exit Prices

The further away your initial stop-loss exit is from your entry, the greater your amount of risk will be. This is an important concept to understand, and Figure 13.1 will help you to visualize it.

The more you visualize what risk looks like on your charts the easier and more automatic it becomes to control and manage that risk. Which brings us to another aspect of the distance between your entry and your exit price on your chart.

### Question

If the distance between your entry and your exit price is larger than $3.25 as in Figure 13.1, and all the other variables are the same, will your trade size be larger or smaller?

### Answer

Your trade size will be smaller.

This is because a larger distance between your entry and exit creates a larger risk amount. The way to manage your risk in this example is to reduce your trade size to account for the larger

**CALCULATING "TRADE SIZE" - S&P E-MINI CONTRACT**

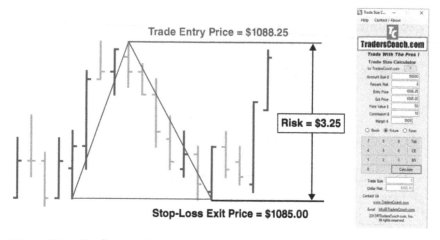

**Figure 13.1** The distance between your entry and your stop loss exit is the amount of risk you will incur. Notice on this S&P E-Mini contract that the amount of risk is $3.25. It's important to visualize the amount of risk on your charts for each trade which makes managing your risk easier.

amount of risk. And of course, the best way to calculate the optimal trade size is to use the trade size formula we have provided in this chapter.

## Trade Size and Risk Psychology

When traders make a killing in the market on a relatively small or average trading account, they are most likely not using sound money management and have not developed a healthy risk psychology.

In cases such as this they are likely exposed to obscene risk because of an abnormally large trade size, possibly using margin and leverage. In this case, they may have gotten lucky, leading to a profit windfall.

To continue trading in this way, the ROR probabilities suggest that it is just a matter of time before huge losses will dwarf the wins.

The psychology behind trade size begins when you believe and acknowledge that each trade's outcome is unknown. Believing that makes you ask yourself, "How much can I afford to lose and not fall prey to the risk of ruin?"

When traders ask themselves this question, they will either adjust their trade size or tighten their stop-loss exit before entering the trade. In most situations, the best method is to adjust the trade size and set your stop-loss exit based on current market dynamics.

During account drawdown periods, risk control and trade size become even more important. Since master traders test their trading systems, they know the probabilities of how many consecutive losses they may incur and what the statistical probabilities are regarding drawdown and their system.

This knowledge enables them to resist the temptation to either give up or to try and get even with the market with revenge trading. They are more likely to maintain an even keel and reap the benefits of future well-managed trades. This risk psychology and confidence takes time and experience to develop.

> *Decrease your trading volume* (or trade size) *when you are trading poorly; increase your volume when you are trading well.*
> —Paul Tudor Jones, original Market Wizard

It comes back to knowing your current win and payoff ratios and your performance statistics at all times. These stats will change and will fluctuate over time. Keep in mind that factors out of your control can affect your performance: your health, changing market volatility, unexpected life events, etc.

## Playing Macho Man with the Market

Paul Tudor Jones has a great quote, see Figure 13.2, where he talks about being careful to not play macho man with the market. Which brings us to an important topic regarding ego.

Needless to say, this pertains to the ladies out there as well, but generally men seem to be more likely than women to "play macho man."

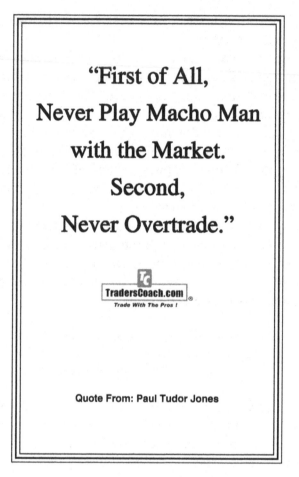

**Figure 13.2**  MINI POSTER—MACHO MAN—Trading too aggressively for your wallet, your account size, and your skill level can lead to disaster. Calculating the proper trade size ensures you won't be trading too big which gives you a better chance of lasting success. Quote from Paul Tudor Jones.

**There are multiple scenarios where traders can fall into the trap of playing macho man, including but not limited to the following:**

- Novice traders with unrealistic confidence
- Revenge trading after a losing streak
- Ignorance and lack of risk management

The markets have an uncanny ability to find our weaknesses and to expose them. Swift and dramatic losses will shine a bright spotlight onto problems such as poor trading psychology, lack of risk control, and the absence of a tested set of trading rules. So as Paul Tudor Jones says, "Never play macho man with the market."

## When Do You Cut Your Trade Size In Half?

An effective strategy to add to your risk management playbook is to sometimes cut your trade size in half. Sometimes a trade set up has promise, but as I like to say, *"All the dots are not connected";* however, enough of the dots are connected to warrant a trade. Meaning, it's a good trade, but your confidence level is not 100%.

**Following are examples of when to cut your trade size in half:**

- The Elliott wave count is not as clear as it could be.
- Using multiple time frame analysis, one of the charts is out of sync, but a trade set up still exists.
- Trading impulsive Elliott waves after a retracement that missed the high probability Fibonacci target zone.
- The trend is mature, and you may be getting in late.

By cutting the trade size in half, your risk is reduced, which allows you to take trades where all the dots don't connect.

# Chapter 14

# Stop-loss Exit Strategies

An excellent way to control trade risk is by setting stop-loss exits. A stop-loss exit is a practical tool used in managing risk, and developing the right strategy is an art.

On one hand, we don't want to set stops that are so tight that we are constantly bumped out of the market and get whipsawed. On the other hand, we don't want to set stops that are so wide that we are taking on too much risk and, as a result, are forced into a very small trade size.

The solution is to find an approach that is a balance of these two goals and is based on market dynamics. A stop-loss strategy should be designed to let a trade breathe with the normal ebb and flow of the current market dynamics and volatility.

## Stop-Loss Essentials

Some finesse is needed to develop an effective stop-loss strategy. Just as with your trading entry rules, depending on changes in market cycles, your stop-loss exit strategy may need to be adjusted at times. Regardless of market cycle, a few rules always apply.

### Essential Stop-loss Exit Rules That Always Apply

- Always set a stop-loss exit for every trade.
- Set this exit before you enter to avoid emotional mistakes that can occur when the trade is live.
- Once in a trade, if the stop-loss exit gets hit, get out immediately; do not second guess it.
- Strive to manage emotions when stopped out to prevent revenge trading.
- Accept that not every trade will be a winner and stop outs are simply a cost of doing business.
- Use current market dynamics to set a stop, such as support and resistance, rather than an arbitrary dollar amount that suits one's wallet.

# Six Risks in Trading

Trading carries a variety of risks, and each one requires a different strategy. An effective money management system is designed to manage as many of these risks as possible.

**Your money management system helps protect you from the following risks:**

1. **Trade risk.** The calculated risk we take on each individual trade is adjusted by changing our trade size.
2. **Market risk.** The inherent risk of being in the market is called market risk, and we have absolutely no control over this type of risk. It includes the entire gamut of risk possible including, but not limited to, world events that create sudden market crashes. For this reason, it is best to not trade with more than 10% of one's net worth.
3. **Margin risk.** This involves risk where we can lose more than the dollar amount in our margined trading account. Because we are leveraged, it is possible to owe the brokerage firm money if the trade goes against us.
4. **Liquidity risk.** If there are no buyers when we want to sell, we experience the inconvenience of liquidity risk. In addition

to the inconvenience, this type of risk can be costly when the price is going straight down to zero and there is no way to get out. Enron shareholders experienced this in 2001 when the company declared bankruptcy. Liquidity risk can also be caused by, or aggravated by, a market risk event.

5. **Overnight risk.** For day traders, this type of risk presents a concern that what can happen overnight, when the markets are closed, can dramatically impact the value of a position. There is the potential to have a gap open at the opening bell where the price is miles away from where it closed the day before. This gap event can negatively impact an account value and can blast through any stop-loss exits that had been in place.

6. **Volatility risk.** A bumpy market may tend to stop out trades repeatedly, creating significant drawdown. Volatility risk occurs when our stop-loss exits are not in alignment with the market and are not able to breathe with current price fluctuations.

## Stop-Loss Exit Strategies

The topic of where to set stop-loss exits generally falls under the heading of trading system. Exits must be carefully coordinated with entries, and this trading skill develops with experience.

Stop-loss selection is often considered a separate topic from money management. But since stops are an integral part of controlling risk, it's important to provide an outline of stop theory as part of this discussion. See Figure 14.1.

### These stop loss exits are a good starting point:

- **Initial stop.** First stop that is set at the beginning of the trade. It is identified before entering the market. The initial stop is also used to calculate trade size. It is the largest loss exposure in the current trade, provided the market does not gap through this stop, and provided there is enough liquidity to exit the market at this point.
- **Trailing stop.** Develops as the market develops. This stop locks in profit as the market moves in the direction of the trade.

**Figure 14.1**   An excellent way to control trade risk is by setting a stop-loss exit on every trade you take before you pull the trigger.

See how, in Figure 14.2, as the market moves up in this bullish trade, the stops are moved up to the bottom of each triangle. Finally at the end of the trend, the trade is exited when the market reverses below the last bullish triangle.

- **Resistance stop.** This is a form of trailing stop used in trends. It is placed just under countertrend pullbacks in a trend.
- **Three-bar trailing stop.** This is used in a trend if the market seems to be losing momentum and you anticipate a reversal in trend.
- **One-bar trailing stop.** When prices have reached your profit target zone, use this stop. You can also use it when you have a breakaway market and want to lock in profits. Use it after three to five price bars move strongly in your favor.
- **Trend line stop.** Use a trend line placed under the lows in an uptrend or on top of the highs in a downtrend. You want to get out when prices close on the opposite side of the trend line.

**A.R.T. Tools In Action!**

If You Just Trading 100 Shares!
Your Gain Would Be $12,305!

TRAILING STOP-LOSS EXIT

A.R.T. TRADE EXIT
AT $165.14

A.R.T. TRADE
ENTRY AT $42.36

TradersCoach.com
Trade With The Pros !

**Figure 14.2**  Trailing stops are useful for locking in profit. As the market moves up in this bullish uptrend, the stops are moved up to the bottom of each triangle until the end of the trend when the trade is stopped out and closed for a profit. The trading system used here is the "ART" system by www.traderscoach.com.

- **Regression channel stop.** Like a regular trend line stop, but the regression channel forms a nice channel between the highs and lows of the trend and usually represents the width of the trend channel. Stops are placed outside the low of the channel on uptrends and outside the high of the channel on downtrends. Prices should close outside the channel for the stop to be taken.

  **REMEMBER:** Not every trade will be a winner and stop-loss exits help prevent a small loss from becoming a large loss.

## Four Major Market Cycles

Just as most climates have four seasons to one degree or another, the financial markets have different environmental cycles. This means you need to quickly identify the changing cycles and then appropriately adapt to them.

If you live in New York City, for example, chances are you will not be going outside for a leisurely stroll down Fifth Avenue in shorts, a T-shirt, and flip-flops in February.

Why is that? Because, if you've lived there for a while and experienced the local seasons, you've already identified that in February it will be pretty darn cold. To appropriately adapt, you will want to wear a heavy winter coat and maybe gloves, a scarf, and earmuffs.

It's the same with the markets. You need to have "lived there for a while" and experienced a variety of market cycles so you know what "to wear," or rather how to adapt, so that you are comfortable in each trade.

Instead of knowing to wear a winter coat in February, you know that in a bracketed market you need to adapt your rules so that you do not get stopped out a lot. Or you may need to recognize a bull market changing to a bear market so that you can exit your position in a timely fashion to lock in profits.

### Here are the four major market cycles:

1. **Trending:** A financial market is moving consistently in one direction, up (bull) or down (bear).
2. **Bracketed:** Also known as a consolidating or sideways market, a bracketed market occurs when the market is stuck in a price range between an identifiable resistance and support level. On a chart it will look like a sideways horizontal channel.
3. **Breakout:** When there is a sharp change in price movement after the market has been consolidating for at least 20 price bars, this is known as a breakout. It will either breakout to the upside (bull) or the downside (bear).
4. **Corrective:** This is a temporary short, sharp reverse in prices during a longer market trend, also known as a correction.

Incorrectly identifying a market cycle can be a costly situation. For example, if you decided that a market entered a new trend, but in fact it was in a correction, you might enter a trade and immediately get stopped out.

For this reason, market experience is the best teacher. Your essential plan of action is constant observation. With that, you will continually improve your ability to read market cycles.

**REMEMBER:** Knowing what market cycle you are in will help to calculate better stop loss exits.

**Figure 14.3** MINI POSTER—TAKE A SMALL LOSS—The struggle is real. Traders must master the ability to take small losses, and if they are unable to do that, their trading psychology needs improvement. Quote from Ed Seykota, Market Wizard.

## The Mother of All Losses

Keeping your losses small and your wins big is considered the number one rule to trading success. And setting a stop-loss exit is one of the best ways to ensure that your losses stay small.

> *If you can't take a small loss, sooner or later you will take the mother of all losses.*
> —Ed Seykota, commodities trader, and Market Wizard

The catch is that sometimes traders fail to adhere to their stop-loss exits; see Figure 14.3. Why do traders struggle with this? Often it is because they can't stand any loss at all. Or being wrong is viewed as negative and unbearable. Regardless of the reason why a stop-loss exit is ignored, when this happens, it is crucial to acknowledge it.

Ultimately, this happens when one's trading psychology is not developed. If you can't learn to take small losses, you will never succeed in trading.

## ◎ Without Risk, There is No Opportunity

Anyone who knows me has heard me say a million times, "Without risk, there is no opportunity."

Which is why I'm so passionate about risk control. After mastering risk control, and learning to set effective stop-loss exits, you can truly benefit from the massive opportunity every day in the financial markets.

# Chapter 15
# Trader's Recordkeeping Forms

These recordkeeping forms take me way back to my days in New York City in the 1990s. Back then I was looking for a recordkeeping system that was custom tailored to trading and investing. There was nothing on the market. So, with the help of my wife Jean, we put together a system that enabled me to look at my trades with both a macro and a micro lens.

The MACRO big picture shows cumulative results on a weekly, monthly, and annual ledger. And the MICRO up close picture shows the minute-by-minute results on daily ledgers and individual trade posting cards.

This approach allowed me to spot my strengths and weaknesses from a bird's eye view on the macro level. Then I could zoom in at the micro level for a deeper understanding of what was working and what to keep repeating. And of course, it was helpful to spot when things were not working and identify the exact trade posting cards to determine how to adjust my strategy.

This chapter is devoted to the importance of tracking profit and loss. These statistics will be valuable in determining what your return on investment (ROI) is, and that is what this business, and every business, is all about.

You are making an investment and risking your time and money to obtain a consistent return. The key is to ensure that your return is just that, consistent. By implementing a recordkeeping system, you will increase your chances of maintaining a consistent profit margin in your trading and investing.

## Start Your Trader's Recordkeeping Right Now

If you have not set up a recordkeeping, bookkeeping, or accounting system specifically designed to track your trading and investing performance, now is the time to start. Every successful business tracks performance daily, and it is the same for traders and investors.

> *"Making good judgements when one has complete data, facts, and knowledge is not leadership—it is bookkeeping."*
> — Dee Hock, Founder and CEO Visa Credit Card Association

Founder and CEO of Visa Credit Card Association, Dee Hock knows that bookkeeping and analysis of such is what provides you complete data and knowledge. Having accurate data and knowledge is the only way for any business to become successful and to stay successful over time.

To help you get started, here are the exact ledgers and posting cards I started using back in the 1990s and still use today. It's a manual handwritten system that enables you to jot down notes on your psychology and strategies the minute they come up before you forget them. Later these gems of insight can reveal how to improve your trading performance in the future.

**The following forms are included:**

1. **Annual Trade Ledger, front,** Figure 15.1 (size 8½" × 11")
2. **Monthly Trade Ledger, front,** (size 8½" × 11")
3. **Weekly Trade Ledger, front,** (size 8½" × 11")
4. **Daily Trade Ledger, front,** (size 8½" × 11")
5. **Daily Worksheet, front,** (size 8½" × 11")

# TradersCoach.com
"The Trader's Assistant" — A Trade Posting and Record Keeping System

YEAR OF LEDGER

## ANNUAL TRADE LEDGER

| MONTH | # TRADES | # WINNING | # LOSING | GROSS $ P/L | COMMISSION $ | NET $ P/L | RUNNING NET $ P/L |
|---|---|---|---|---|---|---|---|
| JANUARY | | | | | | | |
| FEBRUARY | | | | | | | |
| MARCH | | | | | | | |
| APRIL | | | | | | | |
| MAY | | | | | | | |
| JUNE | | | | | | | |
| JULY | | | | | | | |
| AUGUST | | | | | | | |
| SEPTEMBER | | | | | | | |
| OCTOBER | | | | | | | |
| NOVEMBER | | | | | | | |
| DECEMBER | | | | | | | |
| TOTALS: | | | | | | | |

LARGEST WINNING TRADE OF THE YEAR: $
LARGEST WINNING TRADE POSTING CARD #:
AVERAGE WINNING TRADE OF THE YEAR: $

LARGEST LOSING TRADE OF THE YEAR: $
LARGEST LOSING TRADE POSTING CARD #:
AVERAGE LOSING TRADE OF THE YEAR: $

NOTES:

Re-order online through www.traderscoach.com or call (858) 695-1985

111802 Copyright © 2002 by TradersCoach.com, Inc.

**Figure 15.1** Annual Trade Ledger, front, The Trader's Assistant, by Traders Coach.com.

6. **Trading Notes, back of all ledgers,** (size 8½" × 11")
7. **Trade Posting Card (futures), front,** (size 8" × 5")
8. **Trade Posting Card (stocks), front,** Figure 15.2 (size 8" × 5")
9. **Trade Posting Card (options), front,** (size 8" × 5")
10. **Back of all posting cards,** (size 8" × 5")

This system has served me well for many years and is sure to get you on the right track also. To set up the system contact us for the PDF files by emailing support@traderscoach.com. We will email you the PDF files so you can print out the forms in high resolution.

---

# The Trader's Assistant Recordkeeping Forms Are Available in a PDF Printable Format at No Cost to You

As a thank you for purchasing this book, we are happy to provide you with the PDF files that will give you a high-resolution printout of these forms.

### You can access the PDF files two ways:

1. **Email us via:** support@traderscoach.com; be sure to give us your name and email address so that we can send you your files. Sometimes emails get trapped in the spam folder, if you do not receive the files, email us to let us know and we will resend them.
2. **Contact us via this website link:** https://www.trad erscoach.com/book/; you will find an access link on this website page for your files.

We look forward to helping you with your recordkeeping and analysis. Taking the first step to start is the most important, congratulations on taking the first step!

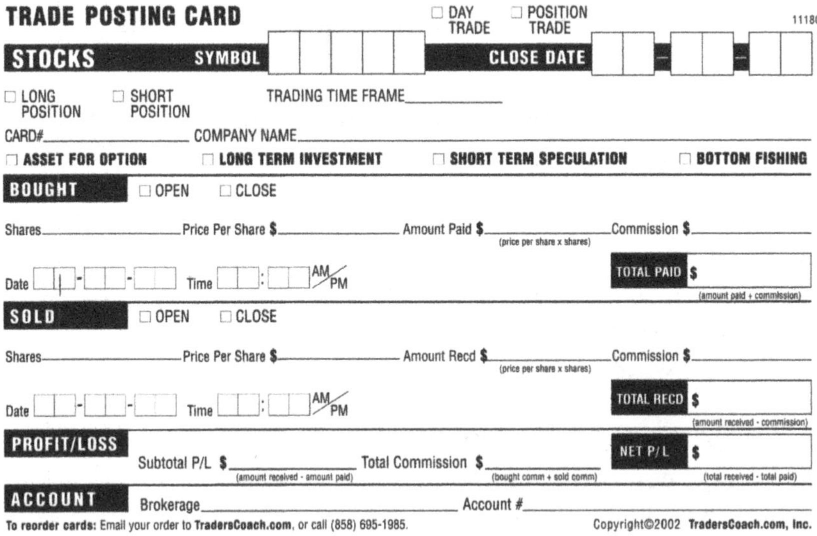

**TRADE POSTING CARD**  ☐ DAY TRADE  ☐ POSITION TRADE                                    111802

**STOCKS**          SYMBOL ☐☐☐☐          **CLOSE DATE** ☐☐ - ☐☐ - ☐☐

☐ LONG POSITION   ☐ SHORT POSITION          TRADING TIME FRAME_____

CARD#_____ COMPANY NAME_____

☐ ASSET FOR OPTION   ☐ LONG TERM INVESTMENT   ☐ SHORT TERM SPECULATION   ☐ BOTTOM FISHING

**BOUGHT**   ☐ OPEN   ☐ CLOSE

Shares_____ Price Per Share $_____ Amount Paid $_____ Commission $_____
(price per share x shares)

Date ☐☐ - ☐☐ - ☐☐  Time ☐☐ : ☐☐ AM/PM          TOTAL PAID $_____
(amount paid + commission)

**SOLD**   ☐ OPEN   ☐ CLOSE

Shares_____ Price Per Share $_____ Amount Recd $_____ Commission $_____
(price per share x shares)

Date ☐☐ - ☐☐ - ☐☐  Time ☐☐ : ☐☐ AM/PM          TOTAL RECD $_____
(amount received - commission)

**PROFIT/LOSS**   Subtotal P/L $_____ Total Commission $_____   NET P/L $_____
(amount received - amount paid)   (bought comm + sold comm)   (total received - total paid)

**ACCOUNT**   Brokerage_____   Account #_____

To reorder cards: Email your order to TradersCoach.com, or call (858) 695-1985.   Copyright©2002 TradersCoach.com, Inc.

**Figure 15.2**   Trade Posting Card (stocks), front, The Trader's Assistant, by
TradersCoach.com.

# Why Track Results?

The ways you'll benefit from setting up a system to track your profit
and loss performance results are infinite. Initially discipline is the
first benefit, and the discipline you develop in your accounting of
profit and loss results, and other vital statistics, will transfer over
into your day-to-day success.

As you fine-tune your machine by evaluating results, it will
become easier to follow your system rules. You'll become more disciplined overall, plus there will be less doubt and more confidence
in your system. It's a perpetual process, and the endless benefits
will reveal themselves over time.

## Scorecard With Your Current Vital Statistics

Have you noticed that when you go to the doctor or hospital, the
nurses are constantly taking your "vitals"? And with good reason

because that is the only way for them to determine what the best prescription and diagnosis for your health will be.

**You will need to track the following financial vital statistics going forward:**

1. Win ratio
2. Payoff ratio
3. Largest winning trade
4. Largest losing trade
5. Average winning trade
6. Average losing trade
7. Largest percentage of draw down
8. Average percentage of draw down
9. Total percent of profit/loss
10. Total dollar value of profit/loss

These scorecard statistics, see Figure 15.3, will give you historical data to adjust your money management system and adjust your trading system to adapt to ever fluctuating market conditions.

## A Trader's Money Management System By Bennett A. Mcdowell

If you are looking for an even deeper dive into how to use the Trader's Assistant Recordkeeping System and analyze your results so that you can diagnose your trading and investing weaknesses and fix them, be sure to pick up a copy of this book:

- **Title:** *A Trader's Money Management System, How to Ensure Profit and Avoid the Risk of Ruin* (Figure 15.4)
- **Author:** Bennett A. McDowell
- **Publisher:** John Wiley & Sons, Inc.

Chapter 12 is especially useful since it includes actual detailed and filled out trade ledgers and posting cards from a student of mine who was generous enough to share his trade posting cards

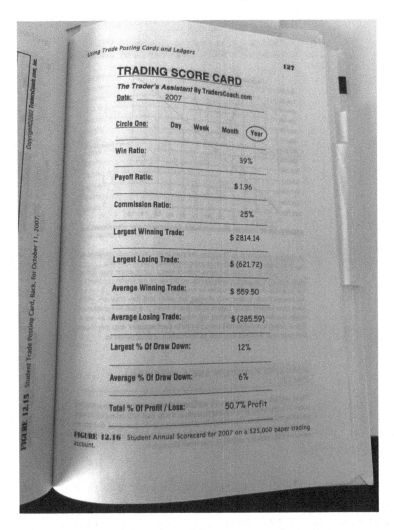

**Figure 15.3** Student Trading Scorecard from page 127 of *A Trader's Money Management System* by Bennett A. McDowell. On this scorecard for the year, you can see that the student had more than 50% profit for the year and yet there is room for improvement in the areas of increasing the win ratio and payoff ratio. The scorecard is a snapshot of your performance so that you can quickly see what to work on to improve.

**Figure 15.4**   *A Trader's Money Management System* by Bennett McDowell published by John Wiley & Sons.

and ledgers over the course of an entire year. His equity curve on a $25,000 account went up to $29,000 down to $27,000 and finally up to over $36,000 in a 12-month period. See Figure 15.5.

His scorecard, see Figure 15.3, for the year boasts more than 50% profit on his account of $25,000. And yet his scorecard illustrates that he has a lot of room to improve since his win ratio is only 39% and his payoff ratio is roughly 1 to 2. Insights on his psychology and strategies written on the back of each trade posting card are useful and show how you too can benefit from this kind of hindsight and debriefing analysis.

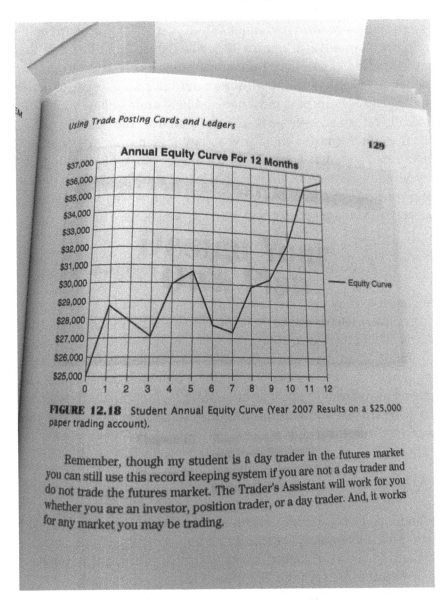

Using Trade Posting Cards and Ledgers

129

**FIGURE 12.18** Student Annual Equity Curve (Year 2007 Results on a $25,000 paper trading account).

Remember, though my student is a day trader in the futures market you can still use this record keeping system if you are not a day trader and do not trade the futures market. The Trader's Assistant will work for you whether you are an investor, position trader, or a day trader. And, it works for any market you may be trading.

**Figure 15.5** Student Equity Curve from page 129 of *A Trader's Money Management System* by Bennett A. McDowell. When observing this equity curve, you can see there are periods of account drawdown, but with effective money management the year ends up, with more than 50% on the account. Every system will have periods of account drawdown; the key is to control the drawdown with a good money management system.

The statistics from my student's one year $25,000 account going up more than 50% in Figures 15.3 and Figure 15.5 illustrate that active trading can deliver impressive returns compared to putting money in a bank account with nominal interest. Successful active trading can also surpass most buy and hold approaches, which historically return an average of 10% per year over the past 50 years.

One must master their psychology and money management before gains shown here can be attained. And active trading and investing is more work than simple buy and hold investing or putting your money into a bank account. Which is why when you are successful you are getting paid for a job well done.

## Accounting is the Language of Business

Accounting may be considered dull by some, but it is the foundation of every successful business, and no one knows this better than Warren Buffett (Figure 15.6).

Life is a numbers game; business is a numbers game; and making money in the financial markets is a numbers game. There's no getting away from it, one way or another to be consistently successful you will have to run the numbers to see which strategies are working or not working.

## A Tale of Two Men: Henry Ford and James Couzens

Which brings me to an interesting story about Henry Ford and the Ford Motor Company, because had it not been for Henry's accountant and business manager James Couzens, you might never have even heard of Henry Ford. See Figure 15.7.

I can almost guarantee you've never heard of James Couzens, which goes to show that accountants and business managers get very little glory. And yet they are the ones that are responsible for ensuring that their companies don't go bankrupt so that their founders and leaders can go on to great fame and fortune.

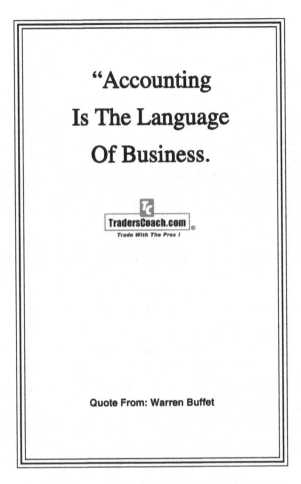

**Figure 15.6** MINI POSTER—ACCOUNTING LANGUAGE—Do you consider yourself to be an articulate trader and investor? Meaning, are you fluent in the language of business? This language is based on your numbers and the accounting of your transactions. When you are fluent in the language of business, you are one step closer to attaining consistent profitability. Quote from Warren Buffet.

As it turns out Henry Ford, a truly creative innovator, was not a fan of accountants and pencil pushers. In his mind they slowed him down and cramped his style. Ford preferred to immerse himself in the romance and passion of his beautiful automobile. Sometimes he forgot about those pesky details of making a "profit."

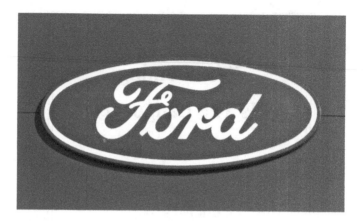

**Figure 15.7**   Henry Ford founded the Ford Motor Company in 1903. This iconic Ford logo has stood the test of time due in no small part to James Couzens, Ford's accountant, and business manager. It was Couzens that kept the company from financial disaster by always keeping an eye on the numbers.
SOURCE: Photo 100896259 Ford @ Josefkubes Dreamstime.com

Do you see any similarities between Ford and our business as traders and investors? I can admit that my passion for trading and investing in the beginning sometimes distracted me from those pesky details of making a "profit."

At one point, Ford didn't have enough money to make payroll, and his employees were not going to get their paycheck. It was then that James Couzens directly disobeyed Ford's order and shipped a railroad car full of 50 automobiles *before* Ford had inspected and approved them.

Ford was furious when he found out the cars had been shipped without his approval, given that he was such a perfectionist. But then, Ford was surprised and happy when he found out how much money he had made because his accountant had shipped them.

Without Couzens, Ford would never have been able to be the visionary that history remembers. Couzens was crucial to Ford's survival because he was able to see the big picture. Couzens could clearly see which priorities mattered . . . and what steps needed to be taken . . . to say in business . . . and not go bust.

It is no different for you as a trader and investor.

# Step IV

# Design Your Trading Rules

# Chapter 16

# The Hardest Rule to Follow

et's start off with the first universal rule that everyone must follow. See Figure 16.1. It's a surprisingly difficult rule to follow; some might say it is the hardest rule to follow. And yet, neglecting to adhere to this rule will ultimately lead to failure. This rule teaches you discipline and will result in greater strength for you in the markets.

## 🎯 Rule 1: Follow Your Rules

The temptation to break the rules is real, even if you are not rebellious by nature. This temptation is rooted in our psychology. In the heat of the moment, when a live position takes an unexpected turn, there may be an impulse to "finesse the rules."

This can be justified by saying, "I'm not breaking the rules. No, I'm trying a better approach." But the reality is the only time to finesse your rules is when testing, not during live trades.

If you find that when evaluating the performance of your current rules, you may have discovered a "better mouse trap," then put it to the test. See if that new approach in fact improves your results,

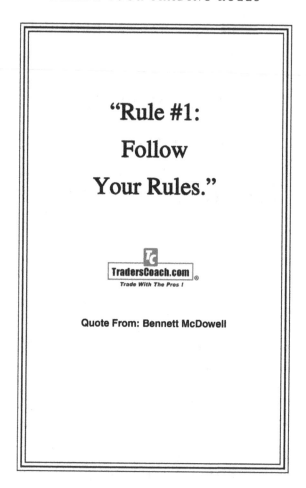

**Figure 16.1**   MINI POSTER—FIRST RULE—If you get nothing else from this chapter, be sure to understand the importance of having enough discipline to stick with your rules, even during draw down and when things are not going well. Quote from Bennett McDowell.

prove to yourself it gives you a greater edge, and you will increase your confidence as a result.

If you're a rule-breaker by nature, be aware of your personal psychology. You'll need to rein in that tendency and channel it elsewhere.

As your psychology in the markets strengthens, the urge to break the rules will lessen and will eventually disappear. This comes from building up your muscle memory by time and time again following the rules. Plus, your confidence in your rules will increase as you see progress and a more profitable equity curve.

> *I always say that you could publish trading rules in the newspaper, and no one would follow them. The key is consistency and discipline. Almost anybody can make up a list of rules that are 80 percent as good as what we taught our people. What they can't do is have the confidence to stick to those rules even when things are going bad.*
>
> —Richard Dennis, Original Market Wizard
> and co-creator of the Turtle Trading Experiment

In his book *Market Wizards*, Jack Schwager interviewed commodity trader Richard Dennis, who conducted the experiment known as Turtle Trading with his partner, William Eckhardt.

He called his students "turtles" after being inspired by the turtle farms he had visited in Singapore and deciding that he could grow traders as quickly and efficiently as farm-grown turtles. See Figure 16.2.

**Figure 16.2**   Richard Dennis and William Eckhardt settled their longtime debate on whether successful trading could be taught by launching their famous Turtle Trader experiment in 1983. As it turns out, Dennis was right, and their experiment proved that successful trading can be taught, and their students averaged 100% profit per year over a four-year period.
SOURCE: Photo 22527429, Turtles @ Woo Bing Siew, Dreamstime.com

This experiment, conducted from 1983 through 1988, was designed to prove that anyone could be taught to trade by giving them a clear set of proven trend trading rules and some training. Surprisingly short, the training was a mere two weeks.

The experiment was a huge success, and what Dennis discovered was that indeed when given a clear set of rules with an edge, all 20 final *Turtle Traders* were exceptionally successful with an average of 100% profit per year each over a four-year period.

## Can Traders and Investors Be Given a Set of Rules and Trained to Be Successful?

You may have heard of the Turtle Traders, who proved that yes, folks with no experience and from all walks of life could be given a proven set of trading rules and could be trained to be exceptionally successful.

*I have a partner who has been a friend since high school. We have had philosophical disagreements about everything you could imagine. One of these arguments was whether the skills of a successful trader could be reduced to a set of rules—that was my point of view—or whether there was something ineffable, mystical, subjective, or intuitive that made someone a good trader.*

*This argument had been going on for a long time, and I guess I was getting a little frustrated with idle speculation. Finally, I said, "Here is a way we can definitely resolve this argument. Let's hire and train some people and see what happens."*

*He agreed.*

*It was an intellectual experiment. We trained them as well as we could. That was the way to do the experiment*

(continued on next page...)

*(...continued from previous page)*

> *right, I thought. I tried to codify all the things I knew about the markets. We taught them a little bit about probability, money management, and trading. It turned out I was right. I don't say that to pat myself on the back, but even I am surprised how well it worked. It's frightening how well it worked.*
>
> —Richard Dennis, Original "Market Wizard" and co-creator of the "Turtle Trading Experiment"

*Source:* Schwager, J. (1989). *Market Wizards*. New York Institute of Finance.

In 1983, Richard Dennis and William Eckhardt ran large print advertisements in some of the biggest financial newspapers with the intent of hiring 10 Turtle Traders.

Out of 1,000 applicants, they interviewed 80, and then selected 21 men and 2 women to train for two weeks in Chicago. The students started with small accounts of $100,000 each, which was increased based on performance. The increased amounts ranged from $500,000 to $2,000,000.

Out of the 23 in total, three were dropped because they didn't do well. The other 20 did very well, averaging 100% profit per year over a period of four years. (These figures are taken from Jack Schwager's interview with Richard Dennis in the book *Market Wizards*.)

Given that each of the 20 traders was said to have kept 15% of their total winnings per year, while Dennis and Eckhardt kept the other 85%, we can all agree that the Turtles as a whole did very well for themselves. Considering that their accounts were completely funded by Dennis and Eckhardt, they risked none of their own capital.

Again, the experiment was a huge success. Debates over whether the Turtle rules from 1983 still work today rage on.

*(continued on next page ...)*

*(... continued from previous page)*

The only way to find out for sure is to test them yourself. Given that the contract the original traders had with Dennis and Eckhardt ended in 1993, the rules were released to the public by some of the original traders.

For more information on the details of the Turtle rules and strategies, refer to this book by one of the original Turtle Traders:

- **Title:** *Way of the Turtle: The Secret Methods That Turned Ordinary People into Legendary Traders*
- **Author:** Curtis M. Faith
- **Publisher:** McGraw Hill

The Faith book outlines important nuances of the rules related to the definition and implementation of $N$, the calculation of a "unit," and more. Of course, with the power of the internet today, doing an online search for "Turtle Traders" will render a variety of free YouTube videos and PDF downloads that will provide you with even more specific information on the exact rules and how to implement them.

**The Moral of the Story:** Successful trading and investing can be taught to ordinary people from every walk of life.

## The Original Rogue Trader, Nick Leeson

The most famous rogue trader of all time had no interest in creating rules or following rules; sadly he created a world of hurt for himself and those around him.

This infamous rogue trader's name is Nick Leeson.

Oftentimes fact is stranger than fiction and can teach us lessons that steer us away from danger in the future. Surely if we cannot learn from our own mistakes and the mistakes of history, then we are doomed to repeat them.

And so it is with the true story of Nick Leeson, who is infamous for causing the collapse of the Barings Bank in February 1995. Barings was the oldest bank in the world, operating for 233 years before the collapse. It had in fact financed the Napoleonic Wars and counted the queen among its clients. See Figure 16.3.

Leeson, a young trader for the bank, allowed small losses to spiral into US$1.3 billion (£600 million) in losses in just three years from 1992 to 1995. Just imagine if those figures were adjusted for today's value.

**Figure 16.3**   The original rogue trader, Nick Leeson, on the cover of *Time* magazine, made history when he brought down Barings Bank in February 1995. His US$1.3 billion in losses caused the oldest bank in the world to no longer exist.
SOURCE: *Time* magazine cover, March 13, 1995.

His own fear, greed, denial, and nonexistent risk control drove him to cover up his losses (in the now famous 88888 account) while he desperately attempted to trade his way back into profitable territory. He stopped at nothing to fund his department's trading activity.

> *I saw the cuttings shreds of paper and glue which I'd used to forge Ron Baker's and Richard Hogan's signatures. I couldn't believe what I'd done. . . . With my scissors, stick of glue and paper and fax machine, I had created £50 million."*
> —Nick Leeson, The Original Rogue Trader

What's even more astounding than Leeson's lies and deceit is that Baring's upper management was oblivious to his deception and did not implement simple checks and balances to prevent just such a disaster. Their own greed and incompetence blinded them to glaring discrepancies that could have been detected and addressed.

---

## Watch the *Rogue Trader* Movie

If you haven't already done so, you really owe it to yourself to watch the movie about the true story of Nick Leeson.

**Title:** *Rogue Trader*
**Studio:** Miramax
**Running Time:** 1 hour, 41 minutes
**Starring:** Ewan McGregor
**Director:** James Deaden

The movie (and 1996 book by Nick Leeson that the movie is based on) are much like a late-night thriller to any trader who has felt the emotions of a trade gone bad, very bad. One reviewer on Amazon stated that he trades for a living and watches the movie once a year to remind himself to use risk control. You probably don't need to go that far, once is no doubt enough, but it does drive the point home.

*(continued on next page...)*

*(...continued from previous page)*

Remember, all large unsurmountable losses start out as a small loss. It is that snowball effect that you've got to watch out for, since the momentum of rogue behavior is difficult to reverse or control.

**The Moral of the Story:** Don't go rogue.

## Who Are You Accountable to and Where Do You Get Support?

If we are to learn anything from the original rogue trader, Nick Leeson, it is that true accountability along with checks and balances go a long way to ensure our survival as traders and investors. If we are to be independent entrepreneurs, we need to consciously institute some type of "overseeing" authority and support person or team.

### Implement Accountability by Enlisting Support
- Wingman or woman
- Trading buddy
- Spouse or friend
- Trading partner
- Accountant or bookkeeper
- Trading coach
- Small trading group, online or in person

When you are too close to a problem, it's difficult to sort out the solution. That is when support from someone on the outside can help. Identify an individual to be your sounding board and eliminate the isolation that can lead to rogue behavior. Healthy accountability will help you resist the temptation to break your rules.

**Your Support Person or Team Needs To**
- Check in to confirm you followed your rules
- Be firm but supportive
- Not judgmental when you make a mistake
- Offer clues and solutions to problems
- Be reliable

Basically, we need someone that we can check in with and be accountable to so that we stay on track and follow the rules we have established for ourselves. And don't be afraid to ask for help when you need it. Working isolated in a vacuum over the long term will hinder your performance.

## Avoid Toxic People

Steer clear of anyone who is toxic and not supportive of your goal when it comes to selecting a person or team. Negative energy will be counterproductive to the cause. Going it alone until you find the right person is okay, but make it a priority. The universe has a wonderful way of delivering what we need at the right time.

A word about spouses: Sometimes they can be fearful; many of my students have expressed concern over this. It is always better to have them on board with your plan. If possible, a little bit of educating your spouse can be helpful. If they understand that this is a business and you are creating a well thought-out plan, it might help to bring them around. Also, when paper trading and testing, show them your results and include them. If all else fails, create boundaries and ways to distance yourself from any fear or negativity.

# Chapter 17
# Understanding Financial Markets

U nderstanding financial markets and how they work requires constant education because they are constantly changing. With every new technological advance and with every new geopolitical structure introduced into the marketplace, the markets will adapt and change. These changes may affect your system rules, so be aware of any changes and adapt your rules as needed.

Prepare yourself to be on the lookout for the latest developments in the markets, since what is written on these pages will no doubt change as the months and years go by. Compared with the simple days of bartering goods in today's world we have a variety of new developments that did not exist until recently:

- Electronic markets have replaced many open-outcry pits.
- The forex market, foreign exchange currency market, began forming during the 1970s, now trades 24 hours a day (except weekends). It's currently the largest and most liquid market with a daily trading volume of $7.5 trillion in US dollars.
- ETFs, exchange traded funds, were introduced in 1993 and have become a popular vehicle for investing and trading.

- The introduction of the euro currency in 1999 replaced the existing currency of 15 European countries at the time.
- Decimalization in the US markets replaced fractions in 2000.
- Computer technology is constantly improving with faster and more powerful computers available to the retail trader and investor.
- Cryptocurrencies first appeared in 2009 and have become a new market to trade.
- Around the clock 24-hour trading for all markets is on the horizon.

In today's world we have new and exciting developments and opportunities which weren't around in 1929, the start of the Great Depression. Who knows what we will have in another 100 years? The financial landscape may be completely different with a new vocabulary to match.

If we go way back to the beginning, finance consisted primarily of a barter system. At one time, a farmer might trade several bushels of grain to a rancher up the road in exchange for a cow. They each got something they needed, and it was a fair trade. In essence, they were trading commodities, which we still do today.

The only difference is that today it's not as literal as it was then. Now the trade generally takes place on paper or over a fiber-optic cable, as opposed to meeting in person and physically handing over a living, breathing cow, in exchange for several bushels of grain.

Barter was essentially the beginning of the financial markets. There were trades being made, and liquidity (or lack thereof) existed just as it does in modern-day markets. The sophistication of today's technology and computers and the many channels an order goes through do not change the essence of it all.

## Buyer and Seller Agree on Price, but They Disagree on Value

It is still the same, where on one side of a trade there is a *buyer* and on the other side of the trade is the *seller*. And this is important;

both the buyer and seller agree on price but disagree on value. The farmer and the rancher exchange commodities; they are buying and selling. They agreed on how much to make the exchange for, but they disagreed on the value of the item they were exchanging. They each had a surplus of one commodity and were willing to give it up for something else.

Many of my students have struggled with the idea that two parties in a transaction disagree on value. How can that be if they both agree to a fair trade? Don't they believe the value to be equal therefore agreeing on value? See Figure 17.1.

Let me try to explain this with another example. Suppose there's a man who owns an automobile that he drives to work every day. This car had value for him until he suddenly lost his eyesight and now must take a taxicab to work. The man decides to sell his car to a young woman, and they both agree on a price of $15,000.

They agree on price, but they disagree on the value of what they are trading. The man does not value the car because he no longer can use it. And the woman does not value the currency because she needs the car more than she needs the cash. In fact, the car enables her to go to work, which helps her generate continuous cash flow. It is a fair trade when they agree on the price and disagree on the value of what they are trading.

## The Financial Order Flow Process

In the world of buy and sell orders, many players contribute to the process. The journey that an order takes from the time it is initiated by the trader or investor until the time it is confirmed by the clearing firm may take just seconds, and yet in slow motion, it is quite an amazing series of events.

Look at Figure 17.2, which is a diagram of a simplified order flow process, to get an idea of how your buy and sell orders are handled. Keep in mind that the process will vary among a variety of

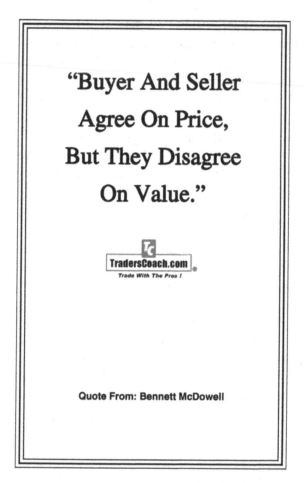

**Figure 17.1** MINI POSTER—DISAGREE ON VALUE—Trading is based on the simple age-old premise of bartering one item for another. For every trade, the buyer and seller agree on the price. Where they disagree is on the value of what they are bartering. When a man sells a car to a woman for $15,000, he values the cash more than the car and the woman values the car more than the cash. Quote from Bennett McDowell.

markets, whether they are stocks, options, futures, ETFs, or forex, but the basic idea is the same.

  The job of all the players is to be a matchmaker for a buyer and a seller and to be sure that the transaction is handled properly so that both the buyer and the seller are treated fairly.

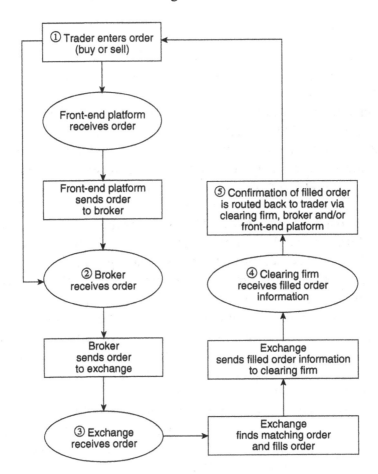

**Figure 17.2**    Order Flow Diagram. This diagram shows the path that a trade takes from the time it is placed to the time it is filled and then cleared.

**IMPORTANT NOTE:** Sometimes one firm functions as a front-end charting platform, broker, and clearing firm all in one. One example of this is TradeStation, because it is a self-clearing broker that has a front-end charting platform as well. There are many other firms that have this same scenario, and they are usually larger firms.

**Processing an order typically takes five steps:**

1. **Trader enters order.** The investor or trader enters a buy or sell order through the front-end charting platform or in some cases calls the broker directly to initiate the order. Different types of orders can be placed, such as a market order, limit order, or stop order. The type of order that is selected is the way that important instructions are communicated on how the order should be handled and filled.

2. **Broker receives order.** The broker then receives the order and ensures that the instructions are carried out correctly. The broker delivers the order directly to the exchange.

3. **Exchange receives order.** The exchange then receives the order and finds a matching order to complete the fill. This filled order information is then provided to the clearing firm.

4. **Clearing firm receives the completed transaction information.** The clearing firm is the player that holds client funds in a segregated bank account in the name of the account holder. The clearing firm then clears transactions at the end of the day and provides daily, monthly, and year-end statements. (Some brokers are self-clearing, which means that they are responsible for both item 2 and item 4 in this order process.)

5. **Trader receives confirmation of the filled, completed order.** The trader or investor will receive a confirmation statement on all transactions and the fill price and net balance on the trader's account from the clearing firm.

Many employees in many different companies worldwide work together to make the system run smoothly, or as smoothly as possible. Basically, there are *a lot of moving parts,* and it is a Herculean effort, to be sure.

When choosing a front-end charting platform, broker, and exchange to trade with, you will need to do your homework to determine which best fits you and your pocketbook. Table 17.1 shows some examples of each of the players to give you a head start on ones to investigate.

**Table 17.1** Some examples of players in today's order flow process.

| Front-end Charting Platforms | Brokers | Exchanges | Clearing Firms |
|---|---|---|---|
| NinjaTrader | NinjaTrader | CME, CBOT, NYMEX, COMEX | NinjaTrader |
| TradeStation | TradeStation | NYSE, NASDAQ, CME, CBOT, CBOE, NYMEX, COMEX | TradeStation |
| eSignal | Dorman Trading | NYSE, NASDAQ, CME, CBOT, CBOE, NYMEX, COMEX | Dorman Trading |
| MultiCharts | Interactive-Brokers | NYSE, NASDAQ, CME, CBOT, CBOE, NYMEX, COMEX | NSCC, National Securities Clearing Corporation |
| MetaTrader 4 and MetaTrader 5 | Forex.com | Not Applicable | JP Morgan |

This table is intended for educational purposes only. Information is subject to change. Readers are advised to consult with their financial advisor for current information.

You will have access to online screenshots and statements and reports of all your trading activity with your front-end charting platform and your broker. This will enable you to monitor your positions and your account balances.

### Here are some of the fields you will find online:

- Account balance
- Orders placed
- Orders filled and canceled
- Open positions
- Closed positions
- Sell, buy, cover, etc.
- Order type: limit, stop limit, market, etc.
- Spread, bid, ask

- Symbols, interval and time frame of chart
- Position short or long
- Quantity filled
- Quantity left
- Time of order placed and filled
- Average price

The look of the statements and online screens will vary depending on which platform you are using, and you will need to acquaint yourself with your chosen platforms so that you can find the information you need to enter and exit your positions as desired.

As with everything, there will be a learning curve with any new platform, and it's best to either paper trade first or place small test trades to get your feet wet before you jump in with your actual trading. Order entry mechanics will also vary from platform to platform, and if you are going to encounter any operator errors, it's best to experience them on a small sample trade or simulated account first.

Once you are up and running, the next important concern is for you to reconcile all your account statements daily. If a glitch in the order flow system occurs, you need to address it immediately. With the volume of transactions and the volume of personnel processing these transactions, there is always a margin for error.

It's like balancing your bank statement and credit card statements every month. You want to catch a problem immediately so that you have grounds to contest it. If you snooze, you lose. You will have less power to prove your point, rectify the situation, and seek reimbursement.

## Types of Trade Orders

The type of order you place is part of your trading and investing rules and can affect your bottom line. You can use many kinds of order types, and not all brokers offer all order types. So check with your broker to find out what is available. The purpose of selecting an order type when you place your order is to achieve several objectives.

**The objective of selecting an order type includes the following:**

- Limit risk
- Control the speed of the fill (as soon as possible or not)
- Control the price of the fill (specific price or not)
- Control when you will be filled (day or time)
- A combination of the above

Depending on market dynamics and liquidity, any attempts to achieve these stated objectives may or may not be possible. This means you may not get filled at the speed and price you desire, or you may not get filled at all. You are at the mercy of the market, and your selection of order type is merely a way to *attempt* to control the outcome of any trade.

**Following are the three most common order types:**

- **Market order.** This is the simplest and most common of the order types. It does not allow any control over the price received and is a buy or sell order to be executed immediately with no limits. As long as there are willing sellers and buyers, market orders are filled. Market orders are used when certainty of execution is a priority over price of execution at current market prices.
- **Limit order.** A *buy limit order* is an order to buy at not more than a specific price. A *sell limit order* is an order to sell at not less than a specific price. This gives the trader control over the price at which the trade is executed; however, the order may never be filled. Limit orders are used when the trader wishes to control price rather than certainty of execution.
- **Cancel order.** This is an order that cancels an existing order already placed.

Sometimes keeping it simple is the best policy, and in that case the three most common order types will work well for you. The limit order, one of the three most common order types, controls the price of the fill. In the next group of order types, the goal is to control the timing of the fill.

**Following are orders that affect the time it takes to fill an order:**

- **Day order.** This order is in force from the time the order is submitted to the end of the day's trading session. For equity markets, the closing time is defined by the exchange.
- **Good till canceled (GTC) order.** This order requires a specific cancel order to close it out. It can persist indefinitely, although brokers may set time limits, for example, 90 days.
- **Good till date (GTD) order.** This order will remain working with the broker system and in the marketplace until it fills or until the close of the market on the date specified.

If you are interested in more complex orders, there are many more to choose from that will combine more than one variable, such as price of fill and speed of fill in the same order. Some orders will also provide a layer of privacy by keeping your strategies hidden from the market. In the end, it is all down to testing which orders yield the best net result in your account.

## Using Margin and Leverage

The definition of margin is borrowed money that is used to purchase market instruments. This practice is referred to as *buying on margin*. Using margin can dramatically increase risk because both gains and losses are amplified. That is, while the potential for greater profit does exist, it comes with a heavy price—the potential for greater loss.

Margin also subjects the trader to additional risks, such as interest payments for using the borrowed money. There is also the possibility of experiencing a *margin call*. This is when traders will need to supply additional funds to their broker immediately if the market goes quickly against them.

Another way to look at margin is purely as a debt, and in the corporate world, debt ratios can determine the health of an entity. Too much debt means a generally unhealthy company. However, debt can also be a positive tool that enables growth and expansion both in trading and in thriving corporations. It can be just a cost of doing business.

For example, using debt as a tool can fund a new start-up company that can change a generation—just as when 20-year-old Mark Zuckerberg got his first investment of $1,000, and a few months later obtained $16,000 to launch Facebook in 2004. In the beginning, Zuckerberg took on proportionally high risk and high debt. This assessment is because at the start, Facebook generated zero revenue.

Now of course today, just 20 years after the launch, Facebook (aka Meta Platforms Inc.) has a market capitalization at 1 trillion USD—yes that is trillion with a t. So, you can see how that turned out.

Ultimately, how you handle margin, leverage, and debt needs to be a calculated business decision on your part. You must carefully weigh the pros and cons of using margin and determine how much to use and when to use it. It's all about risk and managing that risk. The bottom line is this:

## Beware Of the Dreaded Margin Call

My suggestion is that only experienced traders and investors use margin. When novice traders begin to apply this tool, they should do so slowly and carefully. It is crucial that trade size be calculated to prevent overextended risk.

## The Importance of Liquidity and Volume

Liquidity is the degree to which an asset or security can be bought or sold in the market without affecting the asset's price. For the asset's price to be unaffected, there must be a balance of buyers and sellers on both sides of the trade, which offers liquidity to both the buyers and the sellers at the same time.

Volume is the total number of shares or contracts being traded in a given period. Typically, when volume is high, liquidity is high. Volume adds additional pressure to the market system, in that when there is a sudden unprecedented increase in volume, the existing systems can become overloaded.

Then, when there is an imbalance of buyers and sellers, such as when Enron stock was famously falling in 2001 and it was all sellers and no buyers, the stock price will gap down out of control. This type of event will cause low or *zero liquidity* for sellers because the market has no buyers. If you have never heard of the Enron lesson, be sure to Google it; you will learn how devastating a lack of liquidity can be.

Most traders don't fully understand the importance of liquidity until they are faced with an open trade in a market that has zero liquidity such as in the Enron example. Awareness of this possibility is crucial to avoiding devastation to your account. Some risk management techniques are useful in softening the effects of a low liquidity event.

**Following are ways to minimize the effect of low or zero liquidity:**

1. Diversify your trading portfolio among a variety of sectors.
2. Trade with only 10% of your net worth, which limits your overall risk.
3. Seek markets and trading hours that are known for high liquidity due to their higher volume.

Generally, liquidity is reflected in the volume of trades being made on any given day or hour or minute. The number of active traders in the market at any time and place will affect the amount of liquidity.

For example, in the S&P 500 E-mini futures market, liquidity is high during open market hours and low at night. After regular market hours, fewer active traders are in the market; hence, there is less liquidity.

In the forex market, which trades around the clock, there is liquidity throughout the entire day and into the night, except weekends when the market is closed. A lot of night owl forex traders are busy trading when everyone else is sleeping, and that provides more liquidity. But the best liquidity in the forex market occurs during overlapping sessions. One example of this is when the London and New York sessions overlap.

In addition, the forex market is a global market with currencies around the world being traded. When one country ends its day, another country is just beginning, which also contributes to the round-the-clock trading activity in this market.

One more note about liquidity: Speculators, traders, investors, and market makers all create liquidity in the markets. These individuals are seeking to profit from anticipated increases or decreases in market prices.

By doing this, they provide the capital needed to facilitate liquidity. They generate revenue for themselves when they are on the winning side of a trade. In essence, their profits are the price that the world pays in order to maintain adequate liquidity in the financial markets.

## Volatility and Market Gaps

The term *volatility* refers to dramatic, short-term fluctuations of price in a market or individual financial instrument. Quick decreases or increases in price can create *gaps*.

On a chart, a gap looks like a hyperbolic price move to the upside or downside, with just white space and no price bars during the gap. See Figure 17.3. Gaps can happen after a market has been closed, right at the open. This may be caused by some significant event that occurred while the market was closed. Gaps are also common at the beginning, middle, and end of a trend.

### Market gaps and volatility can be caused by the following:

- Overall market crashes, such as occurred in 1929
- Global disasters, such as the Japanese earthquake in 1995
- Terrorist attacks, such as on September 11, 2001
- Breaking news on political, corporate, or other events
- Scheduled Federal Reserve announcements

Generally, traders love volatility because that is when there is movement and traders make money when they are correct about

**Figure 17.3**  *Market Gap Chart Example. Notice the white area in the middle of the chart with no price bars. On February 14, where the price jumps up hyperbolically, that is the area where the gap occurred.*
SOURCE: NinjaTrader. www.ninjatrader.com

which way the market is moving. When there is no movement or volatility in the market, traders are not able to capitalize on their ability to pinpoint what direction the market is moving. And they are not given opportunities to profit from their skills.

Ironically, during the 1929 crash, the market had huge swings to the downside blended in with huge swings to the upside. The market never moves in a perfectly straight line. As I like to say the market *zigs and zags,* which is another way of saying it has ups and downs and volatility.

If you were trading from 1929 through 1933 and could read the market correctly, you would have been able to make an enormous amount of money because of the volatility. Huge swings in price activity to the downside and then to the upside and then to the downside again offer talented traders a unique opportunity to profit.

Unlike buy and hold investors, traders benefit from volatility in the market. In contrast, some buy and hold investors tend to buy during the blind euphoria phase at the top of the market, and they tend to sell during the desperate panic phase at the bottom of a market cycle, which is precisely the wrong thing to do at the wrong time.

**IMPORTANT NOTE:** At times a gap up or a gap down will blast right through your carefully set stop loss exit. This type of event will be out of your control, and you will lose more than your planned risk amount. This is something to be aware of so that you can be quick on your feet and not have your trading psychology thrown off. Keep a cool head in the event of a gap that goes against you.

And in the reverse situation, when you have a gap that goes in your favor, my favorite approach is to scale out a portion of my position to lock in profit and reduce anxiety. This helps while staying in the trade with the remaining portion of my trade.

## How Can the Bid and Ask, Spreads, Fills, and Slippage Affect Profits?

The terms *bid, ask, spreads, fills*, and *slippage* are interconnected in that they can affect your profitability. In reading blogs or trading articles, you will no doubt see lots of conversations about all of these terms. Accusations can abound toward brokers for providing bad fills or that the spreads are too wide. And others will tell you that slippage can kill your profits.

What everyone is really talking about is the bid-ask spread, and how it translates into your profitability (or lack thereof) at the end of the day, week, month, or year.

### Here are some definitions:

- **Bid and ask.** The bid price is the highest price that a buyer, or bidder, is willing to pay for an asset. In bid and ask, the bid price stands in contrast to the ask price. The ask price is the price a seller is willing to accept for the asset.
- **Spread.** The difference between the bid and ask price is called the spread. The size of the spread will differ from one asset to another mainly because of the difference in liquidity of each asset.
- **Fill.** There are three common reasons for a trade to be perceived as receiving a bad fill: *1. Fast-moving markets*—the broker may do everything right but in fast-moving markets the market momentum can be so fast that between the time you entered your order and the time your order was filled the market got away from your ideal entry price. *2. Slow in getting order to exchange*—one broker may be faster than another broker in processing your order due to the quality of their order execution technology. *3. Slow data feed*—this occurs on the front-end charting platform and presents itself when your data feed is either slow or imperfect. This would impact your perception of the quality of the fill because what you were seeing as market reality when you entered the trade was not accurate or was delayed. So, the fill may have been fast and a good fill, but your perception is altered by the quality of the data you were looking at.
- **Slippage.** This is the difference between the expected price of a trade and the price the trade actually executes at. Slippage often

occurs during periods of high volatility when market orders are used and also when large orders are executed when there may not be enough interest at the desired price level to maintain the expected price of the trade.

## Bad Fills Happen More Often With Low Liquidity

Typically, bad fills and slippage are much less of an issue for investors and position traders than for day traders. It is never a good thing when you get a bad fill, but position traders feel less of an impact. In markets that are not liquid, bad fills will happen more often.

## "I Feel the Need for Speed"

As Tom Cruise in the movie *Top Gun* said, "I feel the need for speed." Speed of data, speed of order execution, and the speed of your computer are all important factors that contribute to your success as a trader.

### Here are the areas to check to improve your system speed:

- New computer with good memory
- Fast, hardwired internet connection
- Keeping computer operating system updated
- Keeping charting software updated
- Fast real-time data feed
- A broker known for fast execution

Typically, speed is not as much of a factor for investors to be successful. But for day traders who use faster time frame charts, like tick charts and 1-minute charts, speed is essential. Technology is changing by the minute, and of course the more cutting edge your technology is, the faster it will be.

If you have an old computer, it may hinder your ability to process the massive amounts of data that traders need. Consider upgrading your hardware to meet what the current standards are if you find that your charts are loading slowly.

Also, be conscious of the fact that your *technological hygiene* is critical to maintaining optimum operating speed. For example, we often find that traders neglect to do updates on their charting platform software and on their operating systems of their computers. This can have a significant impact on the functionality of your system.

Your task is to be on the lookout for any advances in technology that can give you an edge and then determine if the benefit of faster technology justifies the expense to attain it.

## How to Choose the Best Broker for Your Needs

There are zillions of brokers worldwide and choosing the best for your needs can be challenging. They each have different niche strengths and varying price models. Your decision will be based on your needs and the costs associated with those needs.

**Consider the following six factors to when choosing your broker:**

1. **Service.** What products and services does the broker provide and is this offering a good match for the products and services you require? Does the broker provide good customer support?
2. **Markets.** What markets will you trade, and what markets will the broker provide? Is it a good match?
3. **Cost.** What are the costs associated with commissions, exchange fees, front-end charting platform, real-time or end-of-day data feed, and any other products and services you may require?
4. **Account size.** What is the minimum account size required for opening and maintaining an account?

5. **Connectivity and compatibility.** What front-end charting platforms is the broker able to connect to, and does the broker provide a quality front-end charting platform itself?
6. **Speed of execution.** What is the quality of the order execution system that the broker has, and how fast can the broker fill your orders?

Many traders and investors maintain a few different brokerage accounts, each serving a different purpose. This is a way to get the best of all worlds in that when you fund a brokerage account you will often get free charting and free real time data for the market(s) that the broker handles.

Other traders may have a one-stop shopping approach and choose one broker that serves all their needs in one place. Depending on your unique situation at this moment in time, you will need to identify priorities and find a broker to match those priorities.

**IMPORTANT NOTE:** Some brokers have an excellent front-end charting platform with real-time data, and some do not. The ones that do not will sometimes offer, free of charge, a connection to a front-end charting platform that you may like. This is a consideration in that it can save you money to not have to pay for live real-time data and/or a front-end platform.

Remember, at any time you can change your priorities and change your broker. So don't feel like you are chained to one provider for life. Both you and the markets are evolving and are a work in progress. Reassess your needs on an annual basis to achieve optimal portfolio performance.

# How to Choose the Best Front-End Charting Platform for Your Needs

Today's technology has dramatically changed the landscape of trading. The speed of execution and the availability of extensive trading tools for a reasonable price have altered the industry as we know it. This has helped level the playing field for the independent trader.

This topic ties in with the power of today's front-end charting platforms. They can do almost anything from enabling traders to place trades with their broker right from their chart, to automating trades, to scanning for opportunities in the market; the possibilities of what they can do for you are endless.

Each one of these platforms has its own individual strengths, just like brokers and data feeds, so you will need to again identify your needs and find the best match for the costs involved.

### There is *overlap* among these providers:

- Brokers
- Front-end charting platforms
- Live data feeds
- Market exchanges
- Prop Firms

A little planning goes a long way because you can save money if you research what the latest offerings are from each of these types of providers.

We've already covered how to choose the best broker for your needs. And what's interesting is that some brokers provide a one-stop shopping opportunity and might be able to give you everything you need all in one place. It comes down to what your personal needs are.

For example, if you want to trade stocks, options, futures, and ETFs and you are a day trader who needs real time data, you could get all of that with the broker TradeStation. You would get a high-end charting platform with all the bells and whistles, real-time data for free, no exchange fees, and scanning tools to boot. But if you wanted to trade forex, TradeStation would not be a good fit for you because it does not carry that market.

On the other hand, a lot of traders need data feeds from a variety of global markets outside the United States. They will need to consider paying for live real time data from eSignal (ICE owns them now), which is a data vendor, and then will have to reverse engineer which broker to use from that. eSignal offers a good chart-ing platform and also excellent data feeds, but it does not have any scanning functionality. For scanning, you can plug eSignal data into MultiCharts, an excellent front-end charting platform, but there is a cost for that.

So, these two examples of TradeStation and eSignal give you a glimpse as to what to look for when choosing your front-end charting platform. Other factors should be considered, depending on how far down the rabbit hole you want to go, just know there are many ways to solve the puzzle, and if you need feedback, contact my team via email: **support@traderscoach.com.**

## How to Choose the Best Live Data Feed for Your Needs

Live streaming price and volume data is your lifeline to the markets and gives you minute-by-minute readings on what is happening in the market at every given moment. You can get data delivered to you in many ways. The quality and speed of the data you receive will vary depending on the source and the way it is delivered.

Very often, but not always, when you get data from a broker, it is filtered and delayed and are not the same quality you would get from a data vendor that specializes in data. It is vital to weigh the importance of the quality of the data you receive versus the cost of getting the data.

Depending on your budget, either quality or cost may be a greater priority, and only you can decide the best solution to achieve the greatest net profit in your trading.

### Paying Exchange Fees

All price and volume data come directly from the exchange that is being traded. Anyone who receives data from the exchange must pay an exchange fee, which covers the exchanges' cost of doing business. Different exchanges charge different prices, and some are more expensive than others. Also, there are two pricing tiers for exchange fees. Professionals pay much more for exchange fees compared to nonprofessionals.

If you are receiving free data through your broker, your broker is paying the fees to the exchange for you. The commissions you pay to your broker indirectly cover the cost of those fees. There's no getting around it; like death and taxes, someone has to pay for the exchange fees.

And the more varied the data you choose, the more you will be paying in exchange fees. For example, if you want to trade multiple markets, in multiple regions, with multiple market exchanges, it can get costly if you are buying direct from a data vendor like eSignal. Which is why many traders choose a broker that provides quality data for free.

## How Fast Does Your Data Need to Be?

You will need to decide on what data speed you will need based on whether you are day trading, position trading, or investing. Rule of thumb is the faster the data, the more expensive it will be.

**Following are a few data speed choices:**

- **Real-time data**—provides 1-minute and tick charts in live streaming data and is the fastest and most expensive data; good for day traders.
- **Delayed data**—usually around a 10-minute delay; good for position traders.
- **End-of-day data**—provides daily, weekly, monthly charts and is the least expensive data; good for position traders and investors.

Plan out your needs and determine the most cost-effective solution. Again, by narrowing your choice of markets and regions you can reduce your costs significantly.

# Prop Firms Offer Free Data And Charting Platforms

Prop firms are an excellent way to obtain not only a way to trade the firms money and not risk your own, but ... they offer free live streaming data for the Futures market. You will find more information on prop firms at the back of this book in the Epilogue.

## Setting Up Your Workstation

Now that you understand the financial markets, it's time to set up your workstation so that you can begin trading. It's pretty simple really, and you can work from anywhere that has a good internet connection.

**Here is what you need to set up your workstation:**

- Computer with enough memory and power
- Monitor
- Back up battery
- Telephone
- Quiet workspace to focus
- Fast hardwired internet connection
- Broker
- Front-end charting platform
- Data-feed to power your charts
- Trader's record keeping system, hand-written
- Educational materials, books, courses
- Trading software for entries, exits, scanning
- Desk, comfortable chair, bookcase, adequate lighting

Once you have set aside a workstation where you can focus and begin, be sure to make it comfortable. If there is something that would inspire you, a photo or painting, display it.

# What Market to Trade?

Choosing the best market(s) for you to trade or invest in may take some time. Eventually, you will settle on your favorites and will develop an understanding of the unique characteristics of each. This gives you an edge in effectively implementing your trading and investing system to generate greater profits.

If you are completely new to the markets, this section is designed to give you an overview and a head start on what direction to go in. Basically, choose the market that seems most "friendly" and that you know the most about for now. That will give you a good start, and you can branch out from there.

**Consider the following seven items when choosing a market:**

1. **Dollar size of your account.** Some markets may be too expensive for you to even consider trading. You may not be able to afford the market, or you cannot trade it and still maintain effective risk control. Sometimes by choosing a lower time frame, you can still maintain effective risk control.

2. **Amount of time you have available to monitor the markets.** Different trading styles require different time obligations. If you day trade, then you need to be available to watch and monitor your trading all day during market hours. However, if you are position trading or investing, then you only need to monitor the markets in the evening. Position trading and investing are great for people who work during the day.

3. **Time frame you want to use.** If you are a day trader, you will choose an intraday time frame to trade, like the 1-minute or 5-minute chart; if you are a position trader, you will choose a daily time frame chart; and if you are an investor or long-term trader, you will choose weekly and monthly charts. Choosing the best time frame is a combination of your trading account size, your risk control approach, and your personal preferences.

4. **Your overall knowledge of the markets.** As you gain experience and knowledge about the financial markets, that will

expand your trading and investing possibilities. For example, most novice students start out with the stock market, but as they learn about other markets, such as options and futures, they may branch out to new areas.

5. **Your trading and investing skill level.** Don't confuse this with your overall market knowledge or the number of years you have been studying. This topic deals specifically with your trading and investing ability. Some markets require a higher level of skill due to their higher level of volatility or movement. You need to work with markets compatible with your skill level.

6. **Personal preference.** Simply stated, what markets do you like best? Some students who are farmers may focus their trading on the commodities markets, such as the grain markets, while others on Wall Street may want to focus their trading and investing on the stock market. It's up to you.

7. **Liquidity and daily movement.** When choosing a market it is crucial to select one that has enough liquidity to give you good fills so that you can enter and exit the markets easily.

Regulatory agencies exist for the purpose of market oversight and help keep the huge financial system running as smoothly as possible.

**Following is a list of financial markets regulatory agencies:**

- **SEC**—The *Securities and Exchange Commission* is the US government agency of the securities industry. It was established in 1934.
- **CFTC**—The *Commodity Futures Trading Commission* is the US government agency of the futures industry. It was established in 1974.
- **NFA**—The *National Futures Association* is a self-regulatory organization that works to protect investors and regulates the financial derivative market in the United States. It was created by the CFTC in 1982.

- **FINRA**—The *Financial Industry Regulatory Authority* is an agency that oversees US broker dealers. It is the successor to the *National Association of Securities Dealers,* NASD. FINRA was established in 2007.

Countless markets are available, but the ones listed in Table 17.2 give you a sample to start with. As you develop your skills and curiosity, you may be interested in exploring other markets, such as bonds, derivatives, cryptocurrencies, insurance, mortgage, capital, and money markets to name a few.

It is important to note that the futures markets are set up for speculating and stock markets are set up for investing. Short-term traders and day traders are speculating and typically choose the futures market. However, a valid argument is that there are more opportunities in the stock market because there are more stocks than futures markets.

### About Cryptocurrency

Another important market to bring your attention to is the cryptocurrency market which first appeared in 2009 when Bitcoin was released as an open-source software. Fast forward to today where now more than 20,000 other cryptos have been added to the marketplace.

Cryptocurrency does not exist in physical form (like paper money) and is typically not issued by a central authority. Instead, it uses decentralized control as opposed to a central bank digital currency. They are digital and are an alternative form of payment created using encryption algorithms.

To use cryptocurrencies, you need a cryptocurrency wallet. Or you can trade cryptos now since the SEC approved the launch of several BTC ETFs on January 10, 2024. The approval order resolves the critical legal and regulatory issues entailed in launching these new ETFs.

Table 17.2 Popular markets.

| | Stocks | Options | Futures | ETFS | Forex |
|---|---|---|---|---|---|
| **Market Types** | Equities | Stocks, futures, indexes | Commodity futures, financial futures | Exchange traded funds | Pairs and cross-markets |
| **Suggested Markets** | All liquid markets, large-cap, mid-cap, small-cap, NYSE, NAS-DAQ, S&P 500, Russell 2000 | Calls, puts, spreads, hedging, trade the option of the underlying asset | S&P e-mini, NAS-DAQ e-mini, Crude Oil, Gold, T-Notes, T-Bonds, Euro, Japanese Yen | QQQ, SPY, SOXS, TLT, IWM, SPXU, UNG, DIA, SPXS, PSQ, GDX, SH, SLV, XLP, | EUR/USD, USD/JPY, GBP/USD, AUD/USD, USD/CAD, |
| **Units** | Shares | Contracts | Contracts | Contracts | Price Ratios |
| **Increments of Movement** | Decimals | Decimals and quarter points | Ticks | Ticks | PIPS (percentage in point) |
| **Suggested Experience Levels** | Master Intermediate Novice | Master Intermediate | Master Intermediate | Master Intermediate Novice | Master Intermediate |
| **Volume and Liquidity** | Are greatest for large cap and blue-chip stocks | Best during normal market hours | Excellent liquidity | Best during normal market hours | 24-hour trading hours (except on weekends) |
| **Notes** | Stocks are good for novice traders learning market basics. | Do not day trade options; the wide bid/ask make day trading difficult. | You can day trade futures, due to excellent liquidity. E-minis and micros offer low price. | ETFs are exchange traded funds and can be bought or sold intraday. | No commissions but brokers make money on spreads; 24-hour market. |
| **Regulatory Agencies for Each Market** | SEC, FINRA | SEC, FINRA, CFTC, and the NFA. | CFTC, NFA, FINRA. | SEC, FINRA. | NFA, CFTC, FINRA. |

This table is intended for educational purposes only. Information is subject to change. Readers are advised to consult with their broker or data provider for current information.

You might note the absence of cryptocurrencies in Table 17.3 with my list of markets to consider. This is because they are so new and untested. And yet, it's an exciting phenomenon much like the internet was when it first appeared in 1983.

Just remember the meteoric rise of the brand new dot.com internet market in the late 1990s and then the subsequent crash around 2000. Like the internet, there have already been bumps in the road along the way for cryptos. This is a new and exciting market, one worth keeping your eye on since it is likely to survive, thrive, and endure.

At the end of the day, you will choose the market that suits your personality and is compatible with where you are now on your journey.

## 🛒 Stock Market

The history of the stock market dates back hundreds of years to the late 1400s in Antwerp, or modern-day Belgium, which became the center of international trade. It wasn't until 1790 that the Philadelphia stock Exchange, PHLX, was formed, and then in 1792 the New York Stock Exchange, NYSE, was formed.

Raising the necessary capital for development or expansion is the primary reason for any company to sell shares of its stock. A stock market or equity market is a public entity for the trading of company stock in shares, and derivatives of stock, at an agreed price.

This gives us the opportunity to buy and sell shares of a large corporation and literally own a piece of the company. The buying and selling creates liquidity in the marketplace.

Often, the first market most investors and traders choose to participate in is the stock market. It is easy to understand the concept of owning shares of a large company, especially if the company creates or does something that we are interested in or know something about.

Plus, there are many stocks to choose from with a variety of sectors so it's easy to find stocks that appeal to most everyone. The choices are virtually limitless and some estimate that more than 600,000 companies worldwide are publicly traded.

### What a stock symbol looks like:

- Single-letter symbols are the most well-known stocks.
- Three-letter symbols are on the NYSE.
- Four-letter symbols are probably on the NASDAQ.

Each company is represented by a *ticker symbol,* which is a short abbreviation used to uniquely identify publicly traded shares of a particular stock on a particular stock market exchange. See Table 17.3.

The phrase *ticker symbol* refers to the symbols that were printed on the tape of a ticker tape machine back in 1870 through the 1960s.

**Table 17.3** Popular stock ticker symbols and their respective exchanges.

| Company Name | Ticker Symbol | Stock Exchange |
| --- | --- | --- |
| 3M Company | MMM | NYSE |
| Automatic Data Processing | ADP | NASDAQ |
| Amazon.com | AMZN | NASDAQ |
| Apple Inc. | AAPL | NASDAQ |
| Applied Materials | AMAT | NASDAQ |
| AT&T | T | NYSE |
| Bank of America | BAC | NYSE |
| Coca-Cola | KO | NYSE |
| Exxon Mobil | XOM | NYSE |
| Facebook (Meta) | META | NASDAQ |
| Ford Motor Company | F | NYSE |
| Google | GOOGL | NASDAQ |
| Hyatt | H | NYSE |
| Kellogg (Kellanova) | K | NYSE |
| McDonald's | MCD | NYSE |
| Netflix | NFLX | NASDAQ |
| Target | TGT | NYSE |
| Tesla | TSLA | NASDAQ |
| United States Steel | X | NYSE |
| Visa, Inc. | V | NYSE |
| Walmart | WMT | NYSE |
| Zillow | Z | NASDAQ |

This table is intended for educational purposes only. Information is subject to change. Readers are advised to consult with their broker or data provider for current information.

The word *ticker* refers to the ticking sound that the machine made as it printed the tape with the updated price and volume numbers.

In the 1960s this machine became obsolete as it was replaced with television and computer monitors to transmit this financial information. After the ticker tape machines were replaced by new technology, the symbols themselves lived on and are still used today.

Occasionally symbols will evolve and change when publicly traded companies merge or change names. For example, in 1999 when Exxon merged with Mobil Oil, Exxon changed its phonetic ticker symbol XON to XOM to reflect the new company merger. And when Facebook changed its name to Meta in 2022, the ticker symbol changed from FB to META. With today's mergers, acquisitions, and name changes, a ticker symbol change is a normal occurrence.

Stock symbols are typically made up of one to five letters. A three-letter symbol means the stock trades on the NYSE. Four letters mean it probably trades on the NASDAQ exchange. Some well-known companies may have a single character, such as the symbol *F* which represents Ford Motor Company.

## Stock Exchanges Around The World

These symbols represent each company and are listed on what is called a *stock exchange*. The activity of the price and volume in the market is reported to the public by the exchange. There are stock market exchanges in virtually every developed country throughout the world. The biggest markets reside in the United States, China, Europe, Japan, Hong Kong, Canada, and the United Kingdom.

There are global opportunities in the stock market. Each market exchange varies in market cap, location, and characteristics. For example, the NYSE (New York Stock Exchange) alone has more than 2,000 companies to choose from. Considering it's been around since 1792 and is estimated to represent one-third of all equities traded in the world, almost everyone trading or investing has heard of it.

The NASDAQ (National Association of Securities Dealers Automated Quotations) is a tech-heavy exchange that responds differently to world events than the NYSE. For example, during the pandemic of 2000, tech stocks enjoyed a strong rally driven by e-commerce and cloud computing, which boosted NASDAQ when other exchanges were plummeting.

Select the specific exchanges and instruments that will work best. You may find that selecting those in your time zone will assist you in trading during normal business hours.

It is also important to research what data feeds are available for the markets you are interested in and the costs involved.

## Market Capitalization

Market capitalization, commonly known as "market cap", is a definitive measure of the total market value of a company's outstanding shares on the stock market. Each company falls within one of the following three categories:

- Large-cap — over 10 billion dollars
- Mid-cap — 2 to 10 billion dollars
- Small-cap — 300 million to 2 billion dollars

Market cap serves as a robust indicator of a company's relative size and value, encompassing critical factors such as risk and market perception.

## About Indexes

Several *stock market indexes* bundle many stocks into one index; see Table 17.4. Following are some of the most popular indexes in the United States:

- DJIA, Dow Jones Industrial Average (See Table 17.5)
- S&P 500, Standard and Poor's 500
- Nasdaq Composite
- Nasdaq 100
- Russell 2000

**Table 17.4**  Popular United States stock index symbols and their exchanges.

| Index Name | Ticker Symbol | Stock Exchange |
|---|---|---|
| DJIA | DJIA, DJI, DOW | NYSE, NASDAQ |
| S&P 500 | SPX, SPY | NYSE, NASDAQ, CBOE |
| NASDAQ 100 | QQQQ, IXIC, COMP | NASDAQ |
| S&P 500 VIX | VIX | CBOE |
| Russell 2000 | RYT RTT | NYSE, NASDAQ |

This table is intended for educational purposes only. Information is subject to change. Readers are advised to consult with their broker or data provider for current information. For a list of worldwide stock market indexes see the Epilogue at the back of this book.

The advantage of trading an index is that a bundle of stocks is included in the index, which gives you diversification as opposed to trading single solitary stocks at a time. Another idea is for you to research the ETF market; I'll cover that later in this chapter. ETFs are available for each of the indexes, and *inverse ETFs* allow you to bet against the market.

### Sectors In The Stock Market

When looking at the global economy, there are a variety of sectors that drive the stock market. Drilling further down into sector analysis, one can also look at specific industries and companies within each sector to gain a better understanding of the overall health of any one sector at a given time.

Some indexes such as the DJIA and S&P 500, are made up of a group of different sectors. They each use a different classification model. For example the DJIA uses the Industry Classification Benchmark (ICB) and the S&P 500 uses the Global Industry Classification Standard (GICS) see Table 17.6.

**Table 17.5** DJIA list of 30 stocks with industry classifications and stock symbols.

| | Company | Industry | Symbol |
|---|---|---|---|
| 1 | Apple | Consumer Electronics | AAPL |
| 2 | Amgen | Biotechnology | AMGN |
| 3 | Amazon.com Inc. | Internet Retail | AMZN |
| 4 | American Express | Banking Payment Card Services | AXP |
| 5 | Boeing | Aerospace & Defense | BA |
| 6 | Caterpillar | Construction Equipment | CAT |
| 7 | Salesforce | Cloud Computing | CRM |
| 8 | Cisco Systems | Communications & Information Technology | CSCO |
| 9 | Chevron | Energy, Oil & Gas | CVX |
| 10 | Walt Disney | Media Entertainment | DIS |
| 11 | Dow Incorporated | News & Publishing | DOW |
| 12 | Goldman Sachs Group | Financial Services | GS |
| 13 | Home Depot | Retailing | HD |
| 14 | Honeywell International | Conglomerate | HON |
| 15 | International Business Machines | Information Technology | IBM |
| 16 | Intel | Semiconductors | INTC |
| 17 | Johnson & Johnson | Pharmaceuticals | JNJ |
| 18 | JPMorgan Chase | Financial Services | JPM |
| 19 | Coca-Cola | Beverages | KO |
| 20 | McDonald's | Fast Food | MCD |
| 21 | 3M | Conglomerate | MMM |
| 22 | Merck | Pharmaceuticals | MRK |
| 23 | Microsoft | Information Technology | MSFT |
| 24 | Nike | Athletic Apparel | NKE |
| 25 | Procter & Gamble | Consumer Goods | PG |
| 26 | Travelers Companies | Insurance | TRV |
| 27 | UnitedHealth Group | Healthcare Insurance | UNH |
| 28 | Visa | Payment Card Services | V |
| 29 | Verizon Communications | Telecommunications | VZ |
| 30 | Walmart | Retail | WMT |

This table is intended for educational purposes only. Information is subject to change. Readers are advised to consult with their broker or data provider for current information.

**Table 17.6** Global Industry Classification Standard (GICS) table illustrating how stock sectors, industries, and individual companies can be observed from a macro to a micro level.

| Code | Sector | Subcode | Industry Group | Company |
|---|---|---|---|---|
| 10 | Energy | 1010 | Energy | Exxon Mobil |
| 15 | Basic Materials | 1510 | Materials | DuPont |
| 20 | Industrials | 2010 | Capital Goods | 3M |
| | | 2020 | Professional Services | ASGN |
| | | 2030 | Transportation | American Airlines |
| 25 | Consumer Cyclical | 2510 | Automobiles | Ford |
| | | 2520 | Consumer Apparel | Under Armour |
| | | 2530 | Consumer Services | McDonald's |
| | | 2550 | Apparel Retail | Foot Locker |
| 30 | Consumer Defensive | 3010 | Food & Staples Retailing | Walmart |
| | | 3020 | Food, Beverage, & Tobacco | Coca-Cola |
| | | 3030 | Household Products | Kimberly-Clark |
| 35 | Health Care | 3510 | Equipment & Services | United Health Group |
| | | 3520 | Pharmaceuticals | Johnson & Johnson |
| 40 | Financials | 4010 | Banks | Bank of America |
| | | 4020 | Financial Services | American Express |
| | | 4030 | Insurance | Aflac |
| 45 | Technology | 4510 | Software & Services | Microsoft |
| | | 4520 | Hardware & Equipment | Apple |
| | | 4530 | Semiconductors | Intel |
| 50 | Communication Services | 5010 | Telecommunication Services | AT&T |
| | | 5020 | Media & Entertainment | Netflix |
| 55 | Utilities | 5510 | Utilities | Chesapeake Utilities |
| 60 | Real Estate | 6010 | Equity Real Estate Investment Trusts (REITs) | GEO Group |
| | | 6020 | Real Estate Management & Development | Zillow |

This table is intended for educational purposes only. Information is subject to change. Readers are advised to consult with their broker or data provider for current information.

*What's a FANG?*

An acronym for the stocks Facebook, Amazon, Netflix, and Google, FANG stocks are famous for their impressive growth and popularity, with each member more than doubling its stock price in recent years.

The stock market is great for novice traders who want to learn about buying and selling instruments with a relatively simple order entry process. After you learn about market dynamics with stocks, it's easier to move to other markets.

# Brief History of the Dow Jones Industrial Average

The Dow Jones Industrial Average (DJIA or Dow) was started in 1896 by *Wall Street Journal* editor Charles Dow. The Dow has come to be known as a barometer of the overall health of the US economy, and by extension the world economy. The original group of companies listed on the DJIA consisted of 12 stocks.

The original list of 12 grew over the years to 20 and then to the current list of 30 stocks. This increase in the number of stocks listed on the index reflected the expanding US economy.

The steady rise of the DJIA over the past 100 years, despite significant downturns from time to time, has led many investors to adopt a passive buy-and-hold strategy, believing they can consistently gain 10% on their money per year over time provided they stayed in the market long enough.

And yet, buy-and-hold has its own set of risks. Should you happen to be caught in a significant downturn or crash, your hard-earned cash could disappear in an instant.

*(continued on next page...)*

*(...continued from previous page)*

**The DJIA has suffered a few significant crashes:**

- 1929—Wall Street crash triggered the Great Depression
- 1987—Black Monday
- 2000—Dotcom bubble
- 2008 to 2009—GFC, Global Financial Crisis
- 2020—Coronavirus crash

With the DJIA at all-time highs today, one must wonder when the next big correction or crash will occur. Only time will tell, but it behooves us all to watch the markets, our investments, and our trading like a hawk so that we don't miss out on either the next big bull or bear opportunities.

## The Continuing Rise And Fall And Rise Again Of The Stock Market

The timeline of the DJIA's fluctuating price story is an interesting one. From the first official closing of the DOW on May 26, 1896 at a price of $31.58 to present day's highest close on May 17, 2024 at a price of $40,003.59, it has been quite a wild ride. See Table 17.7.

Look at Figure 17.4 to see how the 1929 crash took the DJIA high of $381.17 on September 3, 1929 all the way down to a low of $41.22 on July 8, 1932. To date, that was the most dramatic drop in price. And understandably, the market took around 20 years to get back to it's 1929 high. It's hard to forget a crash like that when you lived through it.

Of course we like to think that the 2008 crash was significant, and it was. Yet, the devastation of the Great Depression is one for the history books.

**Table 17.7** Timeline of the DJIA dollar value since its first year in 1896 until 2024.

| Date | Number of Stocks Listed on DJIA | $ Value DJIA @ Market Close |
|---|---|---|
| 5-26-1896—DOW First Official Closing | 12 | 31.58 |
| 1-2-1900—10-year benchmark | 12 | 49.90 |
| 1-3-1910—10-year benchmark | 12 | 72.04 |
| 10-4-1916—Expanded to 20 stocks | 20 | 103.41 |
| 1-2-1920—10-year benchmark | 20 | 108.76 |
| 10-1-1928—Expanded to 30 stocks | 30 | 240.01 |
| 9-3-1929—high | 30 | 381.17 |
| 10-24-1929—Black Thursday Crash | 30 | 299.47 |
| 10-28-1929—Black Monday Crash | 30 | 260.64 |
| 10-29-1929—Black Tuesday Crash | 30 | 230.07 |
| 1-2-1930—10-year benchmark | 30 | 244.20 |
| 7-8-1932—ATL, All-time low | 30 | 41.22 |
| 1-2-1940—10-year benchmark | 30 | 151.43 |
| 1-3-1950—10-year benchmark | 30 | 198.89 |
| 1-4-1960—10-year benchmark | 30 | 679.06 |
| 1-2-1970—10-year benchmark | 30 | 809.20 |
| 1-2-1980—10-year benchmark | 30 | 824.57 |
| 10-16-1987—high | 30 | 2,246.74 |
| 10-19-1987—low—Black Monday Crash | 30 | 1,738.74 |
| 1-2-1990—10-year benchmark | 30 | 2,810.15 |
| 1-3-2000—10-year benchmark | 30 | 11,357.51 |
| 1-14-2000—high—Dotcom bubble | 30 | 11,722.98 |
| 10-9-2002—low—Dotcom bottom | 30 | 7,286.27 |
| 10-9-2007—high | 30 | 14,164.53 |
| 10-10-2008—GFC, Global Financial Crisis | 30 | 8,451.19 |
| 11-20-2008—low | 30 | 7,552.29 |
| 1-4-2010—10-year benchmark | 30 | 10,583.96 |
| 1-2-2020—10-year benchmark | 30 | 28,868.80 |
| 2-12-2020—high | 30 | 29,551.42 |
| 3-23-2020—low—Coronavirus Crash | 30 | 18,591.93 |
| 10-18-2024—ATH, All-time high to date | 30 | 43,275.91 |

SOURCE: https://www.measuringworth.com/datasets/DJA/index.php
This table is intended for educational purposes only. Information is subject to change. Readers are advised to consult with their broker or data provider for current information.

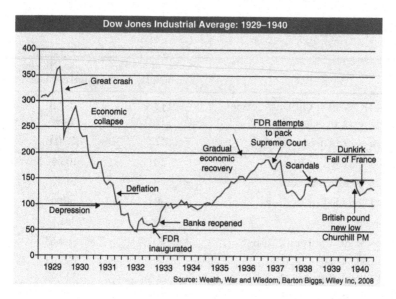

**Figure 17.4**    This chart shows the height of the DJIA at $381.17 in September 1929. The sudden fall to $230.07 on October 29, 1929, triggered a worldwide Great Depression that lasted through 1933. Anyone who hasn't experienced a market crash firsthand must be aware that market crashes have happened before and will happen again. Euphoric bull markets like the one in the roaring 1920s tend to lure unsuspecting participants into the market at the worst possible time.

SOURCE: Biggs, B. (2008). *Wealth, war and wisdom.* Wiley.

# 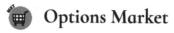 Options Market

Options were introduced in 1973 and have become a driving force in the trading and investing world. Just as with stocks, options have specific symbols that identify exactly which option you are trading. Each broker may have differing symbols, but here is a basic outline of what an option will look like.

### What an Option Symbol Looks Like:

- Stock ticker symbol of underlying asset
- Option expiration month code (See Table 17.8)
- Option exercise price code
- Option exchange code

**Table 17.8**  Option expiration month codes.

| Month | Call | Put |
| --- | --- | --- |
| January | A | M |
| February | B | N |
| March | C | O |
| April | D | P |
| May | E | Q |
| June | F | R |
| July | G | S |
| August | H | T |
| September | I | U |
| October | J | V |
| November | K | W |
| December | L | X |

This table is intended for educational purposes only. Information is subject to change. Readers are advised to consult with their broker or data provider for current information.

An option is a derivative financial instrument that establishes a contract between two parties concerning the buying or selling of an asset at a reference price. A buyer of the option gains the right, but not the obligation, to engage in some specific transaction on the asset, while a seller incurs the obligation to fulfill the transaction if so requested by the buyer.

The price of an option is derived from the difference between the reference price and the value of the underlying asset (commonly a stock, bond, currency, or futures contract) plus a premium based on the time remaining until the expiration of the option.

### Following are a few options definitions:

- **Call**—An options contract that gives you the right to buy stock at a set price within a certain period.
- **Put**—An options contract that gives you the right to sell stock at a set price within a certain period.
- **Expiration Date**—The date when the options contract becomes void. It's the due date for you to do something with the contract, and it can be days, weeks, months, or years in the future.

- **Strike Price**—The price at which you can buy or sell the stock if you choose to exercise the option.
- **Premium**—The per-share price you pay for an option. The premium is based on the following: *intrinsic value*, which is the value of an option based on the difference between a stock's current market price and the options' strike price, and the *time value*, which is the value of an option based on the amount of time before the contract expires. Time is valuable to investors because of the possibility that an option's intrinsic value can increase during the contract's time frame. As the expiration date approaches, time value decreases. This is known as time decay or "theta" after the options pricing model used to calculate it.
- **In the money**—This refers to an option that has intrinsic value. When the relationship between stock price in the open market and the strike price favors the options contract owner, this is considered in the money. A call option is in the money when the stock price is higher than the strike price. A put option is in the money when the stock price is lower than the strike price.
- **Out of the money**—When exercising the option has no financial benefit, it's called out of the money. Meaning, an out-of-the-money option makes buying or selling shares at the strike price less lucrative than buying or selling on the open market. A call option is out of the money if the stock price is lower than the strike price. A put option is out of the money when the stock price is higher than the strike price.
- **At the money**—When the stock price is equal to the strike price, an option is considered at the money.

An interesting part of the options trading story is that sometimes options will expire completely worthless. You might even hear that 90% of all options expire worthless but in fact that is not true.

### The CBOE has provided the following statistics:

- Ten percent of options end up being exercised.
- Fifty-five percent of options are closed out prior to expiration.
- Thirty-five percent of options expire worthless.

Table 17.9   Popular US option exchanges.

| Options Exchange | Market Place |
| --- | --- |
| Chicago Board Options Exchange (CBOE) | Chicago, Illinois |
| New York Stock Exchange (NYSE) | New York, New York |
| Philadelphia Stock Exchange (PHLX) | Philadelphia, Pennsylvania |
| Boston Options Exchange (BOX) | Boston, Massachusetts |

This table is intended for educational purposes only. Information is subject to change. Readers are advised to consult with their broker or data provider for current information.

Trading an option enables you to trade with more leverage than buying the underlying asset outright. In some cases, trading with options can help you increase your trade size, allowing you to implement scaling techniques and better money management.

To help you get started, see Table 17.9 for some of the most popular options exchanges in the United States.

##  Futures Market

Japan's Dojima Rice Exchange opened in 1730 and is the earliest recognized futures trading exchange in the world. Then the Chicago Board of Trade, *CBOT*, commodity trading exchange opened in 1848 in Chicago. Shortly after that the New York Cotton Exchange, *NYCE*, opened in 1870 in New York.

### What a futures symbol looks like:

- ES M 24

Futures contracts are identified with symbols and codes that are different from say, stocks. See Figure 17.5. These codes and symbols consist of three parts:

- Instrument—root symbol
- Contract month
- Contract year

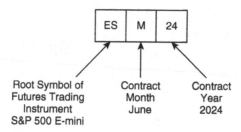

**Figure 17.5** Illustration of futures contract codes: root symbol, month, and year.

These symbols are constantly changing as time passes. The only part of the symbol that is a constant is the root symbol. When looking at a futures contract code or symbol, the contract month is represented by an alpha code, and you will need to know which months are represented by which alpha codes.

See Table 17.10 for a list of alpha codes for each month from January to December. For example, January is represented by the letter F and December is represented by the letter Z. The contract year is represented by the last two digits of the year. For example, the year 2024 is represented by 24.

**Table 17.10** Alpha codes for each month of the year for a futures contract.

| Futures Contract Month | Alpha Code |
| --- | --- |
| January | F |
| February | G |
| March | H |
| April | J |
| May | K |
| June | M |
| July | N |
| August | Q |
| September | U |
| October | V |
| November | X |
| December | Z |

This table is intended for educational purposes only. Information is subject to change. Readers are advised to consult with their broker or data provider for current information.

A futures contract is a standardized contract between two parties to exchange a specified asset of standardized quantity and quality for a price agreed upon today, which is the futures strike price. But the delivery is to occur at a specified future date, the delivery date. The contracts are traded on a *futures exchange*. See Table 17.11.

The party agreeing to buy the underlying asset in the future (the buyer of the contract) is said to be long, and the party agreeing to sell the asset in the future (the seller of the contract) is said to be short. The terminology reflects the expectations of the parties. The buyer hopes the asset price is going to increase, whereas the seller hopes for a decrease.

In many cases the underlying asset to a futures contract may not be traditional commodities at all. That is, for financial futures, the underlying asset or item can be currencies, securities, or financial instruments, as well as intangible assets or referenced items such as stock indexes and interest rates.

Table 17.11   Popular futures exchanges.

| Futures Exchange | Parent Group | Region | Market Place |
| --- | --- | --- | --- |
| Chicago Board of Trade (CBOT) | CME Group | United States | Chicago, Illinois |
| Chicago Mercantile Exchange (CME) | CME Group | United States | Chicago, Illinois |
| New York Mercantile Exchange (NYMEX) | CME Group | United States | New York, New York |
| Commodity Exchange Inc. (COMEX) | CME Group | United States | New York, New York |
| Kansas City Board of Trade (KCBT) | CME Group | United States | Kansas City, Missouri |
| European New Exchange Technology (EURONEXT) | EURONEXT | Netherlands | Amsterdam |
| Intercontinental Exchange (ICE) | ICE | United States | Atlanta, Georgia |

This table is intended for educational purposes only. Information is subject to change. Readers are advised to consult with their broker or data provider for current information.

While the futures contract specifies an exchange to take place in the future, the purpose of the *futures exchange* is to minimize the risk of default by either party. Thus, the exchange requires both parties to put up an initial amount of cash, the margin. Additionally, since the futures price will generally change daily, the difference in the prior agreed-upon price and the daily futures price is settled daily also.

The *futures exchange* will draw money out of one party's margin account and put it into the other's so that each party has the appropriate daily loss or profit. If the margin account goes below a certain value, then a *margin call* is made, and the account owner must replenish the account.

This process is known as *marking to market*. On the delivery date, the amount exchanged is not the specified price on the contract but the *spot value*. This is because any gain or loss has already been previously settled by marking to market.

Unlike an option, both parties in a futures contract must fulfill the contract on the delivery date. The seller delivers the underlying asset to the buyer, or if it is a cash-settled futures contract, then cash is transferred from the futures trader who sustained a loss to the one who made a profit.

In cases where there are tangible assets to be *delivered,* it is important not to let the contract expire and then be required to take delivery on the contract. Imagine taking delivery of cattle, grain, or sugar (as a friend of mine had to take delivery of sugar many years ago, true story!) Futures commodities are much different than trading futures with financial instruments, remember that.

To exit the commitment prior to the settlement date, the holder of a futures position can close out the contract obligations by taking the opposite position on another futures contract on the same asset and settlement date. The difference in futures prices is then a profit or a loss.

You decide which markets are best for you. The e-mini and micro markets are electronic, with fast fills, and excellent liquidity, which is great for day trading. Also, with these markets you can buy more contracts than the regular contract of that market, which can be advantageous, especially when applying "scaling-out" techniques that require multiple contracts. In addition, they can be traded with smaller trading accounts while still operating within proper money management risk controls and trade size.

## 🛒 ETF Market

Exchange traded funds, *ETFs*, are investment funds traded on stock exchanges, much like stocks. They were introduced in 1993 and have gained popularity with traders and investors ever since.

### What an ETF symbol looks like:

- SQQQ—they look very much like stock symbols.

Competing with traditional mutual funds, ETFs hold assets such as stocks, commodities, or bonds. In contrast to an ETF, a mutual fund doesn't settle the net asset value, *NAV*, until it is calculated at the end of each trading day, which means an investor requesting a mutual fund redemption during the trading day can't be sure of what the redemption price will be. ETFs on the other hand trade continuously throughout exchange hours, so the investor or trader benefits from greater flexibility.

Plus, unlike mutual funds, ETFs can be purchased on margin and sold short and may serve as underlying securities for option contracts. And passively managed ETFs tend to have significantly lower expense ratios than actively managed mutual funds. Costs such as management fees, fund account and trading expenses, and load fees related to their sale and distribution drive up a mutual funds expense ratio.

Most ETFs track an index, such as the S&P 500, and are attractive as investments because of their low costs, tax efficiency, and stock-like features. Plus, another key advantage is that they often hold a basket of stocks or other securities, increasing diversification.

The most popular ETFs trade with more liquidity than most stocks, which means buyers and sellers are plentiful, narrowing the bid-ask spreads. Generally, the ETFs with the highest average volume are used widely as trading vehicles among active traders, offering greater liquidity.

ETFs can be a great investment for long-term investors as well as those with shorter time horizons. They can be especially valuable to beginning investors because the time, effort, and experience to research individual stocks isn't required. The cost to own an ETF may also be lower than the cost to buy a diversified selection of individual stocks.

### Diamonds

In *Gentlemen Prefer Blondes* (1953), Marilyn Monroe sang, "Diamonds are a girl's best friend!" We can say we love the diamonds in the ETF market as well. The symbol for the DJIA in the ETF market is DIA and is traded on the NYSE.

### Spiders

You may not be a fan of the creepy crawly kind of spiders, but traders and investors like the SPDR, which is an acronym for Standard & Poor's Depository Receipts, the former name of the ETF now known as SPDR S&P 500 ETF Trust. The ticker symbol is SPY and has excellent liquidity and is also quite popular.

### Inverse ETFs

An inverse ETF bets against the expected daily performance of an asset or market index. During periods of volatility, day traders may use these *short* or *bear* ETFs to reduce their exposure to, or potentially even profit from, downward market moves. See Figure 17.6.

### Dog

The ETF symbol DOG stands for ProShares Short Dow 30 and is an inverse ETF. Figure 17.6 is a daily chart of the DOG versus the DJIA. It helps to visualize how all inverse instruments are a mirror reflection of the instruments they are betting against.

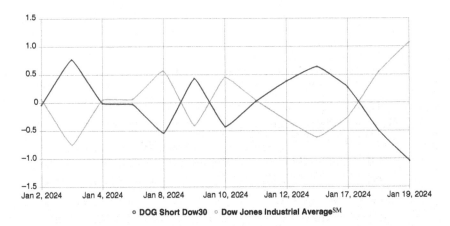

**Figure 17.6**   This chart shows how an inverse ETF mirrors the market it is betting against. This daily chart of the DJIA versus the DOG is literally a perfect mirror reflection. Inverses enable investors and traders to profit from a declining market and can hedge against an expected decline.

SOURCE: https://www.proshares.com/our-etfs/leveraged-and-inverse/dog

Keep in mind that inverse ETFs are risky and speculative investments that aim to achieve goals like short selling. As a result, the US SEC describes inverse ETFs as "specialized products with extra risks for buy-and-hold investors."

# Advantages and Disadvantages to Consider With ETFs

ETFs are investment funds traded on stock exchanges much like stocks. They are an excellent market to trade and invest in, and following are some of the pros and cons to consider.

### Advantages

1. **More diversification**—One ETF can give an investor the ability to own many stocks from a particular industry, investment category, country, or broad market. An ETF

*(continued on next page ...)*

*(... continued from previous page)*

can also provide exposure to asset classes other than equities, including bonds, currencies, and commodities. Diversification reduces your risk, and an ETF helps you do that with less expense and effort than buying individual stocks.

2. **Trades like a stock**—An investor or trader has more flexibility with an ETF than with a traditional mutual fund. Since ETFs are continuously traded throughout exchange hours, they can buy and sell at any time and know what the current price is. With a mutual fund, an investor requesting a redemption during the trading day will not know what the redemption price will be until the fund's net asset value is calculated at the end of the day.

3. **Lower fees**—ETFs are passively managed and tend to have a significantly lower expense ratio than an actively managed mutual fund.

4. **Limited capital gains tax**—ETFs can be more tax-efficient than mutual funds. Consult your tax advisor for details on how this can work to your advantage.

5. **More liquidity**—The ETFs that have the highest daily volumes offer excellent liquidity.

6. **Good for beginners**—You can benefit from not having to research many individual stocks, which is time consuming. You also benefit from the built-in diversification that many ETFs offer, which reduces risk. The cost to own an ETF may be lower than the cost to buy a diversified selection of individual stocks.

### Disadvantages

1. **Less diversification**—For some sectors or foreign stocks, ETF investors might be limited to large-cap stocks due to a narrow group of equities in a market index. A lack of exposure to mid-cap and small-cap companies

*(continued on next page...)*

> *(... continued from previous page)*
>
> could leave potential growth opportunities out of the reach of certain ETF traders and investors.
>
> **2. Higher costs**—Most people compare trading ETFs with trading other funds, which would have higher costs. But when comparing trading ETFs versus trading a specific stock, the ETF costs are higher. The actual commission paid to the broker might be the same, but there is no management fee for a stock as there is with an ETF.
>
> As with all markets you will need to determine if the ETF market is a good fit for your goals and be sure to consider the pros and cons and how they will affect your bottom line.

## 🛒 Forex Market

The modern foreign exchange market began forming during the 1970s, following three decades of government restrictions. Countries gradually switched to floating exchange rates from the previous exchange rate regime, which remained fixed per the Bretton Woods system. It wasn't until the late 1990s when the *little guy* could get into this game; prior to that you needed 10 million USD to even get a seat at the table.

Since the forex market took off for the retail trader, it has now become the largest and most liquid financial market in the world with a daily volume of 7.5 trillion in USD, representing the largest asset class in the world. This daily volume figure is according to the BIS (Bank of International Settlements) Triennial Central Bank survey of FX and OTC derivatives markets. The forex market daily volume is amazingly even larger than the worldwide stock market.

This bustling market trades 24 hours per day, except weekends, and is virtually the market that never sleeps. There are four major live trading sessions per day: the Sydney session, the Tokyo session, the London session, and the New York session. See Table 17.12. Basically, when one currency market is closing, another one is opening. So, even if you are not an night owl, there is just about always a live market open for you to trade, except maybe on the weekends.

But just because you can trade the market any time of the day or night doesn't necessarily mean that you should. The best time to trade is when the market is active with lots of forex traders opening and closing positions, creating a large volume of trades and liquidity.

You can make money trading when the market moves up, and you can make money when the market moves down. But you will have a difficult time trying to make money when the market doesn't move at all.

For the market to move, lots of trades need to occur. And this is why you should focus your energy during specific trading sessions. The four trading sessions are named after major financial centers and are based on the local *workday* of traders working in those cities.

Of course, the more traders that are trading, the higher the trading volume and the more activity and liquidity. The more active a market, the tighter the spreads you'll get and the less slippage you'll experience. In a nutshell, you'll get better order execution.

One of the best times to trade forex is when two sessions are overlapping because when two major financial centers are open

Table 17.12   Forex four global market sessions open and close times.

| Forex Market Session Location | Local Time Open | Local Time Close | EST Open | EST Close |
|---|---|---|---|---|
| 1 Sydney, Australia | 7:00 a.m. | 4:00 p.m. | 4:00 p.m. | 1:00 a.m. |
| 2 Tokyo, Japan | 9:00 a.m. | 6:00 p.m. | 7:00 p.m. | 4:00 a.m. |
| 3 London, England | 8:00 a.m. | 5:00 p.m. | 2:00 a.m. | 11:00 a.m. |
| 4 New York, United States | 8:00 a.m. | 5:00 p.m. | 8:00 a.m. | 5:00 p.m. |

NOTE: This table is intended for educational purposes only. Information is subject to change. Readers are advised to consult with their broker or data provider for current information.

at the same time; the number of traders actively buying and selling a given currency greatly increases. The highest trading volume occurs during the overlap of the London and the New York trading sessions. More than 50% of trading volume occurs at these two financial centers.

Another factor to consider when choosing a time to trade forex will depend on which currency pair you're looking at. Most of the trading activity for a specific currency pair will occur when the trading sessions of the individual currencies overlap.

For example, AUD/JPY will experience a higher trading volume when both Sydney and Tokyo sessions are open. And EUR/USD will experience a higher trading volume when both London and the New York sessions are open.

See Table 17.13 for the major currencies that are traded. You will see that each currency is identified by its ISO code, which is designated by the International Standardization Organization (ISO). For example, the US dollar has an ISO code of USD.

Trading in the euro has grown considerably since the currency's creation in January 1999, and as of today, the EUR/USD is the most

Table 17.13  Top 10 popular forex currencies.

|  | ISO Code | Country | Currency Name | Nickname for Currency |
|---|---|---|---|---|
| 1 | USD | United States | US dollar | Buck, Greenback |
| 2 | EUR | Eurozone | Euro | Fiber |
| 3 | CAD | Canada | Canadian dollar | Loonie |
| 4 | JPY | Japan | Japanese yen | Yen |
| 5 | GBP | United Kingdom | British pound | Cable, Sterling |
| 6 | CHF | Switzerland | Swiss franc | Swissy |
| 7 | AUD | Australia | Australian dollar | Matie, Aussie |
| 8 | NZD | New Zealand | New Zealand dollar | Kiwi |
| 9 | SGD | Singapore | Singapore dollar | Sing |
| 10 | HKD | Hong Kong | Hong Kong dollar | Honkie |

NOTE: Those instruments that are popular today may not be popular tomorrow. This table is intended for educational purposes only. Information is subject to change. Readers are advised to consult with their broker or data provider for current information.

Table 17.14   Top 10 popular forex currency pairs

| | ISO Codes | Base Currency = 1 Unit | Quote or Counter Currency | Nickname for Pair |
|---|---|---|---|---|
| 1 | EUR/USD | Euro | US dollar | Fiber |
| 2 | USD/JPY | US dollar | Japanese yen | Gopher |
| 3 | GBP/USD | British pound | US dollar | Cable |
| 4 | AUD/USD | Australian dollar | US dollar | Aussie |
| 5 | USD/CAD | US dollar | Canadian dollar | Loonie |
| 6 | USD/CHF | US dollar | Swiss franc | Swissie |
| 7 | EUR/GBP | Euro | British pound | Chunnel |
| 8 | USD/RUB | US dollar | Russian ruble | Barnie |
| 9 | GBP/JPY | British pound | Japanese yen | Guppy |
| 10 | NZD/USD | New Zealand dollar | US dollar | Kiwi |

NOTE: Those instruments that are popular today may not be popular tomorrow. This table is intended for educational purposes only. Information is subject to change. Readers are advised to consult with their broker or data provider for current information.

often traded pair. The Bank for International Settlements (BIS) found that the US dollar was on one side of 88% of all reported forex transactions. The question of how long the foreign exchange market will remain dollar centered is open to debate.

### Trading Currency Pairs

The *major* currency pairs all involve the US dollar on one side of the pair such as EUR/USD or USD/JPY. See Table 17.14 for a list of some popular currency pairs. When USD is not on either side of the pair, such as EUR/GBP, it is called a *cross currency* pair.

When trading in currency pairs, currencies are always quoted in relation to another currency. The value of one currency is reflected through the value of the other. For example, if you want to know the exchange rate between the British pound and the US dollar, the quote could be as follows:

- GBP/USD = 1.27

In this example, the currency on the left, GBP, is the *base currency*, and the currency on the right, USD, is the *quote* or *counter currency*. The value of the base currency is always one unit, and the quoted currency is what one unit equals in the other currency. In this example,

- 1 GBP = $1.27 US dollars

The base currency is what you are buying or selling when you buy or sell the pair. The base currency is also the *face amount* of the trade. Continuing with this example following are the outcomes of either buying or selling GBP/USD:

- **Buy GBP/USD** means you bought 10,000 British pounds and sold the equivalent in US dollars, which would be $12,700.
- **Sell GBP/USD** means you sold 10,000 British pounds and bought the equivalent in US dollars, which would be $12,700.

Your profits and losses will be denominated in the base currency, which in this case is the British pound. The mechanics of making money in forex are like the stock market, so if you have experience there, you should pick this up quickly.

The object of forex trading is to exchange one currency for another in the expectation that the price will change, so that the currency you bought will be worth more compared to the one you sold.

Moving along with our example of GBP/USD, let's walk through a hypothetical scenario; see Table 17.15. In this example, the exchange rate between the British pound and the US dollar is 1.27. That means when you bought 10,000 British pounds, they were worth 12,700 USD. When you sold back and exchanged your 10,000 British pounds, their value increased to 13,700 USD. The result is you made a profit of 1,000 USD.

In this example in Table 17.15, the exchange rate between the British pound and the US dollar is 1.27. That means when you bought 10,000 British pounds, they were worth 12,700 USD. When you sold back, and exchanged your 10,000 British pounds, their value increased to 13,700 US dollars, and you made a profit of 1,000 USD.

**Table 17.15**  Example of GBP/USD trade and how to make money in the forex market.

| Your Activity | GBP | USD |
|---|---|---|
| Purchase 10,000 British pounds at the exchange rate of 1.27. | + 10,000 | –12,700 |
| One week later, exchange your 10,000 British pounds back into US dollars at the exchange rate of 1.37. | –10,000 | +13,700 |
| **You earn a profit of 1,000 USD** | **0** | **+1,000** |

NOTE: This table is intended for educational purposes only. Information is subject to change. Readers are advised to consult with their broker or data provider for current information.

**Table 17.16**  Counting PIPs (with classic non-JPY quotes using four digits) in all currency pairs except the JPY.

| Currency Pair | Starting Quote | Ending Quote | PIP Gain/Loss |
|---|---|---|---|
| GBP/USD | 1.2721 | 1.3721 | +1,000 pips |
| GBP/USD | 1.2721 | 1.1721 | –1,000 pips |

NOTE: This table is intended for educational purposes only. Information is subject to change. Readers are advised to consult with their broker or data provider for current information.

### Understanding Quotes and PIPs

A pip, or *percentage in point,* is the smallest unit of movement in the forex. The classic currency pair quotes have four-digits, decimal places, to the right of the decimal point. But now some forex brokers offer quotes with five-digits after the decimal point, which are called *fractional pips* or *pipettes.* They are smaller than classic pips and are a more precise measurement. For clarity, in the following examples we will be using classic quotes and pips. See Table 17.16.

It's important to also note a difference with any currency pair that includes JPY. They will not have the four-digit decimal places to the right of the decimal point. Instead with JPY pairs, there will be only two-digits to the right of the decimal. (In the case of fractional pips, there will be three-digits to the right of the decimal point for JPY pairs.) See Table 17.17.

Another benefit to the forex market is the exceptional leverage available. For example, a trader with $1,000 in an account

**Table 17.17** Counting PIPs (with classic JPY quotes using two digits) with currency pairs that include the JPY.

| Currency Pair | Starting Quote | Ending Quote | PIP Gain/Loss |
|---|---|---|---|
| USD/JPY | 148.38 | 148.58 | + 20 pips |
| USD/JPY | 148.38 | 148.18 | −20 pips |

NOTE: This table is intended for educational purposes only. Information is subject to change. Readers are advised to consult with their broker or data provider for current information.

can control a position of $100,000, which is referred to as having 100:1 leverage. Use caution when implementing leverage and apply risk control to manage your trade size.

As with all markets, the forex market involves risk but also has many benefits, not the least of which is the ability to trade with a small account. Decide which market suits your current ART profile, and maybe the forex market will check off all the boxes.

## The Beauty of the Financial Markets

When you truly understand the financial markets, you can marvel at their beauty. You won't feel they have wronged you or that they are intimidating because you will have a respect for their power and their importance. And you will know how to strategically protect your downside.

It is when traders and investors enter the market with little or no preparation that they can be overpowered by the markets. Risk control and money management are key. So, I invite you to get to know and understand the markets and enjoy their beauty. This will help in your pursuit of trading and investing success.

# Chapter 18

# Customize Your Rules to You

The financial markets have an uncanny knack of ferreting out our weaknesses. In addition, the markets help us to see ourselves with more clarity the longer we are in the ring with them. Every time we falter with operator error or even with a single losing trade, the markets will hold up a mirror to show us who we really are in that exact moment. See Figure 18.1.

It's a mirror that reflects a variety of emotions and reactions to every move the market makes. You may see confidence, pride, regret, happiness, anger, fear, greed, embarrassment, shock, surprise, satisfaction, frustration, disbelief, joy, relief . . . the list goes on. These reflections can enlighten you if look at them with an open mind. Lessons can be learned from the simple cause and effect of market behavior versus your reaction to it.

Ultimately, when looking at your true reflections in that mirror, you will grow and strengthen your psychology to become a better trader and investor and a more insightful person. You will know and understand yourself on a deeper level than you could have ever expected. And you will solve problems as they arise with your trader's mindset.

**Figure 18.1** The financial markets will hold up a mirror to show us who we really are. The reflection we see in that mirror can help us become better at our job if we are willing to look at it with an open mind.
SOURCE: 15697881 Mirror © Fotopitu Dreamstime.com

Which is why, if your system rules are not customized to you and your current unique set of strengths and weaknesses and beliefs, at best you will not reach your full potential. At worst, you will fail miserably.

## ◎ Make Them Your Own

The best way to design rules that you will succeed with is to make them your own. Look in the mirror and figure out who and where you are now. Incorporate those personal characteristics and ingredients into your rules. Then test those rules to prove to yourself firsthand that they give you a proven edge in the markets.

> *One of the things that we repeatedly told the class was: "We are going to teach you what we think works, but you are expected to add your own personal flair, feeling, or judgment."*
> —Richard Dennis, Original Market Wizard and
> co-creator of the Turtle Trading Experiment

So often beginners believe they can take rules off the shelf and be instantly and effortlessly successful. Generally, they will find rules that might have worked well for someone else aren't working for them. Then they ask, "Why?" It's common that this occurs because each of us is different and we need to incorporate a part of ourselves into our rules to succeed.

**To summarize, here's what is needed to be consistently successful with your trading and investing rules:**

- Select rules that are customized to you.
- Write down your rules.
- Prove you have an edge by testing your rules.
- Test a large enough sample size to prove your edge.
- Have genuine confidence in your rules and yourself.
- Follow your proven rules.

As you design your set of rules, and are inspired by other successful traders and investors, as Richard Dennis says, "*. . .add your own personal flair, feeling, or judgment.*" Then and only then can you make these rules your own, which will lead to greater confidence and discipline.

And whether you trade strategies or indicators you have on your charting platform, work to use them in accordance with your personality. This will create your own unique trading edge.

**Note to** TradersCoach.com **Software Users:** For example, along with the TradersCoach.com software, we give you a set of rules and guidelines that include entries, exits, and risk control. Use these structured rules as a starting point. They can be modified in a way so that you are the co-author of your own system, and it is customized to you. Then test your rules to ensure that you have an edge. Keep working on this until you have created your own successful approach.

## Fill Out Your Personal Art Profile

In the quest to customize your rules to you, first it is important to examine who you are right now. Keep in mind that you will be identifying your "current" ART profile as it exists today. This profile may change over time as your experience level, trading style, trading frequency, and preferences change.

One of the key strengths of the ART approach is that you can tailor it to your unique strengths, weaknesses, and preferences, enabling you to become a powerful force in the markets. Creating this profile now helps you to visualize where you are in the journey.

*Fill Out Figure 18.2 With Your ART Profile Personal Information*

The ART profile takes the shape of a triangle and enables you to identify what experience level, style, and trading or investing frequency you fall into. This helps you develop rules based on your current profile.

- **Experience level:** master, intermediate, or novice
- **Trading style:** trend, scalp, or countertrend
- **Trading frequency:** day trader, position trader, or investor
- **Markets:** stocks, options, futures, forex, or other

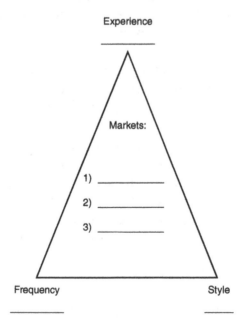

**Figure 18.2**   ART Profile Blank—Fill in the blanks of this template with your current information. It can be adapted as you grow and develop your skills, experience, and preferences in the markets.

As you advance, you may utilize all the "trading styles" and implement multiple "trading frequencies" depending on market conditions. In essence, you will have more than one set of trading rules in your toolbox. For now, focus on creating one set of winning trading rules and then build on that going forward.

**Let us walk before we run.**

# Your Experience Level

Select an experience level that describes your *current* level of experience for your personal ART profile. To select the most accurate level of your current experience, review my descriptions and choose the one that feels right.

## *Master Level of Experience*

Masters are at an expert level of knowledge and skill. Risk control, stop-loss exits, and risk-to-reward minimums are always being used and adhered to.

They understand their own beliefs and know what strengths and weaknesses they have. Trading in accordance with their beliefs, personality, and temperament, they have an intuitive feel for the markets based on experience and operate in a controlled, calm, but fluid way, and in the "zone."

Having the ability to assess the markets quickly, they know when to move on to a higher probability trade. Knowing that there is unlimited opportunity, they are not inclined to force trades when there are none. When there is a messy unclear market, it's easy for them to move on to ones with more clarity.

They understand and accept risk and always operates with risk in mind but are never paralyzed by it. They are not controlled by emotions such as fear and greed. They trade in total awareness and may at times seem to have a carefree attitude. They consistently weigh the risk-to-reward equation.

Moving from one market to another, they can be profitable in a variety of market cycles and can quickly determine which time frames and markets are best to maintain profitability. In other words, they can go from one winning cycle to another with minimal drawdown and can move at lightning speed if needed.

Masters listen to and understand what the market is saying, always thinking of the market as a friend and enjoying the challenge and the process. Consistently profitable, they are not affected by losing trades and account drawdown. It is how these setbacks are managed that sets masters apart from the rest. Risk control is central to their consistent success. Masters represent the top 5% of all traders worldwide.

Individuals at this level have the skill and experience to earn significant net revenue on a consistent basis. This is the level that most "get rich quick" advertisements claim you can achieve instantly with little or no capital.

### Intermediate Level of Experience

Intermediate traders or investors are moderately profitable on a consistent basis, but emotions still get the best of them. Risk control, stop-loss exits, and risk-to-reward minimums are always being used and adhered to.

They have developed enough skill to know what to do to be consistently profitable. They are not nearly as profitable as masters but consistent enough to acknowledge that success is possible and realize how important psychology is.

Personal development is still needed. This is what keeps intermediate traders or investors from being masters. The whole body is not yet integrated with the market and the process. They occasionally have days where they feel and perform like masters, but not consistently.

They have varying forms of anxiety that cause problems. Besides not being as profitable, the difference between the intermediate and the master is abstract. The difference is intangible or nonlinear; it has to do with the "art" of trading. The trader's mind-set is not as developed as the master's.

*Novice Level of Experience*

This category encompasses everyone else who is not making money on a consistent basis for whatever reason—from beginners to those who *know it all* but still can't make consistent money in the markets. To get out of this category requires work on skills, market knowledge, emotional exploration, and practice.

It is important to paper-trade until consistently profitable. Experience a variety of market conditions to experience the feeling of losses and drawdown and see how it affects your psychology. If you can't paper-trade profitably, chances are you can't trade with real money profitably and simply are not ready to trade live.

When your paper-trading is consistently profitable, then trade with real money. Novice traders and investors will remain stuck at this level if they take the *easy* route of rushing into the markets with real money before they are ready.

Diminishing the importance of paper-trading indicates impatience, compulsive behavior, gambling personality, a *get rich quick* mentality, and lack of discipline—all of which will keep one stuck at the novice level. Novices will be unprofitable on a consistent basis until they either acknowledge it is time to change or give up and say that this is not for them.

The novice level has the greatest struggle with emotions. Impatience, anxiety, impulsiveness, fear, and greed cause the most trouble at this level because it is all so new. Don't forget that every master started at this novice level. The length of time you spend here depends on your ability to focus and on how well you work on your emotional stability and development.

## Your Trading or Investing Style

Select a trading or investing style that describes your *current* style for your personal ART profile. To select the most accurate level of your current style, review my descriptions and choose the one that feels right.

## Trend Style

The trend trader or investor likes to trade in the direction of the overall trend regardless of the time frame. A trend is defined as higher highs and higher lows in an uptrend. Or it is defined as lower highs and lower lows in a downtrend. It's important to resist chasing extended markets and mature trends. Instead of chasing markets, focus on how to find and get into trends early.

Stops must be carefully positioned to stay with the trend even during corrections within the trend. Trailing stops are used to lock in profit as the trend moves favorably in the desired direction. They use trend lines and advanced techniques such as the Elliott Wave and classic technical analysis to enhance results with this style.

A day trader could be classified in this category when trend-trading intraday time frames. Trend traders usually are not averse to authority figures, and they feel comfortable *belonging* versus being a *loner*. These tendencies allow for a comfortable fit of going with the crowd of traders in a trend.

Drawdowns with trend strategies are deeper than with counter-trend or scalping strategies. Managing the psychology around drawdowns is important for trading this style successfully.

## Scalp Style

There are many definitions of scalping the markets. Some people believe that any form of day trading at all is considered scalping. This is not always true because scalping has nothing to do with the time frame. It has everything to do with the style of trading.

Scalping is where you take quick profits that occur in between pivot points in channeling markets and during trending markets that are experiencing a correction, regardless of what time frame the chart is.

There are differences between the styles of countertrend and scalping. When you are a scalper, yes, you can scalp corrections in a trend, but you can also scalp in a bracketed market where no trend is in place. This is opposed to a countertrend trader who always enters on the correction of a trend and trades in a trending environment.

Scalpers are high frequency traders. They use the stop-and-reverse technique and may either be long or short almost all the time while using this method. Scalpers like quick action and need to be careful not to overtrade. They should also be careful with trading due to anxiety issues, which also may cause them to overtrade.

Drawdowns with scalping strategies are shallower than with trend trading strategies, which is easier on one's psychology. Due to the fast-moving pace, though, it will require more time in front of your computer screen to monitor trades.

### Countertrend Style

If you are a countertrend trader, you are looking for markets where there is a correction in the overall trend. The concept behind countertrend trading is to find trending markets that either are overextending and ready to correct or are in the beginning of a correction.

Countertrend traders make a profit by taking trades against the overall trend. This is risky because you are going against the flow of the trending market, and while many traders can do well with this technique, you will need to develop your skills. Once corrections end, prices can quickly rebound back in the direction of the trend. You will need to stay alert when countertrend trading.

The countertrend trader isn't afraid to move independently and think differently. They usually do not flow with the crowd and therefore tend to feel uncomfortable going with the herd of traders in a trend.

Drawdowns with countertrend strategies are shallower than with trend trading strategies, which is easier on one's psychology. Due to the fast-moving pace, though, it will require more time in front of your computer screen to monitor your trades.

# Your Trading Frequency (and Time Frame)

Select a trading or investing frequency that describes where you are now for your personal ART profile. In technical analysis terms, the current time frame on your charts will indicate how frequently you place trades. To select the most accurate trading frequency, review my descriptions and choose the one that feels right.

When we talk about time frames, we are discussing the interval of time it takes for one price bar to open and to close on a chart. For example, on a 1-minute chart, there is one price bar generated on your chart every single minute. And on a daily chart, it takes a full day for a single price bar to be generated.

Basically, the lower the time frame, such as a 1-minute chart for a day trader, the more active you will be, and the more frequently you will be placing trades. At the other end of the spectrum, the higher the time frame, such as monthly charts for an investor, the less active you will be and the less frequently you will be placing trades.

## Day Trader Frequency

The classic day trader opens and closes all his trades when the market is open and does not hold positions overnight. Day traders usually base their decisions on 15-second, 1-minute, or 5-minute charts.

### Rule of Thumb: Only Master Traders Should Day Trade

- When day trading, trading time is compressed. Losses and wins come at you faster and more often, which requires a mature, developed trading psychology. Novice traders are usually not seasoned enough to weather the waves of wins and losses.
- You must have the psychology to resist being seduced by the open market—it is important to remain emotionless and objective. This is more difficult when day trading than position trading or investing.
- Your day-trading results can be highly impacted by others trading on higher time frames; the lower your time frame, the greater the effect this will have on you.

- **Exception to the rule:** When paper trading or sim trading any set of rules using technical analysis, day-trading time frames can be used to more quickly learn the art of trading. This will shorten your learning curve for sure. The fractal nature of the markets allows you to learn basics at a lower time frame, and these skills can be applied to all time frames.

**My Favorite Day Trading Markets**

- MCL—Crude Oil Micro
- QM—Crude Oil E-Mini
- CL—Crude Oil
- QI—Silver E-mini
- SI—Silver
- MES—S&P 500 Micro
- ES—S&P 500 E-Mini
- MNQ—NASDAQ 100 Micro
- NQ—NASDAQ 100 E-mini
- M2K—Russell 2000 Micro
- RTY—Russell 2000 E-mini
- MYM—DJIA Micro
- YM—DJIA E-Mini

These day-trading markets are liquid, competitive, fun, and fast and exhibit good intraday trends. In the end, day trading requires more commitment, focus, and discipline than any other trading frequency or time frame. Be prepared to dedicate yourself 100% before choosing this path.

*Position Trader Frequency*

Unlike day traders, position traders will hold positions overnight for a few days, a few weeks, or even a few months if the trend can be maintained. They base their trading decisions on 60-minute, daily, and weekly charts.

Position trading has many advantages, and some believe that it offers the greatest opportunity for net profit out of all the trading frequencies. You'll make fewer trades than a day trader, so there are less expenses from broker commissions. Compared to investing, your capital doesn't get tied up in positions for too long, offering greater liquidity.

See Table 18.1 for the pros and cons of day trading versus position trading. Both have benefits and drawbacks.

**Table 18.1**   Pros and cons of being a day trader and being a position trader.

| Day Traders | | Position Traders | |
|---|---|---|---|
| Day traders close all positions out to cash at night and use intraday time frame charts like the 15-second, 1-minute, and 5-minute charts. Trades can last from minutes to hours. They are not exposed to overnight risk in the markets. | | Position traders hold positions overnight and use end-of-day time frame charts like the daily, weekly, and monthly charts. Trades can last a day, a week, or months at a time. They are exposed to overnight risk in the markets. | |
| **Pros** | **Cons** | **Pros** | **Cons** |
| Have no exposure to overnight risk because all trades are closed out each night. | Cannot capitalize on overnight risk opportunities; all trades are closed out each night. | Can capitalize on overnight risk opportunities. | Have exposure to overnight risk because trades can be held for weeks or months at a time. |
| Can have a smaller trading account size. The risk distance between entry and stop-loss exit is smaller. This is because there is no overnight risk. | They have higher expenses in brokerage commissions because day traders place more trades than position traders do. | Have lower expenses in brokerage commissions because position traders place fewer trades than day traders do. | Requires a larger trading account size. The risk distance between entry and stop-loss exit is larger. This is to accommodate overnight risk. |
| | | *(continued on next page...)* | |

| Day Traders | | Position Traders | |
|---|---|---|---|
| Pros | Cons | Pros | Cons |
| Places more trades than position traders, they gain more experience in a shorter time period. Gets quicker feedback, which helps to analyze system rules. | Day trading requires more skill and experience to be profitable due to the advanced psychology required to manage fast-paced wins and losses. | Position trading is often considered the best time frame for new and novice traders because there is more time to psychologically process wins and losses. | Places fewer trades than day traders, it takes a longer amount of time to gain experience. Gets slower feedback, which means system rule analysis takes longer. |
| Has greater liquidity by closing out to cash every night. | Fatigue occurs from intensely watching the markets all day. | Less fatigue since markets do not have to be watched all day. | Has less liquidity by holding trades overnight and for long periods. |

*(... continued from previous page)*

This table is intended for educational purposes only. Information is subject to change. Readers are advised to consult with their broker or data provider for current information.

## Investor Frequency

Investors hold trades overnight but for longer periods than position traders. Trading decisions are based on weekly, monthly, and yearly charts. Investors are traders when they attempt to time their long-term investments to make greater profit than they would when using a passive *buy and hold* approach. They typically study fundamentals.

They deal with losses but are less comfortable with active trading, where losses can come quickly during drawdown. Day traders and position traders become investors when they neglect to honor their stop-loss exits. In these situations, they may hold onto a position much longer than originally intended.

# Holding Trades Overnight and Assuming Overnight Risk

When holding trades overnight, you are inherently exposed to greater risk. Day traders will close out to cash every night for this very reason. Investors and position traders on the other hand will hold positions overnight knowing that the risk is already built into their risk control plan.

In some cases, though, you may be trading over a shorter time frame and may discover an opportunity to hold a position overnight that offers great profit potential.

For example, if you were trading a 5-minute time frame, your stop loss and position size will be based on the 5-minute chart. But let's say you are 5 minutes from the close of the day and the trade is profitable, and much more profit is possible if you hold the trade overnight based on the longer time frame chart like a 30-minute chart for example.

The key in holding a day trade overnight is you must use a stop based on a high enough time frame to avoid short-term volatility of the lower time frames. Don't set a tight stop that is more likely to get hit due to volatility.

**Five rules of engagement for an overnight trade:**

1. The trade must currently be profitable.
2. The 30-minute chart must indicate a solid trend in place.
3. You must set a new stop loss based on the 30-minute chart.
4. Reduce trade size so that risk remains no more than 2% of your trading account, based on the new adjusted stop based on the higher time frame chart.
5. Monitor the trade at the opening bell the next morning.

*(continued on next page...)*

*(...continued from previous page)*

The key is to be sure to adjust all your money management parameters to allow for the added risk of holding a trade overnight. And then you need to be ready to monitor the trade immediately at the opening bell.

Be prepared for any gap opens where the opening price jumps substantially higher or lower than the previous day's closing price. Gap opens can occur because of some extraordinarily positive or negative news that occurred overnight when the market was closed. If there is a gap open that goes against your position and your stop-loss exit, move quickly to exit.

## Here's the Trick. . .

You won't be able to follow your rules if you don't believe in them, and the best way to believe in your rules is to ". . . develop a system with which you are compatible." Use this chapter to do just that. See Figure 18.3.

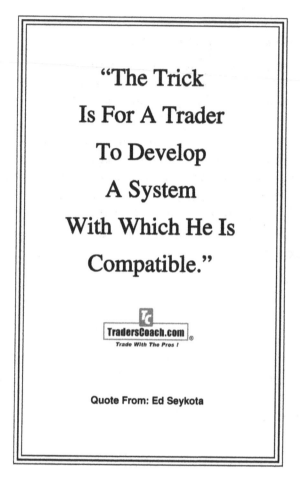

**Figure 18.3** MINI POSTER—THE TRICK—Customizing your system and your rules to you is the key to consistent success in the markets. You must be compatible with the system you develop. Quote from Ed Seykota.

# Chapter 19
# Your *10 Rules* Trading Template

In this chapter we'll focus on the nuts and bolts needed to build and design your personal trading rules. You've already learned that customizing your rules to you is important in creating a system that will win consistently over time. As you move forward with your rules, be sure to focus on tailoring them so that you are comfortable enough to actually follow them.

This chapter is not intended to hand you a set of *off the shelf* rules to follow. Instead, the goal is to give you direction in designing your own custom approach, using time proven principles that will steer you in the right direction.

You may find yourself investigating a variety of approaches that appeal to you. This may help in developing your custom rules. These rules may range from technical analysis to fundamental analysis to everything in between.

### 🎯 Warning Label!

Only testing your rules in real time will determine if they can be consistently viable in the markets. Testing is the best way to determine if the theory behind your rules will actually work for you.

That is the ultimate result, a winning system that has been proven through your own real-time testing.

In Chapter 20, we will outline a detailed testing program to ensure that you have a proven edge in the markets. This chapter is required reading if you want to be profitable.

---

# Use This *10 Rules* Trading Template When Designing Your System

Here is an outline of rules that every system must have to be successful. This template of *10 Rules* is a guide to follow when designing your system:

**Rule 1. Follow Your Rules**
**Rule 2. Decide Where You Are Right Now**
**Rule 3. Determine Daily Dollar Goal**
**Rule 4. Entry**
**Rule 5. Target Zone**
**Rule 6. Risk to Reward**
**Rule 7. Initial Stop-loss Exit**
**Rule 8. Trade Size**
**Rule 9. Trade Order Type**
**Rule 10. Trade Management**

In this chapter, we cover specifics on how to add more detail to each of the *10 Rules*, but remember that sometimes simplicity generates the best result. This is true especially when you are beginning with a new set of rules. Do your best to keep it simple.

---

## 🎯 Tips for Designing Your Rules and Strategies

Here's a heads up with a list of tips you need to know about when working on your rules. Later in this chapter I will give you more detail on these tips, but for now here's a start with what is important to know.

## ◎ Tips Covered in This Chapter

- **Grounded and Ungrounded Assessments:** There are two types of assessments, or signals, when designing your rules: grounded assessments and ungrounded assessments. They are different but are both useful when used correctly.

- **Technical Analysis Signals:** Everything you need to know about a market is represented by price and price patterns. Pure technical analysts do not use fundamentals at all and do not need them. Technical analysis is the use of charts that illustrate the price, volume, and momentum of the markets on a graph to determine entries and exits.

- **Fundamental Analysis Signals:** Fundamental analysis is the use of fundamental data to determine entries and exits into the financial markets. Examples include earnings, growth, etc.

- **News Analysis Signals:** News can be used to draw your attention to markets that are making moves in the financial markets, either up or down.

- **Hybrid Analysis:** Some traders blend a combination of technical, fundamental, and news signals to create their trading rules. They may combine two or more of these methods to create a hybrid approach.

- **Interpreting Signals:** Later in this chapter you will find examples of ways to interpret your signals from technicals, fundamentals, and news signals.

- **Bar Charts Versus Candle Charts:** When looking at technical analysis charts, you can choose from many types of charts. The most popular are *bar charts* and *candle charts*, each having their own unique advantages.

- **Markets Zig and Zag:** Markets rarely move in a hyperbolic straight line; we can profit from the zigs and zags if we know how to read them.

- **Market Cycles:** The four market cycles are trending, bracketed, breakout, and corrective. Incorrectly identifying a cycle can be costly, so mastering identification of cycles is crucial.

- **Trend Lines:** Trend lines are an excellent tool in trend identification and in market cycle identification.
- **Pitfalls of Not Identifying Market Cycles Correctly:** Not identifying a bracketed market means you may get whipsawed by repeatedly entering the market and getting stopped out. Misidentifying a reverse in trend means you might exit a perfectly good trend and miss out on significant profit potential.
- **Trend Exhaustion:** When a trend is extended it may be exhausted. Elliott Wave can help you identify the wave count so you can determine where you are in the trend. Identifying a Wave 3 is helpful in this. Look for trends that are nearing exhaustion so that you can avoid them. Don't chase markets.
- **Breakout Trend Trades Come After Bracketed Markets:** After at least 20 price bars in a bracketed market, a breakout either to the upside or to the downside is likely. This is a good scan for finding potential trade entries to get into the trend early. The more price bars in the bracket, or the longer the market is bracketed, the more significant the trend is likely to be.
- **Fractal Symmetry in Financial Markets:** The ability to apply an indicator over any time frame reflects the fractal quality of price. The fact is that without a label, a series of 15-minute price bars cannot be distinguished from a series of daily price bars. Intraday bars are a microcosm of daily bars, and daily bars are a microcosm of weekly or monthly bars. Traders respond to price changes in repetitive ways whatever the time frame.
- **Moving Averages:** A popular technical analysis tool that smooths out price data by creating a constantly updated average price. The average is taken over a specific period of time, like 20 minutes, 10 days, 30 weeks, or any period the trader chooses.
- **Chart Patterns:** Many chart patterns in technical analysis are useful in determining entries, exits, and risk control. These patterns can serve as signals for certain trading rules you may develop.
- **Chart History:** Sometimes a stock will have very little history because it is newly issued. The more history available the better.
- **Multiple Time Frame Analysis:** Looks at charts of the same financial instrument across multiple time frames to see if the time frames agree or disagree as to what the trend direction is.

- **Timing of the Trade:** Trading at different times of the day, when the markets are open, can yield a variety of results. The open of the market is usually volatile with gaps in price, while the close of the market can also be unpredictable. The middle of the day has less volume and liquidity. Plus, Federal Open Market Committee (FOMC) and earnings releases can drive the markets to be erratic. Timing is everything; test what works best for you.
- **Sector Analysis:** By finding the strongest and weakest companies in a particular sector, you can identify signals to enter and to exit.
- **Seasonality Analysis:** Using historical patterns that repeat themselves over and again from season to season, you can identify signals to enter and to exit.
- **Diversification:** The saying *don't put all your eggs in one basket* refers to the risk you take if that one basket is dropped and you lose all of your eggs. Better to have a few eggs in a few baskets, thus reducing the risk of losing your entire egg collection.

Now that you have a list of the tips in this chapter, you have a better idea of what tools you will be able to put into your toolbox when designing your personal set of trading rules. No doubt you can research further to find additional tips and tools that will help if you decide to do that. But sometimes keeping things simple can generate the best result.

## Traders Mindset Rules

It doesn't matter how good your rules are if you don't have the discipline to implement them. That's where so many fail because they lack a strong mindset. You will notice that on our *10 Rules* template the first three rules require that you have discipline and understand where you are right now.

**Rule 1. Follow Your Rules:** This is the hardest rule to follow until you have developed the trader's mindset and have confidence in your rules.

**Rule 2. Decide Where You Are Right Now:** Fill in the blanks in Figure 18.2, from Chapter 18, so that you know where and who you are right now as a trader.

**Rule 3. Determine Daily Dollar Goal:** To help with your mindset, it is important to determine what your daily dollar goal is. Start small, so that you attain little victories and build your confidence. See the Epilogue at the back of this book for more information on how to determine your daily dollar goal.

We've already talked a lot about the importance of one's mindset in trading, especially in Chapter 6. If after designing your rules and testing them, you find that they are not performing as well as you had hoped, go back and revisit Chapter 6 *before* changing your rules. Instead of changing any rules, work on your mindset, and then re-test your current rules again to see if there is an improvement.

**Win, lose, or draw, you're a winner when you follow your rules.**

In the beginning, regardless of whether you are up or down in your test account, you are winning if you follow your rules. Give your rules enough time during the test; that is the only way to truly know if they are good rules for you. Resist the urge to abandon or give up on them too quickly.

## Entry Rules

In my experience by far, entries seem to be everyone's favorite topic. And while they are important, they only work for you when supported by the rest of your rules. Focus on your entries, but don't get bogged down by thinking they are the magic bullet or holy grail. The true holy grail is using risk control on every trade.

**Rule 4. Entry:** Customize your entry strategy to work for you using the tips in this chapter.

When designing your entry rules, if you haven't done so already, go back to Chapter 18 and fill in the blanks for Figure 18.2, which is your *ART Profile*.

**Your ART profile will identify the following for you:**

- **Experience level:** master, intermediate, or novice
- **Trading style:** trend, scalp, or countertrend
- **Trading frequency:** day trader, position trader, or investor
- **Markets:** stocks, options, futures, forex, or other

By filling in the blanks, you are establishing the foundation upon which all of your rules will be built. For that reason, it is crucial to do this at the very beginning.

## Target Zone and Risk-to-Reward Rules

How far can you go? Once you have found a promising entry, it is crucial to estimate how far the trade has to go. What is the potential? If there is no room to ride the trade to a meaningful profit zone, there is no point in taking the trade at all.

**Rule 5. Target Zone Strategy:** Estimate what the profit target zone is for the trade. There are many ways to estimate the target zone for a trade including Fibonacci extensions, Fibonacci retracements, and Elliott Wave analysis.

**Rule 6. Risk to Reward:** Know what risk-reward amount makes it worth taking the trade. For example, my rules require that there is at least a 1 to 2 risk-to-reward potential. Meaning for every one dollar risked, there is a potential to make two dollars.

I determine my profit target zone two ways: Fibonacci's and Precision Trend Filter (PTF) software. At the back of this book, I go into more detail about how I use these techniques. Other strategies can also generate a price target estimate, such as support and resistance levels, price momentum, etc.

Regardless of what strategy you use to estimate the price target zone, do so prior to pulling the trigger. There is nothing worse than taking a trade that has nowhere to go profit-wise.

Once you have a price target zone estimate, determine what the risk-to-reward ratio is. If your risk is $10 (you would lose $10 if you got stopped out) but your reward is $30 (you would win $30 if you reach the target zone) that means your risk is one dollar for every three dollars you win. The risk to reward is 1 to 3 in this case.

This approach will help you to select only the highest probability and most potentially profitable trade opportunities.

## Risk Control Rules

When it comes to risk control, or money management, it cannot be mentioned enough that you must adopt an effective approach in order to avoid the risk of ruin. As you can see, three rules in your *10 Rules* trading template are completely dedicated to this topic.

**Rule 7. Initial Stop-loss Exit:** Protect your account by setting an initial stop loss exit before you enter each trade. This stop must be placed at a meaningful price level, that if breached, will prove your trade is no longer valid.

**Rule 8. Trade Size:** Carefully calculate the optimal trade size, or position size, to maximize your returns and control risk.

**Rule 9. Trade Order Type:** Choose your order type carefully to prevent paying too much for your trade and to control other risks as well.

Stop loss exits are the backbone of your trading rules, they are the mechanism that gets you out of a trade before you go bust. They are not as sexy as the entry, but any seasoned professional will tell you that without effective stops you are destined to crash and burn.

Refer to Chapter 14, Stop-loss Exit Strategies, for more detailed specifics on the types of stops you can use and also the types of risks that stops protect you from.

Calculating optimal trade or position size is often overlooked. When traders trade the same number of shares or contracts for every trade, regardless of how far away the entry is from the exit, they are disregarding the unique dynamics of each trade.

Refer to Chapter 12, Win Ratio and Payoff Ratio, which covers how to determine what your personal performance statistics are. This will help when calculating trade size. And then, in Chapter 13, Trade Size Matters, you will find formulas to calculate the optimal trade size for every trade.

Finally, your choice of order type is another way to limit risk. The order type is how you tell your broker what your order execution instructions are for the trade. Different order types limit a variety of risks, including the price of the fill and the time of the fill.

Refer to Chapter 17, Understanding Financial Markets, for more detailed information on what order types are available and what they do to limit your trade risk.

Again, keep your eye on the ball and constantly work at limiting and controlling your risk with your trades. That is the way to long-term profitability.

## Trade Management Rules

These guidelines are centered around how to manage the trade, which is really where the trade either makes it or doesn't.

### Rule 10. Trade Management

The entry and initial stop loss exit, Rule 4 and Rule 7 are not the only parameters that determine your long-term win and payoff ratios. That is because, with winning trades, the management can affect the outcome of your win and payoff ratios.

Of course, when a trade goes against you quickly and immediately and gets stopped out, there is no real management other than honoring your initial stop-loss exit. If your mindset messes with you, exiting the trade for a loss may be difficult to execute. In this case, Rule 10 is all about Rule 1, which is to follow your rules and honor your initial protective stop-loss exit.

At the other end of the spectrum, when a trade goes in your favor, you can implement strategies to further manage the trade. Again, this comes down to your confidence level and your strategy.

For example, using a trailing stop strategy, where you lock in profit as a profitable trade moves in your favor, is effective. Another trade management strategy is to scale out of a trade when it has a hyperbolic move in the direction of your price target. This locks in profit, and can reduce stress which helps with the trader's mindset.

## ◎ Grounded and Ungrounded Assessments

Every trading rule, indicator, and analysis strategy falls into one of two categories:

1. **Grounded Assessments:** trading and investing rules, techniques, and approaches that trade the markets as they unfold. For example, using trade entries and exits that are based purely on price and volume would be using grounded assessments.

2. **Ungrounded Assessments:** trading and investing rules, techniques, and approaches that trade the markets by trying to forecast the markets. For example, using MACD, stochastics, Elliott Wave, Fibonacci price targets, and anything that involves a forecast would be using ungrounded assessments. Ultimately current price must verify the ungrounded assessment, or the forecast must be changed.

This distinction is important because ungrounded assessments, though useful, are a forecast of what will happen. Until price and volume action occur to confirm the fantasy or forecast, they are just that, a forecast.

Price must always verify your forecast for it to remain valid. As the market unfolds, your forecast may become invalid. In this case you may need to adjust certain trade parameters, such as stop-loss exits and price target zones.

# 🎯 Technical Analysis Signals

My personal trading style is to find patterns that appear in technical analysis, and chart analysis, and at the end of the day I don't really care what the fundamentals or the news are saying.

This is because for me everything that I need to know is represented by the current price and volume and momentum in the markets. These realities, as I see them, cannot be manipulated or distorted.

**Technical Analysis Signals**
- Price, Volume, and Momentum
- RSI—Relative Strength Index
- ATR—Average True Range
- MA—Moving Average
- EMA—Exponential Moving Average
- OBV—On Balance Volume
- A/D—Accumulation/Distribution
- MACD—Moving Average Convergence/Divergence
- VWAP—Volume Weighted Average Price
- Elliott Wave—See Appendix A
- Fibonacci Retracements—See Appendix A
- Fibonacci Extensions—See Appendix A
- Trend Lines for Identifying Trends
- Channel Lines for Identifying Channels
- Bracketed Market Breakouts
- Volume Profile
- Order Flow
- Range Bar Charts

Technical analysts use charts and graphs to see what the price and volume and momentum activity is in a market. Histograms and software indicators can further illustrate additional information visually to the trader as well.

Price, volume, and momentum are always the truths in the market. Keep in mind that some popular technical indicators are lagging or forecasting indicators, also known as ungrounded assessments, and you must use them with caution.

By looking at historical price and volume patterns in the financial markets, we can determine the probabilities of future activity. Basically, this analysis uses the past to predict probabilities of what the future will be.

## 🎯 Fundamental Analysis Signals

Fundamental signals and analysis rely on data that are widely recognized as being fundamentally factual. A wide variety of information is available, and many subscription services can provide you with in-depth information that may assist you in getting information before the herd gets it.

### Fundamental Analysis Signals
- Corporate Financial Statements
- Sector Analysis
- Market Share
- EPS—Earnings Per Share
- ROE—Return on Equity
- D/E—Debt-to-Equity Ratio
- P/S—Price-to-Sales Ratio
- P/E—Price-to-Earnings Ratio
- PEG—Projected Earnings Growth
- FCF—Free Cash Flow
- P/B—Price-to-Book Ratio
- DPR—Dividend Payout Ratio
- DYR—Dividend Yield Ratio
- COT—Commitments of Traders Reports released by the CFTC Commodity Futures Trading Commission
- Central Bank Interest Rate Decisions
- Unemployment Rates
- Employment Figures
- Inflation Rates
- Durable Goods Orders
- Nonfarm Payroll Reports
- Trade Balance

- Retail Sales Index
- GDP—Gross Domestic Product
- PCE—Personal Consumption Expenditures
- CCI—Consumer Confidence Index
- CPI—Consumer Price Index
- IPI—Industrial Production Index
- Housing Starts
- US International Trade
- USDA Agricultural Reports

A rule of thumb is that the lower, or faster, a time frame you choose to trade, the less you will need to know about the company in terms of fundamentals and news. If you're a long-term investor, you should know a lot about the company you are about to buy, and fundamentals are crucial. Traders and scalpers instead rely more on technical analysis.

## News Analysis Signals

A popular approach is to look at news analysis signals and the impact of world events. News and world events can dramatically shift the markets, and all traders must be aware of their implications.

Often news can draw your attention to a market you might otherwise not look at and can be useful in finding opportunities. Or, if when looking at a technical analysis chart you see a huge gap up or gap down, looking at the news to find out what caused the move is useful.

### News Analysis Signals
- FOMC Meetings
- Economic Calendars
- Weather Reports
- World Currency Reports
- Macroeconomic News
- Leading News Media Headlines

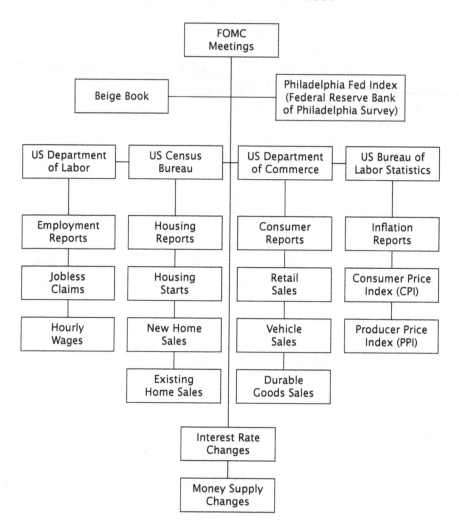

**Figure 19.1**  US Economic Reports. Eight Federal Open Market Committee (FOMC) meetings are held in the United States each year, and this illustration shows some of the data that are released following these meetings, in addition to economic data that are released from other government agencies. Calendars that give you exact dates of each report release are useful in planning on possible market fluctuations due to new report information.

It's also important to note that economic report announcements, such as the FOMC, corporate earnings reports, and the like, can surprise markets and create volatility. See Figure 19.1 for some of the economic data reports that are regularly released and that can drive the markets.

## 🎯 Hybrid Analysis

Depending on your preferences, you may find that you are a true-blue technical trader or a diehard fundamental trader. And you may want to stay in your comfort zone with just one discipline.

But more and more it seems that some fundamental folks are opening up to the technical, and some technical traders are using fundamentals. We call them *hybrid* traders, and blending a variety of signals from technical, fundamental, and news data has many benefits.

The choice is up to you as to what works best.

## 🎯 Interpreting Signals

Here are a few examples of ways to interpret a variety of signals that your rules may be relying on. This is a taste of how technical, fundamental, and news data can give you clues into how to enter and exit the markets.

- Weather forecasts predict severe freezing temperatures in Florida this year, so you go long on the commodity orange juice because the price should go up due to low supply and high demand.
- A cell phone maker's stock is downgraded, so the value of the shares should drop significantly, a reason to short the stock.
- There is unrest in the Middle East, which historically leads to higher prices in oil, so you go long on crude oil.
- There are rumors that the CEO of XYZ Corporation will be indicted for illegal activity, so you short XYZ Corporation.
- A tsunami hits Japan and creates devastation, so you short the Japanese yen, expecting it to drop dramatically.

- The US unemployment report comes out with a rise in new jobs, and the economy looks like it is recovering; the overall stock market rallies.
- The Fed announces a major rise in interest rates, so you go long on bonds.
- Walmart releases higher than expected quarterly earnings, so you go long on Walmart.
- Your analysis determines that the stock you are looking at has just started the beginning of a Wave 3 to the upside, which in Elliott Wave terms means it will be the strongest and longest wave in the pattern. You enter a long position.
- Using Fibonacci analysis, you determine what the target zone for the trade you just entered will be and base your plan on that.
- You see a fry pan bottom channeling chart break out to the downside, so you go short on the stock you are looking at.

**NOTE:** It is crucial that you access and act on information the second it is released, so that you are in front of the herd when entering or exiting the market. In this regard, it is important to have fast, live streaming, real-time data feed that is not delayed. The older the news, fundamental, or price and volume data, the less value it will have for you.

## ◎ Bar Charts Versus Candle Charts

Traders use many types of charts, but the two most popular are candle charts and bar charts. Using technical analysis, you will choose the chart type you prefer, but here is an overview of the difference.

### Bar Chart

Each individual price bar tells a story. One price bar represents the interval of time that the price bar is illustrating. For example, a 1-minute price bar shows you what happened for a 60-second period.

**You will see the following information on this one price bar:**

1. **Open price** with a line to the left
2. **Close price** with a line to the right
3. **High price** the top of the bar
4. **Low price** the bottom of the bar

The OHLC, or the open, high, low, and the close of the bar, tells a complete story in a visually concise format. See Figure 19.2.

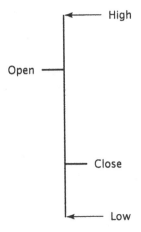

**Figure 19.2**   Price Bar. This is an illustration of a price bar showing the price open and close and the price high and low of this time interval. The acronym for this is OHLC.

### Candlestick Chart

Each individual candlestick tells a story just as with the price bar. One candlestick represents the interval of time that the candlestick is illustrating. For example, a 1-minute candlestick shows you what happened for a 60-second period. You will see the open, close, high, and low of that period. See Figure 19.3.

Names are associated with each area of a candlestick, such as the body (black or white) and an upper and lower shadow (wick). The area between the open and the close is called the real body, and price excursions above and below the body are called shadows.

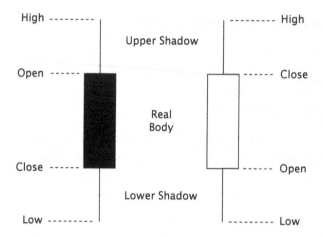

**Figure 19.3** Candlestick. This is an illustration of a candlestick showing the price open and close and the price high and low of this time interval.

If the candlestick closed higher than it opened, the body is *white* with the opening price at the bottom of the body and the closing price at the top. If the candlestick closed lower than it opened, the body is *black*, with the opening price at the top and the closing price at the bottom.

## 🎯 Markets Zig and Zag

Markets rarely move in a hyperbolic straight line; instead, they zig and zag. Just like the natural phenomenon of the ocean with waves and tides that ebb and flow, the markets are an organic and a living breathing entity. The reason they ebb and flow is because of the interconnected psychology in the marketplace.

During moments of exuberance, the herd joins in a strong move, followed by moments of profit taking where the herd cashes in on their current profits. Until the trend changes, this pattern will continue, hence the zigzag pattern.

In technical terms, this pattern can be illustrated with periods of support and resistance. See Figures 19.4 and 19.5.

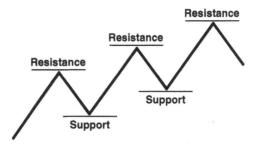

**Figure 19.4** Up trending market example. Notice how support and resistance play a role in the uptrend. A repeating zigzag pattern is created by exuberance followed by profit taking, until the trend changes.

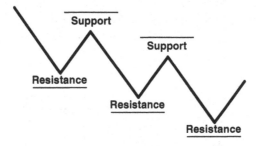

**Figure 19.5** Down trending market example. Notice how support and resistance play a role in the down trend. A repeating zigzag pattern is created by exuberance followed by profit taking, until the trend changes.

The classic definition of an uptrend is where the market experiences a series of successive higher highs and higher lows. This bull trend exhibits a zigzag pattern. See Figure 19.6.

And in reverse, the classic definition of a downtrend is where the market experiences a series of successive lower highs and lower lows. This bear trend exhibits a zigzag pattern. See Figure 19.7.

# 🎯 Market Cycles

You need to learn how to correctly identify four major market cycles. Each market cycle requires a different approach from your trading and investing rules, and adapting to market cycles can improve your profitability dramatically.

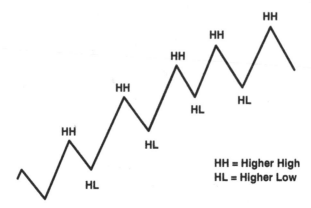

**Figure 19.6** Up trending market example. Notice the series of higher highs and higher lows in this uptrend. The repeating zigzag pattern is created by exuberance followed by profit taking, until the trend changes.

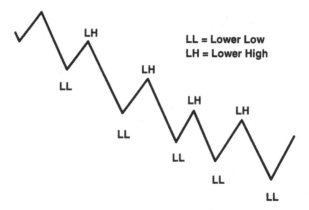

**Figure 19.7** Down trending market example. Notice the series of lower highs and lower lows in this downtrend. The repeating zigzag pattern is created by exuberance followed by profit taking, until the trend changes.

## Following are examples of the four major market cycles:

1. **Trending:** A financial market is moving consistently in one direction, up (bull) or down (bear). Markets tend to trend higher or lower about 25% of the time. See Figure 19.8.

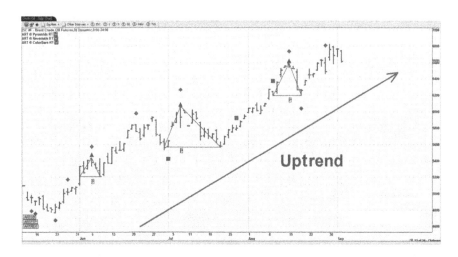

**Figure 19.8** Trending market example. Notice the clear up trend on this chart. Trending markets occur around 30% of the time.

SOURCE: eSignal. www.esignal.com

2. **Bracketed:** Also known as a consolidating or sideways market, a bracketed market occurs when the market is stuck in a price range between an identifiable resistance and support level. On a chart it will look like a sideways horizontal channel. Markets tend to get stuck in sideways bracketed markets 75% of the time. See Figure 19.9.

3. **Breakout:** A sharp change in price movement after the market has been consolidating for a least 20 price bars is known as a breakout. It will either break out to the upside (bull) or the downside (bear). See Figure 19.10.

4. **Corrective:** This is a temporary short, sharp reverse in prices during a longer market trend, also know as a correction. See Figure 19.11.

Incorrectly identifying a market cycle can be a costly situation. For example, if you decide that a market entered a new trend, but in fact it was in a correction, you might enter a trade and immediately get stopped out.

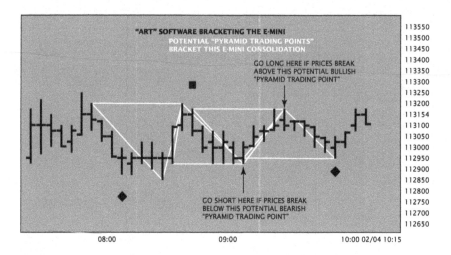

**Figure 19.9**    Bracketed market example. Notice the sideways pattern on this chart. Bracketed markets occur around 75% of the time.
SOURCE: eSignal. www.esignal.com

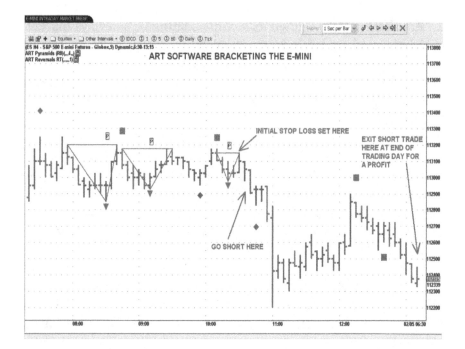

**Figure 19.10**    Breaking out of a bracket market example. Notice the swift drop as the chart shows a bracketed market that breaks out quickly to the downside.
SOURCE: eSignal. www.esignal.com

**Figure 19.11** Corrective market example. Notice the temporary market correction with a brief move to the upside that resumes with a swift move to the downside.
SOURCE: eSignal. www.esignal.com

For this reason, market experience is the best teacher. Your essential plan of action is constant observation. With that, you will continually improve your ability to read market cycles.

## ◎ Trend Lines

Trend lines are a terrific way for you to visualize the support and resistance of any current market cycle, whether it is trending up, trending down, or trending sideways. Visually you will be able to tell when the market movement breaks the trend line.

See Figure 19.12 for an example of using a trend line drawn on the chart to clarify where the trend currently is. Trend lines assist you in identifying what market cycle you're in, and that is an important skill to master.

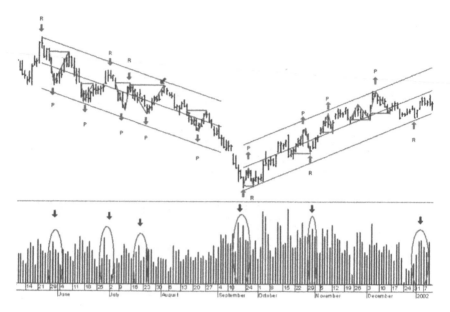

**Figure 19.12**   Trend lines illustrate the downtrend changing into an uptrend on this chart. They are an effective way to visualize the support and resistance of any market and can assist you in identifying market cycles and changes in market cycles.

You can be more relaxed or aggressive in drawing your trend lines, which will depend on your comfort level and your strategy. Aggressive trend lines have a tighter channel, and more relaxed trend lines have a wider channel in which the market moves.

## 🎯 Pitfalls of Not Identifying Market Cycles Correctly

In my experience working with traders and investors over the years, one of the most common reasons for failure is that traders are unable to identify market cycles correctly and do not realize the importance of identifying these cycles.

Sometimes when traders are able to identify a market cycle that their approach does not perform well in, it is difficult for them to sit on the sidelines and not take a trade. Often the best trade is no trade at all, but for some traders, it can be uncomfortable to not be in the game.

Patience is part of the psychological mindset that a trader needs in order to develop the ability to read market cycles effectively. Identifying market cycles is a skill that all successful traders have mastered. It is also essential to know what market cycles your system or approach will work well in and then have the discipline to stay out of the market when necessary.

**Common Pitfalls of Not Identifying Market Cycles Correctly**

- **Not identifying a bracketed market.** Here the pitfall is that you will get whipsawed by repeatedly entering the market and getting stopped out, resulting in paying a lot in commission fees to your broker and not capturing a profitable move in the market. **Solution:** Use trend lines along with software to identify bracketed markets.

- **Misidentifying a reverse in trend.** The pitfall is that you might exit a perfectly good trend and miss out on significant profit potential as the market continues to move in the direction of your original position. **Solution:** Use scaling out techniques for exiting the market so that you still have a portion of your position on the table and can profit from that if the trend is still in play.

Study market cycles and factor this concern into your rules and approach so you can effectively enter the market only when conditions exist for your system to perform well.

## ◎ Trend Exhaustion

I'm not a big fan of chasing markets. The downside of chasing markets is if you get in and the trend is nearly over, there is not enough profit potential to make it worth your while. There really is no upside to chasing markets.

Figure 19.8 shows an up-trending market that is getting close to exhaustion. Notice the triangles on the chart, they are called pyramid trading points and are part of the ART trading software by TradersCoach.com. My rules are such that after four consecutive primary pyramid trading points in a row, I consider the trend exhausted.

Also, having enough history on the chart is extremely important in determining if there is trend exhaustion. By going far enough back, to the left side of the chart, you can identify Elliott Wave patterns and such that provide clues as to where you are in the trend.

Eliotticians know that Elliott Wave 3 is the strongest of all five waves, so distinguishing which wave you are in will also assist in determining trend exhaustion.

Develop your scanning skills so that you can find emerging new trends that give you the most potential for profit and less chance of getting in too late in a trend. The best scans to use for this are for bracketed markets and for Elliott Wave patterns.

## Breakout Trend Trades Come After Bracketed Markets

One way to avoid getting into a trend too late is to find a *breakout* from a bracketed market instead. My favorite approach to this is by scanning for markets that have been consolidating for at least 20 price bars.

The more price bars in the bracket, or the longer and narrower the sideways pattern gets, the stronger the breakout is likely to be. Refer back to Figures 19.9 and 19.10 to review what a bracketed market looks like and how it can lead to a breakout.

Remember, trending markets only occur about 25% of the time. The rest of the time they tend to be in a bracketed pattern. The trick is to not get stuck in the brackets for too long waiting for a breakout but instead to jump in as close to the beginning of the trend as possible.

## Fractal Symmetry in Financial Markets

Fractals are everywhere, in nature and in the markets. Just hold up your hand, and you will see them. Notice that the five fingers on your hand could each represent a price bar. Notice on your hand the price bars, or fingers, trend up until the middle finger which is at the top of the pattern, and then the price bars, or fingers, go down to the bottom of the pattern. This is a fractal pattern, and it is a common chart pattern.

Fractals represent a change in behavior in markets, and fractal price patterns give us clues as to price direction.

Basically, a fractal is a never-ending pattern. They're infinitely complex patterns that are self-similar across different scales. They are created by repeating a simple process over and over in an ongoing feedback loop. Fractals are images of dynamic systems—the picture of chaos.

And yet in a nonlinear world, they are not chaos. Yes, they are dynamic, sometimes complicated, and seemingly chaotic. But if you look closely enough, they boil down to repeating similar patterns. Just like looking through a kaleidoscope. As you turn it clockwise, it generates an infinite number of fractal possibilities.

The term fractal was first coined by Benoit Mandelbrot in the year 1975, and then he expanded on his ideas in 1982 in his book *The Fractal Geometry of Nature*. There has been an explosion of interest in his findings ever since, especially in the financial markets, where fractals occur in chart patterns across all market and time frames. The symmetry of these fractal patterns appears across all time frames, which is why multiple time frame analysis is so effective: the patterns of the lower time frames are found within the patterns of the higher time frames and vice versa.

## 🎯 Moving Averages

Moving averages are a popular tool used by technical analysts looking at charts. See Figure 19.13. There are a number of different types of moving averages, including the simple moving average (SMA), weighted moving average (WMA), and the exponential moving average (EMA). The moving average smooths out price data by creating a constantly updated average price.

For example, to calculate a simple 5-day moving average, you would add the closing price for the last 5 days and divide the sum

**Figure 19.13**   See this meandering moving average line that overlays on top of the OHLC price bar patterns on this chart. This simple technical analysis tool smooths out price data by creating a constantly updated average price. In this chart the average is taken over a period of 50 days. The specific period of time for the averaging can also be 20 minutes, 10 days, 30 weeks, or any period you choose. SOURCE: NinjaTrader. www.ninjatrader.com

by 5. Going forward, each new day's close is added to the previous 4 days and then averaged. With each successive close, the oldest data are dropped off and replaced by new data to keep the average constant. The period for the average can be anything the trader chooses, such as 20 minutes, 50 days, 30 weeks, etc.

One popular strategy when using moving averages is called the *crossover,* which is when the price crosses above or below a moving average to signal a potential change in trend.

Another strategy is to use two moving averages, one longer and one shorter. When the shorter term moving average crosses above the longer term one, it is a buy signal, as it indicates that the trend in shifting up and is called a *golden cross.* In contrast, when the shorter term moving average crosses below the longer term moving average, it is a sell signal because it indicates the trend is shifting down, and it is called a *dead/death cross*.

Moving averages are a common tool that many beginners use when learning about the markets.

# 🎯 Chart Patterns

Everything in technical analysis is based on chart patterns and knowing how to see these patterns. Historically, the same patterns repeat themselves over and over and can give us clues as to future market behavior based on what has happened in the past.

There are books galore on the subject, but for our purposes the idea is for you to know a few of these patterns and understand that *seeing* patterns on the chart is a useful skill. At first you may find that it takes time to see the patterns, and then with practice, you will discover that they are everywhere, and it will become easier for you to find them.

**List of Chart Patterns to Start With**
- Double Top—See Figure 19.14
- Triple Top
- Double Bottom
- Triple Bottom
- Flag
- Pennant—See Figure 19.15
- Triangle
- Head and Shoulders—See Figure 19.16
- Wedges
- Bump-and-Run Reversals
- Cup with Handle
- Dead Cat Bounce

And as I always say, if the chart is messy and looks like spaghetti and you can't find a pattern, do not force it. Instead, move on to another chart; there is an abundance of set-ups in the markets.

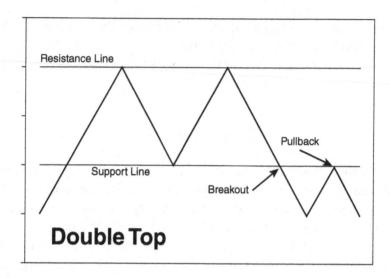

**Figure 19.14**   Double top. Chart pattern with a breakout to the downside.

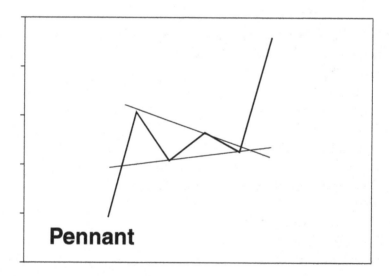

**Figure 19.15**   Pennant. The chart pattern essentially is a channeling market that narrows down into a pennant shape. The breakout occurs at the point of the pennant.

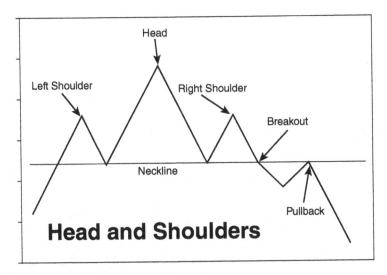

**Figure 19.16**   Head and shoulders. The chart pattern breaks out to the down side with a pullback and another move to the downside.

## 🎯 Chart History

How long a company has been on the stock exchange will determine how much price and volume history is available. Newer companies will have very little history, and older companies may have 100 years of history.

Even with that said, you may or may not be able to access all of the history available on your front-end charting platform because not all platforms carry history back that far. Certain companies like www.StockCharts.com do carry extensive history and can provide charts for you based on that. See Figure 19.17, which has a chart that spans from 1900 to 2024.

Chart history is important because you can see where the company has been and count Elliott Waves based on history, which helps you see where the company is going. Without history, it is more difficult to estimate a price target zone because there is insufficient historical data available to forecast future patterns.

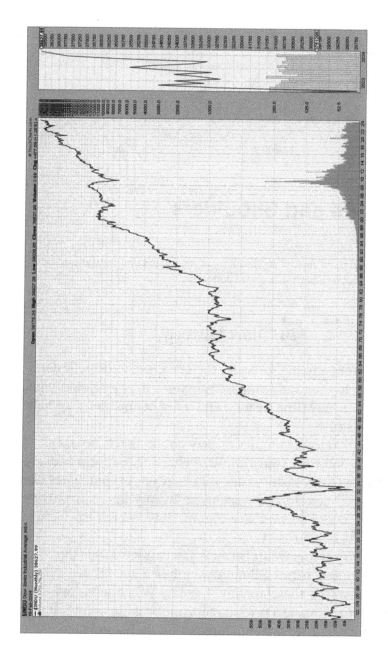

**Figure 19.17** DJIA, Dow Jones Industrial Average chart from January 1900 through January 2024. Take a good look at the 1929 crash, which is clear and dramatic on this chart. You can also see the 1987, 2008, and 2020 crashes as well. The lesson in this is that passive investing can be costly if you happen to be unaware and are fully invested in the markets during a market crash. SOURCE: StockCharts.com. (www.stockcharts.com).

Another note about history—new traders sometimes don't realize that if they load a lot of history onto their chart, their computer may have trouble processing that large amount of data. This can slow down your computer processing and chart loading. Be aware of this.

## 🎯 Multiple Time Frame Analysis

No matter what time frame you are trading or investing in this technique can be used, and it will greatly increase your insight into the markets. By observing the fractal symmetry of price patterns, which are found in all markets, it is possible to determine if momentum is agreeing on more than one time frame. When it does, that identifies a high probability trade. At the back of this book, in the Advanced Techniques section, there is an entire chapter on this topic that will guide you on how to add this strategy to your toolbox.

## 🎯 Timing of the Trade

Timing in life is everything, and the time of day you place trades can affect your profitability. It can also affect how many good set-ups you find. Plus, when there is more volume and activity, there is also more liquidity, which is crucial to getting your desired price for entries and exits.

In addition to the time of day, the day of the week can affect your open positions. Mondays can be famously unpredictable since activity and news over the weekend, when the markets are closed, may trigger a gap opening. Trading days that occur before or after holidays are equally unpredictable because the more consecutive days that the markets are closed, the more unexpected information will come in to hammer the markets when they do open.

You may find a "financial calendar" to be helpful in that it alerts you to these predictable events, such as holidays, FOMC meetings, and earnings reports.

Timing is everything; testing these variables is well worth your time to see which times work for your bottom line and which do not.

# ◎ Sector Analysis

Sector analysis is used by equity traders and stock option traders. If you are trading any time frame under 10 minutes, it becomes impractical to view groups and sectors and focus on that short time frame. These strategies are more suited to traders using 60-minute, daily, and weekly charts.

You can use two approaches to decide what stocks to trade: the *top-down* and the *down-up* approaches.

1. **Top-down Sector Analysis**
    (a) Sector
    (b) Group
    (c) Individual

To use this approach, start the analysis at the sector level and work your way downward to individual stocks. Traders using this approach first look at stock sector charts. Then they analyze the groups, and then pick the best individual stocks to trade within those groups, thus the name *top-down* approach.

You can use this approach by looking for sectors that have been *sleepy* for a while or consolidating for a while. Next, find the sleepiest stock groups within that sector. Then choose the sleepiest individual stock that is in the longest and narrowest channel in that group.

2. **Down-up Sector Analysis**
    (a) Individual
    (b) Group
    (c) Sector

Here you find the individual stock first, and then analyze the group and finally the sector to see how the stock is behaving in relation to its peers. This can be helpful when you're getting a signal to go long on an individual stock, but the volume is a bit low, and you are wondering why.

If you look at the group, it is in a downtrend, and your individual stock is generating a long position on low volume with no positive news out, then you might not want to go long. Again, if it is in play by either momentum traders or position traders, you will see significant volume on the time frame you are trading. The more volume, the more players are participating.

This *down-up* strategy has saved me many times from going into the market when it is not ready to move. It will show you when the market is being manipulated on low volume by market makers. Real trends take outside paper coming from off the floor to move prices significantly.

Many traders worldwide need to participate for a significant trend to develop. Significant trends occur when traders from many different time frames are participating in the trend.

Again, these strategies are best suited to the position trader or the investor. Day traders are less likely to use this approach.

## 🎯 Seasonality Analysis

Seasonality analysis is the use of historical patterns that can be used to predict probabilities of future patterns or trends based on *seasons*. The best-known seasonal trend is the outdoor temperature. This fairly predictable seasonal trend can be used to predict the price of a commodity such as heating oil. For example, oil is less expensive in summer than in winter during the heating season.

The unknown variable is, how hot or cold will this year's seasons be compared to prior years? That variable will determine the actual extent of supply and demand, which will drive prices either higher, lower, or the same as previous years. This example is just one of many in which seasonality can be used in conjunction with your charts to determine price points for entries and exits.

## ◎ Diversification

Diversification is a useful tool for ensuring that you don't blow your entire account on one individual market or trade. Of course, to utilize this tool you need a large enough account size so you can have more than one trade on at a time. It is up to you how much or how little diversification you will put into your plan.

**A few ways to diversify is by limiting the following:**

- Bullish trades
- Bearish trades
- Correlated markets

The idea of diversification is that if one market gets hit hard, or if there is a fast reverse in trend direction, your exposure is limited. That way you don't lose your entire account because all of your eggs won't be in one basket.

## Manage Your Expectations

Once you've designed your rules and are ready to begin testing, it's crucial to realize that some things you may have heard through the grape vine are just not true. For example, when traders, or system vendors, boast that they have a 90% win rate, chances are they are not being completely honest. Maybe they are cherry picking their best trading periods and are telling you about those. But over time, a 90% win rate is just not going to happen.

> In this business, if you're good, you're right six times out of ten. You're never going to be right nine times out of ten.
> —Peter Lynch, Magellan Mutual Fund Manager

So, when you find yourself testing your rules and they are consistently delivering a 60% win rate, that's excellent provided your pay-off ratio is 2 to 1. Don't compare your statistics with what you may have heard is attainable; focus on improving your skills and approach. Keep raising the bar one day at a time.

## Value Investing in a Bear Market

If you've gotten this far in reading *The ART of Trading*, chances are you are already a believer in the advantages of active trading and investing as opposed to passive value investing. But for the record, I want to reiterate some of the reasons it's important to be an active participant in the market as opposed to a passive one.

Value investing is a popular technique made famous by Benjamin Graham and Warren Buffett. Value investors all look extremely smart during a strong bull market, which we have seen many times. The reason value investors look smart during a bull market is because during these periods, for the most part, if they put money in the stock market and wait a few years they are likely to make a comfortable profit.

But during market cycle changes and crashes, such as 1929 and 1987 and 2008 and 2020 and no doubt sometime in the near future, the unknowing value investor usually gets clobbered by a swift and painful wake up call. The buy-and-hold value investing strategy doesn't work then the way it did in the past. Hence the *past performance does not guarantee future* results disclaimer comes to mind. See Figure 19.17 to see that crashes have and will likely continue to occur in the markets.

That's when folks look at their 401k retirement accounts slashed in half, and they wonder how their retirement will look now. Remember, now more than ever, it is important to be educated and to look at the big picture.

If you are a value investor, keep your eye on the ball to be sure that the companies you have selected to invest in are performing the way you had planned. Do not fall prey to the potential devastation of a bear market. Watch your portfolio at all times.

Of course, as an active trader and investor, the volatility of a bear market instead offers you the opportunity to go short and to profit when the bulls are losing. That's where the savvy trader can make money in both bull and bear markets.

## A Quick Word About Shorting the Markets

One of the great advantages to trading as a business is that you can generate revenue in either bull or bear markets. This means that as long as there is volatility and movement, you can make money on both the up swings and the down swings. This is in stark contrast to buy and hold investing and in stark contrast to a typical 9-to-5 job working for an employer.

In a bear market, buy-and-hold investors may watch their net worth decline if they are not savvy enough to exit the market *before* it starts to decline. And when layoffs are rising in companies that are struggling to stay profitable in a bear market, full-time traders who works for themselves are insulated from that loss of income. That is if they are experienced and successful in shorting the markets.

### So, what exactly is *shorting* the market?

Selling short is the process of borrowing shares via your broker and selling them in the open market, with the intention of purchasing the shares back for less cost in the future. See Figure 19.18.

To be clear, you did not own the shares before selling them, which is why you had to borrow them via your broker. The shares must be returned to your broker at some point in the future. Unfortunately, your intentions will not always be fulfilled, and losses can result in a few different ways.

First, you may have to pay more to buy back the stock than you received when initially shorting it. This can result in unlimited losses. Not only that, if you are short the stock when the company declares a dividend, and the ex-dividend date occurs while your position is open, you will owe the dividend to the owner of your short stock. Finally, this type of trade is done in a margin account.

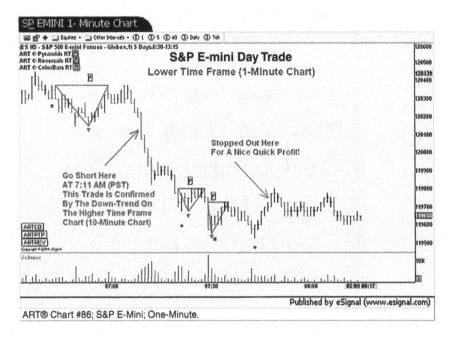

**Figure 19.18** Chart of shorting the market.
SOURCE: eSignal, www.esignal.com

Trading on margin carries additional risks, so please make sure you understand them before opening this kind of position.

With this said, you can in essence short the market by buying inverse ETFs, which can even be done in your IRA retirement account. This tool can be added to your toolbox. The bottom line is that shorting the market gives you greater flexibility in all market conditions and is a good skill set to develop.

# Win or Lose, Everyone Gets What They Want Out of the Market

There's a quote from Ed Seykota that's in Jack Schwager's *Market Wizards* book. See Figure 19.19. The interview that Schwager did with Seykota revealed some interesting insights into the psychology of trading and investing.

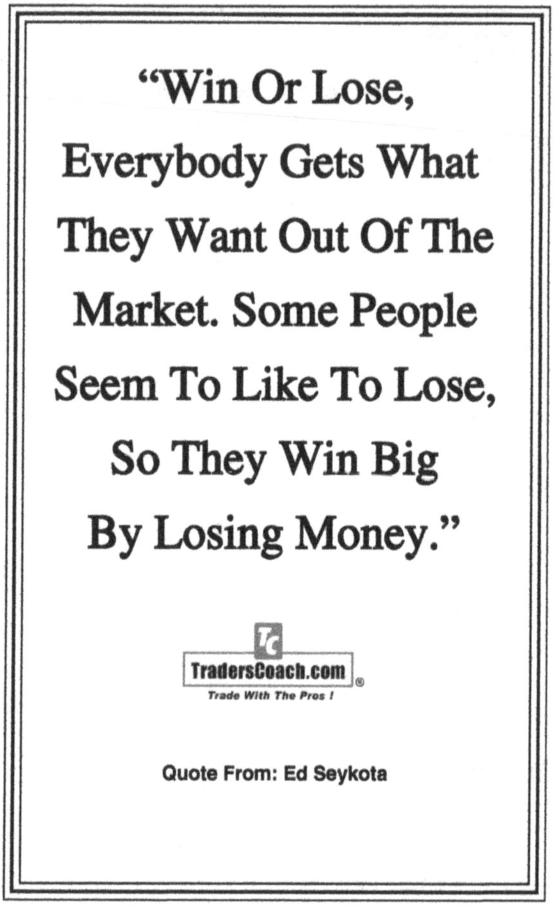

> ## "Win Or Lose, Everybody Gets What They Want Out Of The Market. Some People Seem To Like To Lose, So They Win Big By Losing Money."
>
> **TradersCoach.com**
> *Trade With The Pros !*
>
> **Quote From: Ed Seykota**

**Figure 19.19**    MINI POSTER—WIN OR LOSE—This chapter has focused on designing profitable rules. Remember, that rules alone will not make you profitable; you must have the right trader's mindset as well. Work on developing your mindset alongside your rules. Quote from Ed Seykota.

This brings us full circle to the fact that no matter how phenomenal your rules and your system are, if your psychology and traders' mindset are not strong, you will likely still lose money in the markets.

Once you have designed your trading rules, be mindful of the power of your mindset. Your rules are only as effective as your mindset allows them to be.

## Failure Is Not an Option

I'm visualizing you with your new trading rules, working on your trading at night when you get home from your day job. You've been working steadily, but your paper trading just took a turn for the worse and you've got a 20% drawdown in your practice account. You are feeling pretty discouraged and are just about ready to quit.

This is a time when you will need to look for motivational support from either a trading coach, a trading buddy, or a trusted family member. It is during the times when you want to give up that you have to step back and gain perspective.

You've got to have the feeling that failure is not an option, and then you'll need to just "work the problem people." You've got to have purpose and a reason for achieving this goal of creating a set of trading rules that are consistently profitable.

If you haven't already seen the movie *Apollo 13* about NASA's 1970 Apollo mission that almost did not make it home, you must see it. The remarkable teamwork of the ground crew working together to bring the three flight crew members aboard the ship home safely is a unique and miraculous true story.

### *"Houston, we have a problem . . . ."*

That's probably the most famous line of the movie, when Jim Lovell (played by Tom Hanks), Apollo 13 commander, notifies the ground crew in Houston that all is not well on the Apollo spacecraft.

But my personal favorite line of the movie occurs when Gene Kranz (played by Ed Harris), the flight director, says to his team on the ground very sternly when they are feeling discouraged, *"Gentlemen, listen up! NASA has never lost a man in space, and I'll not let us lose a man in space on my watch. Failure is not an option."* See Figure 19.20.

Gene Kranz was a motivator and had the right mindset to create solutions when everyone else envisioned the likelihood of failure. Another line in the movie that is delivered by the Gene Kranz character is when one of the ground crew is negative while they are waiting for the splash down of the module. Kranz says, *"I believe this will be our finest hour."* And in fact, it was.

**Figure 19.20**    Eugene Kranz, flight director for Apollo 13, is shown here at his flight console in the Mission Operations Control Room in Houston. *"Failure is not an option"* was what Gene Kranz, told his crew in the movie *Apollo 13*. They achieved the seemingly impossible and brought all three crew members home alive from outer space by using the resources they had available, to solve the problems at hand. Even when the Grumman aerospace team said, *". . . the lunar module was not designed to do this . . ."* they used the module to successfully act as a lifeboat. This lesson is designed to show that in your trading you must use all the resources you have available to succeed, especially when the going gets tough.

SOURCE: This file is in the public domain in the United States because it was solely created by NASA. NASA copyright policy states that "NASA material is not protected by copyright unless noted." https://upload.wikimedia.org/wikipedia/commons/6/60/Eugene_F._Kranz_at_his_console_at_the_NASA_Mission_Control_Center.jpg

Only the most focused and positive individuals will be consistently successful in the world of trading and investing. Statistics indicate that 90% of all traders lose money in the markets. To be in the upper 10% you must be determined and confident.

Make sure that you honor the mantra *failure is not an option*, and you will have greater success in designing your rules and winning with them.

# Chapter 20

# Testing and Proving Your Edge

Your rules must be tested to prove they give you an edge in the markets before trading them with real money. The best way to do that is to *paper trade* your rules in real time. This is also known as *simulated* trading and can be done on any front-end charting platform using a real-time simulated account.

Now some people may say, "*I backtested my rules, and they were profitable, so I don't need to paper trade them.*" The problem with backtesting is that it does not consider the human factor.

You see, even if the back test proved that your rules give you an edge, it doesn't mean that you in the heat of the moment will be able to carry out the plan exactly as it is laid out. By paper trading as the market unfolds, you will notice your strengths and weaknesses and adjust accordingly.

Emotions can do funny things. It may surprise you to find that you might not get out at the stop-loss exit your rules told you to. Instead, you may hold on to a small losing trade that then becomes a huge losing trade, all because your ego can't stand a loss.

Better to learn about your emotions in a paper trading environment than when you have real money on the line, right? Well, you say, "*Paper trading doesn't generate the same emotions that trading with real money does."* That may be true to some degree. But if you are doing it right, you will feel the same emotions when you are paper trading your new rules as you would trading real money.

Why? For starters, if you are serious about making money trading, and you aren't going to go live with a real cash account until you are profitable in your simulated account, you will want to get profitable as soon as possible.

Another perk to paper trading is that it hones your skills and builds up *muscle memory* by placing trades using your rules. Trust me, you will want to bulk up those trading muscles, because when you do go live with real money, you will have a much greater chance of knocking the ball out of the park.

## What If You Aren't Profitable Paper Trading?

If you cannot be profitable paper trading your rules, it is unlikely you will be profitable trading with real money. Which is all the more reason to get the bugs out of your rules before risking your hard earned capital.

## Fighter Pilots and Flight Simulators

There is a reason the United States government has all their pilots practice with a flight simulator on the ground prior to even stepping into the cockpit of a zillion dollar fighter jet. See Figure 20.1.

Do you know what that reason is?

It's because the loss of life and property is not something the government is in the habit of doing if they can help it. Now, the cool guys and gals that are like Tom Cruise in *Top Gun* will probably tell you that the simulator doesn't feel exactly the same as when they are flying a real live jet. But they do it anyway.

They do it because it is the smart thing to do.

It is no different for you in your trading cockpit with your control panel and monitors in front of you. The smart thing to do is practice in a paper trading account and conduct multiple simulated

**Figure 20.1**   Flight simulator. Military pilots are required to practice in a flight simulator before they ever step into a real live cockpit. Why? Because it's the smart thing to do. It's the same with your trading and investing. Better to test out your rules in a paper trading account rather than crashing and burning your real live cash account.

trades so that you have experienced virtually any scenario that the market can throw at you, without losing any money.

## Paper Trading Plan

Here is a plan that I use when testing new strategies, and it's a plan that my students have been using since the first edition of *The ART of Trading*. This plan is designed to give you a large enough sample size so that you can be confident in your edge in the markets.

1. **Design your trading rules using the template in Chapter 19.** Write down your rules on paper in a checklist format.
2. **Start to paper trade.** Once you are clear on your rules, start paper trading on the same time frame, in the same financial market, and with the same account size you plan to work with when you use real money.

3. **Evaluate your performance.** Keep track of your paper trading results and approach it as if you were trading with real money. Use the *Trader's Assistant* record keeping forms from Chapter 15 to track your results.

4. **Group in lots of 25 trades.** Group your paper trades in lots of 25 trades each. Calculate your profit/loss, average win/loss, largest win/loss, number of wining trades, number of losing trades, number of consecutive winning trades, and number of consecutive losing trades. A group of 25 consecutive trades that has a profitable outcome is a *profitable lot* of trades.

5. **Practice until profitable.** Analyze *your* paper trading results and practice until you are profitable.

6. **Have three profitable lots of 25 trades each.** Before trading with real money, be sure you have a total of three consecutive profitable lots of 25 trades each while paper trading. It's best to spread your trading over enough days, weeks, or months so you experience uptrending, downtrending, and bracketed markets.

7. **Keep trading in lots of 25 trades.** When trading with real money, keep using the 25-trade lot size to analyze your profit/loss, win/loss, and so on, and see how you're a doing.

8. **Reevaluate your approach.** If you are not profitable trading with real money after trading one lot of 25 trades, stop trading and go back to paper trading again. If at this point you are immediately profitable paper trading, then chances are your psychology is the problem, and you may need some additional help from a trading coach to uncover any self-sabotage issues you may be having. But if your paper trading is not immediately profitable this time, you may have just been lucky the first time and did not paper trade long enough to experience the different types of market cycles. Your trading approach needs to be adjusted. Until you have a qualified approach you will not know if your problem lies in your trading approach or with your psychology.

9. **Experiencing drawdown.** If you experience six consecutive losing trades and/or a drawdown of more than 15%, the market cycle or volatility in the market and time frame you are trading has probably changed. You must adapt to these changes.

10. **During an excessive drawdown, follow these steps:** (a) Stop trading with real money. Keep trading the same market and time frame and go back to paper trading. Wait until you have three winning lots of 25 paper trades before trading with real money again. (b) Adjust your rules to see if doing so eliminates the losses you incurred in your recent drawdown. If so, paper trade again to validate your adjustments. (c) Change time frames until you find the time frame that works best.

## There Will Always Be Losing Trades. How Do You Manage That?

One of the most challenging parts of successful trading, especially in the beginning, is managing the emotions around losing trades. To wrap your brain around that concept, you must navigate real trades and the effect of up and down price action on your emotions. Price action can create a roller coaster of emotions if you allow it to.

Forget about being stopped completely out of a trade. Think about price action just going against you briefly. How do you manage that emotionally?

I can tell you that experience is one of the best teachers, since the more often you see price shooting toward your stop-loss exit, when your heart sinks, but then it reverses for a winning trade, the more you will become immune to the emotional *roller coaster effect*. That immunity comes from confidence in yourself, your rules, and your strategy. Remember this: until your stop is hit, you have not lost anything.

Now let's talk about actual stopped out trades that were stopped out at a loss. Again, the emotions can be difficult. They can drive you to think about breaking your rules and

*(continued on next page ...)*

*(... continued from previous page)*

to think about not exiting a trade when your stop loss tells you to. I confess to being guilty of this early in my trading, not that I'm proud of it, but I want to share with you that if you have these feelings, you are not alone.

Again, until you master your emotions and develop the trader's mindset, not adhering to your stop is a serious issue. What is the first rule of trading? That's right, follow your rules. So, whatever you need to do to follow your stop-loss exits, be sure to do it. If you find yourself breaking that rule, confront the reasons and figure it out. Because, until you do, consistent success in trading will not be possible.

## Common Objections to Paper Trading

Over the years, I've heard it all. Students object to paper trading for many reasons. Here are the most common objections and my answers in response:

- **It doesn't subject you to the same emotions.** That may be true, yet it doesn't seem like an intelligent argument. In medical school, would it make sense for surgeons to operate on live patients before they really know what they are doing? I don't think so. Trading is a life-or-death situation, your financial life or death. Treat it with the respect it deserves.
- **You'll get addicted.** I guess some people feel they'll be afraid to pull the trigger with real money if they paper trade too long. Here's the thing, if you know that your plan says you must have three sets of consecutive trades that are profitable sets before you go live with real money, why would you be afraid to pull the trigger? You've proven you are profitable. Then if you prove to yourself that you can't be profitable, you'd better fix the problem before you go live with real money.

- **Backtesting is the only way to test.** There are lots of ways to backtest. In essence, paper trading is one of the ways you can backtest. Where mechanical back testing fails is that it doesn't test your personal psychology, which is what matters most.
- **It's too much work.** Yes, it requires dedication and work to complete three sets of 25 profitable trades. But then again, anything of real value requires work. The value acquired from this type of paper trading produces results. I've seen it time and time again. The question is this: Are you under the illusion that trading profit will be quick and easy? And if you enjoy the actual process of trading, it won't seem like work since every step of progress will give you great satisfaction.
- **Paper trading is for sissies.** Well, no one has ever really said that to me, but the implication is there. You know, macho men don't need to paper trade, and if you are man enough (or woman enough), you should be trading with real money right away. It's almost as if they are saying "I'm tough enough to get my ass kicked, and that's how I'm going to learn." Thing is, everyone gets their ass kicked sooner or later. At least if you've paper traded successfully first, you'll have a better idea of why.

In the end, it is up to each individual to decide how to test their rules and to prove that they have an edge in the market. My advice to you of course is to paper trade.

## Paper Trading Is A Safe Place

Paper trading is a safe environment that allows you to focus on the art and the science of trading. In other words, hone your rules so they become tested, proven, and second nature. Then if you enter the markets with real money, and fail, you know that you either did not test enough market cycles, or your emotions affected you.

## Every Financial Market Is a Championship Arena

Short-term trading is a zero-sum game. When you enter any financial market, you will be competing against the best of the best. If you enter as a novice, you will be competing against traders who have more skill, more experience, and more capital.

To give yourself a fighting chance, you need to practice and enter the markets as skilled as possible. Anything less will make it hard for you to succeed. See Figure 20.2.

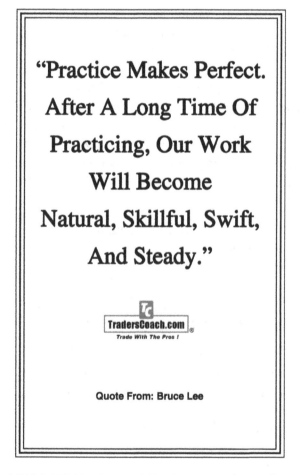

**Figure 20.2** MINI POSTER—PRACTICE—Practice makes perfect. After a long time of practicing, our work will become natural, skillful, swift, and steady. Quote from Bruce Lee.

# Step V

# Scan for Opportunities

# Chapter 21
# Needle in the Haystack

When searching for the best trades, it can feel like looking for a needle in a haystack; With so many markets, and access to thousands of opportunities, beginners may feel overwhelmed. How does one find the highest probability trades or investments?

In the following pages, *Step 5* is here to help you develop strategies to find excellent opportunities for your personal approach. And that is the key: you must identify opportunities that fit your personal system rules. Each financial market is different, and your personal preferences will determine how you search for potential winners.

Another essential aspect of finding the best opportunities is to *not force* trades. Patience is a virtue, and knowing that opportunities are abundant in the financial markets will help you develop that patience. See Figure 21.1.

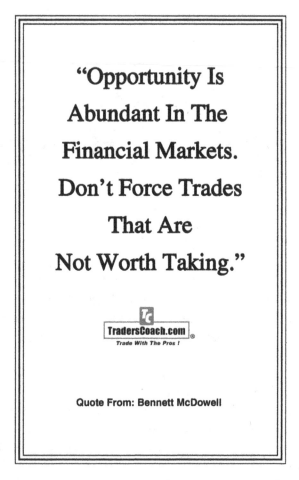

**Figure 21.1**    MINI POSTER—DON'T FORCE THE TRADE—When a chart or set up is not clear, don't try to force it. Just move on and remember, an infinite number of high probability opportunities are in the markets and the universe. Patience in waiting for a trade that meets your criteria will pay off handsomely in the long run. Quote from Bennett McDowell.

If you find yourself looking at a chart or set up and scratching your head trying to make sense of it, just move on to the next chart. If it isn't clear, move on. This can be one of the best filters to weed out weaker trades.

## Scan the Universe of Markets That Fit Your Rules

Once you have designed your trading rules, it will be clear as to what types of scans will render the highest probability trade opportunities.

Refer back to your rules for direction on what markets to scan and what types of scans will find the best opportunities for your personal approach. If you have not developed your rules yet, *Step 4* in this book provides guidelines on creating your own rules.

## 🎯 Specify the Conditions and Criteria for Which You Are Going to Scan

When searching for opportunities, your goal is to begin with a broad universe, a market or group of symbols. You will then narrow down the universe to find the highest probability opportunities. In essence, you are creating an *opportunity funnel* of high probability candidates. See Figure 21.2.

**Figure 21.2**    A funnel is useful in taking a large market, say the S&P 500, and pouring it into the top of the funnel. Then as you take that market and scan for specific conditions, you narrow down the universe to a more manageable list.
SOURCE: Illustration 34199816 Funnel © Natis76 Dreamstime.com

Narrowing opportunities is done by specifying the exact conditions and criteria that need to be met for a high probability set up. These conditions are based on your system rules and your historical performance results. Your previous successful trades will tell you what to look for and the best conditions that must be present.

For example, if you are a trend trader and you have found that after a market has been in consolidation and bracketed for a certain number of price bars, it has a high probability that it will break out into a significant trend, either bullish or bearish, then you can scan for this one condition and create a list.

From this list you can then further narrow down your choices with other conditions based on your rules. This is a simple illustration of the basic idea of scanning for opportunities.

## Create Your Own Stock Picking Service

Many newsletters and stock picking services are available today. You may pay a monthly or annual fee to subscribe to these services. Generally, you won't have access to the inner workings of why these providers are selecting their picks.

But when you produce your own opportunity list based on your specific criteria, you've really created your own stock picking service. And you will have a higher confidence level due to the fact that you know why and how your picks were chosen, which makes managing the trades easier as well.

Now I'm not saying that subscribing to a stock picking service isn't a good idea. In fact, it might be a way to obtain a group of picks to then narrow down from. It can save you time in scanning and analyzing, which can be a good return on your subscription investment.

The idea is to use someone else's picks only as a starting point, not a final destination. Take that list of picks and then visually review each one's chart to decide for yourself if it makes the cut.

Remember, don't blindly follow someone else's picks. When a subscription service gives you picks, review them and clear them for takeoff. Trust and verify every trade you take. Take ownership and make every trade you pull the trigger on your own.

## Take Control of the Haystack

As you gain experience you will see that a seemingly huge haystack of financial instruments can be harnessed by using a few simple strategies. And finding that needle in the haystack is possible, see Figure 21.3.

**Figure 21.3**    For beginners, the process of finding high probability trades can feel like looking for a needle in a haystack. Rest assured, there are excellent strategies for doing just that. You will find them here in the coming pages.
SOURCE: Photo 35815377 @ Vivilweb **Dreamstime.com**

Thanks to the gift of computers and technology, it is easy to scan massive amounts of data quickly, compared to the early days of the markets. Once mastered, these computer scanning skills will serve you well in building your watch list and in finding the best opportunities in the markets.

# Chapter 22

# Scanning Strategies

Depending on your trading rules, you can choose from a variety of scanning strategies. The goal is to find high probability entries quickly and efficiently. In the old days, all my scans were done manually, and it was time consuming.

Now, more than 20 years later, technology has advanced to the point where just about every good charting platform comes loaded with excellent computer scanning tools. And at TradersCoach.com, we have also added a number of proprietary scanning tools to our suite of software studies that plug into the best scanners, including NinjaTrader's Market Analyzer and TradeStation's RadarScreen.

Plus, you can scan all markets and all time frames. And scanning is beneficial for virtually any style of trading, including day trading, position trading, and investing. All of which means that in today's world, you can have software tools at your fingertips that will save you time and allow you to scan huge lists in a matter of seconds.

The benefits of technology are many, and saving time tops the list. Added to that is the benefit of not missing out on opportunities. You can literally load the entire S&P 500, NASDAQ 100, DJIA, or any market of your choice, into a scanner and find the best opportunities that meet your criteria quickly.

The trick is to know how to best use this scanning technology.

## Use Technology to Your Advantage

Keep in mind, the more symbols you load into your scans, the more computer power is required. Which means three things: (1) make sure your computer has the power to handle high-end scans; (2) be mindful of the amount of data you load into your computer; (3) with internet connections, the best practice is to use a hard-wired internet connection and stay away from wireless. See Figure 22.1.

**Figure 22.1** MINI POSTER—COMPUTER SPEED—If you find that your computer speed is slow, or your charts are freezing, you may be loading too much data on your computer for its capacity. Be mindful of this, and if necessary, either upgrade your technology to handle more data or reduce the amount of data you load. Quote from Bennett McDowell.

For more information on how to maximize the speed and efficiency of your technology, be sure to study my *Technology Tips* located in Appendix B.

See Figure 22.2 for an example of a computer scan of the NASDAQ 100. This scan is looking for instruments that meet the criteria and conditions of being in a bracketed market and that are exhibiting high volume. This particular scan generated 25 candidates that met the criteria. This scan was produced using the Turbo Scanner (by TradersCoach.com) on the NinjaTrader charting platform using the Market Analyzer feature.

In this case the broad universe was the NASDAQ 100, which got put into the funnel and generated 25 candidates. You can see that by narrowing the larger list it is easier to zero in on the best opportunities.

Out of the initial 100 candidates, the scan weeded out 75% of the list. This process is crucial in targeting a smaller number to dedicate your time to. Time is money, so any way you can save time is going to benefit you.

| Instrument | Description | Last price | Average daily volume | TURBO Scanner |
|---|---|---|---|---|
| AAPL | Apple Computer, Inc. | 170.94 | 73,817,000 | Bracketed |
| AMZN | Amazon.com, Inc. | 179.99 | 36,437,000 | Bracketed |
| MSFT | Microsoft Corporation | 423.75 | 21,462,000 | Bracketed |
| CMCSA | Comcast Corporation | 42.52 | 21,265,000 | Bracketed |
| CSCO | Cisco Systems, Inc. | 49.71 | 20,467,000 | Bracketed |
| CSX | CSX Corp. | 36.84 | 10,918,000 | Bracketed |
| WBA | Walgreens Boots Alliance, Inc. | 20.63 | 9,302,000 | Bracketed |
| KHC | The Kraft Heinz Company | 36.14 | 8,290,000 | Bracketed |
| SBUX | Starbucks Corporation | 90.71 | 7,787,000 | Bracketed |
| EXC | Exelon Corp. | 37.00 | 7,658,000 | Bracketed |
| MDLZ | Mondelez International, Inc. | 70.85 | 7,599,000 | Bracketed |
| GILD | Gilead Sciences, Inc. | 72.58 | 7,320,000 | Bracketed |
| PEP | PepsiCo Inc. | 172.65 | 6,510,000 | Bracketed |
| AMAT | Applied Materials, Inc. | 208.30 | 6,235,000 | Bracketed |
| TXN | Texas Instruments Incorporated | 170.85 | 5,761,000 | Bracketed |
| TMUS | T-Mobile US, Inc. | 161.12 | 4,654,000 | Bracketed |
| TCOM | Trip.com Group Limited | 44.50 | 4,004,000 | Bracketed |
| FAST | Fastenal Company | 77.01 | 3,799,000 | Bracketed |
| FOXA | Twenty-First Century Fox, Inc | 30.22 | 3,455,000 | Bracketed |
| ADI | Analog Devices, Inc | 190.00 | 3,450,000 | Bracketed |
| AMGN | Amgen Inc. | 280.82 | 3,147,000 | Bracketed |
| NFLX | Netflix | 628.00 | 3,113,000 | Bracketed |
| SWKS | Skyworks Solutions, Inc. | 105.99 | 3,045,000 | Bracketed |
| COST | Costco Wholesale Corporation | 730.96 | 2,622,000 | Bracketed |
| EA | Electronic Arts Inc. | 130.52 | 2,515,000 | Bracketed |

**Figure 22.2**  NASDAQ 100 Scan Example—This is a screen shot showing 25 instruments from the NASDAQ 100 that are in a bracketed market and are exhibiting high volume. This scan was produced using the Turbo Scanner (by TradersCoach.com) on the NinjaTrader charting platform using the Market Analyzer feature.
SOURCE: NinjaTrader (www.ninjatrader.com)

# Like Finding Tesla in 2013

If you had been scanning and found a newcomer named Tesla (TSLA) in 2013, you would have been pleased to be sure. My *Weekly Top Ten Trading Picks* subscribers back in 2013 got access to my scan results, which included TSLA, as it was gaining steam on the NASDAQ.

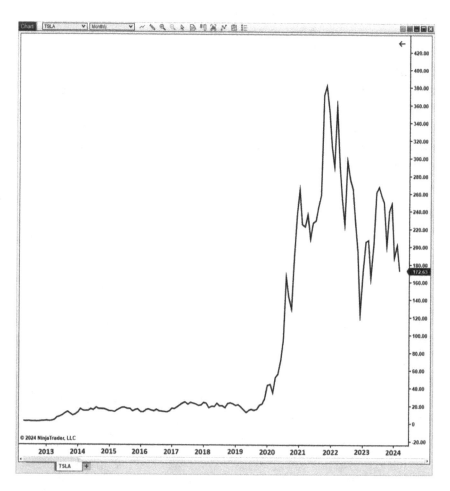

**Figure 22.3** Tesla, TSLA, quadrupled its share price from 2013 to 2014 and continued to skyrocket for the next decade. Your use of technology and scanning may uncover the next best thing, which is why mastering these skills is so important.
SOURCE: NinjaTrader (www.ninjatrader.com)

TSLA went public on June 29, 2010, and steadily gained momentum, when in 2013 through 2014 it quadrupled its share price as you can see on Figure 22.3. TSLA famously continued to skyrocket in the coming decade, and the volatility generated exceptional opportunities both to the upside and the downside.

The reason for bringing up Tesla is that like Apple in 1984, or Amazon.com in 2010, or Bitcoin in 2023, or any number of new opportunities, while producing your scans you may uncover the next big thing. Which is why it's important to do your scanning regularly so that you don't miss the best opportunities.

Plus, finding opportunities early means they are on your radar before the herd catches on. This puts you as an advantage.

## Popular Scanning Tools

Depending on your approach, look for tools that are a good fit for you. Many market scanning tools are available, some are free of charge, and some are included in a paid investment or brokerage product. The more robust scanners generally have a cost associated with them. The following list will give you a head start on finding the best scanners for your needs.

### Popular Scanning Tools:

- NinjaTrader Market Analyzer
- TradeStation RadarScreen
- MultiCharts Market Scanner
- Yahoo Finance
- ChartMill
- Zacks
- Finviz
- Bloomberg
- TradersCoach.com Scanners

As you research which scanners are best for you, take into consideration which scanners are focused on fundamental criteria and which are more tailored to technical analysis. Then find the ones that are geared toward your approach.

# Scanning Tools from TradersCoach.com

A shout out to our clients who own scanners from Traders Coach.com, and for readers who don't own our software tools, if you have questions, you can reach out to support@traders coach.com any time, 24/7.

**The TradersCoach.com Scanners include the following:**

1. Turbo Scanner
2. Elliott Wave Scanner
3. Trade Confirmer Scanner
4. Multiple Time Frame Scanner

A thorough set of software users manuals is located on the companion website portal that is included with your purchase of this book. This portal provides more details on how to use these scanners, which supplements the information in this chapter.

**They all plug into the following charting platforms:**

- NinjaTrader Market Analyzer
- TradeStation RadarScreen
- MultiCharts Market Scanner

As you may have guessed, the scanners developed by TradersCoach.com are all technical scanners. We've listed other popular scanning tools in this chapter as well; again it is a matter of finding the tools that match your approach, whether technical, fundamental, or a combination of both.

# Scanning Strategy Template

Here's a basic template to help you hit the ground running when you start scanning for winners. It's what I do to find the needle in the haystack, and once you get started, you will find that these methods are simple and straightforward.

1. **Your Market of Choice.** Identify the financial market you want to scan.
2. **Funnel Computer Scan.** Set your scan criteria, put the market symbols of choice into the funnel, and run a computer scan to narrow down the larger list.
3. **Opportunity List.** Results from the computer scan make up the candidates on your opportunity list.
4. **Chart Review Filter.** Visually review and analyze each chart generated by your computer scan to filter out the low probability trades and keep the high probability ones.
5. **Trash.** Discard any low probability trades that are not viable.
6. **Watch List.** Put high probability trades that are close but not yet ready to go live onto your watch list for the next review session.
7. **Immediate Live Trade.** Pull the trigger and enter the high probability trades that are ready to go live. Implement all of your rules, including risk control.

If you find that the computer scan you run does not yield many candidates, you can loosen the conditions to increase the number of candidates. These may be lower probability, but during the visual chart review, you may still find good trades.

For the reverse result, a scan that yields too many candidates, tighten the conditions to reduce the number. These will be higher probability candidates, which is a good thing.

# Rinse and Repeat

Once you have developed your scanning approach, it is a matter of rinse and repeat to find the best current candidates. Again, you will regularly be pouring market symbol lists into your funnel and will be narrowing down that universe to a more manageable targeted list each time you do your scans.

It's up to you to decide how often to scan and clean out your watch list. For some it's a daily process, and for others it is weekly and for others it is monthly or something in between. See what works best for you.

## Visually Review and Analyze Charts from Your Opportunity List

It's important to review and analyze each chart your computer scan has identified. Do this manually and visually to see if the patterns are clear and compelling. **You have to see it with your own eyes because the computer scan can only do so much.**

Don't skip the visual review step; it is crucial. After completing a visual review of each chart, determine which of the following three categories the chart falls into:

1. **Trash.** Low probability, discard as not viable.
2. **Watch List.** High probability, close but not ready to take a live trade, goes on watch list.
3. **Immediate Live Trade.** High probability, ready to go live, pull the trigger.

Also, if the patterns are not clear and instead look like spaghetti, move on to the next chart. Or if the setup is close but you could get a better entry after a pull back, put the trade on your watch list for later.

**Remember: Don't force the trade.**

Typically, you will be generating computer scans and doing the sorting and sifting process on a regular basis. This ensures that you won't miss an emerging opportunity.

**Note: Not all scans produce a live trade opportunity.**

It is also important to note here that not all scan results produce a viable and actionable trade. You may find the computer scan results, after visually reviewing them, end up in the trash or on the watch list for later. Again, don't force a trade where there is none.

## Choose Your Scanning Strategy

Run scans that are compatible with your overall approach and your rules, which brings us back to your rules. If you haven't yet outlined and written them down, do so prior to running scans. You will get a better return on the investment of your time if you have thought out exactly what to look for to generate potential trades.

For example, if your rules are based on technical analysis, you will be scanning for technical criteria. I'm listing a variety of popular technical scans here to get you started, but you may find ones that are not on this list that are more tailored to your approach.

**Popular Technical Scanning Strategies:**

- Moving average (MA) scan
- Relative strength index (RSI) scan
- Average true range (ATR) scan
- Accumulation/distribution (A/D) scan
- Bracketed market scan
- Multiple time frame scan
- Elliott Wave scan
- Candlestick pattern scan
- Squeeze scan
- Volatility scan
- Bull/bear flag scan
- Momentum scan

And if you are a fundamental trader, your scans will be focused on fundamental criteria. Here is a list of popular fundamental scans, but you may find ones that are not on the following list that are more tailored to your approach.

**Popular Fundamental Scanning Strategies:**

- Valuation scan
- Profit & loss (P&L) scan
- Price/earnings (P/E) scan
- Earnings growth scan
- Price to sales ratio (P/S) scan
- Projected earnings growth (PEG) scan
- Debt to equity (D/E) scan
- Sector analysis scan
- Market share scan
- Undervalued growth scan
- Dividend payout ratio (DPR) scan
- Dividend yield ratio (DYR) scan

By now you may have noticed, my strategies are primarily technical, so you will not be surprised to find that my favorite scanning approaches are all based on technical analysis.

**My Favorite Scanning Strategies**

- Flat bottom bracketed market scan
- Breakout scan

In the coming pages are step-by-step directions for some of my favorite scans. I haven't included directions for my multiple time frame scan, which I use weekly for my *Market Opportunity Report*. It is rather involved, but if you have questions on that or any of these strategies, you can contact my support team at support@traderscoach.com 24/7.

# 🎯 Flat Bottom Bracketed Market Scan Strategy

This scan is great for building a watch list and can generate some excellent trend trade breakout opportunities for both long and short trades. Figure 22.2 illustrates a NASDAQ 100 scan looking for candidates that are in a bracketed market and are exhibiting high volume.

The definition of a bracketed market is "a market that is stuck in a price range between an identifiable *support* and *resistance* level." On a chart, a bracketed market will be seen as a sideways (horizontal) set of price bars that stay more or less in the same price range. New trends often break out of these bracketed markets.

**Flat Bottom Bracketed Market Scan Strategy Steps:**

1. **Your Market of Choice.** Identify the financial market you want to scan.
2. **Funnel Computer Scan.** Set your scan criteria, put the market symbols of choice into the funnel, and run a computer scan to narrow down the larger list. Look for bracketed markets that have at least *20 price bars* before considering them for a potential trade based on bracketing the high and low of the channel. For higher probability trades, you can set the scan to be more than 20 price bars, but that will yield fewer candidates.
3. **Opportunity List.** Results from the computer scan make up the candidates on your initial opportunity list.
4. **Chart Review Filter.** Visually review and analyze each chart generated by your computer scan to filter out low probability trades and keep high probability ones. Also, the longer and narrower the bracket on your chart, the stronger the probability that it will break out. You can also use Elliott Wave, an advanced technique, as a filter in determining if there is a high probability of breaking out into an impulsive Wave 3 or Wave 5.
5. **Trash.** Discard any low probability trades that are not viable.
6. **Watch List.** Put high probability trades that are close, but not yet ready to go live, on your watch list for the next review session.
7. **Immediate Live Trade.** Pull the trigger and enter high probability trades that are ready to go live. Implement all of your rules, including risk control. Draw a line at the top and bottom of the bracketed channel of each chart. Then place your long trade entry one tick above the upper line and place your short trade entry one tick below the lower line. When the market breaks the bracket and begins to trend, either long or short, you can enter your trade.

For investors and position traders, markets can bracket for weeks and even months, so you don't want to be stuck wasting time in these bracketed markets.

**Remember: Don't tie up your money in bracketed or range bound markets.**

Instead, monitor several markets and instruments simultaneously while they are in a bracket. This way you have a continual stream of trades that are ready to act on when they break out.

For day traders, bracketed markets can last from 20 minutes to hours depending on the time frame you choose. For day traders, the price movement is faster than for position traders or investors, so there is less time in waiting for a set up.

See Figure 22.4, a daily Tesla chart from February 2013 to November 2013. The period from February to March had a narrow flat bottom bracketed market that led to an exceptional breakout into an Elliott Wave 3 through the end of September. Also notice the OWL, Optimum Wave Locator ribbon, at the bottom of the chart, which illustrates the histogram pattern of this move.

It is clear to see that scanning for flat bottom bracketed markets can yield amazing results, in this case it was Tesla in 2013.

## 🎯 Breakout Scan Strategy

Breakout scans are designed to catch a new trend in the beginning so that you can maximize your gain. With trends only occurring 30% of the time, this scan helps you to enter an already existing trend so that you don't waste your time waiting in a bracketed market.

Figure 22.5 shows a scan of the NASDAQ 100 that is looking for either bullish or bearish breakouts. The scan was produced using the Turbo Scanner (by TradersCoach.com) on the NinjaTrader charting platform using the Market Analyzer feature.

Notice the three columns of data: (1) Instrument, (2) Description, and (3) Turbo Scanner. When an instrument meets the criteria of a breakout, it is indicated in the Turbo scanner as either a bear or a bull breakout. This scan was set to look for breakouts that occurred after at least 20 price bars.

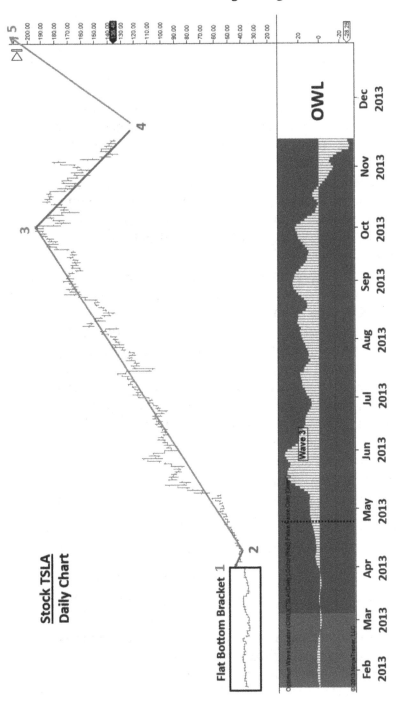

**Figure 22.4** Flat bottom bracket and catching Wave 5 example. This Tesla daily chart from 2013 illustrates how the flat bottom channel scan can identify potential huge trend breakout trades. Notice how from February to March the chart is bracketing in a narrow sideways channel and then begins to break out in April with a bullish uptrend and continues into an Elliott Wave 3 huge move through the end of September. This chart also shows how to catch Wave 5 by estimating the end of Wave 4.

SOURCE: NinjaTrader (www.ninjatrader.com)

# What Is a Bracketed Market?

A bracketed market is one that is stuck in a price range between an identifiable *support* and *resistance* level. On a chart, it will be seen as a sideways set of price bars that stay more or less in the same price range. New trends tend to break out of these bracketed markets. But don't jump in too early and get trapped in a bracketed market.

A bracketed market can go by many names, including choppy, consolidating, range-bound, sideways, nontrending, channeling, trendless, side trending, sleepy, drunk, messy, and a few not listed here.

The psychology of bracketed markets is that, by their very nature, they cannot last forever. They become increasingly unstable with time. Some traders view a bracketed market as a stabilization of price. But in fact, this type of market becomes increasingly unstable the longer it continues.

During the initial formation of a bracketed market, traders are undecided as to value, and the price oscillates. If this bracketed condition continues, perceptions of the asset's value remain the same until new information enters the market to change these perceptions.

The longer or more mature the bracket is, the more significant the new breakout trend will be. While the market waits for new information to arrive, the consolidation becomes narrower and narrower.

**This is where new trends are born.**

And just as important as the length of time the bracket continues is the volatility of prices in recognizing the end of the consolidation before a new trend emerges.

Note that not all significant trends emerge from market brackets. But if you recognize a consolidation in the market, the potential is great for a trend to emerge.

*(continued on next page ...)*

*(... continued from previous page)*

Which is why trend traders use this strategy. By scanning for bracketed markets, they have a watch list of new trends that are waiting to be born. Again, patience is important, since statistically trends only occur about 30% of the time. Leaving you in a bracketed market and waiting for the trend to begin occurs the other 70% of the time.

| Instrum | Description | TURBO Scanner |
|---------|-------------|---------------|
| BIIB | Biogen Idec Inc | Bear Breakout |
| COST | Costco Wholesale Corporation | Bear Breakout |
| GILD | Gilead Sciences, Inc. | Bear Breakout |
| INCY | Incyte Corp. | Bear Breakout |
| MDLZ | Mondelez International, Inc. | Bear Breakout |
| MNST | Monster Beverage Corporation | Bear Breakout |
| NTAP | Network Appliance, Inc. | Bull Breakout |
| ROST | Ross Stores Inc. | Bear Breakout |
| SBUX | Starbucks Corporation | Bear Breakout |
| SPLK | Splunk Inc. | Bull Breakout |

**Figure 22.5** This scan of the NASDAQ is looking for either bullish or bearish breakouts. The scan was produced using the Turbo Scanner (by TradersCoach.com) on the NinjaTrader charting platform using the Market Analyzer feature. Notice the three columns of data: (1) Instrument, (2) Description, and (3) Turbo Scanner. When an instrument meets the criteria of a breakout, it is indicated in the Turbo Scanner as either a bear or a bull breakout.
SOURCE: NinjaTrader (www.ninjatrader.com)

### Breakout Scan Strategy Steps:

1. **Your Market of Choice.** Identify the financial market you want to scan.
2. **Funnel Computer Scan.** Set your scan criteria, put the market symbols of choice into the funnel, and run a computer

scan to narrow down the larger list. Look for instruments that have already broken out of a bracketed pattern of more than 20 price bars.

3. **Opportunity List.** Results from the computer scan make up the candidates on your initial opportunity list.

4. **Chart Review Filter.** Visually review and analyze each chart generated by your computer scan to filter out low probability trades and keep high probability ones. For these breakouts, the longer the bracketed market and the narrower the channel, the more likely the breakout trend will be significant.

5. **Trash.** Discard any low probability trades that are not viable.

6. **Watch List.** Put high probability trades that are close, but not yet ready to go live, onto your watch list for the next review session.

7. **Immediate Live Trade.** Pull the trigger and enter the high probability trades that are ready to go live. Implement all of your rules, including risk control.

The chart on Figure 22.6 shows a bullish breakout trade example. Notice the horizontal lines that identify the top and bottom of the channel, which is more than 20 price bars. When the price bar breaks above the top of the channel, it signals the entry of a bullish trade.

The next chart on Figure 22.7 shows a bearish breakout trade example. Notice the horizontal lines that identify the top and bottom of the channel, which is more than 20 price bars. When the price bar breaks below the bottom of the channel, it signals the entry to a bearish trade.

## Now Go Scan Something!

Next step is for you to go scan something and begin your ongoing watch list. If scanning is new for you, this will be a turning point in your trading and investing career because, from this point forward, you will always have a constant flow of new candidates to consider acting on.

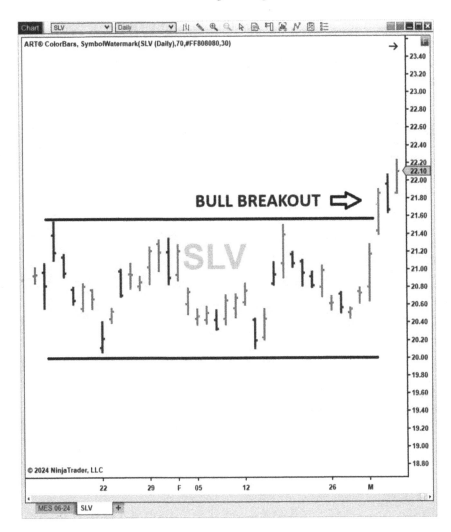

**Figure 22.6** Bull Breakout Trade Example. On this daily chart of SLV, you can see the horizontal lines that identify the top and the bottom of the channel. When the price bar breaks out of the channel, it signals the entry to a bullish trade.

SOURCE: NinjaTrader (www.ninjatrader.com)

NOTE: The Breakout Scan is different than the Flat Bottom Bracketed Market Scan. Although they both focus on bracketed markets, the breakout scan generates more immediate trade setups than the flat bottom scan which is excellent for building a strong watch list

Remember, when you have this constant supply of opportunities, you will never settle for mediocre trades. Instead, you will only choose the best of the best, which will improve your overall performance.

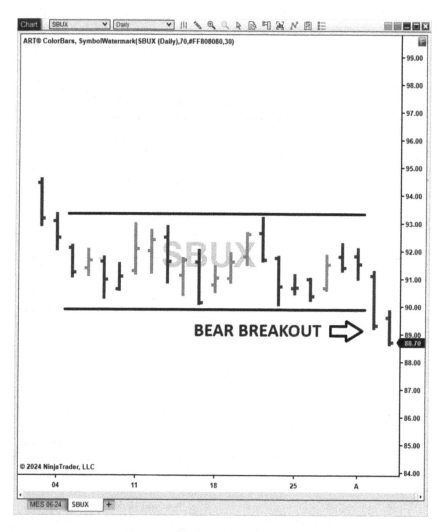

**Figure 22.7**   Bear Breakout Trade Example. On this daily chart of SBUX, you can see the horizontal lines that identify the top and the bottom of the channel. When the price bar breaks out of the channel, it signals the entry to a bearish trade.
SOURCE: NinjaTrader (www.ninjatrader.com)

# Chapter 23

# Building Your Watch List

**B**uilding a rich watch list is the natural result of a well thought-out scanning routine. Invariably, your computer scans will deliver high probability opportunities that are close to being ready, but not quite there yet. When this happens, they are diamonds in the rough, and you can put them right on your watch list.

To a less skilled craftsman, who may not see the possibilities, these gems might get lost or tossed. For you though, when these gems are safely saved on your manageable watch list, you can patiently wait until the ideal time to pull the trigger. A rich watch list is priceless.

Now that we've covered specific scanning strategies in the last chapters, let's fine-tune the entire process, including how to build a strong watch list.

## Watch List Essentials

A watch list is a group of instruments or symbols that a trader or investor monitors for emerging opportunities. After you conduct your initial scans, you can put the opportunities that are close but not quite ready onto your watch list. Many brokerages and financial charting platforms allow for easy construction and viewing of watch lists.

This feature can be helpful in that when you click on a symbol on the watch list, you immediately pull up a current chart of that instrument. If you have customized your chart templates, you can instantly do a visual chart review to see where each symbol on your list currently stands.

For example, my chart templates are set up to show three time frames so that I can visually determine if my primary time frame is supported by the current higher and the current lower time frame. Multiple time frame analysis is one of my most effective filters. You can learn more about how to use this method in the *Advanced Techniques*, Appendix A section at the back of this book.

Plus, when using brokerage and financial charting platforms for your watch list, they often can send alerts via text message or email when certain changes in criteria occur. This timely information can enable you to get in at the best price ahead of the herd. Depending on how robust you want your watch list technology to be, both paid and free models are available through a variety of financial websites.

An organized watch list is the best watch list. You may find it helpful to create a number of watch lists so that it is easier to focus on one thing at a time when doing your visual chart reviews.

**You can have several watch lists:**

- Markets Indexes such as NASDAQ 100, S&P 500, etc.
- Market Sectors such as Energy, technology, etc.
- Large, mid, small cap stocks
- Setup strategies such as breakout, Elliott Wave, etc.
- Specific types of markets such as stocks, bonds, mutual funds, ETFs, cryptos, etc.
- Bullish versus bearish entries

Novice beginners may be tempted to track as many stocks and have as many watch lists as possible. In this case, less is more; don't try to track everything at once. Focus on the best of the best and use your filters to trim down your lists to a manageable group of genuinely viable candidates.

## Love My Watch Lists!

Lists help me stay on track and get the job done without missing anything. Once I jot down my list, it's locked in, and important details don't get lost. Some folks like handwritten lists, and some prefer digital lists on their phones and computers. If you aren't a watch list person right now, get in the habit of creating one. Your trading and investing efficiency are sure to improve.

## Filter and Clean Your Lists

List hygiene is crucial to your scanning success. It's important to filter out and clean your watch list and opportunity lists regularly. Basically, you are cleaning out the bad charts and keeping only the good charts.

Think of how a HEPA air filter takes out all the bad allergens and dust particles from the air. Your respiratory health improves, and you can breathe easier. With scanning, it is exactly the same (see Figure 23.1).

**Figure 23.1** Dedicate yourself to cleaning out bad charts from your opportunity and watch list by using chart review filters. You'll find a number of good filters to start with in this chapter. Just know that filtering out weak trades will result in healthier trading and investing profits. It's no different than using a HEPA filter to clean the air, so you maintain better respiratory health.
SOURCE: Photo 72743179 Filter @ Vchalup Dreamstime.com

The best way to clean out the bad charts is to do a visual chart review and use filters to determine if each chart is up to your standards or not. The following visual chart analysis filters are a good starting point.

1. **Reward-to-risk ratio good?** When entering a trade, determine if it is worth taking the risk. First determine the target zone using Fibonacci or another method, then determine the stop-loss exit. Once you know how much the risk is and how much reward is, you can determine the risk-to-reward ratio. Don't take a trade that doesn't have at least a 2-to-1 reward-to-risk ratio. This means you have the potential to earn $2 reward for every $1 risk if the trade gets stopped out.

2. **Is there enough liquidity and volume?** Depending on the time of day, or on seasonality, and other factors, there may be low liquidity for the instrument you are looking at. This can be costly and comes with risk. Evaluate the current liquidity to be sure it is adequate for a good fill. And for some set ups, confirm that there is enough volume to make the set up valid.

3. **Is the current volatility good for your strategy?** Each strategy performs differently in varying market conditions. Know your strategy and whether it performs better in higher or lower volatility and then make sure the best conditions are present for your approach.

4. **Is the estimated time to reach the target okay?** Tying up your money in a stagnant or bracketed market can be costly. Determine whether you are comfortable with a long-term trade or investment, or if you prefer short-term moves.

5. **Multiple time frame analysis, are conditions favorable?** By looking at the activity on the higher and the lower time frames, you can trust and verify that the activity on the primary time frame is confirmed. You can see the big picture of the market to determine if your primary time frame agrees with the time frames above and below.

6. **Could any calendar events affect the trade?** This affects day traders more than investors. Look for any big announcements, earnings reports, FOMC meetings, etc. that could affect the overall strategy by gapping up or down, which could cause a stop out.

Generally, the market reaction to these events is a wild card and very unpredictable. See Figure 23.2.

7. **Is the trend exhausted and too late to get in?** Using Elliott Wave or other types of technical analysis, you can estimate the target for when a trend will end. If your entry point is toward the end of an exhausted trend, it may be too late to get in.

8. **Is the chart pattern clear or messy**? Last but not least, if the chart is messy and unclear, move on to another chart.

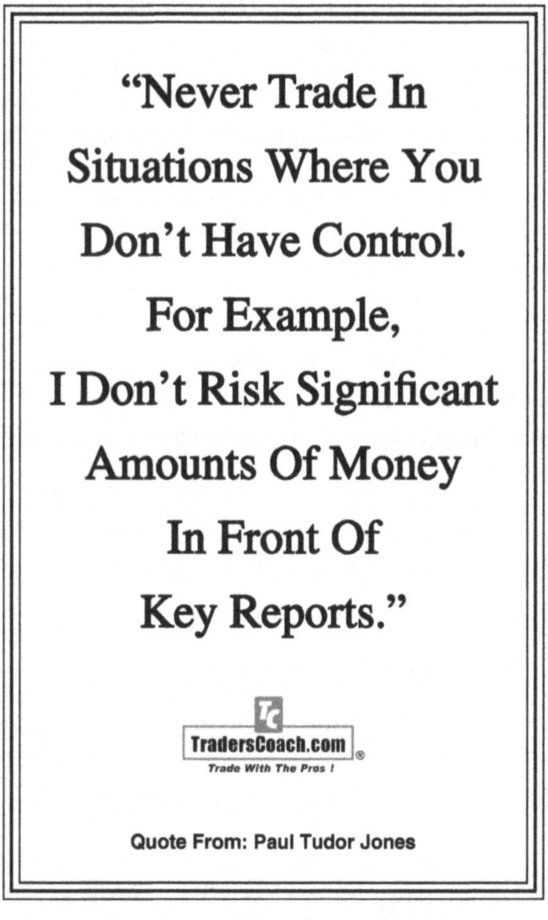

> ## "Never Trade In Situations Where You Don't Have Control. For Example, I Don't Risk Significant Amounts Of Money In Front Of Key Reports."
>
> **TradersCoach.com** ®
> *Trade With The Pros !*
>
> **Quote From: Paul Tudor Jones**

**Figure 23.2** MINI POSTER—CONTROL—An economic calendar that lists important dates for key reports, FOMC meetings, and the like can be a wealth of information. You have no control over the market's unpredictable reaction to these events. Quote from Paul Tudor Jones.

Everyone develops favorite filters, and this list has many of mine. The more practice you get in using them the faster and better you will get at cleaning your lists.

## ◎ Visually Review and Analyze Your Charts from Your Watch List

It's important to review and analyze each chart on your watch list on a regular schedule. Do this manually and visually, to see if the patterns are clear and compelling.

**What may have been on your watch list yesterday, or two days ago, or last week, may not stay on your watch list today.**

Don't skip the visual review step, it is crucial. After completing a visual review of each chart, determine which of the following three categories the chart falls into:

1. **Trash.** Low probability, discard as no longer viable.
2. **Watch List.** High probability, close but not ready to take a live trade, stays on watch list.
3. **Immediate Live Trade.** High probability, ready to go live, pull the trigger.

Also, if the patterns are not clear and instead look like spaghetti, move on to the next chart. Or if the setup is close but you could get a better entry after a pull back, keep the trade on your watch list for later.

**Remember: Don't force the trade.**

Typically, you will be generating computer scans and doing the sorting and sifting process on a regular basis, which means your watch list can be your best friend when properly maintained.

## Scanning Recap and Flowchart

In the last few chapters, we've covered a lot of ground on how to effectively scan and find the needle in the haystack. Since there are a number of moving parts, it seemed like a good idea to give you a picture, which hopefully is worth a thousand words. See Figure 23.3.

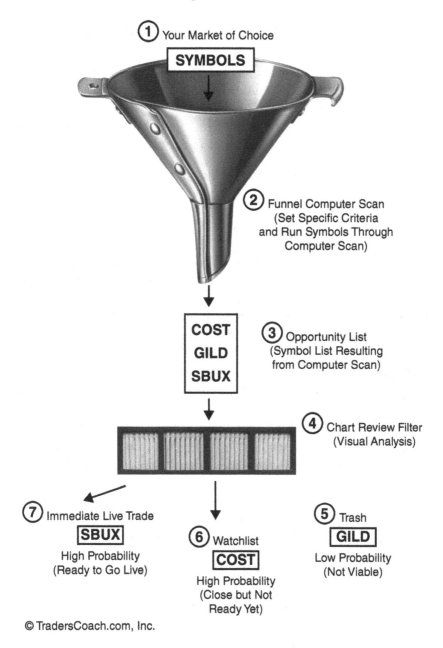

© TradersCoach.com, Inc.

**Figure 23.3** To find a steady stream of high probability trades you need an effective scanning routine. This flow chart is for illustration purposes and shows how the NASDAQ market scan from Chapter 22 on Figure 22.5 looking for the criteria of breakouts, produced a live SBUX trade as shown in Figure 22.7 also from Chapter 22.
SOURCE: © TradersCoach.com, Inc.

## Scanning Flowchart Example and Explanation

The chapters in "Step V, Scan for Opportunities" in this book are designed to give you a foundation so that you can develop your own scanning strategies. Figure 23.3 is a flowchart that illustrates the seven steps in the scanning process. What follows is a thorough explanation of each of the steps in this flowchart.

### Seven Step Scanning Flowchart:

1. **Your Market of Choice:** NASDAQ.
2. **Funnel Computer Scan:** Criteria set as looking for breakouts both bull and bear.
3. **Opportunity List:** In this illustration, the symbol list that resulted from the computer scan included COST, GILD, and SBUX. See actual scan in Figure 22.5 from Chapter 22.
4. **Chart Review Filter:** Upon the visual analysis and chart review, each of the symbols was categorized as either trash, watch list, or immediate live trade.
5. **Trash:** The GILD chart was reviewed, and not enough profit potential was found, so it was filtered out and put into the trash category.
6. **Watch List:** The COST chart was reviewed, and enough profit potential was found, but a better entry price could be attained by waiting for a pullback. Therefore, it was put into the watch list category.
7. **Immediate Live Trade:** The SBUX chart was reviewed, enough profit potential was found, and the entry was ideal. It qualified as an immediate live trade. See Figure 22.7 from Chapter 22.

This flow chart example shows you the methodical steps involved in a well thought-out scanning routine. The more you practice these steps, the more automatic they will become.

# Step VI

# Manage the Trade

# Chapter 24

# It Ain't Over Till It's Over

Once you've pulled the trigger and your trade is live, that's when the real work begins. Managing the trade and your emotions is an acquired skill set. But with experience it gets easier and becomes second nature.

The most important thing to remember is that until you close out a trade, "It ain't over till it's over." (See Figure 24.1 and Figure 24.2.) In the sports world, this is a common phrase because you really don't know the outcome of any game or any trade until "it's over."

**Anything is possible, in sports, trading, and in life.**

So, if your emotions are generating fear or anxiety, the reality is that there is no reason for negative feelings. The trade is a success until it actually gets closed out at a loss. And even if it gets closed out at a loss, you must remember that losing trades are all part of the game in any successful plan.

When a trade is live, emotions can disrupt a well-thought-out plan if the trader does not have a strong mindset. The work involved in developing one's mindset, and in managing the trade, is crucial in attaining consistent long-lasting success.

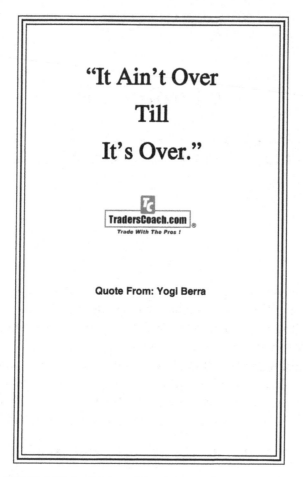

**Figure 24.1**  MINI POSTER—IT AIN'T OVER—Don't let emotions distract you from effectively managing the trade. Remember, the trade isn't over until you close it out for a profit or a loss. If there is a stop loss level in your rules, follow it. If your rules say stay in the trade until the target zone, stay in it. Stick to your plan. Quote from Yogi Berra.

## Emotions in Managing the Trade

The list of emotions that can interfere with trade management is an interesting and sometimes unexpected one. Coping with these emotions if you haven't experienced them can be a challenge, but here are a few tips.

### Trade Management Emotions

1. **Fear.** The trade catapults in your direction, and you fear losing the profit that the trade has quickly given you. If your rules tell

**Figure 24.2** The Yankees All Star Yogi Berra is credited with saying "It Ain't Over Till It's Over." During his 19 seasons playing baseball for the major leagues, and for many years after, he is famous for his "Yogi-isms." This one in particular is a perfect lesson for traders and investors in understanding that until a trade or investment is closed, it most certainly "ain't over."
SOURCE: Photo 60181160 Yogi Berra @ Jerry Coli Dreamstime.com

you to, you can scale out a portion of the trade to lock in profit. This will alleviate the fear of loss.

2. **Panic.** When you enter a trade, and it immediately goes against you there can be a knee-jerk panic to get out of the trade. If your stop is not hit, stay in the trade.

3. **Anxiety.** The trade is meandering at a loss level but has not been stopped out. Anxiety can set in, and you want to do something, anything. The discomfort of sitting and waiting for the trade to evolve is unbearable. In this case, set alarms to notify you of needed actions. And then find something else to do.

4. **Impatience.** If it is difficult for you to sit still and watch a trade evolve, test out a shorter and faster time frame. You may need more action if you have any version of an attention deficit disorder.

5. **Regret.** If you pull the trigger and immediately regret the trade, you may need to do more testing to prove to yourself that your rules in fact give you an edge. The doubt and regret may reflect a lack of confidence in yourself and your approach.

6. **Surprise.** A gap or unexpected event throws your trade off completely. Your stop loss is hit, but you want to stay in the trade because the unexpected event should not have happened. Therefore, you think it must be a temporary anomaly. Resist any temptation to ignore your stop-loss exit. Exit regardless of how surprising the market activity may be.

7. **Greed.** The trade is going against you, but you want it to be a winner, so you add on to a losing position. Your greed convinces you that you have the power to force the market to do what you want. Never double down; it is a recipe for disaster.

8. **Anger.** You accidentally hit the sell button when you meant to hit the buy button. This scenario applies to any other operator errors that you can't believe were possible. The anger prevents you from thinking straight; you are tempted to stay in the position with the error. Resist that temptation; terminate the trade immediately.

9. **Tilted.** Trader's sometimes refer to emotional trading as "tilted". When stuck in a period of emotional trading, take a break. Walk away from the screen, clear your head and get back in the zone.

Again, when managing the trade, you are always honing your trader's mindset. Be aware of emotions that arise that may be new and possibly unpleasant. Work on understanding what has triggered these emotions and on how to prevent them from disrupting your plan.

## Yogi Berra's Lifetime in Baseball and the Beauty of His "Yogi-isms"

Lawrence Peter Berra was born May 12, 1925, in St. Louis, Missouri, to Italian immigrants Pietro and Paolina Berra. His professional Major League baseball career began in 1946 as a catcher for the New York Yankees at the age of 21.

*(continued on next page...)*

*(...continued from previous page)*

As a player, Berra was with the Yankees (American League) and later the New York Mets (National League) for a total of 19 seasons. Though not as famous as some of the players of his time, like Joe DiMaggio, Micky Mantle, and Jackie Robinson, some of his stats were better than all of them combined. After his days as a player, he even went on to successfully coach and manage the New York Mets.

Yogi won more World Series rings than any other player in history, a total of 10. He caught three no-hitters including the only no-hitter in a World Series in 1956 pitched by Don Larsen. He won the American League's Most Valuable Player Award three times (1951, 1954, and 1955) and was an All-Star 15 consecutive times. Elected into the National Baseball Hall of Fame in 1972, Yogi remains one of baseball's most entertaining and loved figures.

With all his talents and accomplishments, he may best be known for his "Yogi-isms." They often took the form of an apparent witty contradiction, but always with underlying humor and wisdom.

**Here are some of my favorites:**
- It ain't over till it's over.
- When you come to a fork in the road, take it.
- I tell the kids, somebody's gotta win, somebody's gotta lose. Just don't fight about it. Just try to get better.
- Slump? I ain't in no slump . . . I just ain't hitting.
- No one goes there nowadays, it's too crowded.
- If the world were perfect, it wouldn't be.
- I never said most of the things I said.

Yogi wasn't flashy, yet he always got the job done with professionalism. A lesson to be learned is that it is important to focus on developing the skills needed to succeed instead of being drawn to the shiny objects that distract us.

## Psychology of the Right Side of the Chart

How do you manage the emotions associated with the right side of the chart? The uncertainty as a trade unfolds can be difficult to process. This is the core of our job, to emotionally manage the right side of each chart.

When we enter a trade and have a set of rules that give us an edge, it is a probabilities game. So, with a strong mindset along with proven rules that give you an edge, the right side of the chart should not present any emotion at all. We should be able to execute every trade like a machine and reap the benefits.

**With experience, you can become a machine.**

If you are new and do not have enough experience in every type of market situation, it may take time to execute every trade like a machine. So, work on developing the confidence to be emotionless, to carry out your rules and stick to the plan.

## Like a Moth to the Flame

When managing a trade, there can be an impulse to do the wrong thing, such as to not follow one's rules. For inexperienced traders, when a trade doesn't behave as expected and they get stopped out, it may seem less painful to just ignore the stop-loss exit. This is like a moth being attracted to a bright light.

Invariably, moths are irresistibly drawn to something that is harmful, and yet they can't help themselves. It is similar with novices who don't get out of a trade when their stop-loss exit tells them to. This behavior is a perfect example of lack of discipline. Again, they can't help themselves.

**Every large loss starts as a small loss.**

Don't be like a moth to a flame. Follow your stop-loss exits to the letter and get out when you are supposed to. Hesitating for even a moment can be disastrous, and by hesitating you are likely to get burned.

## Instrument Flight Rules—IFR—Follow Your Instruments

Back in the 1980s, while in the Navy, I got my private pilot's license at the Navy Flying Club in Coronado, California. (See Figure 24.3.) Obtaining my license along with some IFR training enabled me to read my flight instruments in order to pilot the aircraft safely.

Things are not always as they seem when flying. Clouds, fog, rain, and other weather conditions can limit visibility and prevent you from seeing the horizon. During these conditions, pilots often experience *spatial disorientation* and are literally unable to determine the orientation of their plane.

My flight instructor trained me to understand this firsthand, by blindfolding me while in flight and then turning the plane upside

**Figure 24.3** That's yours truly with my Cessna before taking off for flight from North Island Coronado in San Diego, California, circa 1980. The lessons learned in getting my private pilot's license prepared me for navigating through weather conditions with limited visibility. When you know how to read your instruments and indicators, you will never fly blind.

down. That's right, I couldn't tell the orientation of the aircraft regardless of whether it was right side up, upside down, or headed toward the ground.

When you are in a live trade or investment, it is imperative to rely on your instruments and indicators just as a pilot does. Depending on your rules, you can rely on technical indicators such as price, volume, and momentum. You may also be charting your course based on a number of fundamental instruments such as earnings, market share, and seasonality.

Every trader and investor in the markets has a varying degree of training, expertise, and skill. Mastering your instruments will put you at the head of the pack.

# Chapter 25
# Trade Management Strategies

**M**ost trade management strategies are only as effective as the individual implementing them. Meaning, if you have not developed a strong mindset, it can be difficult to follow your rules and manage a trade effectively.

If you feel your trader's mindset could be stronger, this may be a good time to revisit the section at the beginning of this book covering developing the trader's mindset. Half of trade management has to do with sticking to the plan, and that requires discipline.

## Living in the Moment

For starters, it is imperative to live in the moment and be aware of the current market. Not the market yesterday or last week or last year. Which brings us to a lesson I've learned and have shared with my students over the years. (See Figure 25.1.)

If our minds stray from the current moment and cause us to focus on our last trade, it can disrupt our trade management abilities.

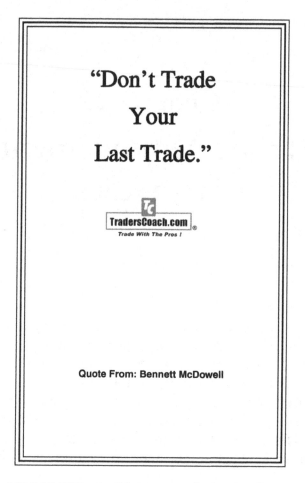

**Figure 25.1** MINI POSTER—LAST TRADE—Whether your last trade was a defeat or a victory, you must live in the present moment. The past has no bearing on this moment; this is the only way to effectively manage the current trade with no emotion and no bias. Quote from Bennett McDowell.

Regardless of whether the past trades were defeats or victories, it is dangerous to focus on the past and not on the present.

For example, many traders who get stopped out, only to find the market then reverse and reach their original target, will feel extreme frustration. So, on the next trade they do not adhere to their stop because of the prior frustration and suffer a large loss. This negative behavior can repeat itself over and over again.

I call this the *trader's ping-pong syndrome*: the trader is trading the current trade based on what happened on the previous trade. Traders suffering from this condition base every new trade on their last trade, thus ignoring their trading rules. Their actions are emotionally based and not rule based.

This is a sure way to end up as a losing trader. Instead, trade your proven tested system and stay with the probabilities and always follow your stop-loss exit.

Another example of this syndrome is where, say, your last trade was a complete disaster, with trade errors causing the trade to close out at a loss, and your confidence is undermined. You are so focused on the previous trade and loss that it's almost a self-fulfilling prophesy that you make the same mistakes again.

These examples illustrate a common dilemma. Remember, the only trade that matters is the one you are in right now. Become an emotionless machine. No ego, no pride, no regret, no doubt, just carry out the plan.

## Set Your Sails for Success

My love of sailing goes back to childhood. My father taught me how to sail, and he said I could single-handedly sail his 35-foot *Allied Sea Breeze* by the time I was eight years old. And I loved every minute of it. We had many adventures up and down the East Coast from Long Island, New York, to Newfoundland, Canada. (See Figure 25.2.)

The most exciting sail we had was from Long Island, New York, to Bermuda circa 1975. During those days and nights, I learned a lot about ocean sailing, unpredictable weather, and adapting to ever changing conditions. Regardless of the ferociousness of the ocean swells or the intensity of any storm, I never feared the ocean.

**I had respect for the ocean, but I never feared it.**

Whenever a halyard broke at the top of the mast in the middle of a storm, I was the guy that shimmied up to fix it. The mast often swayed violently back and forth in those seas, but rather than

**Figure 25.2** That's me and my Dad in our yellow foul weather gear, ready for any type of storm. The ocean is a great metaphor, and just like the financial markets, it can be chaotic and unpredictable. It taught me at an early age to live in the moment and adapt to ever-changing conditions.

fearing the worst, for me it was beautiful to look out over the ocean. My lack of fear came from the confidence that I was in my element. This was my wheelhouse, and I was good at it.

Just as with trading and investing, when you have a set of rules that give you an edge, and the experience that generates confidence in your abilities, you will not fear the markets. Instead, you will have respect for them.

Plus, you will have mastered your tools to navigate the current conditions whether stormy or calm. Just as setting the storm sails when the winds are blowing, you will know how to use the right risk control for each situation.

Most importantly, you will adapt to the current conditions, the here and the now. If a weather report says that a storm is coming, but the skies are sunny, proceed for the current conditions. No storm sails are needed until the winds start kicking up.

If the market is moving upward right now and is bullish, but all logic says that it should be moving downward, go with the reality of the here and now. If it is sunny, but the weather report says a storm is coming, you don't need to wear your foul weather gear until the current conditions actually change from sunny to rainy. Live in the moment.

**Set your sails for the current conditions and for success.**

As you gain experience with the unpredictability of the markets, you will become better at managing every possible scenario. You will have the needed tools onboard and will set the correct sail for the current condition. Remember to have respect and a love of the markets, just as a sailor does for the sea.

## Trade Management Strategies

As your trade progresses and the market unfolds, your rules should guide you every step of the way. If as you fine-tune your rules, you realize that some alterations would make them more complete, you can make those changes after the current trade has closed.

**Trade Management Strategies:**

- **Trailing stops:** Figure 14.2 in Chapter 14 shows how trailing stops develop as the market develops. When a position moves in your favor, you can adjust your stop to lock in profit. Basically, you are tightening the stop as the market moves in your direction.
- **Scaling out:** This is effective in reducing the anxiety when a position moves in your favor quickly. Sometimes the fear of losing a gain creates discomfort and may tempt you to close out of a position. Rather than closing the entire position, it is better to scale out of one third of the position to lock in profit. If you had

three contracts, for example, you would close out one of them for a profit. Then the idea is to let the remaining contracts stay live in an attempt to reach the target zone.

- **Scaling in:** When your position is profitable and you still have a way to go to reach the target zone, you scale in or add on to your position. This strategy enables you to profit even more from a position that has proven itself to be worthy of adding on to.
- **Making it to the target zone:** Impatience can make it uncomfortable to wait for a trade to develop and get to the target zone. Withstanding profit-taking pull backs and corrections in the overall trend can create doubt in the initial analysis. Focus on strengthening your psychology and confidence in the edge that your rules are giving you.
- **Stop-loss exits:** The most common mistake novices make is that they don't follow their stop-loss exit. An overabundance of ego can cause novices to bargain with the markets. They believe they can force the market to do what they want. The reality is that stop losses are part of the game for every trader. The sooner it becomes comfortable to take a small loss and move on, the faster consistent profitability will be attained.
- **Stepping away from the computer:** For day traders, this is a big issue, but not so much for investors and position traders. When there is a live trade on, stepping away from the computer can spell disaster if the market moves swiftly against you. For lunchtime, or when you need a restroom break, or if your better half comes in to ask a question, be sure you have automated triggers in place to manage your trade for you.
- **Double checking your orders:** Mistakes happen, and it is better to catch them early. When I'm working on a home improvement project, I always measure twice and cut once. With my broker, it is the same in placing orders. I take an extra minute to double check all the particulars, the entry, the exit, the trade size, etc. Better safe than sorry.
- **Workspace set up:** Managing a trade is easier when your workspace is customized to your needs. Make sure you have a set up

that provides you with the right technological support and tools, peace and quiet so that you can focus, and access to monitors to see the progress of your trade clearly.

These are a good start to your trade management strategies, but you may find additional strategies that assist you in making your job easier and more successful. Be on the lookout for anything that helps you boost your bottom line.

## 🎯 Expect the Unexpected

The financial markets are never boring, and you must be prepared for the unexpected. The spectrum of events that can throw off a perfectly planned trade are varied, and it is important to plan for them in advance if possible.

### Potential Unexpected Events

1. **Operator Error**. We're all human and believe me, there will be times that you hit the sell button when you meant to hit the buy button. Regardless of the operator error, stay calm and terminate the trade as soon as you realize something is awry. It is not the error itself that can ruin you; instead, it is the reaction to the error that can destroy your confidence and trade management ability.
2. **Market Gap**. Markets can gap unexpectedly right through your stop-loss exit. Do not let sudden market behavior catch you off guard; instead, terminate the position asap.
3. **Market Halt**. During times of manic markets, mechanisms are in place that will halt all activity in the markets. The purpose is to slow down the momentum of a market crash. If you haven't experienced this, be aware that though a rare occurrence, a halt can dramatically affect any open positions. It may even affect your psychology as well. (See Table 25.1.)
4. **Market Closure**. Very similar to a market halt, mechanisms are in place that attempt to slow down a market crash and will completely close the market for the entire day. Again, though a

rare occurrence, they have a significant effect on one's portfolio and psychology. (See Table 25.1.)

5. **Zero Liquidity.** There are a number of zero liquidity examples including the aforementioned *market halt* and *market closure*. (See Table 25.1.) Another example of zero liquidity also occurs when a company has a mass exodus of buyers, and there are only sellers. Enron is a perfect example of this; google it to see the history of Enron in December 2001 when it went bankrupt.

6. **Power Outage.** Brownouts and blackouts are now more common than ever. With the grid overloaded in many areas, it is possible that you may lose power for a short or long period. It is imperative that you have a backup battery on your computer system that gives you a good 20 minutes to close out any positions that you many need to tend to. Have your broker's phone number on hand and a fully charged cell phone if needed.

7. **Power Surge.** To protect your equipment be sure that you have surge protectors in place so that you don't unexpectedly have your computer get fried in a power surge. To lose your computer completely puts you at a huge disadvantage when a live position is open. Again, be sure to have your broker's phone number on hand and a fully charged cell phone if needed.

8. **Unexpected News or Financial Announcements.** When an unexpected FOMC announcement, financial report, news or world events occur, the markets can swiftly and significantly react. These reactions may move the markets dramatically and can affect your position.

9. **Unexpected Price Activity.** As you may have heard before, "past performance does not guarantee future results" meaning that even if your strategy of reading price activity has worked before, it may unexpectedly not work in the future. This can be an anomaly, or a change in market cycle, and can disrupt your mindset.

10. **Margin Call.** A margin call occurs when the percentage of your equity in a margin account falls below the broker's required amount. A margin account contains positions purchased with a combination of one's own money and money borrowed from

the broker. A margin call refers to a broker's demand that you deposit additional funds into the account so that the value of the account rises to a minimum value indicated by the *maintenance requirement*. This can be disastrous if you do not have the funds to meet the requirement and indicates that the position has decreased in value.

11. **Physical Delivery of a Commodities Contract.** The delivery month for a commodity is the month stipulated in a futures contract for cash settlement or for physical delivery. The dilemma can be when you may have inadvertently forgotten about the delivery month and suddenly have a delivery of sugar arrive at your front door, as happened to a friend of mine back in the day. It is a real issue to be aware of.

Personally, I've experienced a number of the aforementioned unexpected events, and no matter what, they are not pleasant to deal with. But you can live to trade another day if you take just a few precautions beforehand or, most importantly, if you keep a cool head amidst any unexpected events and the possible ensuing chaos.

**Table 25.1** The first circuit breaker system (Rule 80B) was instituted on October 19, 1988, by the New York Stock Exchange (NYSE). The levels (of market drop) have changed over the years to reflect the increase in the NYSE value from year to year. This table reflects the latest update from April 9, 2019.

### NYSE CIRCUIT BREAKER SYSTEM (RULE 80B)

| Percent Drop in Market | Time of Drop in Market | Amount of Time Trading Closed |
|---|---|---|
| Level 1: 7% | After 9:30 a.m. ET and before 3:25 p.m. ET | Marketwide halt for 15 minutes |
| Level 2: 13% | After 9:30 a.m. ET and before 3:25 p.m. ET | Marketwide halt for 15 minutes |
| Level 3: 20% | Anytime during day | Marketwide close for remainder of trading day |

This table is intended for educational purposes only and is subject to change. Readers are advised to consult with their broker for current information. Source: Securities and Exchange Commission Release No. 34-85560: File No SR-NYSE-2019-19.

**Table 25.2**   Examples of NYSE Special Closings. This list of closings is a partial list but gives you an idea of the types of events that can trigger a closing.

NYSE SPECIAL CLOSINGS

| Date(s) | Period of Closing (Times Noted in ET) | Reason for Closing |
|---|---|---|
| July 30, 1914, to Dec. 12, 1914 | Market completely closed for 4 months | Closed pending outbreak of World War I. |
| June 13, 1927 | Closed all day | Charles Lindbergh parade for first transatlantic flight from New York to Paris |
| Feb. 20, 1934 | Opened at 11:00 a.m. | Delayed opening due to severe snowstorm |
| Nov. 22, 1963 | Closed at 2:07 p.m. | Assassination of President John F. Kennedy |
| July 7, 1969, to Sept. 26, 1969 | Closed at 2:30 p.m. every day for more than 2 months | Paperwork crisis |
| July 22, 1969 | Closed all day | US Apollo 11 spacecraft landed first man on moon |
| July 14, 1977 | Closed all day | Blackout in New York City; no electricity |
| Mar. 30, 1981 | Closed at 3:17 p.m. | Assassination attempt on President Ronald Reagan |
| Oct. 23–30, 1987 | Closed at 2:00 p.m. every day for 1 week | Shortened hours after market fall of Oct. 19, and record-breaking volume |
| Nov. 9–11, 1987 | Closed at 3:30 p.m. | Shortened hours due to trading floor and clerical staff strike |
| Oct. 27, 1997 | Closed at 2:35 p.m. for 30 minutes | Circuit breakers triggered for first time, after DJIA dropped 350 points |
| Sept. 11–14, 2001 | Market completely closed for 4 days | Terrorist attack on the World Trade Center in New York City |
| Oct. 29–30, 2012 | Market completely closed for 2 days | Hurricane Sandy flooding and power outages |
| Mar. 23–May 26, 2020 | Trading floor closed with all transactions done electronically | COVID-19 pandemic forced the trading floor to be closed |

This table is intended for educational purposes only.

# Zero Liquidity Is Rare but Possible

There are rare occasions when you will be faced with zero liquidity, meaning there is no volume at all because no one is able to trade. A variety of events can occur to affect an exchange's ability to function, including snowstorms, hurricanes, acts of war, excessive volume that overloads the system, labor strikes, computer failures, and circuit breaker halts and closings. (See Table 25.1 and Table 25.2.)

**Following are few examples of zero liquidity:**
- Marketwide halt and/or marketwide close
- Plummeting stock with all sellers and no buyers such as the Enron bankruptcy debacle in 2001

Typically, when a market halt or market closing occurs, at the market reopen there can be a gap opening.

**Following are examples of gap opens after a market halt or close:**
- World War I closing in 1914: when the market reopened, the DOW surged 4.00%.
- Charles Lindbergh closing in 1927: when the market reopened, the DOW surged 1.00%.
- President John F. Kennedy assassination closing in 1963: when the market reopened, the DOW surged 4.50%
- Apollo 11 moon landing with Neil Armstrong as the first to set foot on the moon in 1969: when the market reopened, the DOW dipped 1.94%
- September 11, 2001, terrorist attack on New York City: when the market reopened the DOW sank 7.10%.

This kind of unexpected event is challenging to be sure. Emotionally it is difficult to sit on your hands and watch all the while having absolutely no control over current events. With that said, it is these types of events that your money management strategies can protect you from to some degree.

## The Pattern Day-trading Rule

When managing your trade, it is important to be aware of the *pattern day-trading* rule (PDT) in the United States because it may affect the management of your trades. This rule is applicable to stock trades on margin but not futures or foreign currency trades. It does not apply to Canada and other countries. A day-trade is defined as a trade that is opened and closed (a round trip) in the same day.

According to FINRA (Financial Industry Regulatory Authority), if you make four or more day-trades over the course of any 5 business days, and those trades account for more than 6% of your account activity over that period, your margin account will be flagged as a *pattern day-trader* account.

For example, under the PDT rule, if you're trading with an account of less than $25,000 and you decide to trade two round trips on a Monday and one more on Tuesday, then you cannot day trade until the following Monday.

If you do day-trade more than this, even inadvertently, you'll be required to maintain a minimum balance of US$25,000 in the flagged account on a permanent basis. If you are short of the minimum at the close of any business day, you'll be limited on the following day to making liquidating trades only.

Basically, when your account is flagged as a *pattern day-trader* account, a number of restrictions will be permanently put on your account. If you want to be a more active trader, or occasionally do a little day trading, be sure to keep tabs on the current applicable limits if your account balance is under the $25,000 amount.

FINRA and the US Securities and Exchange Commission created the pattern day-trader designation after the tech bubble burst back in 2001, with the goal of holding active traders to higher standards than those who trade less frequently.

Again, if you don't want to hold $25,000 in your account at all times, pay close attention to your trades to make sure you don't end up with a flagged account. That said, most brokers allow a one-time exception to clients who may have been flagged as day traders, so long as they make a commitment to not doing so again.

### The PDT rule doesn't apply to a cash account.

The PDT rule only applies to stock margin trading accounts. Margin trading allows you to use leverage, borrowing money from the broker to trade. Say you open a $5,000 margin account with a broker, and the broker allows four times leverage. The buying power is $20,000, but this account will be subject to the PDT rule.

On the other hand, you could open a $5,000 cash account with your broker. The upside of a cash account is that you are not subject to the PDT rule and are not limited to only three round trip day-trades per 5 trading days. The downside is that you will need to wait for your cash to settle, which can take 2 days for most brokers.

**IMPORTANT:** This information is for educational purposes only. Consult with your broker and/or financial advisor before placing any trade.

## The Calm Voice of Chuck Yeager

You can google it; it's a thing. The use of Chuck Yeager's style and tone of voice is legendary in aviation, military command, emergency medical services, and beyond.

Most often you will hear commercial airline pilots say, "Welcome aboard. We are going to climb to 30,000 feet; sit back and enjoy the ride." And on other rare occasions you might hear them say, "This is your captain speaking. We are having engine failure, but not to worry, just remain calm and buckle your seat belts."

### Regardless of what the message is, they are always calm.

Tom Wolfe, in his book *The Right Stuff*, first documented this folksy, calm, West Virginia Chuck Yeager drawl. Regardless of whether Yeager was flying a combat mission in World War II or breaking the sound barrier, his radio voice was the same: calm, unruffled, slowed down, clear, and professional.

**No matter what the markets throw at you, be Chuck Yeager, calm, cool, and collected.**

Keep that voice in your head and your entire temperament calm and unperturbed. Maintain your cool and work the problem. This temperament and mindset will serve you will when managing the trade. See Figure 25.3.

**Figure 25.3**  Chuck Yeager flew many combat missions in World War II shooting down 11 enemy aircraft and also was the first person to break the sound barrier on October 14, 1947. His legendary calm radio style was taught to new pilots in aviation, and later taught in the military and other fields. Regardless of the crisis in the cockpit, Yeager kept his cool. No matter what the financial markets throw at you, it's important to stay calm, cool and collected, just like Yeager.

# Step VII

# Debrief the Trade

# Chapter 26
# Learn from History

Here's where we focus on the debrief. Your trade or investment is now closed and posted at a profit or a loss. Either way, it's time to use your recordkeeping system to record all the details of your transaction(s) so that you can debrief your trade.

Refer to Chapter 15 of this book, and the Money Management section of the companion website that is included with your purchase of this book. Which is chock full of forms and ledgers to help you track your positions, unless you already have a system that is doing that for you. The purpose of this recordkeeping is to learn from your historical performance.

**Following are the historical data you need to track:**
1. Win ratio
2. Payoff ratio
3. Largest winning trade
4. Largest losing trade
5. Average winning trade
6. Largest percentage of drawdown
7. Average percentage of drawdown

Just as with studying world history, it's important to study our financial performance history. It's the only way to improve profitability and consistency. In essence, your recordkeeping books are your personal financial history books. Study them closely; they are your best friend when striving to increase your revenue over time.

> *Those who cannot learn from history are doomed to repeat it.*
> —George Santayana, Spanish-American
> philosopher and poet

The good, the bad, and the ugly, it all has to be put under a microscope so that you can see where things went right and where they went wrong. And it's important to know what outcomes to expect from your trading system.

Figure 26.1 is an annual trading ledger from a student of mine during his first year of trading. This ledger originally appeared in my book *A Trader's Money Management System* (published by John Wiley & Sons), and it shows the macro level of a full year of paper trading.

Not many students will paper trade for a full year. Usually students paper trade for less time, but this is such a good example of the actual journey of a real student and seems like the perfect way to illustrate effective recordkeeping.

**NOTE:** Refer to Chapter 20 where there is a complete set of guidelines on paper trading so that you can test your rules in a safe and effective environment before going to a live account. When paper trading, the debrief is done in the same way as with live trades.

By looking at the big macro picture of the annual trade ledger (Table 26.1) and at the annual equity curve graph in Figure 15.13 (in Chapter 15), you can see that there were ups and downs. No one's equity curve goes straight up all the time.

Next, look a little closer at the micro picture of the monthly statistics. You can really get a feeling of this journey's progression. For example, January started out of the gate with a big net profit for the month of $3,694.08. Immediately followed by February and March, which both posted net losses, bringing the running net profit and loss down to $2,096.62.

A TRADER'S MONEY MANAGEMENT SYSTEM

104

## TradersCoach.com
"The Trader's Assistant"—A Trade Posting and Record Keeping System

YEAR OF LEDGER
2007

### ANNUAL TRADE LEDGER

| MONTH | # TRADES | # WINNING | # LOSING | GROSS $ P/L | COMMISSION $ | NET $ P/L | RUNNING NET $ P/L |
|---|---|---|---|---|---|---|---|
| JANUARY | 46 | 21 | 25 | 4295.00 | (600.92) | 3694.08 | 3694.08 |
| FEBRUARY | 28 | 9 | 19 | (320.00) | (459.74) | (779.74) | 2914.34 |
| MARCH | 13 | 5 | 8 | (615.00) | (202.72) | (817.72) | 2096.62 |
| APRIL | 32 | 14 | 18 | 3345.00 | (524.90) | 2820.10 | 4916.72 |
| MAY | 28 | 9 | 19 | 1062.51 | (325.80) | 736.71 | 5653.43 |
| JUNE | 29 | 7 | 22 | (2600.00) | (325.80) | (2925.80) | 2727.62 |
| JULY | 23 | 8 | 15 | (5.00) | (394.58) | (399.58) | 2328.04 |
| AUGUST | 33 | 14 | 19 | 2837.50 | (275.12) | 2562.38 | 4890.42 |
| SEPTEMBER | 16 | 5 | 11 | 650.00 | (162.90) | 487.10 | 5377.52 |
| OCTOBER | 21 | 9 | 12 | 2237.50 | (191.86) | 2045.64 | 7423.16 |
| NOVEMBER | 33 | 13 | 20 | 3937.50 | (224.44) | 3713.06 | 11'136.22 |
| DECEMBER | 21 | 9 | 12 | 850.00 | (285.98) | 564.02 | 11'700.24 |
| TOTALS: | 323 | 123 | 200 | 15'675.00 | (3974.76) | 11'700.24 | |

| | | |
|---|---|---|
| LARGEST WINNING TRADE OF THE YEAR: $2814.14 | LARGEST WINNING TRADE POSTING CARD #: 297-07 | AVERAGE WINNING TRADE OF THE YEAR: $559.50 |
| LARGEST LOSING TRADE OF THE YEAR: $(621.72) | LARGEST LOSING TRADE POSTING CARD #: 315-07 | AVERAGE LOSING TRADE OF THE YEAR: $(285.59) |

NOTES:

My first year of trading ended well

I am UP 51%

My annual pay-off ratio is: $1.96 to $1.00

My annual win ratio is: 39%

111802

**FIGURE 12.1** Student Annual Trade Ledger On $25,000 Paper Trading Account for 2007, 50.7 Percent Gain.

**Figure 26.1** This annual trade ledger from a student of mine first appeared in my book *A Trader's Money Management System* (published by John Wiley & Sons). It shows a full year of statistics from this student's paper-trading futures account. You can see in the *running net $ profit and loss* column that the student was up $11,700.24 for the year on a $25,000 account. That equates to a 51% return on his money in a 12- month period.

SOURCE: © www.TradersCoach.com

As you can imagine, psychologically, 2 losing months in a row can take the wind out of a trader's sails for sure. April and May posted 2 months of gains, again followed by 2 months of losses in June and July. The month of June posted a net loss of $2,925.80, the largest monthly loss of the year.

And then for the rest of the year, 5 months straight, the equity curve shows a steady increase of the running net profit and loss with not a single losing month. With experience, this first-year trading student was able to refine his approach to attain 5 months of straight winning months. It was his debriefing skills that enabled him to improve his consistency.

**Table 26.1** This is the actual data from my student's annual ledger (see Figure 26.1) in table format, so it is easier to read. On a $25,000 account, he had a 51% ($11,700.24) total net profit. He went from $25,000 to $36,700.24 in 1 year on this paper-trading account. Notice though, there were months of drawdown (see the Net $ P/L Column) before reaching the 51% annual profit, which is normal for any equity curve.

### ANNUAL TRADE LEDGER (FROM STUDENT)

| Month | # Trades | # Wins | # Losses | Gross $ P/L | Comm. $ | Net $ P/L | Running Net $ P/L |
|---|---|---|---|---|---|---|---|
| JAN | 46 | 21 | 25 | 4,295.00 | (600.92) | 3,694.08 | 3,694.08 |
| FEB | 28 | 9 | 19 | (320.00) | (459.74) | (779.74) | 2,914.34 |
| MAR | 13 | 5 | 8 | (615.00) | (202.72) | (817.72) | 2,096.62 |
| APR | 32 | 14 | 18 | 3,345.00 | (524.90) | 2,820.10 | 4,916.72 |
| MAY | 28 | 9 | 19 | 1,062.51 | (325.80) | 736.71 | 5,653.43 |
| JUN | 29 | 7 | 22 | (2,600.00) | (325.80) | (2925.80) | 2,727.62 |
| JUL | 23 | 8 | 15 | (5.00) | (394.58) | (399.58) | 2,328.04 |
| AUG | 33 | 14 | 19 | 2,837.50 | (275.12) | 2,562.38 | 4,890.42 |
| SEP | 16 | 5 | 11 | 650.00 | (162.90) | 487.10 | 5,377.52 |
| OCT | 21 | 9 | 12 | 2,237.50 | (191.86) | 2,045.64 | 7,423.16 |
| NOV | 33 | 13 | 20 | 3,937.50 | (224.44) | 3,713.06 | 11,136.22 |
| DEC | 21 | 9 | 12 | 850.00 | (285.98) | 564.02 | 11,700.24 |
| Totals | 323 | 123 | 200 | 15,675.00 | (3,974.76) | 11,700.24 | |

This table is intended for educational purposes only. No representation is being made that any account will or is likely to achieve profits or losses similar to those discussed.

**Table 26.2**   This is the actual data from my student's trading scorecard (which correlates to Figure 15.14 from Chapter 15) in table format, so it is easier to read. Using a scorecard is incredibly helpful in nailing down all the essential information on your statistics into one easy to read sheet. This is the exact information you will need on your own trades to conduct your macro debriefing.

### TRADING SCORECARD (FROM STUDENT)

| Metric | Annual Results |
| --- | --- |
| Win Ratio | 39% |
| Payoff Ratio | $1.96 |
| Largest Winning Trade | $2,814.14 |
| Largest Losing Trade | $(621.72) |
| Average Winning Trade | $559.50 |
| Average Losing Trade | $(285.59) |
| Largest % of Drawdown | 12% |
| Average % of Drawdown | 6% |
| Total % of Profit / Loss | 50.7% Profit |

This table is intended for educational purposes only. No representation is being made that any account will or is likely to achieve profits or losses similar to those discussed.

Next let's look at this same first-year student's trading scorecard, Table 26.2, which correlates to Figure 15.14 from Chapter 15. These data are the exact data you will need on your own trades in order to conduct your trade debriefing.

Notice how the information on the scorecard is a distillation of the more detailed information on the annual trade ledger. The distilled information from the scorecard is a macro version of the performance as a whole for the entire year. And as you can see, it was a profitable year with a 51% gain on the account.

But if you move down to the more micro version, that being the annual trade ledger, you get much more information to evaluate. Here you get to see the losing months and how the year progressed. Again, the debrief is essential to improve the statistics going forward.

And you can then move down further, to the most micro version, that being the actual individual trade posting cards. Here there are data on not only the profit and loss, but the actual strategies and mindset during each trade.

This is where the real magic can happen, when you discover which strategies and mindsets are creating the winning trades. Conversely, it's useful to see which strategies and mindsets are creating the losing trades. (See Figures 26.2 and 26.3.)

## Importance of Sample Size

When paper trading or live trading, evaluating a strategy or approach, you have to give it enough time and a large enough sample size to be a valid test. Often inexperienced traders will hop from one strategy to another and will not give the strategy enough time to either prove itself or not.

This again comes back to sample size. When conducting your debrief, if you are considering a change in your rules or approach, be sure you have given the current rules enough of a test, or sample size, to make the test meaningful.

## Failures and Mistakes Are the Greatest Teachers

Whatever you call them, mistakes, or failures, they can be the greatest teachers. Ask any successful person and they will probably tell you they failed their way to the top. And the more colossal the failure or mistake, the more you can potentially learn from it.

Trading and investing are no different than any other profession in that you have to persevere to succeed and you have to be willing to take on risk. The inevitable result of taking on risk is to experience failure and to make mistakes. How you deal with failure and making mistakes will determine your ability to do great things.

Many famous and successful people failed and made mistakes before they ever enjoyed success. So, you see, sometimes failure is just the first step toward success. Just watch the Biography Channel for inspiration from great men and women throughout history that proves this very point.

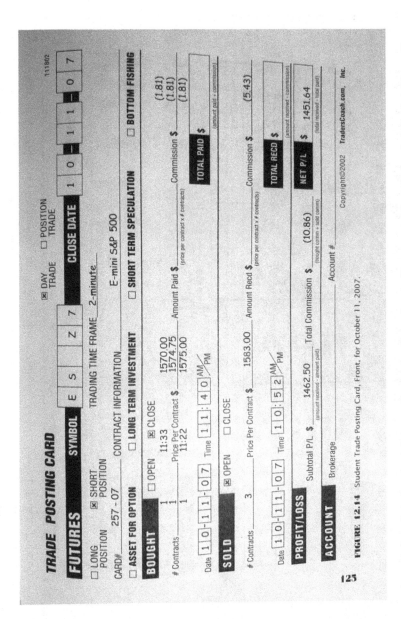

**Figure 26.2**  This trade posting card, Front, from a student of mine first appeared in my book *A Trader's Money Management System* (published by John Wiley & Sons). It shows the ultra-micro level of the trade, that being the actual trade posting card itself.

SOURCE: © www.TradersCoach.com

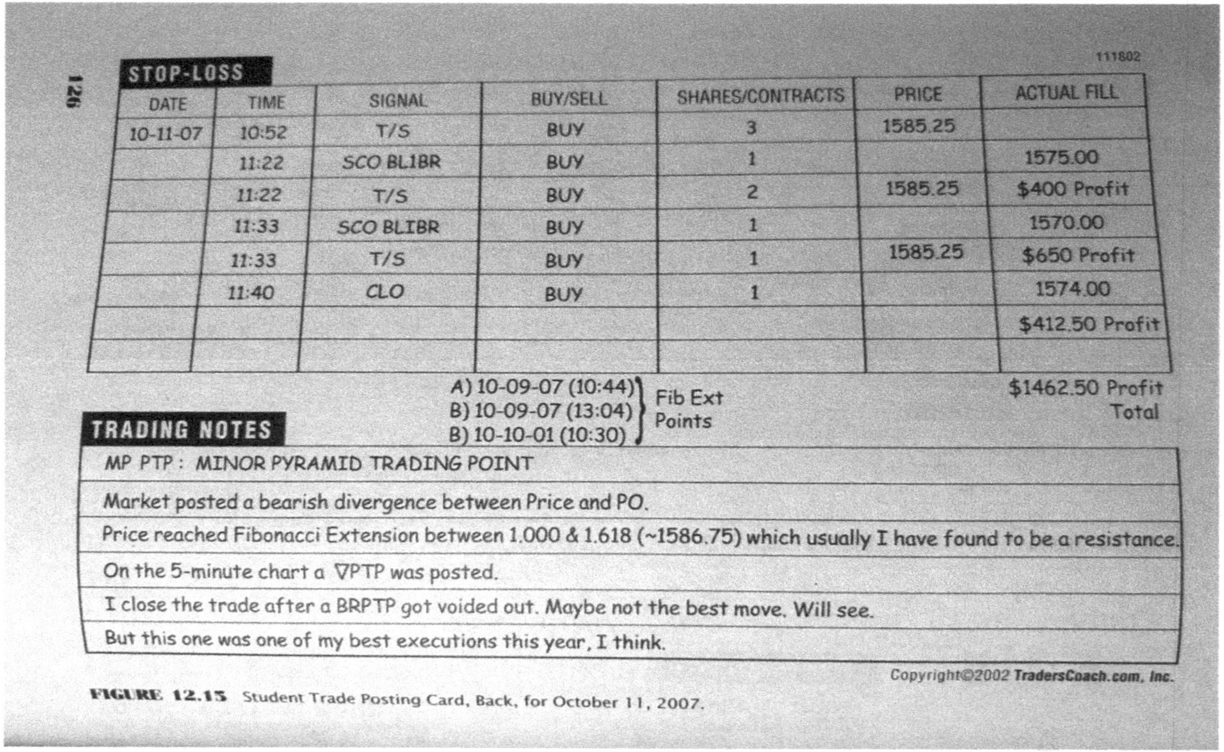

**STOP-LOSS**

| DATE | TIME | SIGNAL | BUY/SELL | SHARES/CONTRACTS | PRICE | ACTUAL FILL |
|------|------|--------|----------|------------------|-------|-------------|
| 10-11-07 | 10:52 | T/S | BUY | 3 | 1585.25 | 1575.00 |
| | 11:22 | SCO BLIBR | BUY | 1 | | $400 Profit |
| | 11:22 | T/S | BUY | 2 | 1585.25 | 1570.00 |
| | 11:33 | SCO BLIBR | BUY | 1 | | $650 Profit |
| | 11:33 | T/S | BUY | 1 | 1585.25 | 1574.00 |
| | 11:40 | CLO | BUY | 1 | | $412.50 Profit |
| | | | | | | $1462.50 Profit Total |

A) 10-09-07 (10:44) ⎫ Fib Ext
B) 10-09-07 (13:04) ⎬ Points
B) 10-10-01 (10:30) ⎭

**TRADING NOTES**

MP PTP : MINOR PYRAMID TRADING POINT

Market posted a bearish divergence between Price and PO.

Price reached Fibonacci Extension between 1.000 & 1.618 (~1586.75) which usually I have found to be a resistance.

On the 5-minute chart a ▽PTP was posted.

I close the trade after a BRPTP got voided out. Maybe not the best move. Will see.

But this one was one of my best executions this year, I think.

126

111802

Copyright©2002 *TradersCoach.com, Inc.*

**FIGURE 12.15** Student Trade Posting Card, Back, for October 11, 2007.

**Figure 26.3** This trade posting card, Back, of Figure 26.2, from a student of mine first appeared in my book *A Trader's Money Management System* (published by John Wiley & Sons). It shows the ultra-micro level of the trade, that being the actual trade posting card itself.

SOURCE: © www.TradersCoach.com

**A Few Examples of Successful Failures:**

- **Henry Ford** failed at five businesses that left him broke before he founded the Ford Motor Company.
- **Thomas Edison** was told by his teachers that he "was too stupid to learn anything," and he made more than a thousand attempts at inventing the light bulb before finally designing one that was commercially viable.
- **Orville and Wilbur Wright** both battled depression and failed repeatedly before ever creating an airplane that could get airborne and stay there.

During your trade debriefings, you are bound to review a trade where you failed and made mistakes. Being human is part of the process. It is important to remember that mistakes and failures are part of the growing and learning process. Henry Ford, founder of Ford Motor Company, shared a valuable insight during an interview in 1929 on this very topic (see Figure 26.4).

## Learn from the Mistakes of Others

In addition to learning from our own mistakes, by searching out the guidance of other experts in our field, we can learn from their mistakes. Case in point is to study other successful traders and investors and to learn as much as we can from their mistakes.

> *Learn from the mistakes of others. You can't live long enough to make them all yourself.*
> —Eleanor Roosevelt, Former First Lady of the United States

Far better to not have to make the mistake firsthand. Although, I've seen that to truly learn some lessons, certain individuals will have to experience the intensity of the mistake themselves prior to genuinely learning from it.

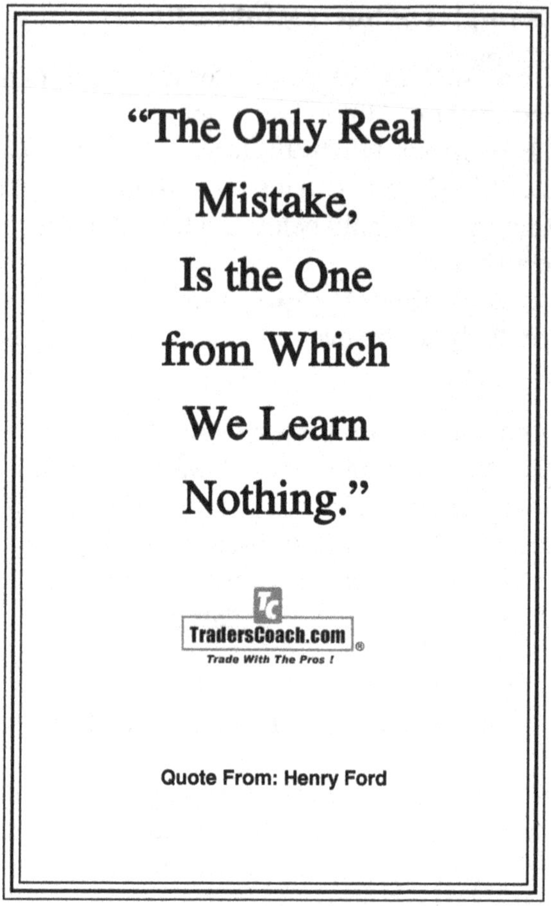

**Figure 26.4**    MINI POSTER—REAL MISTAKE—It's crucial to learn something from every mistake and failure. That is how we will improve and grow as traders and investors. Quote from Henry Ford.

# Chapter 27

# Debriefing Strategies

The process of debriefing your trades and investments involves sifting through the data to determine what worked and what didn't and to see if your goals have been met. Next, it's a matter of focusing on doing more of what worked and doing less of what didn't and reassessing goals going forward.

Studies show that when done correctly, debriefs work. According to Scott Tannenbaum's study, those who practice regular debriefing outperform those who do not by about 25%. In his February 2013 article in the journal *Human Factors*, "Do Team and Individual Debriefs Enhance Performance? A Meta-analysis," he states that debriefs work equally well for teams as they do for individuals.

When comparing teams to individual traders, from personal experience, I can attest to the fact that in my weekly group day-trading room, when the participants in the live online room share thoughts and debriefs about each trade, it genuinely boosts the entire group's performance. And in contrast, when I debrief my own trades, as an individual it also improves my performance.

It stands to reason that if conducting a regular debrief increases our performance by 25%, then we owe it to ourselves to add this to our routine.

## Socrates Was Humble Enough to Admit This

The great philosopher Socrates originally said, "I only know that I know nothing," which has been modernized into a catchier version. (See Figure 27.1.) If everyone in the world were as humble as Socrates, we might have more successful traders and investors.

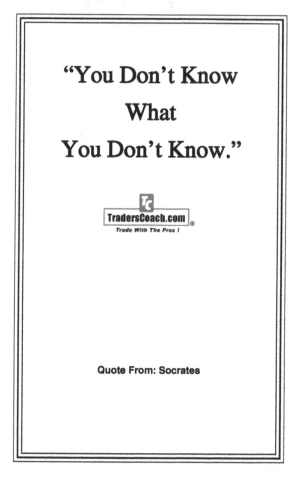

**Figure 27.1**    MINI POSTER—YOU DON'T KNOW—This intentionally redundant phrase is a modern version of a quote from the philosopher Socrates when he said, "I only know that I know nothing." Meaning, we can only work with the information that is available to us now, and there is much information that we just don't know yet. Quote from Socrates.

In truth, being humble as a trader or investor is a valuable quality. It enables you to realize that you can't possibly know everything and to admit that you have a certain amount of ignorance, no matter what your level of success is. This awareness allows you to improve and to actively seek out better or more complete information when needed.

By developing a humble mindset, you will be likely to get more out of your debriefings.

## The Dunning-Kruger Effect Is Real

It is commonly accepted that most active traders lose money in the live markets. Brokerage firms truly know these statistics, since they see all the trades that get processed. Some even say that 90% of all traders are losing money, which is a startling statistic.

**And we have to wonder why.**

It may very well be due to the Dunning-Kruger effect, first described and studied by Cornell University researchers Justin Kruger and David Dunning in 1999. This phenomenon is defined as the tendency of people with low ability in a specific area to *overestimate* their ability. This cognitive bias can be detrimental if not addressed. And we are all terrible at estimating our own ability.

> *Not knowing the scope of our own ignorance is part of the human condition. The problem with it is we see it in other people, and we don't see it in ourselves.*
>
> —David Dunning, American social psychologist
> and college professor

Take a look at the graph in Figure 27.2, which is from the study that Dunning and Kruger conducted. The top line at the left of the chart is the perceived test score, and the bottom line is the actual test score of the participant. Not only did most participants in this study overestimate their performance, but the least competent participants, the ones that scored in the bottom quarter, were the most likely to overestimate themselves.

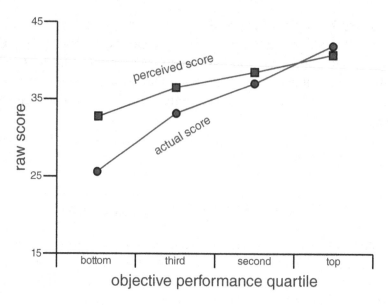

**Figure 27.2**  The Dunning-Kruger effect is an interesting phenomenon where people with the most limited abilities tend to *overestimate* how good they are. It's considered to be a cognitive bias that was first described by Justin Kruger and David Dunning in 1999. (Ironically, in contrast, those with the very top abilities tend to *underestimate* how good they are. See where the two lines cross over.) The top line at the left of the chart is the perceived score, and the bottom line is the actual score of the bottom, third, and second performance quartile.
SOURCE: Phlsph7 httpscommons.wikimedia.orgwikiFileDunning-kruger_effect_-_raw_score.svg

## The less they knew, the more they thought they knew.

It's reasonable then, given the Dunning-Kruger effect study, to expect that novice traders and investors might unknowingly overestimate their skill level. This effect might even apply to those who don't consider themselves novice, and yet have not attained consistent profitability.

Consider the trader that may have had a huge win, but actually just got lucky and didn't use any risk control. They might be overconfident because they just "Don't know what they don't know."

It makes complete sense that they are confident and are feeling knowledgeable because the dollar amount in their account increased. But "what they don't know" is the very thing that will catch them off guard, and possibly wipe out their account in the future.

*This meta-ignorance (or ignorance of ignorance) arises because lack of expertise and knowledge often hides in the realm of the "unknown unknowns."*
—David Dunning, American social psychologist
and college professor

And so here is the conundrum: If you don't know what you don't know, how can you know? Fortunately, there is a solution, and that is to develop *meta-cognitive* skills, which means *thinking about thinking*. This is an essential process to help you determine the best strategies for learning and problem solving as well as knowing when to apply them.

## Make the Leap from Meta-ignorance to Meta-cognition

So how do we go from *meta-ignorance* to *meta-cognition*? First, we have to exercise our brains, as if we were going to the gym, to make them more receptive to new information. Then we have to consciously remain open-minded to the possibility that we might not know everything there is to be known.

**Here are a few ways to exercise your brain:**

- **Block time for self-reflection and debriefing.** Journaling has many science-based benefits. Beyond its many health benefits, it's an incredible tool for meta-cognition. Whether as a weekly review or in another format, make sure to spend some time honestly evaluating your progress and your skills.
- **Use second-level thinking to make decisions**. Instead of jumping to the most obvious conclusion, use second-level thinking by asking yourself, what are some potential blind spots, what information am I missing? Drill down a little deeper.
- **Take lots of smart notes.** It's much easier to notice gaps in our knowledge when we have a way to visualize our knowledge. That's where taking notes comes in handy. By building a

note-taking habit, you will be able to identify thought patterns and mental shortcuts more easily.

- **Be aware of cognitive biases that may cloud your judgment.** For instance, confirmation bias may reinforce the Dunning-Kruger effect by turning wishful thinking into actual beliefs. Learn about cognitive biases and reflect on your own biases when you notice them.

These exercises will help to rewire and strengthen your brain to be open to new information and ideas. As your *meta-cognitive* abilities grow, your critical thinking will become more effective. When faced with obstacles, it will feel more like you are working on a puzzle as opposed to being saddled with a burden.

## The Four Stages of Competence, a Learning Model

By conducting a regular debriefing, you will be *thinking about thinking* and will develop stronger *meta-cognitive* skills, which will enable you to become more competent. Following are the four stages of competence as first outlined in a 1960 textbook *Management of Training Programs,* written by three management professors at New York University.

**The Four Stages of Competence:**

- **Unconscious incompetence:** When you don't know what you don't know. You do not understand or know how to do something and don't yet recognize the deficit. You may deny any usefulness of the skill. You must recognize your own incompetence and the value of the new skill before moving on to the next stage. The length of time you spend in this stage depends on how motivated you are to learn.
- **Conscious incompetence:** When you're aware of what you don't know but haven't learned it yet. You do not understand or know how to do something, you recognize the deficit, as well as

the value of the new skill in addressing the deficit. Making mistakes can be integral to the learning process at this stage.

- **Conscious competence:** When you're gaining knowledge. You know how to do something. It may be broken down into steps, and there is heavy conscious involvement in executing the new skill. However, demonstrating the skill or knowledge requires concentration, and if the concentration is broken, you may lapse into incompetence.
- **Unconscious competence:** When you've mastered something. You have had so much practice with a skill that it has become *second nature* and can be performed easily. As a result, the skill can be performed while executing another task. You may be able to teach it to others.

This learning model, the four stages of competence, has been developed further since its first debut in 1960. Management trainer Martin M. Broadwell called the model *the four levels of teaching* in an article published in February 1969. Paul R. Curtiss and Phillip W. Warren mentioned the model in their 1973 book, *The Dynamics of Life Skills Coaching*. Then the model was used at Gordon Training International by its employee Noel Burch in the 1970s; see Figure 27.3.

During your debriefings, it will be useful to see where you are in the four stages with regard to each of the individual skills that are needed to become consistently profitable. Of course, the book you are reading now has outlined the various skills needed, and you can self-evaluate to determine which skills are the most important areas to work on first.

## Debriefing Strategies

The process of debriefing originated in the military, to mitigate the psychological impact of traumatic war events, alleviate acute stress response, and reduce the frequency of post-traumatic stress disorder (PTSD). The success of the debrief in the military environment immediately crossed over into other fields.

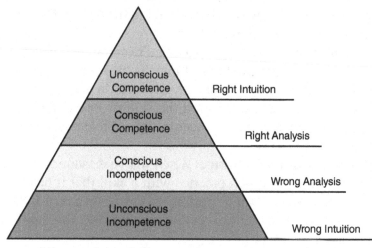

## Hierarchy of Competence

**Figure 27.3** The four stages of competence learning model relates to the psychological states involved in the process of progressing from incompetence to competence in a skill. These stages suggest that individuals are initially unaware of how little they know, or they are unconscious of their incompetence. As they recognize their incompetence, they consciously acquire a skill, then consciously use it. Eventually, the skill can be utilized without it being consciously thought about. That is the mastery level where they have acquired unconscious competence.
SOURCE: Wikimedia – by Tylzael - https://en.wikipedia.org/wiki/Four_stages_of_competence#/media/File:Competence_Hierarchy_adapted_from_Noel_Burch_by_Igor_Kokcharov.svg

In the business world for example, organizational debriefings have become standard operating procedure to increase the effectiveness of both teams and individuals. Debriefs can be instrumental in project management, project acceleration, managing difficult objectives, and innovating novel approaches.

Knowing studies have shown that individuals who debrief outperform those who don't by 25% makes it a no brainer to add this to our trading and investing strategy.

Here is a list of steps to help you implement your debriefing strategies:

- **Schedule a regular time and place.** Make the debriefing a regular part of your routine. Whether in a group or as an individual, you become accustomed to the structure and will expect to regularly debrief every day, week, or month. Eventually, the more you debrief, the more effective the process becomes.

- **Create a learning environment.** Expectations should be set so everyone knows that learning is what's most important, again this applies to both a group and/or individual. Allow all participants to admit to mistakes, make errors, and to be vulnerable. This is how progress and learning will develop. Being humble and honest with others and ourselves is the best way to improve our skills.

- **Review four key questions:**

  1. **What were we trying to accomplish?** Every debriefing should start by restating the objective you were trying to hit. If there's lack of clarity here, the rest of the debriefing will be of little value because you won't know how to judge your success. In the beginning, the first objective is to follow your trading rules. If you did this, did you met your objective? As you grow, your objective may evolve to be a daily or weekly dollar target. Or your objective may be to test a new strategy.

  2. **Where did we hit (or miss) our objectives**? If your objectives and rules are clear, it is a straightforward conversation as to whether did or didn't hit your objectives.

  3. **What caused our results?** This is the root-cause analysis and should go deeper than the obvious, first-level answers. If you were shooting for a $300 per day profit and you averaged at $100 per day profit, dig deep to find the root-cause(s) of the decrease in daily revenue. An effective tool for getting

to the root cause is *the five whys*. For every answer you give, ask why that is the case. By the time you answer the question five times, you've usually uncovered some fundamental issues that are holding you back.

4. **What should we start, stop, or continue doing?** Given the root causes uncovered, what does that mean for the plan changes? Specifically, what should be done next? Now that we know what we know.

- **Codify lessons learned.** Be sure to write down all the lessons learned during the debrief in a usable format, so that you can refer to them later. Maybe create a debrief notebook that you use for each session.

The biggest challenge to debriefing is starting to do it. Once you begin, you quickly realize how natural and intuitive it is. And how beneficial to your bottom line it is.

## Put Your Trades Under a Microscope

Rather than looking at only one number on your broker statement, that of your profit and loss, the most effective debrief is where you actually put your trades under a microscope. It's the only way to understand the real meaning behind that profit and loss number each day, week, month, and year.

**By looking at the microscopic details of each trade you can accomplish the following:**

- Understand causes of operator error.
- Optimize your rules.
- Improve risk management strategies.
- Reduce drawdown periods.
- Identify and reduce overtrading.
- Strengthen your trader's mindset.
- Pivot more quickly when market cycles change.

This process is effective and allows you to see clues that might not have been noticed on first glance. By digging down to the micro level and magnifying the information, you can see ways to do your job better, which ultimately will make you more profitable.

Refer to Chapter 15 of this book to find ways to evaluate the microscopic details of each trade, such as win ratio, payoff ratio, etc. See Figure 27.4.

**Figure 27.4**   Putting every trade under a microscope during the debriefing process is crucial in developing and growing as a trader or investor. Looking at the microscopic details of each trade, such as your win ratio and payoff ratio, will help you become more profitable and consistent.
SOURCE: Photo 38904868 Microscope @ Phartisan Dreamstime.com

# Take Accountability for Yourself and Reject the Victim Mindset

At the conclusion of each debrief, it is important to be accountable. Remember, it is okay to make mistakes; that is how we learn. Resist the temptation to blame the markets, or someone else, for things that have gone wrong. Being humble and clear minded is the quickest way to get to the root cause of any mishap. And that is the quickest way to prevent a mishap in the future.

Ultimately, you must reject the victim mindset to be consistently profitable in the financial markets. If you believe that bad things will keep happening to you and that the world is against you, that belief system will permanently take hold.

### Manifestations of a Victim Mentality:

- Identifying others as the cause for an undesired situation and denying any personal responsibility for one's own circumstances. "It's not my fault."
- Attributing negative intentions to others when there are none.
- Believing that others are generally more fortunate.
- A sense of relief or pleasure from self-pity, "poor me," resulting in sympathy and attention from others.
- Displays of entitlement and selfishness.
- Defensive behavior, even when others are genuinely attempting to help.
- Black and white thinking, no gray area. Circumstances are either good or bad; there is no middle ground.
- Exhibiting learned helplessness.
- Need for recognition that they are being unfairly treated.
- Moral elitism where there is a perception of moral superiority of themselves and moral inferiority of others.
- Lack of empathy because they are concerned with their own deep suffering; they tend to ignore the suffering of others.
- Rumination where there is a focus on the distress rather than on solutions to the distress, sometimes leading to revenge.

A victim mindset often plagues those who were abused and manipulated and were the victim of some trauma in the past. The past trauma may trap an individual into a victim self-image for life. The mindset may have also been taught to them at an early age by family members.

Their psychologic profile includes a variety of feelings and emotions, such as a pervasive sense of helplessness, passivity, loss of control, pessimism, negative thinking, strong feelings of guilt, shame, self-blame, and depression.

As was covered in Chapters 6 through 10 in this book, *Step 2: Develop the Trader's Mindset,* one's mindset will determine the outcome of any trader's profitability. If during the debriefing process you discover that you have underlying issues that are holding you back, it is important to work on healing the past trauma or to seek help from a qualified therapist or coach.

You can see how if you feel the market wronged you or is against you, making you a victim of the atrocities of the markets, there can be significant negative ramifications. It may be uncomfortable to burst the protective bubble of victimhood. Doing so puts you more in control of your destiny, and doing so means you take accountability.

## Go Out and Do Something Great

Okay, now it is time to be brave and fearless and to go out and do something great. It's okay if you make mistakes; that is how you will learn and grow. Debrief on a regular basis so that you can learn from your mistakes by looking at them and dissecting them under a microscope.

> *The only man who makes no mistakes is the man who never does anything. Do not be afraid to make mistakes providing you do not make the same one twice.*
>
> —Theodore Roosevelt, 26th president
> of the United States

Remember that all successful people fail their way to the top. They put themselves out there to achieve great things more often than others. Thus, they painfully fail more often than others. But they never give up and the victory is sweeter when they finally do achieve their dreams.

I am confident that if you set your mind to it, you will do great things. This is not to say you will not fail. The key is to get back up and keep working to get better every day. And as Roosevelt says, try to not make the same mistake twice.

# Epilogue: Trading Is the Perfect Business

T rading is the perfect business. It can be a part-time or full-time occupation, depending on your preferences. And there are examples of people who have built successful trading and investing businesses around the world. If you haven't done so already, it is now your turn to join this elite club of entrepreneurs.

## How Is Trading the Perfect Business?

Let me count the ways in which trading and investing as a business beats most other professions. My personal bias aside, from a purely practical standpoint, it has many upsides.

### 12-Reasons Why Trading Is the Perfect Business

1. Live and work anywhere in the world.
2. Work in the comfort of your home.
3. Be your own boss.

4. Employees not needed.
5. Coworkers not needed.
6. Not dependent on the local economy.
7. Not dependent on appreciating assets.
8. Unlimited profit potential.
9. Prop firms offer funding.
10. Revenue in bull and bear markets.
11. Day trade, position trade, or actively invest.
12. College degree not needed.

You can see why independent minded and entrepreneurial people around the world are attracted to this profession. There are many benefits, but just know that the possibilities are limitless.

## Live and Work Anywhere in the World

This is an important benefit to a trading and investing business. We live in a global economy and when you are an independent trader or investor, you can literally live and work anywhere in the world . . . provided you have access to good internet.

Of course, if you live in a country without internet access, and there are a few, this profession is not a good fit. But pretty much everyone else is good to go. The freedom to live almost anywhere is huge. Add to that the benefit of mobility and of being able to pack up your computer any time and go anywhere you choose.

Consider this: say you live in New York City, which is certainly expensive, you could move to a less expensive location, and you can still do your job. Or maybe a family member is in need, and you must travel to assist them, and you can still do your job.

### Liberating Flexibility

Now, let's take a look at the global opportunities available to you in the financial markets. There are currently 69 major global stock exchanges that range in size and trading volume—from the New York Stock Exchange to tiny local exchanges. This figure is from the *World Federation of Exchanges* (WFE), which was founded in 1961.

### The Trillion Dollar Club

Out of the 69 exchanges that are members of the WFE, only 18 currently have a market capitalization of more than US$1 trillion (see Table E.1). This group of exchanges are considered to be members of the *Trillion Dollar Club*, which is a nickname given to the exchanges in this category.

Table E.1   The *Trillion Dollar Club* is the nickname given to the 18 exchanges around the world that currently have more than US$1 trillion in market capitalization.

| Rank | Stock Exchange | Headquarter | Country | Market Cap In Trillions (USD) |
|------|----------------|-------------|---------|-------------------------------|
| 1 | NYSE | New York City | United States | $28.42 |
| 2 | NASDAQ | New York City | United States | $25.43 |
| 3 | Euronext (is unique in that it connects seven European economies) | Amsterdam, Brussels, Dublin, Lisbon, Milan, Oslo, Paris | Europe | $7.22 |
| 4 | JPX | Tokyo | Japan | $6.66 |
| 5 | SSE | Shanghai | China | $6.55 |
| 6 | NSE | Mumbai | India | $4.65 |
| 7 | SZSE | Shenzhen | China | $4.10 |
| 8 | HKEX | Hong Kong | Hong Kong | $3.87 |
| 9 | LSEG | London | UK | $3.42 |
| 10 | TSX | Toronto | Canada | $3.21 |
| 11 | Tadawul | Riyadh | Saudi Arabia | $2.93 |
| 12 | FWB | Frankfurt | Germany | $2.30 |
| 13 | Nasdaq Nordic | Stockholm | Sweden | $2.04 |
| 14 | TWSE | Taipei | Taiwan | $2.02 |
| 15 | KRX | Busan | South Korea | $1.98 |
| 16 | SIX Swiss Exchange | Zurich | Switzerland | $1.95 |
| 17 | TSE | Tehran | Iran | $1.77 |
| 18 | ASX | Sydney | Australia | $1.68 |

SOURCE: https://ceoworld.biz/2024/05/19/revealed-largest-stock-exchanges-in-the-world-by-market-capitalization-2024/. This table is intended for educational purposes only. Information is subject to change. Readers are advised to consult with their broker or data provider for current information.

The New York Stock Exchange (NYSE) is the largest stock exchange globally, boasting an equity market capitalization exceeding US$28.42 trillion. Following closely behind are the tech-heavy NASDAQ, at US$25.43 trillion, Euronext, at US$7.22 trillion, and the Japan Exchange Group (JPX) at US$6.66 trillion.

The NYSE and the Nasdaq, the top two exchanges in the world, together account for 42.4% of global market capitalization. Since 2016, the NYSE has grown by 35.1%, while the Nasdaq has seen a staggering 189.3% increase in market cap. The Shanghai Stock Exchange (SSE) holds the fifth position globally with a market cap of US$6.55 trillion, and the National Stock Exchange of India (NSE) ranks sixth with a market cap of US$4.65 trillion.

These market capitalization numbers of course vary from year to year depending on the local activity in each market's exchange, so the figures on Table E.1 will change from time to time. It is interesting to also note the ranking for each market exchange.

To get an idea of how global the markets are, take a look at the map on Figure E.1, where you can see there is opportunity in literally every hemisphere of the world. This further illustrates that you can truly live and work just about anywhere you want to.

Many countries have a stock market index representing a segment of their economy. These indexes are often used as a barometer of the overall health of the economy of the countries they represent.

### 10 Popular Worldwide Stock Market Indexes

1. **Dow Jones Industrial Average (DJIA), United States, Founded 1885**: Groups together the prices of 30 of the most traded stocks on the NYSE and the Nasdaq; helps investors determine the overall direction of stock prices.

2. **Deutscher Aktien Index (DAX), Germany, Founded 1988:** A popular index in Europe; measures the performance of the Frankfurt Stock Exchange's 30 largest companies.

3. **Russia Trading System (RTS), Russia, Founded 1995:** 50 of the most liquid stocks listed on the Moscow Exchange.

## Stock Market Exchanges Around The World

**Figure E.1**    This world map illustrates that there are trading and investing opportunities in literally every hemisphere in the world. This map shows some of the world's largest stock market exchanges and the cities where they are located, from New York to London to Sao Paulo to Mumbai to Tokyo to Sydney and elsewhere. SOURCE: Photo 148451219 @ Oleksandr Kyrylov Dreamstime.com

4. **Nikkei 225, Japan, Founded 1950**: N:eading and most-respected index of Japanese stocks; composed of Japan's top 225 blue-chip companies traded on the Tokyo Stock Exchange.

5. **Toronto Stock Exchange (TSX), Canada, Founded 2002**: - The S&P/TSX Composite Index tracks the performance of the largest companies listed on Canada's primary stock exchange; the equivalent of the S&P 500 index in the United States.

6. **Financial Times Stock Exchange (FTSE), England, Founded 1992:** Informally known as "Footsie,"; United Kingdom's best-known index; name is derived from the names of two companies that launched it: *Financial Times* and London Stock Exchange.

7. **EURO STOXX, Switzerland, Founded 1998**: An index of Eurozone stocks designed by STOXX, an index provider owned by Deutsche Börse Group; composed of 50 stocks from 11 countries in the Eurozone and one of the most liquid indices for the Eurozone.

8. **Bolsa de Valores de São Paulo (BOVESPA), Brazil, Founded 1890**: One of the largest exchanges in the Americas and part of the B3 (Brasil, Bolsa, Balcão); in 2008, merged with the Brazilian Commodities & Futures Exchange.

9. **NIFTY, India, Founded 1996**: One of two national indices, the other being SENSEX, a product of the Bombay Stock Exchange; owned by the India Index Services and Products (IISL), which is a fully owned subsidiary of the National Stock Exchange Strategic Investment Corporation Limited.

10. **Hang Seng Index (HSI), Hong Kong, China, Founded 1969**: Compiled of a selection of the largest companies in Hong Kong; conceived with the idea of creating a DJIA for Hong Kong.

This list of 10 worldwide stock market indices is in no way a complete list of all indices worldwide, but it will give you a broad view of some of the largest indexes in the world. See Figure E.2. Again, there are opportunities worldwide.

**Figure E.2**  These 16 different stock market indexes spanning the globe show that no matter where you live, there are trading and investing opportunities in your time zone.
SOURCE: Photo 24046281 © The Dreamstime.com

## Work in the Comfort of Your Home

Especially after the COVID-19 lockdown and social distancing of 2020, it became clear to just about everyone that being able to work at home remotely is a plus. And now, it has become a way of life for workers around the world. Seems like at the point of the crisis everyone started to add office space to their homes and were putting up accessory dwelling units (ADUs) in their backyards.

Of course, for me as an independent trader, my home addition with a view was built 20 years ago in San Diego, California. That's because I recognized the value and convenience of working at home even before the pandemic.

Back then, in 1999, I was also a financial advisor for a firm in Del Mar and commuted back and forth to work every day, which involved additional expenses such as gas, wear-and-tear on my car, and most of all the cost of my time.

Plus, the contract I had with my brokerage firm included a monthly payment to pay for my office space. In the end, it was a no brainer to add on to my house, increasing my home value, and decreasing these other many expenses. And to top it off, I didn't have to wear a suit every day, so no more dry-cleaning expenses!

You can see the benefits of giving up office life and transitioning into a work-at-home lifestyle, and maybe you've already done that or are considering it. It can be as simple as sectioning off an extra room to be your office at home. We can thank advancing technology and high-speed internet for making this possible.

In contrast, certainly many independent traders and investors prefer to have an official office space, and they have factored those costs into their bottom line. It is a personal choice, and you can determine what is best for you.

## Be Your Own Boss

You are the boss. Which gives you the control to call the shots and to control your destiny. Corporations can be fickle, and politics are always in play no matter where you are on the corporate ladder. Personalities are not always compatible, and even if you are great at what you do, your boss may not advance you or give you the credit you deserve.

> *When dealing with people, remember you are not dealing with creatures of logic, but with creatures of emotion.*
>
> —Dale Carnegie,
> author of *How to Win Friends and Influence People*

Then there are times when even with a great boss, you may get fired, downsized, or become redundant, due to circumstances out of your control and out of their control. In the corporate world, it's a numbers game, and if the economy is suffering, cutting staff is the first solution upper management will turn to in an effort to stop the bleeding. Or if there is a corporate merger and your job becomes redundant, you may find yourself on the unemployment line.

So, when you are not the boss, you are at the mercy of the corporate machine and are not in control of your own destiny, on so many levels. And it can be frustrating to be sure. The beauty of being your own boss is that you call the shots and have job security.

## Employees Not Needed

With today's global labor shortage, if you own a business that requires employees, it can be a Herculean task to retain a competent staff. There are many skill-set shortages in the labor force, and it is getting more and more difficult to find qualified staff. See Table E.2. Plus, the cost of employee acquisition is hefty, with headhunter fees and the cost of new employee training.

Add to that the problem of rising wages. For example, if you are running a restaurant where labor costs are increasing dramatically, you end up cutting back staff to cover the cost of the higher wages. But that reduces the quality of the customer experience since all of your staff are working the job of two people. Not an easy dilemma to be faced with.

**Table E.2**   The worldwide labor shortage has exploded since t 2018 when the shortage was a mere 45%. Today the global average is at a staggering 77% and climbing.

| Country | Region | Labor Shortage |
| --- | --- | --- |
| | Global Average | 77% |
| Taiwan | Asia | 90% |
| German | Europe | 86% |
| China | Asia | 81% |
| Brazil | South America | 80% |
| India | Asia | 80% |
| United Kingdom | Europe | 80% |
| Australia | Oceania | 79% |
| Canada | North America | 79% |
| Japan | Asia | 78% |
| South Africa | Africa | 76% |
| United States | North America | 75% |
| Mexico | North America | 69% |
| Colombia | South America | 64% |

THIS table is intended for educational purposes only. Information is subject to change.
SOURCE: https://explodingtopics.com/blog/labor-shortage-stats#top-labor-shortage-stats

Last but not least, let's not forget the task of managing employees. Even if you have a human resource team, this has challenges as well. There are risks, liabilities, and expenses for every employee you employ.

Whatever the initial cost of the hourly wage, or salary, the actual cost to your bottom line is double that. There are insurance, taxes, and managerial expenses associated with each person on your payroll.

If you are an entrepreneurial individual, and thrive in an independent business environment, you can see that any business model requiring employees has certain limitations.

Fortunately, an independent trading and investing business does not require hiring employees. You may choose to outsource your accounting but there is very little need to hire any employees unless that is your personal preference.

## Coworkers Not Needed

Workplace politics is a real thing. You may love the actual work of your job, but if you happen to fall into a toxic workplace, it can be exhausting. Many people think of politics at work as a game. The thing is, if you are not good at playing the game, your compensation and advancement may be negatively affected.

By building your own circle of trading buddies, that you have personally vetted, you are in control of your surroundings. There's no water-cooler gossip, or boardroom manipulation, there's just you doing your job. It doesn't get any better than that.

## Not Dependent on the Local Economy

To some degree, there are a lot more businesses that are not dependent on the local economy than ever before. With the advancement of the internet and our access to it, we can shop online, learn online, and do almost anything online.

And yet, many businesses still do rely on the local economy, which limits their ability to prosper when the local economy suffers. For example, restaurants, brick and mortar shopping malls, service companies such as heating and cooling are all completely dependent on their local economy.

When the local economy suffers, these businesses are trapped in their physical location, which puts them at greater risk than other businesses. They still have all the other risks that every business has, it's just that they are forced to add one more risk to the list. For traders and investors, we probably have the most agile and mobile business in the world, which is a good thing.

## Not Dependent on Appreciating Assets

In real estate, everyone looks like a genius when the market is going up. Because when the market is going up and appreciating, the value of your portfolio is continually increasing. Same with retirement accounts, they are dependent on the stock market going up.

### So, what happens when these assets are depreciating?

Bingo, you got it. When real estate or the stock market are going down, you are losing money if you own these assets. And there is virtually no way around it, which makes many folks vulnerable without them even knowing it.

Typically, when a downturn occurs, it is fast and furious, so maneuvering is no longer an option once the downturn begins. The only option is to liquidate at a significant loss or to wait out the length of the downturn.

My concern is that not everyone is as conscious of the possibility of a downturn as they should be. The younger folks haven't experienced a recession firsthand, so they don't fully understand what the far-reaching impact can be. And the older folks may underestimate the risks they are exposed to.

When you are a trader, you can quickly pivot to any change in the marketplace. Being more aware and more liquid than others puts you at an advantage.

## Unlimited Profit Potential

Once you have developed the skill and experience to consistently generate revenue, it's a matter of upping your game and increasing your win percentage to increase your profit. It is a growing process, and the goal of striving to get better each and every day is an important one to put into your trading rules. See Table E.3.

Another way to increase profit is to add an additional zero at the end of your trading account. This would mathematically increase your winning dollar amount immediately. You can do this by adding available risk capital to your account. See Table E.4.

**Table E.3** Day Trading Daily Goals: Notice how when you improve your skills and increase your win percent per day from 0.50% to 1.00%, your daily goal revenue doubles.

| Day Trading Account Size | Average Win % Per Day 0.50% | Average Win % Per Day 1.00% |
|---|---|---|
| $1,000 | $5 goal | $10 goal |
| $5,000 | $25 goal | $50 goal |
| $10,000 | $50 goal | $100 goal |
| $25,000 | $125 goal | $250 goal |

This table is intended for educational purposes only. No representation is being made that any account will, or is likely to, achieve results like those discussed.

**Table E.4** Day Trading Daily Goals: Notice how when you add a zero to the end of your account size, you increase your daily goal revenue by 10 times when compared with Table E.3.

| Day Trading Account Size (added a zero) | Average Win % Per Day 0.50% | Average Win % Per Day 1.00% |
|---|---|---|
| $10,000 | $50 goal | $100 goal |
| $50,000 | $250 goal | $500 goal |
| $100,000 | $500 goal | $1,000 goal |
| $250,000 | $1,250 goal | $2,500 goal |

This table is intended for educational purposes only. No representation is being made that any account will, or is likely to, achieve results like those discussed.

Say your account size is $10,000 and you add one zero to that, you would then have a $100,000 account. If on the smaller account, you were making an average of $100 per day, by adding one zero to your account, would immediately boost your average daily revenue to $1,000 on the larger account. See Figure E.3.

You can also consider the use of margin in your account. Provided you have good credit, your broker may offer up to 50% margin, which would boost your winning dollar amount by the amount of margin you access. Doing so requires that you sign a margin agreement, which acts as a loan agreement. There are certain risks, but the reward potential on a winning system may warrant the risk.

**Figure E.3**   As an independent trader, you have unlimited profit potential to earn, whether it's a stack of dollars, pounds, euros, yen, francs, or any other currency you prefer.
SOURCE: Photo 148451219 © Oleksandr Kyrylov Dreamstime.com

### Again, the profit potential is unlimited.

When pushing the envelope to grow and increase your profit, you will find that sometimes emotional roadblocks get in the way. Your trader's mindset might need to get used to adding a zero to the end of your account, so be patient with yourself. Your psyche may also need to get used to the pressure of striving to increase your average daily win percentage.

### Find your comfort zone.

My suggestion is to always use the baby step approach and build gradually. Find your comfort zone, and once you've mastered it, then you can push yourself to step out to keep growing, because that is where the magic happens.

**IMPORTANT:** Depending on whether you are a day trader, position trader, or investor, your profit goals must be tailored to your frequency of trading. Rule of thumb is that day traders work with a *daily goal*, position traders work with a *weekly goal,* and investors work with a *monthly goal.* You can of course choose something different than this rule of thumb. What type of goal works for you is a personal choice. See Tables E.5, E.6, E.7, and E.8.

**Table E.5**    Position Trading Weekly Goals: Notice how when you improve your skills and increase your win percent per week from 1.00% to 2.00%, your weekly goal revenue doubles.

| Position Trading Account Size | Average Win % Per Week 1.00% | Average Win % Per Week 2.00% |
|---|---|---|
| $1,000 | $10 goal | $20 goal |
| $5,000 | $50 goal | $100 goal |
| $10,000 | $100 goal | $200 goal |
| $25,000 | $250 goal | $500 goal |

This table is intended for educational purposes only. No representation is being made that any account will, or is likely to, achieve results like those discussed.

**Table E.6**    Position Trading Weekly Goals: Notice how when you add a zero to the end of your account size, you increase your weekly goal revenue by ten times when compared with Table E.5.

| Position Trading Account Size (added a zero) | Average Win % Per Week 1.00% | Average Win % Per Week 2.00% |
|---|---|---|
| $10,000 | $100 goal | $200 goal |
| $50,000 | $500 goal | $1,000 goal |
| $100,000 | $1,000 goal | $2,000 goal |
| $250,000 | $2,500 goal | $5,000 goal |

This table is intended for educational purposes only. No representation is being made that any account will, or is likely to, achieve results like those discussed.

**Table E.7**   Active Investor Monthly Goals: Notice how when you improve your skills and increase your win percent per month from 2.00% to 4.00%, your monthly goal revenue doubles.

| Active Investor Account Size | Average Win % Per Month 2.00% | Average Win % Per Month 4.00% |
| --- | --- | --- |
| $1,000 | $20 goal | $40 goal |
| $5,000 | $100 goal | $200 goal |
| $10,000 | $200 goal | $400 goal |
| $25,000 | $500 goal | $1,000 goal |

This table is intended for educational purposes only. No representation is being made that any account will, or is likely to, achieve results like those discussed.

**Table E.8**   Active Investor Monthly Goals: Notice how when you add a zero to the end of your account size, you increase your monthly goal revenue by 10 times when compared with Table E.7.

| Active Investor Account Size (added a zero) | Average Win % Per Month 2.00% | Average Win % Per Month 4.00% |
| --- | --- | --- |
| $10,000 | $200 goal | $400 goal |
| $50,000 | $1,000 goal | $2,000 goal |
| $100,000 | $2,000 goal | $4,000 goal |
| $250,000 | $5,000 goal | $10,000 goal |

This table is intended for educational purposes only. No representation is being made that any account will, or is likely to, achieve results like those discussed.

# Dollar Profit Goals: Daily, Weekly, Monthly

Depending on whether you are a day trader, position trader, or investor, your profit goals must be tailored to your frequency of trading. Rule of thumb is that day traders work with a *daily goal*, position traders work with a *weekly goal*, and investors work with a *monthly goal*.

*(continued on next page ...)*

*(... continued from previous page)*

Your recordkeeping will tell you where you are as per your average win percentage and your average dollar goal. That is what you will start with as your baseline.

**How to Calculate Your Dollar Goal:** Say you are a day trader and trade 2 days a week. Your average weekly revenue is $1,000 over the past 3 months. Since you trade 2 days per week and your average revenue per week is $1,000, then your average daily dollar goal is $500.

**For Example:** If your daily dollar goal is $500, keep trading until you reach your $500 goal. Once you reach your goal amount and are in the black, you can finish your day and feel really good about it. If you end the day at a loss, remember that tomorrow is another day.

**Little Victories:** I'm a big believer in the baby steps approach. It's better to take one step at a time and walk before you run. Take those little victories and build confidence. So, starting with a small daily, weekly, or monthly dollar goal is AOK. If you are consistently making $10 per day and are trading 20 days a month, that's something to be proud of.

Once the current profit range becomes consistent, you can consider upping your game. Remember, every time you push to improve, you may experience some internal resistance. We as humans don't like change, even when it is good change. Growing pains are normal. It can take time to adjust to making more money, but you can do it.

## Prop Firms Offer Funding, So Why Risk Your Own Money?

Funded prop firms are exploding right now. And for good reason, as they allow you to day trade without having to risk your own money. Instead, you trade prop firm trading accounts, of various sizes, depending on your needs. So, even if you don't have a significant amount of cash to trade, you can generate sizable payouts and revenue if you have a profitable system and get funded.

There is minimal risk since during the evaluation phase your only real expense is a monthly subscription fee, and in exchange for that fee, you get a free real-time data feed and charting platform. Plus, most of these firms have promotions where they offer a steep discount when signing up, so if you time it right, you can save a lot.

Then, after you pass the evaluation phase and are qualified to become funded, there is usually a funding activation fee. But, going forward as long as your account is in good standing, you will no longer pay the monthly evaluation fee.

This type of funding is relatively new, the first company of this type that I remember is *TopstepTrader*, which was founded by then-floor trader Michael Patak on the floor of the Chicago Board of Trade in 2012. Since then, many other firms have opened, with much better terms. You can see a current list of excellent prop firms at this link: https://www.traderscoach.com/book/.

Here is an overview so you can consider if this is a good fit for you. In essence, it is not that the firm is funding you with actual cash, but they do pay you anywhere up to 90% of your account's profits. Meaning if you earn $10,000 in a month, they will send you a payout of $9,000.

Prop firms make their money by charging a variety of fees, such as monthly evaluation and reset fees. Given that we know 90% of all traders and investors are losing money, that certainly gives them consistent recurring revenue from fees alone.

Given that one prop firm (that is on our preferred list) is averaging payouts of more than $23 million per month over the last 3 months, and averaging more than $10 million in payouts per month over the last year, you can see that they have many consistently profitable traders as clients.

With regard to time frames, most prop firms will only support day trading, although there are a few exceptions. The markets supported by each firm vary with a majority of them allowing you to trade futures. Other markets offered include stocks, options, forex, commodities, indices, cryptocurrencies, and metals.

## How Does Prop Trading Work?

There are a number of hoops to jump through to get funded, but once you accomplish that you can start getting regular payouts. And many of the hoops are actually geared toward money management, so if you have implemented the strategies covered in Chapters 11 through Chapter 15 of this book, you will be well on your way. Take a look at Table E.9 for an example of what the parameters are that you will need to be aware of.

For example, when looking at Table E.9, if you sign up for a $25,000 size prop account, the parameters to get funded are that you must reach a profit goal of $1,500 on that account while at the same time not having a drawdown or trail loss of $1,500 or more. This is the minimum threshold for getting a funded account. Once you are funded, you must then have an account balance of more than $26,600 before you can qualify to request a payout withdrawal.

Compare an account of $25,000 with one of $250,000, and you will see a stark contrast in what the parameters are for achieving a funded account. In short, the larger the account, the more difficult it is to get funded. In this example where we have added one zero

**Table E.9**  Funding Parameters for a Typical Prop Trading Firm. These are hypothetical parameters to give you an idea of how the system works. Notice the account sizes range from $25,000 to $250,000 and the allowed contracts and micros vary depending the size of the account. The profit goal figures are the amount of profit you need to generate on an account in order to get funded. The trail loss figures represent the dollar amount of drawdown allowed before an account gets shut down.

FUNDING PARAMETERS FOR A TYPICAL PROP TRADING FIRM

| Account Size | $25K | $50K | $75K | $100K | $250K |
|---|---|---|---|---|---|
| Contracts | 4 | 10 | 12 | 14 | 27 |
| Micros | 40 | 100 | 120 | 140 | 270 |
| Profit Goal | $1,500 | $3,000 | $4,250 | $6,000 | $15,000 |
| Trail Loss | $1,500 | $2,500 | $2,750 | $3,000 | $6,500 |
| Min Acct Size For Payout | $26,600 | $52,600 | $77,850 | $103,100 | $256,600 |

THIS table is intended for educational purposes only. No representation is being made that any account will, or is likely to, achieve results like those discussed.

at the end of the $25,000 account and compare it with an account size of $250,000, we can see that the parameters do not scale up consistently.

When working toward getting funded, the profit goal amount on these two account sizes scales up at the same consistent rate by going from $1,500 to $15,000. But when looking at the trail loss, or drawdown allowance, it does not scale consistently. Instead of the trail loss increasing from $1,500 to $15,000 it increases from $1,500 to only $6,500. Which means that if your drawdown at any time goes over $6,500, your account will be shut down.

**Blowing out your Prop account can and will happen.**

Just about every prop trader has had multiple blown accounts; it is part of the process. Since all prop firms have strict rules that can change at any time, it is important that you fully understand the nuances involved. Basically, if you break any of the rules in an account, that account will be closed, and you will lose any profits you may have accrued. See Table E.10.

There are two types of prop firm accounts, which are the personal evaluation account and the funded account. Everyone starts off with the personal evaluation account at the account size of their choice. They pay a monthly subscription fee for the privilege of working toward getting a funded account.

Once they meet the profit goal of their chosen account, and abide by the rules, they can then get a funded account after they pay an activation fee. Then they no longer pay a monthly fee and are eligible for payouts if their performance warrants it.

If a personal evaluation account gets blown out, the owner can either pay a reset fee for immediate reinstatement or wait until their monthly subscription renews. Any profits they may have accrued in that account will be lost.

If a funded account gets blown out, the owner must go back to the beginning and pay a monthly subscription for a personal evaluation account. Any profits they may have accrued will be lost. The trader must also pass the evaluation again in order to be eligible to get a funded account and to receive payouts in the future.

**Table E.10**    There are two types of prop firm accounts available. They are the personal evaluation account and the funded account. You must pass the evaluation in order to qualify for a funded account.

| | Two Types of Prop Firm Accounts | |
| --- | --- | --- |
| | Personal Evaluation Account (PA) | Funded Account |
| Status? | Has not passed evaluation | Has passed evaluation |
| Charged a monthly fee for subscription? | Yes | No |
| What if an account blows out? | Pay a reset fee for immediate reinstatement or wait until your monthly subscription renews | Go back to square one, must pay for monthly evaluation subscription again and pass evaluation before getting funded |
| Payouts? | Not eligible | Eligible |
| Free data feed and charting platform? | Yes, most firms offer this benefit. | Yes, most firms offer this benefit. |
| Free education and support? | Yes, most firms offer this benefit. | Yes, most firms offer this benefit. |

This table is intended for educational purposes only. Consult with your prop firm to verify their terms and conditions prior to purchasing a subscription. Their terms and conditions may or may not be the same as those outlined here.

There are many tricks of the trade when it comes to prop trading, and one of the most common is *trade copying*. Basically, it is a strategy where you copy your trades over multiple accounts. It requires that you use a *trade copier* that can be purchased for a reasonable fee and in some cases is included in some platforms.

**Trade copying is a popular technique.**

Say you have a total of 10 accounts, you could literally copy one exact trade onto all 10 accounts simultaneously. So, if the trade generated a profit of $500 for one account, you would in fact have earned $5,000 because you had that trade on 10 accounts. When you have a winning edge, this is how the big money is made.

Obviously, it is a no brainer that this strategy is great when you are winning. But if you have a loss of $500 on one copied trade, you would in effect have a loss of $5,000 over the 10 accounts that you copied the trade to. And in trading no one wins 100% of the time, so it is important to factor this reality into your strategy.

### Delaying payouts and building a buffer.

You might think that the minute you have qualified profits that you can get a payout on, you would want to cash out as soon as possible. But there are other considerations when looking at your long-term goals. This is due to the fact that traders have their own strategies, some of which work better in the prop arena than others.

If your approach has large drawdown swings, even if the ultimate profit is huge, it might not work well within the prop trading set of rules. Which is why prop traders will often keep their winnings in their account to act as a buffer to their drawdowns.

Again, looking at Table E.9, on a $25,000 account you are allowed to have a drawdown no greater than $1,500. Say you generated enough winning trades to bring that account up to a $30,000 value, and you haven't taken any payouts.

In essence, you would then be allowed to have a drawdown of no greater than $6,500, because your $5,000 profit acts as a buffer and adds to your trailing drawdown amount. Building a buffer is another trick of the trade, and it's up to you to see what works best for your style of trading and your mindset.

Considering the list of prop rules, trading after you make a payout request can throw a curve ball at you. This is because by requesting to withdraw funds you are also removing your buffer.

Say for example you had a payout request for $5,000 on an account that had a $30,000 value, that brings your account back down to its starting point of $25,000. You may not realize that even if the funds have not been removed from the account yet, due to your payout request, your thresholds will be enforced as if the payout had already occurred.

Well, that about covers the opportunities that prop trading offers along with some of the restrictions and rules to be aware of. When considering this route, recognize that scalpers find this rule environment easer to navigate than intraday trend traders, due to the drawdown limitations.

Intraday trend traders just have to be more diligent in controlling their drawdown risk. And a lot of the things you would do in a prop account you would not do with real money. There are idiosyncrasies of the game each trader needs to become comfortable with, but the revenue opportunities are limitless.

## Revenue in Bull and Bear Markets

A bear market is defined as a price increase on the S&P 500 Index of more than 20%, and in reverse, a bear market is defined as a price decrease on the S&P 500 of more than 20%. Bull markets tend to last longer than bear markets, in part because stock prices tend to trend upward over time.

Historically bull markets have lasted an average of twice as long as bear markets and bull markets also tend to see prices rise more than double than what they had fallen in bear markets.

The problem for most businesses is that during a bear market the economy slows down and buyers stop buying. That is compounded by low employment, low disposable family income, weak productivity, and an overall drop in business profits.

Although bear markets happen less frequently than bull markets, they can be financially devastating. Mass layoffs occur, and the world at large has to figure out how to make ends meet. And they tend to hit when the average individual least expects it.

**Job security at its finest.**

Fortunately for traders, they can generate revenue in both bull and bear markets, which is a rather unique aspect of the business. By shorting the market, a trader can generate revenue even during a downturn. Rather than getting fired from their job, a trader can quickly pivot and shift from long positions to short positions at a moment's notice.

## Day Trade, Position Trade, or Actively Invest

You can set up your business however you decide is best for you. Depending on a variety of personal factors, you may choose day trading, position trading or active investing. Chapter 18 of this book goes into great detail on the pros and cons of each of these choices and will be helpful in determining what is best for you.

If you are a beginner, and as you gain skill and experience, it is important to maintain a steady income from whatever job you may currently have. Conducting a parallel test in this way while you are learning is the best way to reduce stress and to make progress.

Which means, your time may be limited, and your best choice might be to position trade or actively invest as a part time job. This allows you to gain experience and confidence while constantly improving your earning ability.

Or maybe you are an experienced trader with a proven edge and track record. For you, day trading full time is the best choice, since you are making consistent revenue and can rely on this job as your sole source of income. This is just business as usual.

The flexibility of being able to work part time or full time on whichever time frame suits your schedule is empowering. Remember, one day at a time is the best path. You may decide to move from being a position trader to become a day trader or the reverse.

## College Degree Not Needed

The cost of a college degree has gotten more expensive over the years to the point where most college students must take out loans in order to pursue that path. In the last 58 years, the average cost of college tuition in the United States for undergraduate students has more than tripled, according to data from the National Center for Education.

And yet the value of a college degree today may very well not be worth the increased cost. The employment landscape is shifting, with artificial intelligence (AI) on the horizon, the job market may change dramatically as AI replaces more positions in the coming years.

While learning to successfully trade and invest does require education, there are no barriers to entry in this industry such as needing an expensive high-level ivy league college degree. There aren't even job interviews, and there is no discrimination of any kind because the only thing that matters is that you are a profitable trader.

## May the Force Be with You

My sincere heartfelt best wishes go out to you now as you embark on either a new journey, or a continuing journey, in making trading the perfect business for you. See Figure E.4.

**Figure E.4**  MINI POSTER—THE FORCE—Much of our success can be accelerated by focusing on our own inner and external force. Allow that positive energy to guide you in all that you do. Quote from Obi-Wan Kenobi, Star Wars.

# Appendix A

# Advanced Techniques

# Technique 1

# Elliott Wave and Fibonacci

B oth Elliott wave and Fibonacci techniques are cornerstones
to my trading and investing analysis. They are commonly
used together by traders and investors worldwide. Having
used these techniques for most of my career, they have become second nature to me.

For those who are new to these ideas it may take some time
to become proficient because they are most certainly advanced
techniques. I must admit, in the beginning it took me a while to
get the hang these approaches. With that said, these approaches
will add massive insight into your analysis and are well worth the
time and effort to master them. I can't imagine trading or investing
without them.

One important note to make before diving into these specific
techniques is that these approaches are ungrounded assessments.
They enable us to determine high probability forecasts of price
movement and direction, but it is crucial to use grounded assessments to make your actual entry and exit decisions.

## Elliott Wave Analysis Is the Road Map to the Markets

A form of technical analysis, the *Elliott Wave Principle* discovered by Ralph Nelson Elliott during the 1930s, states that financial markets unfold in price patterns that are referred to as waves.

The principle further states that there are five waves in every trend, and that after the fifth wave in a trend is complete, the trend will end and a new trend in the opposite direction will begin. These patterns occur in both bull and bear markets. See Figure T1.1.

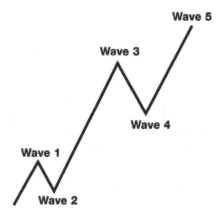

**Figure T1.1**    An Elliott Wave pattern consists of five saves in a trend. After the fifth wave is complete, the trend will end and will begin a new trend in the opposite direction. These patterns occur in both bull and bear markets.
SOURCE: @TradersCoach.com.

Elliott published his discovery in his book *The Wave Principle* in 1938. The principle provides a comprehensive structure as to where price patterns in the market are most likely to go.

**And that structure is the best market road map I know of.**

Elliott's concept of waves is borrowed from the phenomenon of waves in the ocean. Waves are subject to the force of tidal patterns driven by the moon orbiting around the earth and the gravitational pull between the two. This creates an ebb and flow where tides rise and fall in predictable patterns.

In the markets, the overriding force is human emotion and crowd behavior. Many, believe that it is human emotion that moves markets in the same way that the force of the moon orbiting around the earth moves the ocean's tides. See Figure T1.2.

**Figure T1.2**    Elliott Wave patterns resemble the ocean's waves as they ebb and flow. The only difference is that instead of the moon's gravitational pull that creates the ebb and flow in the ocean, in the financial markets it is collective human emotions and crowd behavior that moves the markets.
SOURCE: Photo 14582420 @ Irabel8 Dreamstime.com

The beauty of the Elliott Wave is that it creates a clear structure with which to forecast future price movement based on historical prices and patterns. Although there is no way to predict the future with absolute certainty, the Elliot Wave can predict the most probable future regarding the direction of market prices.

The Elliott Wave is the most powerful forecasting tool I have ever seen. It has an uncanny way of behaving like a crystal ball in predicting future market price activity. When you master this tool, the probable direction of future price will be clear. What won't be clear is the fundamental cause of the impending price action.

Not until after the fact, will your predicted price action be defined and explained by world economic and behavioral aspects of the environment. Global events like war, economic depressions, political developments, and so-called acts of God such as earthquakes, fires, and tsunamis have all consistently been forecasted by the Elliott Wave . . . before they happened.

If you predict and then observe a dramatic move in price, there is usually a fundamental underlying reason this move. You as an analyst will have no idea what the trigger will be when you are creating the forecast. It will only be after you observe your forecast develop into an actuality that you will know the entire story.

## Classic Approach with Elliott Wave Rules Based Purely on Price Patterns

When Ralph Nelson Elliott published his book *The Wave Principle*, he outlined the definitions of specific price patterns based on his theory that there are five waves in any trend that alternate between bullish and bearish moves. These clearly defined rules have been handed down through the ages and are an effective tool in analyzing market behavior past, present, and future.

### There are five waves in a trend.

Within the five-wave trend, the first distinction to be made is that there are both impulsive and corrective waves in every trend, hence the zigzag pattern. See Figure T1.3 and Figure T1.4.

Every trend has five waves, including three impulsive waves which are Wave 1, Wave 3, and Wave 5, and two corrective waves which are Wave 2 and Wave 4. An impulsive wave is defined as a wave that moves in the direction of the trend and a corrective wave is one that moves in the opposite direction of the trend.

The classic approach to wave analysis focuses only on price action, but there is also a modern approach to Elliott Wave analysis that will be covered in the coming pages. The modern approach utilizes computer programs and technology to further improve

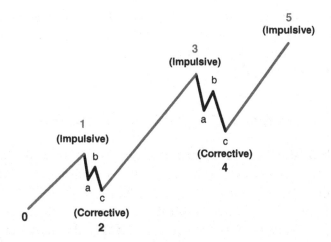

**Figure T1.3** Bullish five wave pattern with impulsive and corrective waves. Impulsive waves move in the direction of the primary trend and corrective waves move in the opposite direction of the primary trend.

SOURCE: @TradersCoach.com.

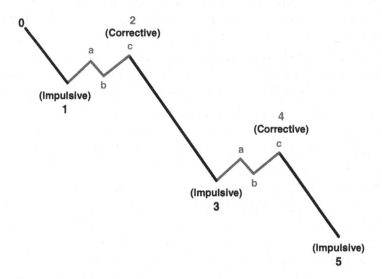

**Figure T1.4** Bearish five wave pattern with impulsive and corrective waves. Impulsive waves move in the direction of the primary trend and corrective waves move in the opposite direction of the primary trend.

SOURCE: @TradersCoach.com.

our forecasting accuracy. My experience is that by combining both the classic and the modern approach, you can eliminate much of the subjectivity that can sometimes be associated with Elliott Wave forecasts.

# Descriptions for All Five Elliott Waves

For each of the five waves in the Elliott Wave pattern, there are unique characteristics and price patterns that apply. Once you know what these patterns are, when looking at a chart you will know where you are in the Elliott Wave sequence, which gives your entry and exit decisions more strength. **NOTE:** the percentages and probabilities outlined here are approximate.

### Description of the Five Waves

- **WAVE 1 Description (impulsive):** This wave is rarely obvious at its inception. Depending on market conditions, Wave 1 may break out of a narrowing channel and is identified when Wave 5 of the previous trend has completed. One of the best ways to identify the beginning of Wave 1 is to determine the target zone for the previous trend and determine when Wave 5 of the previous trend is expected to complete. At the beginning of a new *bullish* Wave 1, the economy does not look strong, fundamental news is negative, and sentiment is decidedly still bearish. The previous bearish trend is still strongly in force. For example, when Wave 1 of a new bullish market begins, the market will ignore good news. (The opposite is true for a *bearish* Wave 1. Fundamental news is still positive, the previous trend is still strong, and sentiment is still bullish. Basically, the market ignores bad news.) As it gains strength, the new impulsive Wave 1 will break the previous trend and mark the beginning of a new trend. Start watching for a pullback after Wave 1 starts. This first pullback will be Wave 2. When you see this pullback, you will be able to identify the end of Wave 1.

- **WAVE 2 Description (corrective):** This wave can be either simple or complex. If Wave 2 is simple, then Wave 4 will usually be complex and vice versa. Prices may create a simple Elliott Wave a-b-c zigzag corrective pattern, which can easily be seen. This is the most common. Or instead, prices may meander sideways for an extended period, forming a complex correction that is not as easily seen and represents chaos as prices move in pennants and channels with hard to follow volatility. This pattern corrects Wave 1 but can never extend beyond the starting point of Wave 1. Volume is lower during Wave 1 than Wave 2. Here is where you begin looking for a trade entry, and this sets up your first pullback scenario. The idea is to get on board at the beginning of a new trend, either bullish or bearish, and to catch Wave 3. In Wave 2 prices will retrace anywhere from 23.6% to 100% of the length of Wave 1.

- **WAVE 3 Description (impulsive):** This is the steepest and the strongest of all five waves, giving the greatest opportunity for profit. It also has the highest volume. While it can be, it is not always the longest wave in terms of time. That is why we want to get ready during Wave 2 (the pullback) so we can jump in immediately as Wave 3 is beginning to unfold. You must wait for Wave 3 to exceed the final price level of Wave 1. That is the signal that Wave 2 is over, and any price bar that goes beyond the final price level of Wave 1 must be Wave 3. In a bull market news is now positive, and fundamental analysis start to raise earnings estimates. Prices rise quickly, and corrections are short lived and shallow. Wave 3 exceeds Wave 1 anywhere from 100% to 261.8% or more. Exit, or at least scale out, during Wave 3 since you don't want to lose your profits when the market reverses in the corrective Wave 4 move.

- **WAVE 4 Description (corrective):** This wave can be either simple or complex. If Wave 2 was simple, then Wave 4 will usually be complex and vice versa. Prices may create a simple Elliott Wave *a-b-c* zigzag corrective pattern, which can easily be seen. This is the most common. Or instead, prices may meander sideways for an extended period, forming a complex correction that is not as easily seen and represents chaos as prices move in pennants and channels with hard to follow volatility. Wave 4 prices retrace 23.6% to 76.4%. This wave is pretty disappointing for those who get in too late at the end of Wave 3, thinking that the Wave 3 move will continue. Instead, when Wave 4 begins it is the signal that the best part of the trend is over. The best part of the trend is always Wave 3.

- **WAVE 5 Description (impulsive):** This wave moves in the direction of the overall trend but is usually sluggish and not as dynamic as Wave 3 of an Elliott Wave cycle. Wave 5 marks the last burst of buying (in a bull trend) or the last burst of selling (in a bear trend) before a new trend starts. Wave 5 is the final leg in the direction of the dominant trend. In a bullish scenario, the news is almost universally positive, and everyone is bullish during Wave 5. Unfortunately, this is when many unknowing investors finally buy, right before the end of Wave 5. Volume is lower in Wave 5 than in Wave 3, and many momentum indicators start to show divergences. At the end of a major bull market, bear forecasters may be ridiculed and are in the minority. In a bearish scenario, the opposite occurs, and the news is almost universally negative, and bull forecasters may be ridiculed and are in the minority. Forecasters are slow to declare a change in trend.

The most profitable and tradeable waves in the five-wave pattern are the impulsive waves of Wave 1, Wave 3, and Wave 5. Out of these three impulsive waves, Wave 3 by far is the greatest opportunity for profit. There is also opportunity for profit when trading the corrective Wave C in Wave 4, but this is an advanced technique and should be used with caution.

## Statistics for All Five Elliott Waves

The statistics needed to accurately count Elliott Waves and estimate targets are based on Fibonacci ratios, which will be covered later in this chapter. These ratios and patterns are often found in nature and play an integral part in the counting of Elliott Waves. **NOTE:** the percentages and probabilities outlined here are approximate.

**Statistics of the Five Waves**

- **WAVE 1 Statistics (impulsive):** Wave 1 will begin after Wave 5 of the preceding trend ends. Wave 1 will usually be steep and short. Depending on market conditions, Wave 1 may break out of a narrowing channel.
- **WAVE 2 Statistics (corrective):** Use Fibonacci retracement tools to determine the price target zone. Fifteen percent of the time this wave will retrace between 23.6% and 38.2% of Wave 1. And 70% of the time it will retrace between 38.2% and 61.8% of Wave 1. Leaving 15% of the time this wave will retrace between 61.8% and 100% of Wave 1.
- **WAVE 3 Statistics (impulsive):** Use Fibonacci extension tools to determine the price target zone. Fifteen percent of the time it will extend from 100% to 161.8% of Wave 1. Then 45% of the time Wave 3 extends from 161.8% to 175% of Wave 1. And 30% of the time Wave 3 will extend from 175% to 261.8% of Wave 1. Leaving 10% of the time, in unusual cases, where Wave 3 extends more than 261.8% of Wave 1.
- **WAVE 4 Statistics (corrective):** Use Fibonacci retracement tools to determine the price target zone. Using two anchors, anchor the drawing tool at the end of Wave 2 and the end of Wave 3. With this anchor strategy, 15% of the time it retraces between 23.6% and 38.2% of Wave 3. Then 70% of the time this wave retraces between 38.2% and 61.8% of Wave 3. And finally, 15% of the time it will retrace between 61.8% and 76.4% of Wave 3.
- **WAVE 5 Statistics (impulsive):** Use Fibonacci extension tools to determine the price target zone. Using three anchors, anchor the drawing tool at the end of Wave 2, the end of Wave 3, and the end of Wave 4. With this anchor strategy, 15% of the time it will extend 38.2% to 61.8%. Then 70% of the time it will extend 61.8% to 100%. And lastly, 15% of the time it will extend 100% to 161.8%.

The percentages in these Elliott Wave statistics may seem unusual to you with numbers like 23.6, 38.2, and 61.8 to name a few. As mentioned before, these numbers are based on Fibonacci ratios, which will be covered in more depth in the coming pages.

You can use these unusual numbers to determine what the likely target is for the various waves in a trend. And in most charting programs such as NinjaTrader and TradeStation, you will find Fibonacci drawing tools that enable you to illustrate the extensions and retracements on your chart that are based on these numbers as well.

Keep in mind that my way of calculating extensions and retracements is different than other Elliotticians in the industry. Refer to Figure T1.18 and Figure T1.19, my cheat sheets, later in this chapter which have guidelines on how to use your Fibonacci drawing tools in your charting platform, and how to set up anchors to get the most accurate target zones.

## Volume Characteristics for All Five Elliott Waves

Understanding the role that volume plays in each of the five waves will help you identify the Elliott Wave pattern more effectively. This section will give you guidelines on what to look for in each wave with regard to volume. These guidelines apply to both bullish and bearish trends.

### Volume Characteristics of the Five Waves

- **WAVE 1 Volume (impulsive):** Volume might increase a bit as prices move in the direction of the first wave, but not always enough to alert many technical analysts.
- **WAVE 2 Volume (corrective):** Volume is usually lower during Wave 2 than during Wave 1.
- **WAVE 3 Volume (impulsive):** Highest volume occurs in Wave 3. You will see some peak volume spikes. Momentum of price movement is usually highest here too.
- **WAVE 4 Volume (corrective):** Volume is well below that of Wave 3.
- **WAVE 5 Volume (impulsive):** Volume is lower in Wave 5 than in Wave 3.

Volume analysis, like Fibonacci levels, is also considered part of the classic approach to Elliott Wave analysis. The main thing you need to know about volume is that during Wave 3, volume is at its highest of all the waves in the trend.

The reason for this is that as Wave 3 unfolds, prices are moving dramatically in the direction of the overall trend. Market participants take notice, and this move is usually accompanied by supporting news in the direction of the trend. Hence the high volume on Wave 3.

After Wave 3 and Wave 4, Wave 5 emerges in the direction of the trend and prices reach higher new levels in a bullish trend, and lower new levels in a bearish trend. However, the volume on Wave 5 will not be as high as it was during Wave 3. We expect this since there is less enthusiasm during Wave 5 than during Wave 3, meaning there is less trading.

This is because the previous Wave 4, which is a nasty corrective wave pattern, usually creates havoc and destroys the enthusiastic sentiment that occurred during Wave 3. So even though Wave 5 exceeds Wave 3 in price, it lacks the emotional sentiment that was present during Wave 3. You can locate Wave 3 using a volume indicator as it will display the highest volume.

Be mindful of how volume can provide clues in confirming or denying that your wave count is correct. Again, remember to be diligent in monitoring your Elliott wave counts as they progress to catch any failed wave counts. It is best to catch them earlier rather than later.

## Two Types of Corrective Elliott Wave Patterns

Corrections can be difficult to master. Most experienced Elliotticians earn the bulk of their profit trading during an impulsive pattern, like Wave 1, Wave 3, and Wave 5. We try to avoid corrections.

Less experienced traders that know Elliott wave techniques, along with those who don't, tend to give back much of their winnings to the market during corrective cycles, Wave 2 and Wave 4. Which is why it is important to understand these corrective cycles.

### Corrective Patterns Fall Under Two Categories

1. **Simple corrections:** Known as zigzag or an a-b-c correction.
2. **Complex corrections:** There are three types of complex corrections which are flat, irregular, and triangular.

Within a single trend there are two corrective waves which are Wave 2 and Wave 4. What is important to remember is that if Wave 2 is simple, then Wave 4 will usually be complex and vice versa. This is known as the alternation rule for corrective waves.

### Corrective Patterns and Their Characteristics

- **Simple Correction or a-b-c Correction, See Figure T1.5:** The simple correction is called a zigzag correction or an a-b-c correction and is made up of three waves. This is the most common and easy to spot correction. The underlying structure of the simple

**Simple ABC Zig-Zag Correction Pattern**

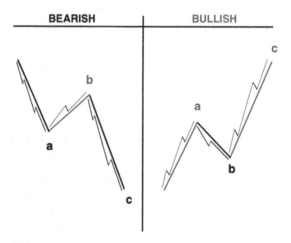

**Figure T1.5**    Simple a-b-c zigzag corrective pattern.
SOURCE: @TradersCoach.com.

correction includes an *a wave* which looks like a minor pullback in a current trend, but instead it is the first leg of a significant correction. The *a wave* and the *c wave* in the zigzag always consist of five subwaves. In contrast, the *b wave* consists of only three subwaves. The subwaves of this a-b-c pattern illustrate the fractal symmetry of the wave structure that we will investigate later. *a wave* **statistics**—There are five subwaves in *a wave*. It is the first leg of a swing in the opposite direction of the previous impulsive trend. *b wave* **statistics**—There are three subwaves in *b wave*. The length of *b wave* is usually 50% of *a wave* and should not exceed 76.4% of *a wave*. *c wave* **statistics**—There are five subwaves in *c wave*. The length of *c wave* is likely to be 1 times *a wave*, or 1.618 times *a wave*, or 2.618 times *a wave*. These are Fibonacci extension numbers.

- **Flat Complex Correction, See Figure T1.6:** In this correction, there are three subwaves and the length of each sub wave is identical and creates a channel. After an impulse pattern, the market begins its correction in *a wave*. It then reverses and begins *b wave*. Finally, the market corrects one last time in *c wave*. Then the market breaks into the next impulsive wave.

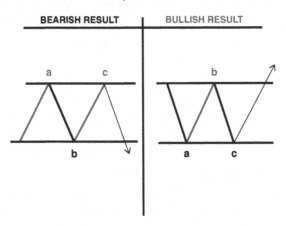

**Flat Complex Correction**

Figure **T1.6**    Flat Complex corrective pattern.
SOURCE: @TradersCoach.com.

### Irregular Complex Correction

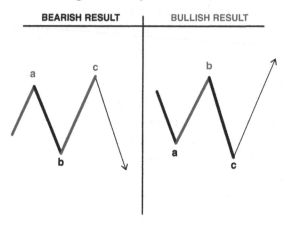

**Figure T1.7**  Irregular Complex Corrective Pattern.
SOURCE: @TradersCoach.com.

- **Irregular Complex Correction, See Figure T1.7:** In irregular complex corrections, there are three subwaves and *b wave* makes a new low when this type of correction occurs in a bearish impulse trend, and a new high in a bullish impulsive trend. Also, the final *c wave* may rise to the beginning of *a wave* in a bearish impulsive trend and vice versa in a bullish impulsive trend. ***b wave* statistics**—this wave is 1.15 to 1.272 longer than *a wave*. ***c wave* statistics**—this wave is 1.618 to 2.618 longer than *a wave*.
- **Triangular Complex Correction, See Figure T1.8:** This complex correction is different from the flat and the irregular complex corrections, in that they only have three subwaves. The triangular complex correction in contrast has five subwaves that are designated as a, b, c, d, and e, in sequence. These patterns are where pennants form, which are a type of technical analysis signal marking price compression followed by a significant move when the pennant pattern is broken. Triangles are, by far, most common in Wave 4. They can be tricky and confusing. One must study the pattern carefully prior to acting.

## Triangle Complex Corrections

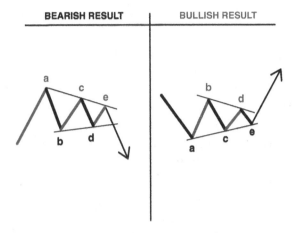

**Figure T1.8**    Triangular Complex Corrective Pattern.
SOURCE: @TradersCoach.com.

Prices tend to shoot out of the triangle formation in a swift thrust coming out of a correction and can be an excellent place for a trade entry.

Corrective waves behave differently than impulsive waves in a five-wave trend with regard to volume.

### Volume in the Corrective Wave 3 a-b-c Trend:

- *a Wave:* Increased volume and remains stable in relation to Wave 3. The fundamental news is still positive (in a bull pattern) or still negative (in a bear pattern). Most analysts see the *a Wave* as just a correction.
- *b Wave:* Volume during *b Wave* should be lower than in *a Wave*.
- *c Wave:* Volume picks up, and by the third leg of *c Wave,* almost everyone realizes that a reverse in trend is firmly entrenched.

Again, as you become more familiar with Elliott Wave patterns and their unique characteristics, all of this information will become second nature.

## Fractal Symmetry Exists in Nature and Within the Elliott Wave

A fractal is generally a rough or fragmented geometric shape that can be subdivided in parts, each of which is (at least approximately) a reduced size copy of the whole. The term fractal was coined by Benoit Mandelbrot in 1975.

Natural objects that approximate fractals to varying degrees include snowflakes, clouds, mountain ranges, lightning bolts, and coastlines. See how this photo, Figure T1.9 of a real snowflake, demonstrates the repeating pattern of a natural fractal found in nature. It might surprise you that human behavior and the financial markets are also made up of fractals.

In a financial market's price action, if one looks at the monthly, weekly, daily, and intraday bar charts, the structure has a similar appearance. The patterns are the same and repeat themselves.

Because they appear similar at all levels of magnification, fractals are often considered to be infinitely complex. The next section

**Figure T1.9**   You can see the fractal symmetry in this photograph of a real snowflake magnified on a black background.

SOURCE: Photo 76875550 Crystal © Chaoticmind Dreamstime.com

in this advanced techniques appendix covers multiple time frame analysis, which is also based on fractal symmetry.

So, you can see that fractal symmetry appears all around you, in both nature and in the Elliott Wave patterns on your chart. The more you start to be aware of fractal symmetry, the more often you will see it on your charts and all around you.

## Waves Within Waves Illustrate Price Symmetry

This is where the real fun begins! Price symmetry and fractal symmetry are present in all Elliott Waves, and Figure T1.10 illustrates the concept of waves within waves. What you can see on this diagram is that if you examine the same market and same chart on different time frames, you will be able to see predictable wave patterns on all of the time frames.

For example, on Figure T1.10, looking at the bullish impulsive Wave 1 on say a 60-minute chart it will look like a straight line. But, if you go to a lower time frame such as a 5-minute chart you will see much more detail and information, and there you

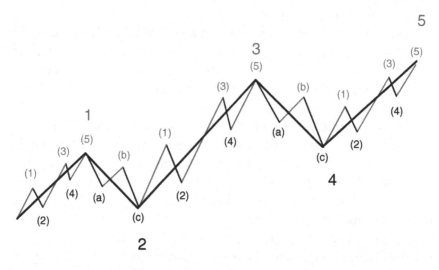

**Figure T1.10**   Waves within waves diagram.
SOURCE: @TradersCoach.com.

will discover a five-wave pattern inside the higher time frame pattern. Remember, all the same rules and statistics that you have learned for a 5-wave pattern, will apply to these five sub waves that appear inside Wave 1.

Then when you look at the corrective Wave 2 in Figure T1.10, which is bearish, you can see that there is a 3-wave pattern, an a-b-c sub wave pattern, inside the higher time frame pattern. Again, all of the rules and statistics that you have learned for a corrective 3-wave pattern, a-b-c pattern, will apply here as well.

And this continues through all of the waves in impulsive Wave 3, corrective Wave 4, and impulsive Wave 5. If you really want to go down the rabbit hole, like Alice in Wonderland, you should know that within each sub wave there is an entire additional set of sub waves. This can continue on into infinity.

Without going too far down the rabbit hole, the goal is instead to look at both the micro (the lower time frame) and the macro (the higher time frame) to get a more complete picture of what is happening in the market.

Later in Appendix A, which covers advanced techniques, you will discover more about my use of multiple time frame analysis, but for now just know that looking deeper into the chart by going to a lower time frame is illuminating.

One more note about waves and sub waves is that the larger scale waves are sometimes referred to as *parent waves,* and the smaller scale waves are sometimes called *child waves.* Just to give you context in case you hear these terms in Elliott Wave circles of conversation.

Last but not least, we can't talk about the topic of waves within waves without me showing my absolute favorite chart on this topic, See Figure T1.11. It is a daily chart showing the uptrend of Apple from the year 2011 to 2012 where you can see the macro parent waves one through five. What a perfect Wave 3 this chart displays.

Then on Figure T1.12, which is also the same daily Apple chart from 2011 to 2012, but instead I've taken the liberty of drawing in the sub waves, or child waves, within the parent waves. There within Wave 1 you can see on a real chart what the five sub waves look like in a real-life example. Then Wave 2 shows clear as a bell

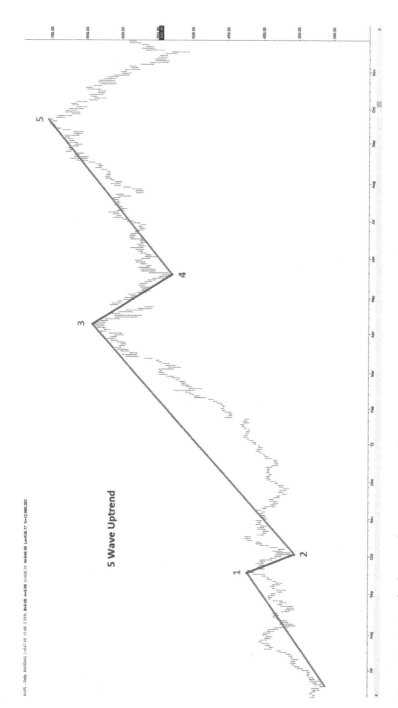

**Figure T1.11** Apple chart with parent wave only.
SOURCE: @TradersCoach.com.

433

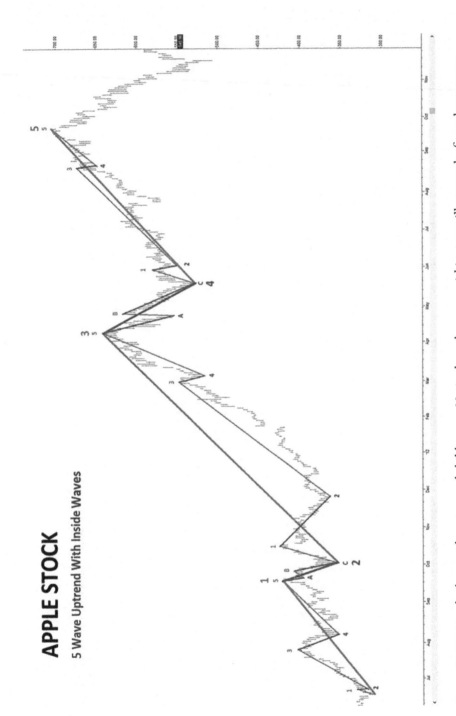

**Figure T1.12** Apple chart with parent and child waves. Notice how the waves within waves illustrate the fractal symmetry that exists in the markets.

SOURCE: @TradersCoach.com.

what the a-b-c corrective move looks like. Then look at that classic and massive Wave 3, with five sub-waves. And of course, the Wave 4 corrective wave with an a-b-c pattern. Ending with the final Wave 5 and its five sub-wave pattern.

Again, you know I'm a big fan of clear charts, and it doesn't get any clearer than this.

## Nine Degrees of Elliott Wave Cycles

Elliott stated that markets grow from small price movements to larger price movements, as you can see in the nine degrees of wave cycles that range from the smallest Sub-Minuette to the largest which is the Grand Super Cycle.

**There are nine degrees of waves:**

1. **Grand Super Cycle**—multiple century
2. **Super Cycle**—multiple decade, about 40 to 70 years
3. **Cycle**—one year to several years, even several decades
4. **Primary**—a few months to two years
5. **Intermediate**—weeks to months
6. **Minor**—weeks
7. **Minute**—days
8. **Minuette**—hours
9. **Sub-Minuette**—minutes

When Elliott wave patterns are linked together to form larger five-wave and three-wave structures, they exhibit self-similarity and are applicable on all time frames. This self-similarity is an example of the fractal symmetry that occurs amongst these varying degrees.

As you can see, Elliott laid out a structure that helps us to envision the large picture and investigate all the way down to the microscopic level. The distinction between these degrees helps all traders and investors to use the wave approach on any strategy of their choosing. It can be used on a day trading, position trading, and also on an investing approach.

# Alternate Wave Counts Are Possible and Your Hypothesis Can Fail

Wave counts can change, and it may turn out that your original hypothesis is wrong. It is also possible to have alternate wave counts when you are first looking at a market. This is why you must be diligent in your preliminary analysis and also in monitoring your wave counts as the market unfolds.

For example, you may think you are in a Wave 4 correction until the correction exceeds its maximum retracement level and instead turns into a continuation of an impulsive Wave 3. In this scenario, you must adhere to your stops to protect your account from excessive losses in the event of a failed wave count.

**IMPORTANT NOTE:** At times when counting Elliott waves, you may see two possible wave counts if the markets have not yet revealed enough information to give you a clear reading. In times like this, if both alternate wave counts agree with each other and put you in a trade pointing in the same market direction (whether bullish or bearish), that is a good enough reason to go ahead and take the trade. Only do this when your entry and exit trading system (which is a grounded assessment) gives you an entry.

Always be on the lookout for price action that isn't doing what it is supposed to do based on your initial Elliott wave count. When there is a red warning flag, reassess the trade to see if the current price action is in conflict with your original assumption. If you discover a conflict and your stop loss is hit, immediately scrub the trade and move on.

# If the Chart Is Messy, Forget It and Move On

My students hear me say this all the time, and my advice is to stay out of messy or unclear markets. Remember, there is unlimited opportunity in the universe and the markets, and it is pointless to try and force a wave count on a chart that simply doesn't have one. You may find that going to a higher or lower time frame of the same market might reveal a pattern with more clarity.

Typically, messy markets are going to end up becoming complex corrections, and yes, I'm sure there are traders that enjoy trading these markets, but I'm not one of them. I find that my time is better spent on the higher probability trades. In the final analysis you must choose the strategies and approaches that work best for you.

# Ralph Nelson Elliott's Story

The story of how Ralph Nelson Elliott (1871–1948) discovered the wave principle is a fascinating one to be sure, and it seems fitting to provide a brief biography here.

He began his career in 1896 as an accountant, meaning he was good at numbers. For 25 years he worked for a number of railroad companies in Mexico, Central America, South America and in the United States. In 1903 he married Mary Elizabeth Fitzpatrick, and they lived a comfortable life in both Mexico and later in the United States due to Elliott's distinguished career.

In 1920, Elliott and his wife obtained a residence in New York City. Then, seemingly out of nowhere, Elliott developed an illness caused by an organism known as *Entamoeba histolytica*, which he most likely contracted during decades of living in Latin America. The organism may have been lying dormant for many years, but it did not to show symptoms until around 1926 when he was 55 years old.

Robert Prechter describes the onset of Elliott's condition in his *book R.N Elliott's Masterworks*. "In December 1927, just when Elliott's future appeared its brightest, his independence and financial security seeming assured, disaster struck. Instead of recovery from his illness, Elliott's condition worsened. By 1929, his affliction had developed into a debilitating case of pernicious anemia, involving chronic fever, dysentery and weight loss, leaving him bedridden.

*(continued on next page ...)*

*(... continued from previous page)*

Several times over the next five years, he came extremely close to death. Each time he managed to recover."

With time on his hands due to his illness, Elliott studied patterns of market behavior. He had not been involved in the stock market before, but soon focused on examining, yearly, monthly, weekly, daily, hourly, and even half-hourly charts of the various indexes covering 75 years of stock market dating back to 1857.

Somewhere around 1932, Elliott read Robert Rhea's book *The Dow Theory* and was one of the first subscribers to Rhea's stock market service, *Dow Theory Comment* (1932–1937). Around May 1934, just two months after his final brush with death, Elliott's mission began to be fulfilled. His numerous observations of general stock market behavior began falling together into a general set of principles that applied to all degrees of wave movement in the stock price averages.

On February 19, 1935, Elliott mailed Charles J. Collins 17 pages of his treatise entitled *The Wave Principle*. Collins was president of Investment Council, Inc. Elliott sent 12 more pages and five additional charts. Collins was hooked and began to correspond with Elliott on a regular basis, even introducing him to the Fibonacci number sequence, which was similar to Elliott's own discoveries.

On March 13, 1935, Elliott sent Collins a telegram stating the following: "NOTWITHSTANIDNG BEARISH (DOW) IMPLICATIONS ALL AVERAGES ARE MAKING FINAL BOTTOM." Elliott's call proved to be so precise and correct using his wave principle, as the market continued on its upward climb, that Collins became a lifetime fan of Elliott's work. So much so that he wrote the book that would later be known as *The Wave Principle,* published in 1938. The copyright was in both Elliott and Collins's names, but the full credit of the wave discovery went to Elliott.

**Figure T1.13**   Ralph Nelson Elliott developed the wave principle in the 1930s and it is still as effective today as it was then.

## *Elliott Wave Techniques Simplified* by Bennett A. McDowell

Ralph Nelson Elliott, see Figure T1.13, changed my trading for the better. And, if you are looking for an even deeper dive into how to use Elliott Wave and Fibonacci techniques to better master them, be sure to pick up a copy of this book:

- **Title:** Elliott Wave Techniques Simplified, *How to Use the Probability Matrix to Profit on More Trades* (Figure T1.14)
- **Author:** Bennett A. McDowell
- **Publisher:** McGraw Hill Education

This book delves into the nuances of using both the classic and the modern Elliott Wave approach to get the most accurate wave counts. You'll find that in Chapter 7 there is a probability matrix enabling you to trust and verify your trading signals. This matrix scores each trade set up, to see if it is high probability or not. Plus, Chapter 8 has real-life case studies with step-by-step instructions on how to implement my favorite Elliott Wave trades.

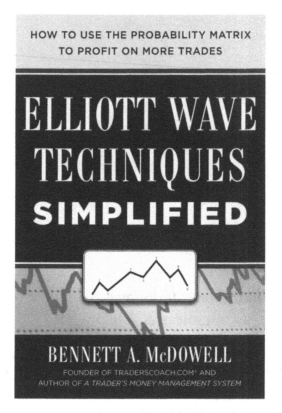

**Figure T1.14** *Elliott Wave Techniques Simplified* by Bennett A. McDowell published by McGraw Hill Education.

## How Did Elliott Find Out About the Fibonacci Number Sequence?

Elliott's analysis of the mathematical properties of waves and patterns eventually led him to conclude that they were essential to his approach. See Figure T1.15. Numbers and ratios from the Fibonacci sequence repeatedly surfaced in Elliott Wave structures, but Elliott developed his market model before he even realized that it reflected the Fibonacci sequence.

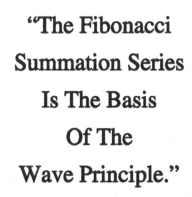

**Figure T1.15** MINI POSTER—ELLIOTT AND FIBONACCI—The numbers and ratios from the Fibonacci sequence repeatedly surfaced in Elliott Wave structures, but Ralph Nelson Elliott developed his market model before he even realized that it reflected the Fibonacci sequence. It wasn't until his friend and colleague Charles J. Collins sent him a book on Fibonacci that he discovered the similarities between the two. Quote from Ralph Nelson Elliott.
SOURCE: @TradersCoach.com, Inc.

*When I discovered the Wave Principle action of market trends, I had never heard of the Fibonacci Series.*
                                                    —Ralph Nelson Elliott

It was Charles J. Collins who first introduced Ralph Nelson Elliott to the concept of Fibonacci numbers, and he even sent Elliot a number of books including one on Fibonacci numbers and their occurrence in nature. Their close friendship lasted decades and if you read any biography of Elliott, you will see how they worked together to bring this remarkable approach to the world.

They came to know each other because Collins was president of *Investment Counsel,* Inc. in Detroit, Michigan and published a stock market publication that Elliott subscribed to.

## Elliott's Famous Telegram to Collins in 1935

On Wednesday, March 13, 1935, Elliott sent a telegram to Collins and stated the following: "NOTWITHSTANDING BEARISH (DOW) IMPLICATIOINS ALL AVERAGES ARE MAKING FINAL BOTTOM."

*Two months after his telegram, Elliott's market call had proved so precisely and dramatically correct as the market continued on its upward climb that Collins, 'impressed by his dogmatism and accuracy,' wrote and proposed that Investment Counsel subscribe for payment to Elliott's forecasts and commented, 'We are of the opinion that the Wave Principle is by far the best forecasting approach that has come to our attention'.*
                        —Excerpted from *R.N. Elliott's Masterworks,* page 57, edited by Robert R. Prechter, Jr.

When Elliott proved to Collins that his approach had value, Elliott then asked him to write the book that would later be known as *The Wave Principle*. The copyright of the book was in both their names but credit for the discovery and development of the Wave Principle went solely to Elliott.

Collins only agreed to write the book if Elliott's forecasts in timing the market were successful and accurate for two full years. At the end of the second year in March 1937, Collins, as promised, began working on Elliott's first monograph which was based on the original treatise.

The final book was published on August 31, 1938, with an estimated 500 copies printed. The size was 81/2 by 11 inches, and it had a dark blue cover with no text. As they say, the rest is history.

## The Fibonacci Number Sequence

Leonardo Fibonacci of Pisa (1170–1250), Italy, was a thirteenth century mathematician, and many would say the greatest mathematician of medieval times. See Figure T1.16.

**Figure T1.16**   Leonardo Fibonacci of Pisa, Italy, was mathematician that made the Fibonacci number sequence popular in the thirteenth century. Ralph Nelson Elliott discovered that Fibonacci's number theory was nearly identical to the math he used in The Wave Principle.

Although he introduced the Fibonacci number sequence to the Western world in the thirteenth century, some say it was originally discovered by Indian mathematicians hundreds of years earlier. Regardless of who originally identified this remarkable series of numbers, it is used today by traders and investors around the world.

The Fibonacci number sequence is based on a pattern of numbers wherein each number is derived by adding the two numbers before it. For example, the number sequence progresses like this: 0, 1, 1, 2, 3, 5, 8, 13, 21, 34, 55, 89, 144, and out to infinity.

What is remarkable is that in this sequence each number is approximately 1.618 (the Golden ratio number) times greater than the preceding number. So, when you multiply a number in this Fibonacci series by 1.618, the result approximates the following number in the series.

For example, if you multiply 89 by 1.618 it equals 144.002 (which is the next number in the Fibonacci sequence). The ratio becomes more precise as the numbers increase. See Table T1.1.

Table T1.1   This table shows the structure of the Fibonacci number sequence.

### FIBONACCI NUMBER SEQUENCE

| Formula To Find Next Number In Sequence | Fibonacci Number Sequence | Formula Of Golden Ratio Multiplied By Fibonacci Number |
|---|---|---|
| First Number | 0 | |
| Second Number | 1 | |
| $0 + 1 = 1$ | 1 | $1.618 \times 1 = 1.61$ |
| $1 + 1 = 2$ | 2 | $1.618 \times 2 = 3.23$ |
| $1 + 2 = 3$ | 3 | $1.618 \times 3 = 4.85$ |
| $2 + 3 = 5$ | 5 | $1.618 \times 5 = 8.09$ |
| $3 + 5 = 8$ | 8 | $1.618 \times 8 = 12.94$ |
| $5 + 8 = 13$ | 13 | $1.618 \times 13 = 21.03$ |
| $8 + 13 = 21$ | 21 | $1.618 \times 21 = 33.97$ |
| $13 + 21 = 34$ | 34 | $1.618 \times 34 = 55.01$ |
| $21 + 34 = 55$ | 55 | $1.618 \times 55 = 88.99$ |
| $34 + 55 = 89$ | 89 | $1.618 \times 89 = 144.00$ |
| $55 + 89 = 144$ | 144 | $1.618 \times 144 = 232.99$ |

When a Fibonacci number is multiplied by 1.618 the sum is the next number in the sequence.

NOTE: This table is intended for educational purposes only.

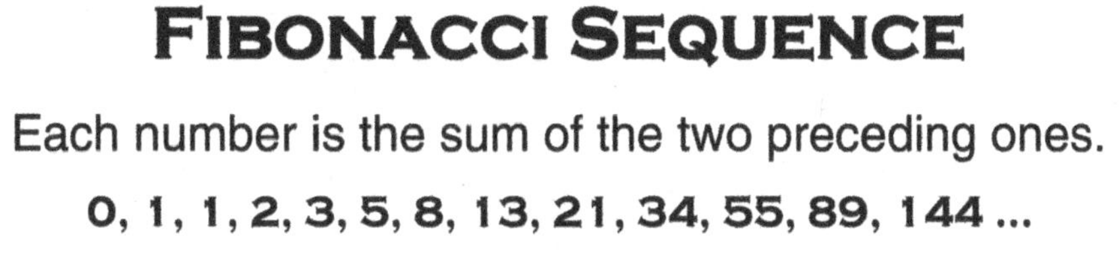

# FIBONACCI SEQUENCE

## Each number is the sum of the two preceding ones.

### 0, 1, 1, 2, 3, 5, 8, 13, 21, 34, 55, 89, 144 ...

**Figure T1.17**    The Fibonacci number sequence is based on a series of numbers with a pattern wherein each number is derived by adding the two number before it. SOURCE: @TradersCoach.com, Inc.

This number sequence is a fascinating pattern found naturally occurring throughout nature, geometry, and architecture and has enabled traders and investors to unlock a number of secrets to the financial markets. Ralph Nelson Elliott found that these very numbers and their ratios enabled him to find predictable patterns in the financial markets. His wave principle is intertwined with the Fibonacci sequence. See Figure T1.17.

## Cheat Sheets with Fibonacci Target Zones and Anchor Guidelines

As you can see, there are a lot of rules and statistics to memorize when first studying Elliott Wave analysis. Rest assured; you will know this information like the back of your hand once you begin seeing these patterns on your charts. In the beginning though, refer to the cheat sheets here while you are getting familiar with this material. See Figure T1.18 and Figure T1.19.

These essential cheat sheets cover not only the approximate probability of each outcome, but also the details on how I use Fibonacci extensions and retracements to determine target zones for each of the waves. It is crucial to refer to my guidelines for anchors when using Fibonacci drawing tools on your charting platform. These guidelines will give you the most accurate targets.

| | FIBONACCI TARGET ZONES | % PROBABILITY (APPROXIMATE) |
|---|---|---|
| **WAVE 2** Price Retracement | 23.6% - 38.2% of Wave 1 length | 15% |
| | 38.2% - 61.8% of Wave 1 length | 70% |
| | 61.8% - 100% of Wave 1 length | 15% |
| **WAVE 3** Price Extension | 100% - 161.8% of Wave 1 length | 15% |
| | 161.8% - 175% of Wave 1 length | 45% |
| | 175% - 261.8% of Wave 1 length | 30% |
| | Greater than 261.8% of Wave 1 length | 10% |
| **WAVE 4** Price Retracement | 23.6% - 38.2% of Wave 3 length | 15% |
| | 38.2% - 61.8% of Wave 3 length | 70% |
| | 61.8% - 76.40% of Wave 3 length | 15% |
| **WAVE 5** Price Extension | 38.2% - 61.8% (see anchor guidelines) | 15% |
| | 61.8% - 100% (see anchor guidelines) | 70% |
| | 100% - 161.8% (see anchor guidelines) | 15% |

**Figure T1.18**    Cheat Sheet of Fibonacci Target Zones for Elliott Waves. This cheat sheet is intended for educational purposes only. NOTE: Most charting platforms have "Fibonacci" drawing software tools that when properly used will illustrate these target zones visually on your charts. It is important you understand where to place the multiple anchoring points when using your Fibonacci software drawing tools so that you get the most accurate targets. See Figure T1.19 for exact anchor settings.
SOURCE: TradersCoach.com.

| | GUIDELINES FOR ANCHORS WHEN USING FIBONACCI DRAWING TOOLS |
|---|---|
| **WAVE 2** Price Retracement | Anchor the drawing tool at the beginning of Wave 1 and at the end of Wave 1. |
| **WAVE 3** Price Extension | Anchor the drawing tool at the beginning of Wave 1 and the end of Wave 1. (To use three anchors, anchor the drawing tool at the end of Sub-Wave 2, the end of Sub-Wave 3 and the end of Sub-Wave 4.) |
| **WAVE 4** Price Retracement | Anchor the drawing tool at the end of Wave 2 and at the end of Wave 3. |
| **WAVE 5** Price Extension | Anchor the drawing tool at the end of Wave 2, the end of Wave 3 and the end of Wave 4. |

**Figure T1.19**    Cheat Sheet of Guidelines for Anchors When Using Fibonacci Drawing Tools. This cheat sheet is intended for educational purposes only. NOTE: Most charting platforms have "Fibonacci" drawing software tools where you can anchor the drawing tool as these guidelines suggest. This will assist you in identifying Elliott Wave target zones on your charts and will give you the most accurate targets.
SOURCE: TradersCoach.com.

# How to Draw Fibonacci Target Zones on Your Chart

The first step in drawing target zones is to find the Fibonacci drawing tools located in your computer charting platform. For example, NinjaTrader, TradeStation, eSignal, and MultiCharts charting platforms all have these drawing tools available. If you are using a different charting platform and need assistance, be sure to contact the support team.

**Use these two Fibnoacci studies to draw in targets:**

1. **Fibonacci Price Retracement**—This enables you to draw a target zone that estimates where corrective Wave 2 and Wave 4 will go.
2. **Fibonacci Price Extension**—This enables you to draw a target zone that estimates where impulsive Wave 3 and Wave 5 will go.

Be sure to refer to the cheat sheets I provided to you. Figure T1.18 gives you Fibonacci target zone percentages and the probabilities associated with each. Figure T1.19 provides detailed anchoring instructions to get the most accurate result.

Then study Figure T1.20 carefully to learn how to anchor your Fibonacci drawing tools correctly for a retracement to obtain a

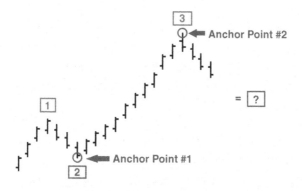

**Figure T1.20**   Anchor Point Diagram for Retracements. This diagram illustrates how to use your Fibonacci drawing tools on your charting platform and to apply two anchor points to obtain the highest probability Wave 4 target zone.
SOURCE: @TradersCoach.com, Inc.

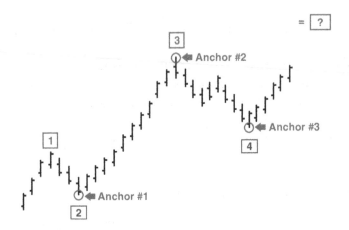

**Figure T1.21** Anchor Point Diagram for Extensions. This diagram illustrates how to use your Fibonacci drawing tools on your charting platform and how to apply three anchor points to obtain the highest probability Wave 5 target zone.
SOURCE: @TradersCoach.com, Inc.

Wave 4 target zone. Figure T1.21 is a diagram that illustrates the best anchoring strategy for an accurate Wave 5 target zone.

Now that you have all the guidelines for drawing targets, take a look at Figure T1.22 to see what a target zone on a real chart looks like. On this chart you can see that Wave 1, Wave 2, Wave 3, and Wave 4 are identified. The plan is to determine what the *target* will be for Wave 5.

To anchor your Fibonacci drawing tools on three places, first click with your mouse on the end of Wave 2, then move your cursor to the end of Wave 3 and click, and finally move your cursor to the end of Wave 4 and click. This strategy will give you the best target zone.

You can see on the upper right side of the chart the Wave 5 target zone is identified with a box around it. If price action moves anywhere inside that box, it has reached the target zone. The Fibonacci ratios used to determine the target zone in this example are between 61.8% and 100%, which is reached 70% of the time.

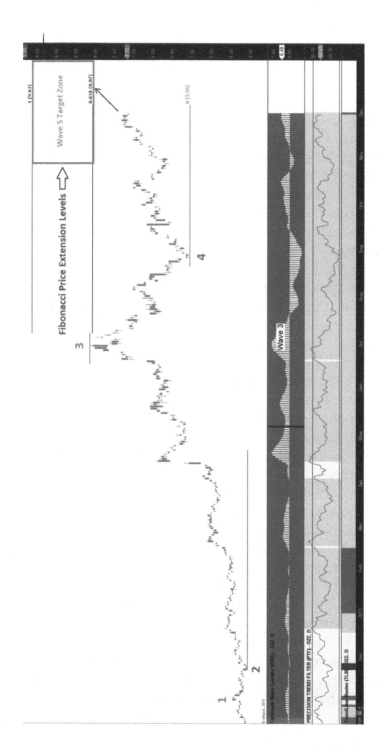

**Figure T1.22** Illustration of Wave 5 Target zone with fib price extension levels. Anchor your Fibonacci drawing tools on three places which are the end of Wave 2, the end of Wave 3, and the end of Wave 4. The drawing tool will identify the Wave 5 target zone with is between 1 and 0.618.

SOURCE: @TradersCoach.com, Inc.

# The Golden Ratio of 1.618 and Fibonacci Ratios

The golden ratio is a ratio between two numbers that equals approximately 1.618. Usually written as the Greek letter *Phi*, it is strongly associated with the Fibonacci sequence. The companion to *Phi* is 0.618 and is called *phi*. The Golden Ratio is also known as *Golden Mean* or *Divine Proportion*.

This common relationship between every number in the Fibonacci sequence is the foundation of the ratios used by technical traders and investors to determine retracement and extension levels.

For example, when you divide any Fibonacci number by its larger neighbor it approximates 0.618, or *phi*. So, if you take 89 and divide it by 144 it equals 0.6180. Or when you divide any Fibonacci number by its smaller neighbor, it approximates 1.618, or *Phi*. When you take 89 and divide it by 55 it equals 1.618.

Several variations of how to identify a Fibonacci ratio are in Table T1.2. The formulas do not always produce an exact result, but the ratios become more precise as the numbers increase.

More fun math exercises include the fact that Fibonacci ratios can be added, subtracted, multiplied, or divided and the result will be another Fibonacci ratio. For example, 1 minus 0.618 equals 0.382. Or 1 plus 0.618 equals 1.618. And 0.382 times 0.618 equals 0.236. Lastly, 1.618 divided by 0.618 equals 2.618.

And if you are interested in finding the inverse ratio, here is a formula to help with the calculations. Consider a number $x$ where $x$ is not equal to zero. Then the inverse of the number $x$ is the reciprocal of the number that is 1 divided by $x$. Example: Inverse of the ratio 1.618 is 1 divided by 1.618 which comes out to 0.6180. See Table T1.3 for the most common Fibonacci ratios and their inverse counterparts.

Last but not least are the Fibonacci ratios that are squared. A square root produces a specified quantity when multiplied by itself. An example of this in round numbers is 5 times 5 equals 25, and the square root of 25 is the number 5.

**Table T1.2**  This table shows how some of the mathematical Fibonacci ratios are arrived at. When using these formulas, the figures are not always exact, but they are very close.

### 13 FAVORITE FIBONNACI RATIOS

| | Ratio | Ratio Percentage | Formula To Find Ratio | Formula Description |
|---|---|---|---|---|
| 1 | 0.146 | **14.6%** | 89 ÷ 610 = 0.1459 | Divide any Fibonacci number by the number that is four spots to the right. |
| 2 | 0.236 | **23.6%** | 89 ÷ 377 = 0.2360 | Divide any Fibonacci number by the number that is three spots to the right. |
| 3 | 0.382 | **38.2 %** | 89 ÷ 233 = 0.3819 | Divide any Fibonacci number by the number that is two spots to the right. |
| 4 | 0.500 | **50%** | 1÷ 2 = 0.5000 | Divide the Fibonacci number 1 by the Fibonacci number 2. |
| 5 | 0.618 | **61.8%** | 89 ÷ 144 = 0.6180 | Divide any Fibonacci number by the number that is one spot to the right. |
| 6 | 0.786 | **78.6%** | 0.786 × 0.786 = 0.6177 | 0.786 is the square root of 0.618 |
| 7 | 1.000 | **100%** | 89 ÷ 89 = 1.0000 | Divide any Fibonacci number by itself. |
| 8 | 1.272 | **127.2%** | 1.272 × 1.272 = 1.6179 | 1.272 is the square root of 1.618. |
| 9 | 1.618 | **161.8%** | 89 ÷ 55 = 1.6181 | Divide any Fibonacci number by the number that is one spot to the left. |
| 10 | 2.000 | **200%** | 2 ÷ 1 = 2.0000 | Divide the Fibonacci number 2 by the Fibonacci number 1. |
| 11 | 2.618 | **261.8%** | 89 ÷ 34 = 2.6176 | Divide any Fibonacci number by the number that is two spots to the left. |
| 12 | 4.238 | **423.8%** | 89 ÷ 21 = 4.2380 | Divide any Fibonacci number by the number that is three spots to the left. |
| 13 | 6.846 | **684.6%** | 89 ÷ 13 = 6.8461 | Divide any Fibonacci number by the number that is four spots to the left. |

NOTE: This table is intended for educational purposes only.

**Table T1.3** This table shows how the inverse Fibonacci ratios are arrived at. When using these formulas, the figures are not always exact, but they are very close.

FIBONACCI INVERSE RATIO TABLE

|   | Ratio | Inverse Ratio | Inverse Ratio Percentage | Formula to Find Inverse Ratio |
|---|-------|---------------|--------------------------|-------------------------------|
| 1  | 0.146 | 6.846 | 684.6% | $1 \div 0.146 = 6.8493$ |
| 2  | 0.236 | 4.238 | 423.8% | $1 \div 0.236 = 4.2372$ |
| 3  | 0.382 | 2.618 | 261.8% | $1 \div 0.382 = 2.6178$ |
| 4  | 0.500 | 2.000 | 200%   | $1 \div 0.500 = 2.0000$ |
| 5  | 0.618 | 1.618 | 161.8% | $1 \div 0.618 = 1.6181$ |
| 6  | 0.786 | 1.272 | 127.2% | $1 \div 0.786 = 1.2722$ |
| 7  | 1.000 | 1.000 | 100%   | $1 \div 1.000 = 1.0000$ |
| 8  | 1.272 | 0.786 | 78.6%  | $1 \div 1.272 = 0.7861$ |
| 9  | 1.618 | 0.618 | 61.8%  | $1 \div 1.618 = 0.6180$ |
| 10 | 2.000 | 0.500 | 50%    | $1 \div 2.000 = 0.5000$ |
| 11 | 2.618 | 0.382 | 38.2 % | $1 \div 2.618 = 0.3819$ |
| 12 | 4.238 | 0.236 | 23.6%  | $1 \div 4.238 = 0.2359$ |
| 13 | 6.846 | 0.146 | 14.6%  | $1 \div 6.846 = 0.1460$ |

NOTE: This table is intended for educational purposes only.

This relates to Fibonacci ratios as in this example where 0.618 multiplied by 0.618 produces a result of 0.3819 (which rounds up to 0.382). Which means that the square root of 0.382 is 0.618. See Table T1.4.

The relationship between the Fibonacci numbers is important only in that they are the foundation of the Elliott Wave principle. The tables included in this chapter are designed to help you see where these ratios came from and why they are important in our Elliott Wave forecasting.

**Table T1.4**   This table shows how the squared Fibonacci ratios are arrived at. When using these formulas, the figures are not always exact, but they are very close.

FIBONACCI SQUARED RATIO TABLE

| | Ratio | Squared Ratio | Squared Ratio Percentage | Formula To Find Squared Ratio |
|---|---|---|---|---|
| 1 | 0.146 | 0.021 | 2.1% | $0.146 \times 0.146 = 0.0213$ |
| 2 | 0.236 | 0.055 | 5.5% | $0.236 \times 0.236 = 0.0556$ |
| 3 | 0.382 | 0.146 | 14.6% | $0.382 \times 0.382 = 0.1459$ |
| 4 | 0.500 | 0.250 | 25% | $0.500 \times 0.500 = 0.2500$ |
| 5 | 0.618 | 0.382 | 38.2% | $0.618 \times 0.618 = 0.3819$ |
| 6 | 0.786 | 0.618 | 61.8% | $0.786 \times 0.786 = 0.6177$ |
| 7 | 1.000 | 1.000 | 100% | $1.000 \times 1.000 = 1.0000$ |
| 8 | 1.272 | 0.618 | 61.8% | $1.272 \times 1.272 = 1.6179$ |
| 9 | 1.618 | 2.618 | 261.8% | $1.618 \times 1.618 = 2.6179$ |
| 10 | 2.000 | 4.000 | 400% | $2.000 \times 2.000 = 4.0000$ |
| 11 | 2.618 | 6.846 | 684.6% | $2.618 \times 2.618 = 6.8539$ |
| 12 | 4.238 | 17.960 | 1796% | $4.238 \times 4.238 = 17.9606$ |
| 13 | 6.846 | 46.867 | 4686.7% | $6.846 \times 6.846 = 46.8677$ |

NOTE: This table is intended for educational purposes only.

## Fibonacci Golden Spiral

The geometry of the Fibonacci number sequence forms patterns and geometry that are found everywhere in nature. Golden spirals are self-similar, and the shape of them is infinitely repeated when magnified. It is based on the golden ratio of 1.618

If you look at Figure T1.21, you can see how the Fibonacci number sequence fans out into a spiral. Then look at Figure T1.22 and you will see the same spiral is clearly evident in this nautilus shell. Although the Fibonacci numerical sequence is very precise and specific, in nature and in the financial markets it takes on its own shape.

The beauty of the pattern is that in nature it doesn't always match up exactly and yet, visually once you start looking you can spot it everywhere.

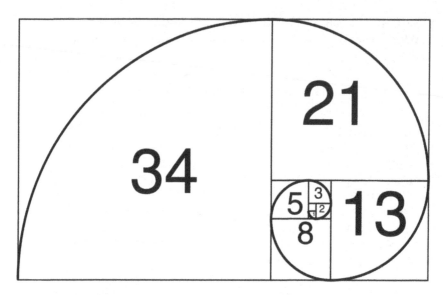

**Figure T1.23**    Fibonacci number spiral.

**Figure T1.24**    Nautilus shell spiral.
SOURCE: Photo 69471844 @ Andersastphoto Dreamstime.com

# The Modern Added to the Classic Elliott Wave Approach Improves Your Accuracy

In this chapter we have covered the classic Elliott wave approach in great detail. The classic strategies directly from Ralph Nelson Elliott are based purely on price action. In the 1930s Elliott didn't have computers that we have available to us today.

Which is why by adding the modern approach that involves various computer strategies, you can dramatically improve your forecasting accuracy. The modern approach blends several technical indicators together to further improve your analysis.

**Modern Elliott Wave analysis utilizes the following tools:**

1. **Price oscillator histogram using McDowell's secret settings (OWL)**
2. **Relative Strength index (RSI) using McDowell's secret settings (PTF)**
3. **Multiple Time Frame analysis**

All of these tools are explained in great detail on the website that comes with your purchase of this book.

For now, know that using a combination of the classic and the modern approaches will greatly enhance the accuracy of your Elliott Wave forecasts.

# Have Fun Counting Waves!

Now that you know the basics of using Elliott wave theory in combination with the Fibonacci sequence and ratios, you are ready to start counting waves on your charts.

If you are new to this approach you will be thrilled when you first begin to identify Wave 3, which the easiest wave to identify, and can then build your trading and investing plan on that. And of course, if you are a seasoned Elliot pro, you will continue to use this approach every day as your roadmap to the markets.

Enjoy!

# Technique 2

# Multiple Time Frame Analysis

No matter what time frame you are trading or investing in this technique can be used. If you are a day trader, swing trader, or an investor, this approach will improve your insight.

Significant trends involve traders and investors from many time frames that are trading in the same market direction. By looking at the time frame above, and the time frame below your primary time frame, you can uncover important data.

The reason why multiple time frame analysis works is because fractal symmetry produces similar price patterns across all financial markets and across all time frames. This is also why technical analysis systems should work on any market and any time frame.

## Price and Price Patterns Reveal Important Information

Technical analysts rely on the realities of the markets, price, volume and momentum, to guide them with regard to entries and exits. There are patterns that can identify key levels enabling traders and investors to determine the probabilities of future market direction.

And when it comes to multiple time frame analysis, there is no greater reality than price. Does price represent all known information in the current market? The answer is a resounding YES! Which means that by digging deeper into price patterns on more than just one time frame, we can see the entire picture.

**Price and price patterns reveal the following:**

- Support price levels
- Resistance price levels
- Fractal symmetry in price patterns

We know that history tends to repeat itself, and that is especially true in the world of price patterns. So when we have an understanding of current price activity, probabilities of what future price activity might be can be established.

And by looking at price patterns on multiple time frames, we can see if the support, resistance, and fractal symmetry agree on more than one time frame. When price patterns do agree on more than one time frame, that increases the probability of success.

## Fractal Symmetry Is the Foundation of Multiple Time Frame Analysis

The term *fractal* was first coined by mathematician Benoit Mandelbrot in 1975. He based this new word on the Latin *fractus*, meaning broken or fractured. The 1982 publication of Benoit's *The Fractal Geometry of Nature* brought fractals into the mainstream of professional and popular mathematics.

What's interesting is that long before 1975, Ralph Nelson Elliott actually went much further in describing the patterns of fractals than others in more recent mathematical circles. Elliott explained these fractal patterns and how they link together, in *The Wave Principle* in 1938, before the word fractal even existed. See Figure T2.1

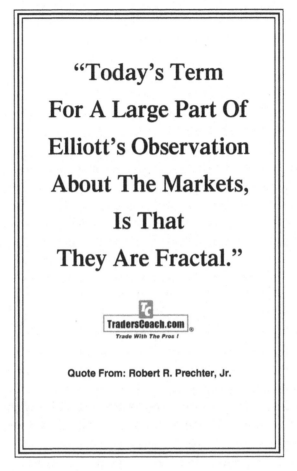

"Today's Term
For A Large Part Of
Elliott's Observation
About The Markets,
Is That
They Are Fractal."

**TradersCoach.com** ®
*Trade With The Pros !*

**Quote From: Robert R. Prechter, Jr.**

**Figure T2.1**  MINI POSTER—FRACTAL—Nearly 40 years before the word fractal had been coined by Benoit Mandelbrot, Ralph Nelson Elliott described these same self-similar patterns in his book *The Wave Principle* published in 1938. Quote from Robert R. Prechter, Jr.
SOURCE: @TradersCoach.com.

Fractal symmetry occurs all around us in nature, mathematics, the arts, and even the financial markets. A fractal can be defined as a self-similar geometric shape that can be subdivided into parts, each of which is a reduced size copy of the whole. Fractal symmetry is the foundation for multiple time frame analysis.

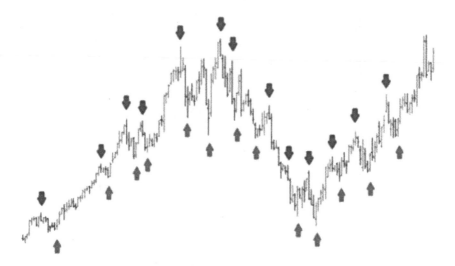

**Figure T2.2**   This chart illustrates the many repeating fractals that occur in this financial market. Notice the arrows pointing down indicating a period of bearish movement. And then there are arrows pointing upward that are indicating a period of bullish movement. The patterns continue to repeat themselves in varying degrees over and over again.
SOURCE: @TradersCoach.com.

Just like a fractal, the underlying structure of any price pattern in the market is a self-similar copy of itself. And remember that human behavior and crowd psychology are equally self-similar and repetitive, which means that fractal symmetry occurs in the realm of psychology as well. This concept ties in with how crowd psychology can move the markets, and that movement can be forecasted using Elliott Wave analysis.

On a chart, a fractal looks much like a pivot point. Nature and financial markets typically take the path of least resistance so that when a market hits the resistance of a fractal, it changes direction. This is a continuous self-repeating pattern that occurs over and over again. See Figure T2.2.

The concept of self-similar symmetry is also important to discuss. For example, when you look at a naked chart there is no way

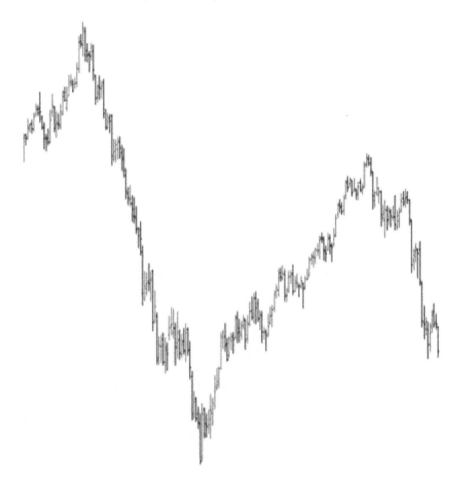

**Figure T2.3**   This is a Daily chart of the Futures symbol "CL" which is light crude oil. Looking at a naked chart, there is no way to determine what the market or the time frame is. This is due to the self-similar symmetry across all markets and all time frames.

SOURCE: @TradersCoach.com.

to determine what financial market it represents or what time frame the chart is based on. That is because all markets, and all time frames, contain the same patterns. There is symmetry across the board. See Figure T2.3 and Figure T2.4.

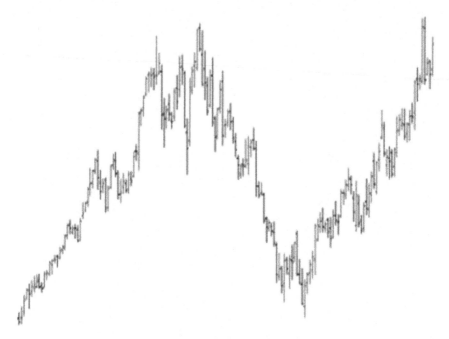

**Figure T2.4**    This is a Weekly chart of the Stock symbol "AMAT" which is Applied Materials, Inc. Looking at a naked chart, there is no way to determine what the market or the time frame is. This is due to the self-similar symmetry across all markets and all time frames.
SOURCE: ©TradersCoach.com.

## Benefits of a Three Time Frame Approach

In my experience using three time frames provides the best insight into where the market is headed when using a multiple-time frame approach. At one time I used only two time frames, but I've found that using three time frames is a far more accurate approach.

Again, this structure works for day traders, position traders, and investors. My recommendations for time frames and their associated correlation are outlined in Table T2.1. Notice that there are a variety of choices for you to choose from regarding the time frame correlations. It is a matter of testing to see what works best for you and your personal approach.

**Table T2.1**  Cheat Sheet for Using Three Time Frames in Your Multiple Time Frame Analysis.

### MULTIPLE TIME FRAME ANALSYIS CHEAT SHEET

| Trading Type (Frequency) | Lower Time Frame | Intermediate Time Frame (Primary Chart) | Higher Time Frame |
|---|---|---|---|
| Day Trader | 3-Second | **15-Second** | 2-Minute |
| Day Trader | 15-Second | **1-Minute** | 5-Minute |
| Day Trader | 20-Second | **2-Minute** | 10-Minute |
| Day Trader | 1-Minute | **5-Minute** | 25-Minute |
| Day Trader | 2-Minute | **10-Minute** | 60-Minute |
| Swing Trader | 5-Minute | **30-Minute** | 150-Minute |
| Swing Trader | 12-Minute | **60-Minute** | Daily |
| Position Trader | 60-Minute | **Daily** | Weekly |
| Investor | Daily | **Weekly** | Monthly |

NOTE: This table is intended for educational purposes only.

There will be times when the trend is not clear on the primary time frame you are trading. This is when multiple time frame analysis can give you more clarity. By looking at what traders' and investors' activity is on the lower and higher time frames, the market may provide more direction.

Even when the trend is clear on the primary time frame, another use of this approach is to use it as a confirmation tool. When the lower and higher time frames are in agreement with your primary time frame, that is a strong confirmation signal. In contrast, there will be times when you find that the other time frames are not in agreement with your primary chart, and in these cases you may decide to pass on the trade.

As we begin to paint in the broad brush strokes of how to use this approach, take a look at Figure T2.5, Figure T2.6, Figure T2.7, and Figure T2.8. In a very simple format with these diagrams, you can see how eventually you will be lining up three separate charts right next to each other, all from the same market, but on different time frames.

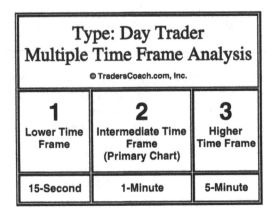

**Figure T2.5**  Example of Day Trader multiple time frame analysis recommendations. Using three time frames produces the best analysis result. Refer to Table T2.1 for more time frame correlations. Test to see what combination works best for your approach.
SOURCE: @TradersCoach.com.

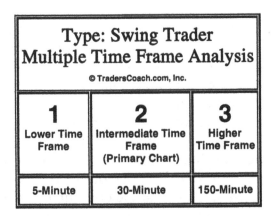

**Figure T2.6**  Example of Swing Trader multiple time frame analysis recommendations. Using three time frames produces the best analysis result. Refer to Table T2.1 for more time frame correlations. Test to see what combination works best for your approach.
SOURCE: @TradersCoach.com.

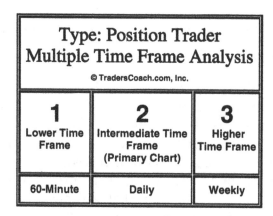

**Figure T2.7**  Example of Position Trader multiple time frame analysis recommendations. Using three time frames produces the best analysis result. Refer to Table T2.1 for more time frame correlations. Test to see what combination works best for your approach.

SOURCE: @TradersCoach.com.

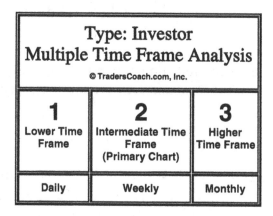

**Figure T2.8**  Example of Investor multiple time frame analysis recommendations. Using three time frames produces the best analysis result. Refer to Table T2.1 for more time frame correlations. Test to see what combination works best for your approach.

SOURCE: @TradersCoach.com.

## Day Traders, Position Traders, and Investors Use Different Time Frame Correlations

As you can see in Table T2.1, the three time frames you will select for each of your three charts will vary depending on whether you are a day trader or investor or somewhere in between.

This is because depending on the time frame you are making your entry and exit decisions on, which is your primary and center chart, the lower time frame and higher time frame must be correlated correctly. It is important that the lower and higher time frames are not too far away and yet not too close to the center chart.

Considering that day traders close out their positions to cash every night, the information they look at is different from position traders that are holding their positions overnight. They both use different risk control strategies and must look at different information.

## How to Set Up Three Charts Side by Side on Your Workspace

To benefit from the multiple time frame approach, you will need to use your charting platform and create a new workspace naming it "Multiple Time Frame Analysis."

### How to Set Up Three Charts Side by Side

1. **Create a brand new workspace**—Open your charting platform and create a new workspace naming it "Multiple Time Frame."
2. **Create one master chart with the studies you like**—Make this chart perfect, just like you want it. Include any studies or indicators you like and add any other bells and whistles. You will be copying this chart so the more perfect the better.
3. **Duplicate the chart you created in Step 2**—Create two copies of the master chart, so that you will have three individual charts on your workspace that are laid out side by side.
4. **Link all chart symbols together; do NOT link the time frames**—The goal is to have three charts showing the same

market symbol, but each chart will have its own time frame. The three time frames, from left to right, will be lower time frame, intermediate time frame, and higher time frame.

5. **Adjust the time frames on all three charts**—Refer to Table T2.1 for the recommended lower time frame, intermediate time frame, and higher time frame correlation. Then adjust each charts' time frame to customize it to your needs.

6. **Save this master template**—This template with these time frames is now ready to be saved to your workspace in a safe place. Label it accordingly. This way you will not have to recreate this layout again.

7. **Type in any new market symbol**—Now that you have this master template, as long as it is *symbol linked* to the three charts, you can make as many copies as you like with as many different symbols as you like.

The initial set up takes a few minutes, but once you have built your workspace the way you want it, you are good to go. Take a look at these examples of actual charts set up for multiple time frame analysis on Figure T2.9 and Figure T2.10.

**Set up your three charts in this order from left to right:**

1. Lower Time Frame
2. Intermediate Time Frame (Primary Chart)
3. Higher Time Frame

When your charts are set up side-by-side, your primary chart will be in the middle. That way you can focus on the center chart the most, using it for your entry and exit decisions.

Looking to the left at the lower time frame chart, you can see if that pattern confirms the center chart or not. The same applies to when you look at the chart on the right. You may have additional signals that also confirm or deny whether the center chart is a high probability trade or not.

For example, when looking at my charts on Figure T2.9 and Figure T2.10, I use the ribbons at the bottom of my charts which give me signals from the OWL, PTF, TLM, and ERI. The OWL gives me

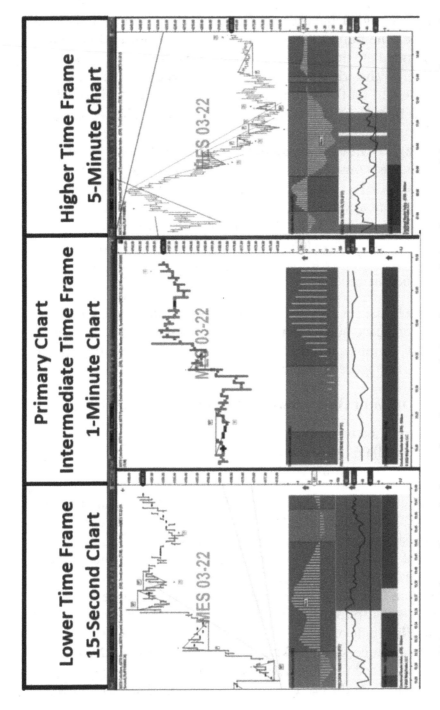

**Figure T2.9** MES day trading multiple time frame layout with three charts, including the 15-second chart, 1-minute chart, and the 5-minute chart.

SOURCE: @TradersCoach.com.

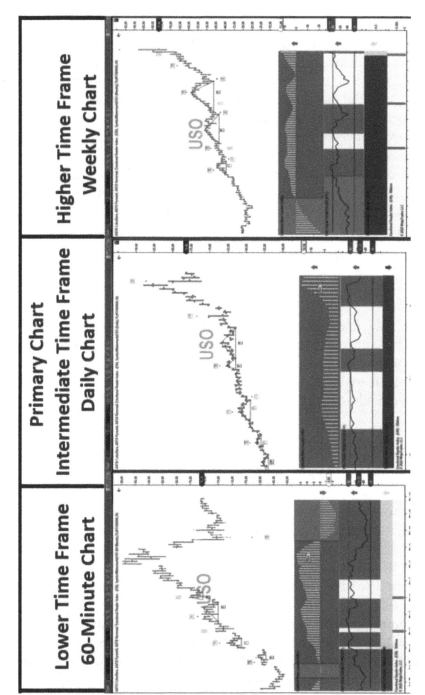

**Figure T2.10** USO position trading multiple time frame layout with three charts including the 60-minute chart, daily chart, and the weekly chart.

SOURCE: ©TradersCoach.com.

469

Elliott Wave counts, the PTF tells me if there will be higher highs or lower lows, the TLM indicates the trend direction (or lack thereof), and the ERI is my emotional reader index.

My approach is to look at price action on the actual chart and make an initial assessment based on that. Then by using the ribbons below, I can see more information such as if we are in an Elliott Wave 3 or if we have a high probability of reaching new highs or new lows.

Of course, you will be using your own personal approach but remember that by looking at price action and other signals on more than one time frame, you can increase your understanding of where the market is likely to move next.

## Using a Scanner or Quote Bar Is Helpful

If you have just one monitor, you may want to use a scanner or quote bar and locate that at the top of your three charts. When you link that to the charts you can click and toggle to different market symbols. It makes it easy to pull up market symbols on all three charts quickly.

## You May Discover an Opportunity That Is Not on Your Center Chart

The center chart is the one that you initially plan to use for determining the speed of your trade. However, you can use any of the time frames of the three charts, if you spot a trading opportunity. So, be flexible and know that there are times when you may suddenly find an ideal trade set up, that is not on your center chart.

In this case, if you are switching time frames, be sure to base your entry and exit signals, and also your trade size and risk control, on the time frame of the chart where you actually identify the opportunity. It is also important to locate the price target on the chart where you identify your opportunity.

## Set Profit Targets Using the Center Chart

Your targets should be set using the primary time frame, or the center chart. A profit target that exists on the higher time frame chart, usually cannot be reached if the chart that is used for risk control and position sizing, is on the lower time frame chart.

The reason is because the volatility on the lower time frame will usually stop you out before you reach the higher time frame's price target. If you want to shoot for the target on the higher time frame chart, make the switch so that the higher time frame chart becomes the primary and center chart. In this case, act accordingly and select entry, exit, risk control, and price targets based on the primary center chart.

## When Momentum Agrees on All Three Time Frames, That's a High Probability Trade

Best case scenario is when momentum signals agree on all three of your charts. The probabilities of a trade's success increase dramatically when the momentum of a trend is in agreement on the lower time frame, intermediate time frame, and the higher time frame all at the same time. The next best-case scenario is if momentum on the lower time frame chart is moving in the same direction and agrees with your center chart.

Short of these two scenarios, be on the lookout for any signals that are in the opposite direction of your primary center chart. Any signals on the lower or higher time frames that are in opposition to your center chart indicate that the trade may not be viable. Sometimes it means that you can put the trade on your watchlist and wait for market conditions to move in your favor.

## Waiting to Get a Better Entry Price

A trade that looks good on the primary time frame on the center chart may show an opposite short-term movement on the lower time frame chart. In this case, it is possible to get a better trade entry price by waiting. In this event, put the trade on a watchlist and wait for a better price to enter on.

## Using Multiple Time Frame Analysis on Every Trade

This approach has become an essential part of my analysis, and once you get the hang of it, my bet is it will help you too. I've already tweaked my template so that it is exactly the way I want it. Look at Figure T2.11 for a glimpse of my workstation.

This screenshot is from a live event I did last week and shows how my screen looks. Here you can see my scanners located at the top of the chart so that I can click and toggle to pull up symbols quickly.

Also notice the horizontal lines on the middle and left charts, these are my Fibonacci price target zones. And lastly, on the bottom of the screen are ribbons for my OWL, PTF, TLM, and ERI signals. I'm excited to show you my approach to multiple time frame and hope that you have great success with it as well.

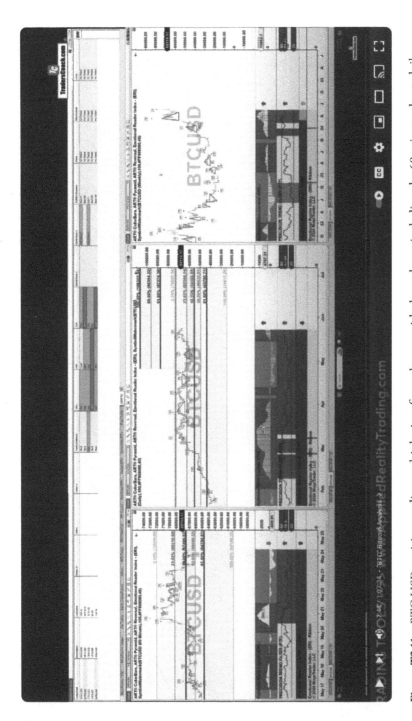

**Figure T2.11** BTC USD position trading multiple time frame layout with three charts including the 60-minute chart, daily chart, and the weekly chart. This screenshot from my live event last week shows how my screen looks. Notice my scanners located at the top of the chart so that I can click and toggle to pull up symbols quickly. Also notice the horizontal lines on the middle and left charts, these are my Fibonacci price target zones. And lastly, on the bottom of the screen are ribbons for my OWL, PTF, TLM and ERI signals.

SOURCE: @TradersCoach.com.

# Technique 3

# Scaling Out of and Into Trades

Scaling out of positions is one of my favorite strategies because it locks in profit and reduces stress. And of course, scaling into a position is also an excellent strategy to get a larger position of an already successful trade.

You cannot use scaling out of a position at the exact same time as when you are scaling into a trade because these two techniques are in direct conflict. You can however scale into a position, adding on shares or contracts, and then scale out later during the same period of a trend trade.

Thus, there are times to scale in which are different than the times to scale out. The following pages detail the best conditions for benefiting from each of these techniques.

## Scaling Out of Trades to Lock In Profit and Reduce Stress

A primary goal of trend trading is to stay in the trend as long as possible. As they say, cut your losers short and let your winners ride. But sometimes when a trend takes off and catapults into a

APPENDIX A: ADVANCED TECHNIQUES

significantly profitable territory, it is difficult emotionally to resist the temptation to liquidate and take all of your profits right then and there. You have probably experienced this.

The problem is, if you exit the trade before it matures or before you reach your target zone, there is money left on the table. That is, if the trade in fact makes it to the target zone. Herein lies the conundrum, from a trader's mindset point of view, how confident are you that this trade will reach the target zone? That kind of confidence is built over time using a consistently winning approach.

Here's where the strategy of scaling out comes in. While you are building confidence, and strengthening your trader's mindset, this strategy enables you to reduce the stress associated with a profitable trade, and to lock in profit. See Figure T3.1.

The exact parameters you choose for using this strategy can be written into your trading rules. Think of it as a happy medium or the best of both worlds. Rather than liquidating the entire profitable position thus not benefitting from the potential continuation of the trend . . . or . . . rather than staying in the entire position and risking being stopped out at a loss . . . you instead lock in a small profit and still stay in the trend.

## Select a Reversal Signal to Scale Out On

When scaling out, as with all of your trading rules, it is important to scale out based on an actionable signal that current market dynamics are exhibiting. Don't randomly scale out based on an emotional reason. Instead find a reversal signal that your approach uses to tell you what the market is saying.

And scale out only when the position has displayed a certain amount of profit. Determine this benchmark ahead of time and include it in your trading plan rules. For example, you could say that your trade must produce a 10% or 20% profit prior to any scale out. This amount is something that you can test and fine tune to determine the optimal amount.

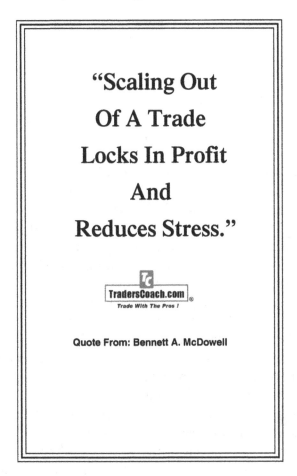

**Figure T3.1**   MINI POSTER—SCALING OUT—Scaling out of a trade is an ideal way to reduce stress and lock in profit when your trade reaches significantly profitable territory. The fear of losing profits from a possible market reversal can be lessened by scaling out a third of your position to lock in profits. This strategy is helpful while you are building confidence and a stronger trader's mindset. Quote from Bennett A. McDowell.
SOURCE: @TradersCoach.com.

## Scale Out No More Than Two Times per Trade

To scale out of trades effectively, your initial trade size must be large enough so you can reap the benefits. The technique can be used for both long and short positions and on all markets and all time frames. Scaling out more than two times per trade is not recommended.

In the Futures market for example, if you have a position with three contracts, you could scale out of one contract for your first time scaling out. Then you could scale out your second time with the second contract. This would mean you could leave the final and third contract on until your position was stopped out. That is the idea of having a large enough trade size to reap the benefits.

## Scaling Out Example for a Bearish Trade

Using the Emini as an example, see Figure T3.2, on this 1-minute chart you can see a bearish downtrend in place that began around 7:00 am, on the left side of the chart. Notice the second triangle from the left that is facing downward and has a "P" symbol located above the flat part, or base leg of the triangle.

That second downward facing triangle gives us an entry signal that occurs when price moves beyond the apex, or the point of the triangle. The initial stop-loss exit is located at the flat part of the triangle and will be hit if price action becomes bullish and exceeds 11560. So now the trade is in place.

Notice the third triangle from the left that has a "P" on top of the flat part of the triangle, it is moving in the direction of the trend which is bearish. To tighten our *initial stop,* and lock in profit, we use an adjusted stop which is known as a *trailing stop.* The initial stop is moved from the flat part of the second triangle and is trailed to the flat part of the third triangle.

Next a fourth triangle from the left appears with a "P" on top, it is also moving in the direction of the bearish trend. Again, we will use another trailing stop and move the stop position from the flat part of the third triangle to the flat part of the fourth triangle.

When the fifth triangle from the left appears with a "P" on top, again moving in a bearish direction, we will now scale out of 30% of our position to lock in profit. The reason for the scale out is that the trend is becoming mature and has a probability of reversing after the fourth triangle in this trend's pattern.

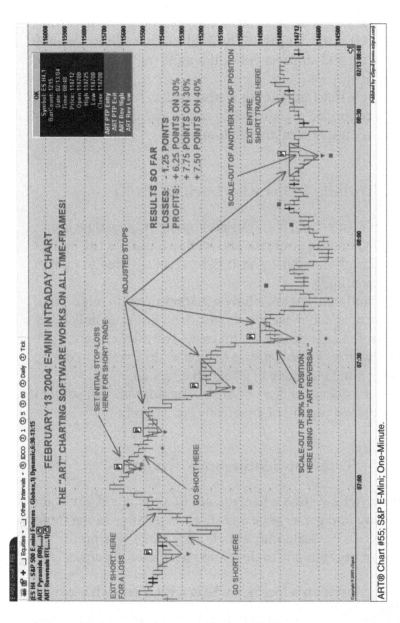

**Figure T3.2** Scaling out on the Emini with a bearish 1-minute chart. Notice how scaling out of a mature trend, as defined by four consecutive ART Pyramid Trading Points, can lock in profit. An added strategy to lock in profit is to use *trailing stops*, labeled as adjusted stops on this chart. By tightening the stops as the trend goes in your favor, you are more likely to ride the trend to the end. This chart is from the first edition of *The ART of Trading*, hence the 2004 date.

SOURCE: www.eSignal.com

Look at the sixth triangle from the left with a "P" on top, again this reversal signal that is at a mature place of the trend and is an ideal place to scale out another 30% of the position. The new *trailing stop* is placed at the flat part of the final triangle. Market activity begins to reverse and stops us out of the trade on the final trailing stop, at a profit.

This example illustrates how a methodical scaling out approach can deliver a controlled and profitable result. Test this approach for yourself and see if it boosts your bottom line.

## Trailing Stops Also Lock In Profit

As you saw in Figure T3.2, the adjusted stops, or *trailing stops* are an effective way to control your risk and lock in profit. As the market moves significantly in your favor, it is an excellent idea to tighten your stops accordingly.

Keep in mind that you must have a market signal to rely on that lets you know where to move the stop to; don't just randomly move your stops. In the case of this Emini trade, the market signals are the triangles with a "P" on top, also known as the Pyramid Trading Points, that continue to move in a bearish direction.

Another consideration is to be sure your stops are not so tight that volatility stops you out of a perfectly good trend.

## Rules for Scaling into Trades

Scaling into a trade is used when you are in a trend and you want to be aggressive and get as large a position as possible as the trend moves in your favor. Scale into a trade only when it is profitable. Scaling into an unprofitable trade is known as doubling down.

**Doubling down on a losing trade is a high-risk strategy.**

When scaling into a profitable position, you will be adding to your position when additional signals are triggered. There are many variations to this technique, and you may not want to scale in if the trend is matured, since a mature trend is likely to soon reverse.

Before adding on to a winning position, recalculate your trade size. Since the position is profitable, be sure you have eliminated any risk that you initially had. Next it is a matter of calculating how many shares or contracts you can add on to maintain proper risk control for the larger trade size.

## Key Point: Do Not Increase Your Trade Risk When Scaling In

Only scale in when your position is profitable, this profit is based on your trailing stop in relation to your initial trade entry. The trailing stop exit must ensure a trade profit before you can scale into a trade. The key here is to not increase your trade risk.

Once the initial trade risk is removed, because your trailing stop exit has removed the initial trade entry risk, you are then clear to scale into the trade. For example, if your trade risk was 2% on the initial entry, you want to maintain no more than a 2% risk even after you have scaled in with additional shares or contracts. Trailing your stops allows this.

## Dollar Cost Averaging

Another way to look at a common  strategy of "dollar cost averaging" is that you are in essence adding onto your position. Many investors will deposit a fixed dollar amount into the stock market every month. Over time, the markets tend to rise, so this strategy is a way to continually grow their account with the understanding that they will sometimes get in at a higher or lower price per share depending on market fluctuations. Typically this is considered to be an investing strategy as opposed to a day trading strategy.

# Appendix B
# Resources

# Resources 1

# Brokers, Data Feeds, and More

Here is where I get to share with you my *little black book* or *yellow pages* of the financial industry and its suppliers. This appendix has lots of great information at the time of printing, but as you can imagine, this space is rather fluid and can change over time. So for the latest information on my recommendations, you can go to the following webpage:

https://www.traderscoach.com/BOOK

Keep in mind that we do not make any guarantees that you will be successful using the following resources, but these are some of my current favorites. We are not affiliated with these companies, and as such, if you need more information or support, you can reach out to them directly.

As in all things in life, it is what you do with the resources you are presented with that makes all the difference. So, cultivate your resources and manage them. A vendor may even need to be replaced on occasion, if in the future a better solution that meets your needs presents itself. Your needs may change, these providers may change, so be mindful of this and act accordingly. Give us your feedback on who your favorites are; we would love to hear from you. Just drop us a line at:

**Support@TradersCoach.com**

You may find some vendors that overlap across all of the categories, and as such you may notice some repetition. For example, the firm TradeStation is a one-stop solution offering brokerage services, charting platform, and data feed all in one, so they are listed under each of the categories that follow. Kinetick data feed, however, is only listed under data feed. My advice to you is to carefully study *Chapter 17* in this book, *Understanding Financial Markets,* pages 19 through 23, which goes into more detail on how to select the best vendors for your unique needs.

### The Categories of Resources Included Here

- Brokers
- Charting platforms
- Data feeds
- Prop firms

A little planning goes a long way because you can save money if you research what the latest offerings are from each of these providers. And as mentioned earlier, some providers overlap services, so you want to be sure you are not paying for the same service twice.

We do have clients who benefit from having multiple providers in all of the categories included here. These clients may be more advanced than most and are looking to have a rich and comprehensive suite of tools. Plus, many traders have multiple providers acting as insurance; if one of the services goes down, there is a backup.

**IMPORTANT NOTE.** The information in this chapter is for educational purposes only and is subject to change. Readers are advised to consult with their financial advisor.

# Brokers

There are many brokers worldwide, and choosing the best for your needs can be challenging. They each have different niche strengths and varying price models. Your decision on which broker or brokers to choose will be based on your needs and the costs associated with those needs.

You may find that having more than one active brokerage account can actually reduce costs by getting real-time data, charting platform, and a variety of tools for free, as part of your brokerage package.

### There are different levels of brokers:

- FCM (Futures Commission Merchant)—main futures broker dealer
- RFED (Retail Foreign Exchange Dealer)—main forex broker dealer
- IB (Introducing Broker)—smaller referring broker

There are bigger and smaller brokerage firms. In the futures space, an FCM is the larger main broker dealer, such as NinjaTrader. An FCM or RFED must be registered with the National Futures Association (NFA).

And then there are IB (introducing broker) firms that are smaller like Forex.com, which is an introducing broker and clears through its RFED, which is GAIN Capital.

Then there is the connectivity between brokers, charting platforms, and data feed providers. This is accomplished with an application programming interface (API), which enable us to fluidly connect all of our vendors together.

My advice to you is to carefully study Chapter 17 in this book, *Understanding Financial Markets*, which goes into more detail on how to select the best broker for your unique needs.

# Brokers

The history on the brokerage industry, particularly regarding the cost of commissions before 1975 and after 1975, is enlightening and worth sharing here. On May 1, 1975 (*Mayday*), the New York Stock Exchange (NYSE) Board of Governors made the unanimous decision to discontinue the practice of fixed commission rates in favor of competitive negotiated commission rates.

A 183-year-old tradition of fixed commission rates, that were exorbitantly high, in effect was a blockade for lower net worth individuals to enter the financial markets. The change in 1975 opened the doors to *discount online brokers* like Charles Schwab to offer investment opportunities to virtually everyone. See Figure R1.1.

The famous 1975 date was referred to as *Mayday*, by Morgan Stanley chairman Robert Baldwin, as he felt the need for the *international distress call* was in order. The old-boy network was not in favor of deregulating the commission structure, and one hundred investment banks did fail as a result of the change, but the lean and efficient firms that survived went on to flourish in the new deregulated environment.

Robert Hack, former NYSE president, got the ball rolling with a speech in 1970 advocating negotiated commission rates. In an interview in 1988, he said, "My speech still reads pretty good, if I may make a conceited statement." Meaning it all turned out pretty well for the financial industry.

I remember that my very first personal online trades were with Charles Schwab back in the beginning, and the idea that you could place a trade for $9.95 instead of $300 back then was a game changer. Of course, Charles Schwab was one of the very first retail online discount brokers. And with that, active trading was born and hasn't looked back since.

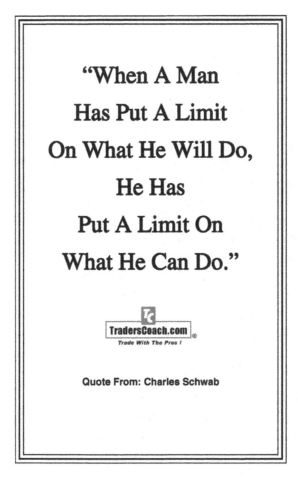

**Figure R1.1** MINI POSTER—NO LIMITS—Charles Schwab was a pioneer in his time at the forefront of the discounted online brokerage industry on Wall Street. This quote is one of his core beliefs and is inspiring to anyone who is exploring new frontiers. Quote from Charles Schwab.
SOURCE: @TradersCoach.com.

### Broker: NinjaTrader

- Website: https://www.NinjaTrader.com
- Market(s): futures
- Charting platform: NinjaTrader, included

- Scanner: Market Analyzer
- Data feed: real time included
- Compatibility: connects with all TradersCoach.com software
- US phone: 800-496-1683
- US phone: 312-262-1289
- Email: support@ninjatrader.com

NinjaTrader is a US-based broker with a 4.5 out of 5 score from BrokerChooser.com. It was founded in 2003 by Raymond Deux as a charting platform and became a broker in 2014. Fun fact is that Raymond and I met at a trade show when he was starting, and the ART software was the second or third software program developed for Ninja. NinjaTrader provides one of the best charting platforms available with an excellent scanning feature called Market Analyzer. The charting platform along with real-time data are provided for free when opening a funded brokerage account. NOTE: If you are in a paper testing mode and do not trade each month, you will be charged a small monthly *inactivity fee*.

### Broker: TradeStation

- Website: https://www.TradeStation.com
- Market(s): stocks, options, futures, ETFs, and funds
- Charting platform: TradeStation, included
- Scanner: Radar Screen
- Data feed: real time, included
- Compatibility: connects with all TradersCoach.com software
- US phone: 800-822-0512
- TradingView: 800-328-9861
- US phone: 954-652-7900
- Email: sales@tradestation.com

TradeStation is a US-based broker with a 4.4 out of 5 score from BrokerChooser.com. It was founded in 1982 by two brothers, William Cruz and Rafael Cruz, as a charting platform and became a broker in 2001. TradeStation is equal in excellence to NinjaTrader and has a scanner called Radar Screen. The charting platform along with real-time data are provided for free when opening a funded brokerage account. One downside is that the commission fees are high; for example they are about five times the cost of IB (InteractiveBrokers) for stocks, which has one of the lowest priced commissions. NOTE: If you are in a paper testing mode and do not trade each month, you will be charged a small monthly *inactivity fee*. The real-time data feed from your TradeStation account can be imported into the MultiCharts charting platform. By importing real-time data, you can save money by not paying for data from a separate vendor.

### Broker: InteractiveBrokers, IB

- Website: `https://www.InteractiveBrokers.com`
- Market(s): stocks, options, futures, forex, bonds and funds
- Charting platform: IBKR, included
- Data feed: real time included
- US phone: 877-442-2757
- US phone: 312-542-6901

IB is a US-based broker with a 4.9 out of 5 score from `Broker Chooser.com`. It was founded in 1977 by Thomas Peterffy and was later incorporated in 1993 as a US broker dealer. Fun fact is that as of 2024, *Forbes* magazine estimate Peterffy's net worth at US$34 billion, making him the 46th richest man in the world. From a purely cost standpoint, IB probably has the lowest commissions of any broker, which makes them popular with professional traders. There are a few downsides, such as IB is not geared toward inexperienced traders. Also, its charting platform is not as robust as NinjaTrader and TradeStation's, although it is provided for free along with a free data feed with all funded accounts. The real-time data feed from IB can be imported into the NinjaTrader and the MultiCharts charting platform. By importing real-time data, you can save money by not paying for data from a separate vendor.

### Broker: Charles Schwab

- Website: https://www.Schwab.com
- Market(s): stocks, options, futures, ETFs, forex, cryptocurrency, bonds, and funds
- Charting platform: thinkorswim (TOS), included
- Data feed: real time included
- US phone: 800-435-4000

Charles Schwab is a US based broker with a 4.7 out of 5 score from BrokerChooser.com. It was founded in 1971 by Charles Schwab as the first online broker to offer multiple stock order entry for all online trading accounts. Having acquired TD Ameritrade's holdings in 2023, Schwab customers now have access to the award winning *thinkorswim* charting platform, also known as TOS. The real-time data feed from your Charles Schwab account (aka TOS platform) can be imported into the NinjaTrader charting platform. By importing real-time data, you can save money by not paying for data from a separate vendor.

### Broker: Oanda

- Website: https://www.Oanda.com/us-en
- Market(s): forex and cryptocurrencies
- Charting platform: MetaTrader 4, included
- Data feed: real time included
- US phone: 877-626-3239
- US phone: 212-858-7690

Oanda is a US-based broker with a 4.5 out of 5 score from BrokerChooser.com. It was founded in 1996 by Michael Stumm and Richard Olsen. You can choose from a variety of charting platforms, including MetaTrader 4 and TradingView. The real-time data from your Oanda account can be imported into your MultiCharts charting platform. By importing real-time data, you can save money on not having to pay for data from a separate vendor.

**Broker:** Forex.com

- Website: https://www.Forex.com/en-us
- Market(s): forex
- Charting platform: MetaTrader 5, included
- Data feed: real time included
- US phone: 877-367-3946
- US phone: 908-731-0750
- Email: newaccounts@forex.com

Forex.com is a US-based broker with a 4.5 out of 5 score from BrokerChooser.com and was founded in 2001. Forex.com is a subsidiary of GAIN Capital Group LLC, which is a wholly owned subsidiary of StoneX Group Inc. According to the 2023 monthly Retail Forex Obligation reports published by the CFTC, based on client assets it is the number 1 forex broker in the United States.

### Broker: Optimus Futures

- Website: https://optimusfutures.com/
- Market(s): futures
- Charting platform: Optimus Flow, TradingView, Sierra Chart, included
- Data feed: real time included
- US phone: 800-771-6748
- US phone: 561-367-8686
- Email: support@optimusfutures.com

Optimus Futures is a US-based broker with a 4.5 out of 5 score from BrokerChooser.com. It was founded by Matt Zimberg in 2004. Its trading commissions are low and in the same ballpark as IB. Another upside is there is no *inactivity fee*.

### Broker: AMP Futures

- Website: https://www.NinjaTrader.com
- Market(s): futures
- Charting platform: MetaTrader 5, MultiCharts.net, TradingView, Sierra Chart, included

- Data feed: real time CQG or Rithmic, included
- US phone: 800-560-1640
- US phone: 312-893-6400
- Email: support@ampfutures.com

AMP Futures is a US-based broker with a 4.2 out of 5 score from BrokerChooser.com. It was founded in 2009 by Dan Culp. A big plus of AMP Futures is its low commission rates, even lower than IB, which is usually the lowest priced broker. Another upside is there is no *inactivity fee*. Plus, the company provides many high-quality educational materials, including videos and articles. One downside is it has a high wire withdrawal fee.

## BrokerChooser.com

You can also check out a website called BrokerChooser, which pulls up data for you to conduct side-by-side comparisons for about 100 brokers. It has information on what markets, charting platforms and more about each regulated broker in its system. Here is the link: https://brokerchooser.com/.

When using this website, know that they are not necessarily as interested in a robust charting platform so it gives higher ratings to some brokers than I would have. The flexibility of a platform to be compatible with a number of third-party tools is a big plus. Both TradeStation and NinjaTrader can do that.

## Charting Platforms

Your choice of charting platform will depend on what markets you trade and the charting tools your approach requires. Of course, cost is an issue as well. Both NinjaTrader and TradeStation offer professional grade charting tools and are free if you have a funded brokerage account.

*(continued on next page ...)*

*(... continued from previous page)*

Currently the cost to open a brokerage account is nominal, so it may be the most cost effective solution to get a quality charting platform with real-time data. Determine what markets and tools you need and which platforms offer those markets and tools at the best price.

Go back to Chapter 17 in this book, *Understanding Financial Markets,* which goes into more detail on how to select the charting platform for your unique needs.

# Charting Platforms

Your charting platform is your canvas. This is where your creativity and ingenuity can be expressed to develop a custom approach that works and is profitable for you.

Each charting platform offers a variety of different tools from the basics, like moving averages all the way to the more complex Elliott Wave and Gann studies. Do a little research depending on what your preferred approach is, and you can find the right fit for you.

### Charting Platform: NinjaTrader

- Website: `https://www.NinjaTrader.com`
- Computer language: NinjaScript, Microsoft C# based language
- Scanner: Market Analyzer
- FREE version of charting platform is available with end of day Kinetick data
- Can import data from these brokers: Charles Schwab, thinkorswim (TOS), Interactive Broker, `Forex.com`, FXCM
- Can import data from these data vendors: eSignal, Kinetick, DTN/IQFeed,
- Supported brokers and connectivity: InteractiveBrokers, Charles Schwab, `FOREX.com`, FXCM

- Compatibility: connects with all `TradersCoach.com` software
- US phone: 800-496-1683
- US phone: 312-262-1289
- Email: `support@ninjatrader.com`

NinjaTrader is a US-based broker and charting platform. It was founded in 2003 by Raymond Deux as a charting platform provider and became a broker in 2014. NinjaTrader provides one of the best professional grade charting platforms available with an excellent scanning feature called Market Analyzer. The charting platform along with real-time data are provided for free when opening a funded brokerage account. This charting platform is compatible with a variety of brokers for order execution and a variety of data vendors for real-time data feeds. There are also a large number of third-party developers, including `TradersCoach.com`, that sell add-on indicators for this platform.

### Charting Platform: TradeStation

- Website: `https://www.TradeStation.com`
- Compatibility: connects with all `TradersCoach.com` software
- Computer language: EasyLanguage
- Scanner: Radar Screen
- Data imported from broker: TradeStation (must open a brokerage account to use this charting platform)
- Data imported from data vendor: not applicable
- Compatibility: connects with all `TradersCoach.com` software
- US phone: 800-822-0512
- US phone: 954-652-7900
- Email: `sales@tradestation.com`

TradeStation is a US-based broker and charting platform. It was founded in 1982 by the brothers William Cruz and Rafael Cruz as a charting platform and became a broker in 2001. TradeStation is equal in excellence to the NinjaTrader charting platform and comes complete with a scanner feature called Radar Screen. The charting platform along with real-time data are provided to you for free when opening a funded brokerage account. One downside is that the commission fees are high; for example, fees are about five times the cost of IB for stocks. (IB has one of the lowest priced commissions.)

### Charting Platform: MultiCharts

- Website: https://www.MultiCharts.com
- Compatibility: connects with all TradersCoach.com software
- Computer language: PowerLanguage (which is very similar to EasyLanguage originally created and produced by TradeStation)
- Scanner: Market Scanner
- Data imported from broker: InteractiveBrokers, Oanda, AMP, TradeStation
- Data imported from data vendor: eSignal, barchart, Rithmic, CQG, iQFeed
- Supported brokers: InteractiveBrokers, Oanda, AMP, TradeStation, Rithmic
- Compatibility: connects with all TradersCoach.com software
- US phone: 888-340-6572
- US phone: 614-285-3456
- Email: support@ninjatrader.com

MultiCharts is a US-based charting platform founded in 2004 by Denis Globa. Built on the same foundation that the TradeStation charting platform is built on, it is similar. Unlike NinjaTrader, there is not a free version of MultiCharts available at this time. This charting platform is compatible with a variety of brokers for order execution and a variety of data vendors for real-time data feeds. There are also a large number of third-party developers, including TradersCoach.com, that sell add-on indicators for this platform.

### Charting Platform: MetaTrader 4, MT4

- Website: https://www.metatrader4.com/en
- Brokers offering MT4: Oanda, FXCM, Gain Capital
- Computer language: MQL4

- Scanner: none
- Compatibility: connects with all TradersCoach.com software (except scanners)
- Email: support@metaquotes.net

MetaQuotes, the parent company of MetaTrader 4 (MT4) is a Cyprus-based company founded in 2000 by Renat Fatkhullin. This charting platform is one of the most popular among forex traders since 2005. Although MT5 has many advanced analytics, forex traders prefer MT4 for forex trading. Many brokers offer this platform for free when you fund a brokerage account.

### Charting Platform: MetaTrader 5, MT5

- Website: https://www.metatrader5.com/en
- Brokers offering MT5: Oanda, Forex.com
- Compatibility: connects with all TradersCoach.com software except scanners
- Computer language: MQL5
- Scanner: none
- Email: support@metaquotes.net

MetaQuotes, the parent company of MetaTrader 5, MT5, is a Cyprus-based company founded in 2000 by Renat Fatkhullin. Released in 2010, MetaTrader 5 is different from MetaTrader 4 in that it offers enhanced analysis tools, including more built-in technical indicators. The new MT5 is considered to be superior to MT4 for stock trading and order management. Many forex brokers offer this platform for free when you fund a brokerage account.

### Charting Platform: eSignal

- Website: https://www.eSignal.com
- Charting platform: eSignal
- Computer language: EFS, eSignal Formula Script (an extended version of JavaScript)
- Scanner: none
- Data imported from broker: Interactive Broker, Rithmic

- Data imported from data vendor: eSignal
- Compatibility: connects with all `TradersCoach.com` software (except the scanners)
- US phone: 770-999 4511
- Email: `retailtechnicalsupport@theice.com`

eSignal is a US-based data provider and charting platform that was founded in 1983. It was acquired by ICE (Intercontinental Exchange) in 2015. When `TradersCoach.com` first released the ART (Applied Reality Trading) software in 2003, eSignal was the first charting platform I programmed for.

### Charting Platform: TradeNavigator

- Website: `https://www.tradenavigator.com/`
- Supported brokers and connectivity: InteractiveBrokers, AMP Futures, Optimus Futures
- US phone: 800-808-3282
- US phone: 719-262-0285
- Email: `sales@tradenavigator.com`

TradeNavigator is a US-based charting platform and was founded in 1983 by Glen Larson. Their custom programming services enable the company to provide custom studies to customers with its platinum product.

**PROP TRADING NOTE:** Opening a proprietary (prop) firm account is an inexpensive way to get real-time live streaming data and an excellent free charting platform. If you are a day trader, and primarily a futures trader, you can get remarkable value from just one account. This field is quickly evolving; if you want further information, go to this webpage:

`https://www.traderscoach.com/BOOK`

There you will find extensive current information on prop firms if you are interested. In addition, all the material in this Appendix B is updated on that webpage, so you will always have access to the latest and greatest information.

# Data Feeds

Go back to Chapter 17 in this book, *Understanding Financial Markets,* which goes into more detail on how to select the data feed for your unique needs.

**Here are three data speed choices:**

1. **Real-time live streaming data:** provides 1-minute and tick charts and is the fastest and most expensive data; good for day-traders
2. **Delayed data:** usually around a 10-minute delay but can still generate 1-minute charts, good for position traders
3. **End-of-day data:** provides daily, weekly, and monthly charts and is the least expensive data; good for position traders and investors

The highest quality data feed is typically live streaming from a dedicated data vendor. Lower quality data can sometimes (not always) be offered free from your broker. Also, at times brokers will *throttle* data to save money.

What that means is they will provide delayed data, as the default. If you suspect this is the case, you may be able to call customer service at the broker to request a real-time data feed, which they may provide at no charge.

Although, in my current experience both NinjaTrader and TradeStation offer extremely high-quality data free to funded brokerage accounts, with no throttling.

## Data Feeds

Your live streaming data feed is your direct connection to the markets and is an important consideration. Finding the right balance between your needs, the cost, and the quality, is the goal.

### Consider the following factors with data:

- **Markets:** The more markets, such as stocks, options, futures, forex, crypto, etc., that you sign up, for the higher the cost.
- **Regions:** The more regions, such as North America, Asia Pacific, Europe, that you sign up, for the higher the cost.
- **Symbols:** The more symbols that you choose to view at one time, such as 100, 500, or over 500, the higher the cost.
- **Amount of History:** Data vendors only hold data back a certain amount of time, meaning if you are looking to get a chart that goes back to 1920, many vendors will not offer that.
- **Exchange Fees:** Depending on the exchanges you are choosing, such as NYSE, NASDAQ, CBOT, CME, the exchanges' fees vary. Typically, stock exchange fees tend to be less expensive than future, forex and cryptocurrencies.
- **Speed:** Real-time data that provides 15-second or tick charts is the most expensive. End of day data is less expensive.

Plan out your needs and determine the most cost-effective solution. By narrowing your choice of markets and regions, you can reduce your costs significantly.

### Data Feed: eSignal

- Website: https://www.eSignal.com
- Can import data to broker: InteractiveBrokers, NinjaTrader
- Can import data to charting platform: NinjaTrader, MultiCharts
- US phone: 770-999 4511
- Email: retailtechnicalsupport@theice.com

eSignal is a US-based data provider and charting platform that was founded in 1983. It was acquired by ICE in 2015. They have the largest selection of paid data feeds, including virtually every worldwide region and every exchange and every asset class. In my experience, one of the most cost-effective packages the company offers is a delayed data package based on region. That is currently, one of the best bangs for your buck if you are a position trader or investor.

### Data Feed: Kinetick

- Website: https://kinetick.com/
- Can import data to broker: NinjaTrader
- Can import data to charting platform: NinjaTrader

Kinetick is a US-based company founded in 2014 by NinjaTrader and was sold sometime after that to a company in Nevada. Kinetick is actually a white label for data that are provided from DTN/IQFeed, and the data quality is excellent. Kinetick provides all of the free end-of-day data that the free version of the NinjaTrader charting platform provides. See DTN/IQFeed, which you will find in the following listing, for more information.

### Data Feed: DTN/IQFeed

- Website: https://www.iqfeed.net/
- Can import data to broker: NinjaTrader
- Can import data to charting platform: NinjaTrader, Multi Charts, Sierra Chart
- US phone: 800-475-4755
- US phone: 402-255-8435
- Email: sales@iqfeed.net

DTN/IQFeed is a US-based data provider that was founded in 1984. It has exceptional data quality with the band width and backup infrastructure to ensure the fastest, most complete, and reliable data available. Their domestic quote data are direct from each exchange. When data are not resold from a third party, the data delivery speed is faster because there is no middle man to slow it down. It provides 180 calendar days of tick history. Plus, it provides 11 years of 1-minute OHLCV historical data and 80 years of daily historical data. Kinetick data is a white label of DTN/IQFeed's data and is equally excellent.

### Data Feed: barchart

- Website: https://www.barchart.com/
- Can import data to broker: Dorman Trading
- Can import data to charting platform: MultiCharts
- US phone: 800-238-5814
- US phone: 866-333-7587
- US phone: 312-554-8122
- Email: solutions@barchart.com

Barchart is a US-based data provider that was founded in 1995 by Logical Systems, Inc. It provides a variety of asset classes, including stocks, futures, options, forex, crypto, indexes, funds, and more.

### Data Feed/Broker Bridge: Rithmic

- Website: https://yyy3.rithmic.com/
- Can import data to charting platform: NinjaTrader, MultiCharts, Trade Navigator, Sierra Chart, Medved Trader
- US phone: 877-748-4642 (877-Rithmic)
- Email: sales@rithmic.com

Rithmic is a US-based data provider and charting platform that was founded by Jonathan Walden. A leader in the prop firm landscape, Rithmic provides live streaming data to many prop firms in the industry.

### Data Feed/ Broker Bridge: Tradovate

- Website: https://www.tradovate.com/
- US phone: 844-283-3100
- US phone: 312-283-3100
- Email: info@tradovate.com

Tradovate is a US-based data provider, charting platform and brokerage that was founded in 2014 by Rick Tomsic. NinjaTrader acquired Tradovate in 2022, further strengthening NinjaTrader's position in the futures brokerage field. On the prop firm landscape, Tradovate has dominated in providing the data feed engine to many prop firms in the field. It offers its cloud-based platform on a variety of devices, allowing you to monitor and trade on your desktop, mobile, and tablet.

## Prop Firms

The proprietary (prop) firm industry is relatively new, with the first of its kind established in 2012. They can be an excellent solution to accessing a live streaming data feed and professional grade charting platform. You can choose from a number of firms, most of which offer opportunities to futures day traders. A limited number of firms also cater to other markets, such as stocks, options, forex, commodities, indices, cryptocurrencies, and metals.

Plus, prop firms offer a genuine opportunity to get monthly payouts on a percentage of your profits, without putting up or risking your own money. During the evaluation phase, there is a monthly subscription fee, but after you pass the test and are funded, the subscription fee is eliminated.

Review the *Epilogue* in this book, where I go into more detail on how to best navigate and benefit from prop trading. If you are interested in pursuing the prop field, you can obtain a significant discount with some of the best firms in the industry by clicking the following link and also access the latest information:

`https://www.traderscoach.com/book`

There you will find extensive current information on prop firms if you are interested. In addition, all the material in this Appendix B is updated on that webpage, so you will always have access to the latest and greatest information.

# Resources 2

# Technology Tips

Technology and your use of it can help you do great things in the financial markets. It is crucial to be aware of the ever changing landscape of the technological world and adapt to it as needed. Here are the areas of greatest concern, which can assist you in getting the most out of your current technology.

**Your Technology Health Check List:**

**A.** Check Data Feed Speed
**B.** Perform Weekly Updates
**C.** Slow Chart Loading Causes (and Solutions)
**D.** Best Computer for Traders
**E.** Suggested Computer Specifications for Traders
**F.** When All Else Fails . . .

My technology team works with traders every day, and surprisingly many issues that come up can be easily prevented or corrected using the technology health check list included here in this chapter. Of course, if you have other technology questions, you can always contact my team via email:

`support@traderscoach.com`

Much has changed over the last 10 or 20 years in the technological space. Those that leverage the power of computers and their processing abilities can compete with other traders and investors on a much more level playing field than existed ever before.

And yet it is not just the technology that makes the difference; it is what you do with it. It is your creativity and ingenuity in applying these modern tools in a way that makes you more successful. As Steve Jobs said, "Think Different." See Figure R2.1.

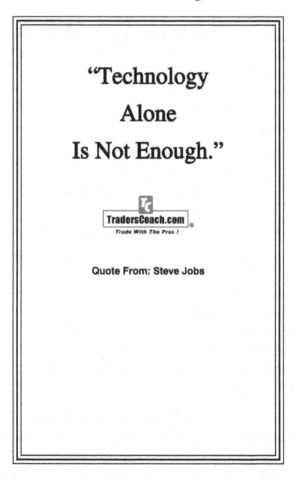

**Figure R2.1**   MINI POSTER—TECHNOLOGY—When it comes to using modern technology to succeed in the financial markets, buying expensive computers is not enough to make you profitable. It is what you bring to the table that makes the difference. Meaning all the flat screen trading monitors in the world will not make you profitable, if you do not add your own inspiration, motivation, and talent to the equation. Quote from Steve Jobs.
SOURCE: @TradersCoach.com.

# A. Check Data Feed Speed

Your data feed provides you the data that your entry and exit decisions are based on, so it needs to be as fast and accurate as possible. In this *Appendix B Resources,* you will find more information on data. Plus, in Chapter 17 in this book, *Understanding Financial Markets,* there is more information on this important topic.

1. **Check your data feed regularly.** Some of our clients have experienced *throttling* or *slowing down* and *down grading* of their free data feeds. For example, on both TradeStation and thinkorswim (TOS), clients have been unaware that what had previously been a *real-time* free data feed was converted to a delayed data feed without them being notified. In some cases, historical data range was shortened as well.

2. **How do I check my data feed?** If you find that suddenly your *data loading* becomes slow and it takes your charts longer to load than usual, there is a possibility your data are being *throttled* by your broker. It seems most clients have discovered their data was not *real time* when their charts didn't match Bennett's charts during live webinars. Also, some clients in our trading rooms would compare charts with each other and discover that they did not match. We suggest you attend a live event and pull up your charts and compare with the presenter and/or with other members of a live trading room.

3. **Important note about data feeds:** Intraday data feeds (15-second, 1-minute, etc.) can and will vary from data provider to data provider. This is because their servers can be slightly different during real-time data processing and because each data provider delivers based on their own band width. All data providers are NOT created equal; some are just faster than others. This speed can vary from time to time for a variety of reasons. We have had a number of clients conduct side-by-side testing between different providers to prove this. Also charting platform settings can vary as well, producing different results. The bottom line is that even if your data are not being *throttled,* sometimes

comparing your chart to someone else's chart can produce a different result.

4. **How do I fix my throttled data feed?** In the cases we are aware of with both TradeStation and TOS, all it took was a phone call to the vendor, and they turned the *real-time* data back on.

5. **Why are the data being throttled?** We've seen this happening more frequently, and it most probably is due to the high cost of *real-time* data. By only providing *real time* to clients that go to the trouble of asking for it, they save a lot of money. Think of it like when you go to a restaurant now, and you have to ask for a glass of water. In the old days, everyone got a glass of water in restaurant whether they wanted it or not. This is the "new normal."

6. **Paid data feeds.** If you are paying for your data feed with eSignal or Kinetick for example, chances are they will not *throttle* your data. But just to be safe, it is best to check periodically as outlined in item number 2.

Data is so important to successful trading; it is paramount to your survival. Keep an eye out for any erroneous price bars, or anything odd on your charts. Glitches do occur, and better to be aware of them.

## B. Perform Software Updates Weekly

It's a little bit like cleaning your house and not leaving old fast-food packaging around. If it piles up, it creates bigger problems than just being unsightly. With your updates, if you don't do them weekly, your technology will suffer as a result.

Many people think all updates are done automatically, but the fact of the matter is that some are not. And not only do you need to keep your operating system on your computer updated, there are brokerage and charting platform updates that need to be done as well.

1. **Operating system updates.** You may already do this, but you would be amazed at how often our technical support technician finds that clients have sometimes never done their Windows

updates. This is bad for your computer health and bad for your trading health. **IMORTANT:** Many of the cumulative major updates must be done manually. Remember to update!

2. **Brokerage and charting platform updates.** Once again, you probably already do this, but if you were unaware that this is needed, update, update, and update some more!

3. **Don't know how to update?** If you do not know how to update your operating system either pay us to do it for you with Platinum Care, or pay the "geek squad," or get your kids, or niece or nephew to do it for you. As Nike says, just Do It!

4. **What happens if you don't update?** Well, let's just say it is not pretty. Your computer will get very slow, and the functionality will suffer. Things that used to be so easy will be harder, and sometimes everything will lock up and freeze. And Mark's favorite (he's our software technician) is that when a client hasn't done any of their updates, it can take hours, and in some cases days, for the updates to process and complete. As the saying goes, "a stitch in time saves nine."

Bravo to you if you are already doing weekly updates! If you are not, there's no time like the present to start.

---

# Technology Troubleshooting

There are excellent online resources you get access to as a benefit of your purchase of this book *The ART of Trading*. Videos and written, updated current material that can assist you in troubleshooting your technical problems. Chances are, if you are experiencing a technology issue, someone else has as well.

**Get access to this information here:**
https://www.traderscoach.com/book

Again, technology is advancing all the time; the information written in this book may become out of date at some point. But the previous access link will have the updated information posted there.

## C. Slow Chart Loading Causes (and Solutions)

Time is money, and there is nothing worse than slow charts. They are usually easy to fix, once you understand what is causing the slowness. The most common problem is too much data being loaded, but there are other causes as well.

1. **Windows/Mac parallels operating system updates not installed.** Solution: Install all updates weekly. If you have not done this for some time, do not be alarmed if it takes many hours to process. Patience is a virtue. The payoff in speed will be worth it.
2. **Charting platform updates not installed.** Solution: Install all updates weekly. And refer to number 1.
3. **Using a wireless internet connection (hard wired internet connection recommended).** Solution: When live trading only use a hardwired internet connection. Do not take a chance on wireless no matter how fast you think it is.
4. **Throttled data feed.** Solution: Test your data feed, and if you find it is throttled, call the provider and have it restored.
5. **Too much data loaded, too many symbols, history, etc.** Solution: Limit the number of symbols and history you load on your charts. Less is more.
6. **Using intraday charts with unusually lengthy amounts of data history.** Solution: When day trading, you do not need historical data that goes back to 1999. Again as earlier, less is more.
7. **Too many browser windows open at the same time drain the system.** Solution: When you fail to close browser windows that are not currently needed, you will see a significant slowdown of your system. Do you really need 20 browser windows open at a time? Again, as earlier, less is more.
8. **Old and outdated computer with low memory and weak CPU processor.** Solution: As of this writing, the recommended specifications for your system are as follows: latest I-7 chip or better; 16 gigabytes of memory or better; 1 terabyte hard drive or better; hardwire broadband, high speed internet.

Slow charts can delay your entry and exit decisions, so it's important to keep them loading quickly.

## D. Best Computer for Traders

The best trading computer is not determined by the brand you purchase as much as it is about the specifications you select. And it's not even about how much money you spend on your system, although some boutique trading computer firms will have you believe you need to spend a lot of money. Truth be told, you can usually go to Costco and get an awesome system that is the best bang for your buck.

Refer to the following "Section E" for our recommendations for the best specifications for a powerful enough computer to trade with.

Also, regarding monitors, as the saying goes, "If you can't make money using one monitor, you won't be able to make money using 10 monitors." But having plenty of "real estate" in the monitor department is not a bad thing. If you have questions about video cards and monitors contact us via support@traderscoach.com.

**NOTE FOR MACINTOSH COMPUTER USERS:** Most traders tend to have a Windows operating system since the software we use is often Windows based. With that said, we have many Mac users who trade using Parallels as an interface that works well.

## E. Computer Specifications for Traders

As a trader you need the best technology you can afford. It is not so important as to what brand computer you purchase, as it is important to get the correct specifications. Following is an outline of items of what we currently recommend.

1. Latest I-7 chip or better
2. 16 gigabytes of memory or better

3. 1 terabyte hard drive or better
4. Hardwire broadband, high speed internet whenever possible
5. Battery backup for unanticipated power outages, brown outs, power surges, etc.
6. Macintosh users will need to use Parallels software for running Windows. It's an excellent solution for Mac users.

Technology is advancing all the time, so the information provided here may become out of date at some point. But the following access link will have the most current information posted there:

```
https://www.traderscoach.com/book
```

Remember, in the old days many traders would go to high end computer vendors that specialized in supporting traders, and they were expensive. Technology has advanced to the point where you can purchase a system from your local electronics store, or even from Costco, and get excellent quality. Just be sure to purchase the highest level specifications available in the current environment.

One last thought to mention. Unlike a hot classic 1953 Corvette with a new shiny new paint job, computers and technology do not improve with age. Meaning, if you have a computer that is 10 years old, no matter how many memory cards you add, it just can't compete with a current model flaunting the most current processing technology. With lower prices of computers now, for not much money you can get a screaming fast processor and retire your old computer for good.

## F. When All Else Fails . . .

**REBOOT.** Yes, just a reboot of your computer can sometimes do the trick. Sometimes your computer just needs a fresh start.

# Resources 3

# Books, Movies, and Websites

This chapter has many of my absolute favorite books, websites, movies, and more listed for your enjoyment. Discovering knowledge is an integral key to success. My hope is that this chapter introduces you to a new source of knowledge, or insight, to help you along on your journey.

And just like the quote on the corner of 13th Street and Fifth Avenue in New York City above the Lone Star café, "Too Much Ain't Enough." The never ending quest for knowledge is what makes life worth living. See Figure R3.1.

Plus, I'm always looking for new sources of knowledge as well; be sure to drop me a line to support@traderscoach.com to let me know what is helping you. Thanks in advance for your feedback.

## Books

One of the best ways to keep up to date with current (and classic) trading and investing approaches is to read, read, and read some more. What I find is that when reading a variety of material, one new idea or approach may be all it takes to cultivate a more profitable approach. I may not agree with or use every idea of each author, but if their observations and commentary open my eyes by presenting the material in a way not expressed before, it can be valuable.

513

**Figure R3.1**    When it comes to knowledge, "Too much ain't enough." This photo of the Lone Star Café, circa 1980, on the corner of 13th Street and Fifth Avenue in New York City shows off that very saying.
SOURCE: © Bob Minkin Photography

If you've been in this business very long, you know that books we as traders and investors benefit the most from are generally not in the local public library or book store. The reality is that active traders and investors are a small segment of the population.

The books we are looking for are sometimes difficult to find, Amazon.com seems the easiest source for me. And honestly, sometimes getting a used copy of a book saves money. I'm generally writing notes in the margins and using a highlighter to mark important information, so having a brand new book isn't essential.

**Technical Analysis Books**

- *The ART of Trading,* 2nd edition, Bennett A. McDowell, John Wiley & Sons, 2024
- *Technical Analysis of the Financial Markets: A Comprehensive Guide to Trading Methods and Applications,* John Murphy, New York Institute of Finance, 1999
- *Technical Analysis: The Complete Resource for Financial Market Technicians,* 2nd edition, Charles Kirkpatrick, FT Press, 2010
- *The Encyclopedia of Technical Market Indicators,* 2nd edition, Robert Colby, McGraw Hill, 2002
- *Encyclopedia of Chart Patterns,* 2nd edition, Thomas Bulkowski, John Wiley & Sons, 2005
- *Technical Analysis for Dummies,* 4th edition, Barbara Rockefeller, John Wiley & Sons, 2019

**Fundamental Analysis Books**

- *The Intelligent Investor,* 3rd edition, Benjamin Graham, Harper Business, 2024
- *How to Make Money in Stocks: A Winning System in Good Times and Bad,* 4th edition, William J. O'Neil, McGraw Hill, 2009
- *The Secrets of Economic Indicators: Hidden Clues to Future Economic Trends and Investment Opportunities,* 3rd edition, Bernard Baumohl, FT Press, 2012
- *Stock Trader's Almanac 2024,* 57th edition, Jeffrey A. Hirsch, John Wiley & Sons, 2023
- *The Wall Street Journal Guide to Understanding Money and Investing,* Kenneth M. Morris, Lightbulb Press, 1999
- *Fundamental Analysis for Dummies,* 3rd edition, Matthew Krantz, John Wiley & Sons, 2023

**Elliott Wave and Fibonacci Analysis Books**

- *Elliott Wave Techniques Simplified: How to Use the Probability Matrix to Profit on More Trades,* Bennett A. McDowell, McGraw Hill, 2016

- *Elliott Wave Principle: Key to Market Behavior,* 10th edition, Robert R. Prechter, New Classics Library, 2005
- *R.N. Elliott's Masterworks: The Definitive Collection,* 3rd edition, Ralph Nelson Elliott, Edited by Robert R. Prechter, New Classics Library, 2017
- *Elliott Wave Explained: A Real-World Guide to Predicting & Profiting from Market Turns,* Robert C. Beckman, McGraw Hill, 1992 (Originally published as *Powertiming*)
- *Fibonacci Trading: How to Master the Time and Price Advantage,* Carolyn Boroden, McGraw Hill, 2008
- *Fibonacci Applications and Strategies for Traders,* Robert Fischer, John Wiley & Sons, 1993

**Money Management and Risk Control Books**

- *A Trader's Money Management System: How to Ensure Profit and Avoid the Risk of Ruin,* Bennett A. McDowell, John Wiley & Sons, 2008
- *Money Management Strategies for Futures Traders,* Nauzer Balsara, John Wiley & Sons, 1992
- *The Mathematics of Money Management: Risk Analysis Techniques for Traders,* Ralph Vince, John Wiley & Sons, 1992
- *Portfolio Management Formulas: Mathematical Trading Methods for the Futures, Options, and Stock Markets,* Ralph Vince, John Wiley & Sons, 1991

**Psychology Books**

- *Trading Iin the Zone: Master the Market with Confidence, Discipline and a Winning Attitude,* Mark Douglas, Prentice Hall Press, 2000
- *The Disciplined Trader: Developing Winning Attitudes,* Mark Douglas, John Wiley & Sons, 1990
- *Trading to Win: The Psychology of Mastering the Markets,* Ari Kiev, John Wiley & Sons, 1998
- *The Courage to Fail: Art Mortell's Secrets for Business Success,* Art Mortell, McGraw Hill, 1992

## Candlestick Books

- *Japanese Candlestick Charting Techniques: A Contemporary Guide to The Ancient Investment Techniques of the Far East,* 2nd edition, Steve Nison, Prentice Hall Press, 2001
- *The Candlestick Course,* Steve Nison, John Wiley & Sons, 2008

## Options Books

- *McMillan on Options,* 2nd edition, Lawrence G. McMillan, John Wiley & Sons, 2004
- *Options as a Strategic Investment,* 5th edition, Lawrence G. McMillan, Penguin Publishing Group, 2012

## Trading, Financial History, and Interview Books

- *Rogue Trader: The Original Story of the Banker Who Broke the System,* Revised edition, Nick Leeson, Sphere, 2016
- *Reminiscences of a Stock Operator,* Edwin Lefevre, John Wiley & Sons, 2006 reprint of the original 1923 edition
- *Market Wizards: Interviews With Top Traders,* Jack D. Schwager, John Wiley & Sons, 2006
- *The New Market Wizards: Conversations with America's Top Traders,* Jack D. Schwager, John Wiley & Sons, 2008
- *Manias, Panics, and Crashes: A History of Financial Crises,* 8th edition Robert Z. Aliber and Charles P. Kindleberger, Palgrave Macmillan, 2023
- *How I Made $2,000,000 In the Stock Market,* Nicolas Darvas, Reprint of the original 1960 edition, Martino Publishing, 2011
- *The Wizard of Lies: Bernie Madoff and the Death of Trust,* Diana B. Henriques, St. Martin's Griffin, 2012
- *The Smartest Guys in the Room: The Amazing Rise and Scandalous Fall of Enron,* Bethany McLean and Peter Elkind, Portfolio Hardcover, 2003
- *Wealth, War & Wisdom,* Barton Biggs, John Wiley & Sons, 2008

### Inspirational and Motivational Books

- *You Can Heal Your Life,* Louise Hay, Hay House LLC, 1984
- *Think and Grow Rich,* Reprint of the original 1937 edition, Napoleon Hill, Sound Wisdom, 2016
- *The Secret,* Rhonda Byrne, Atria Books, 2006
- *What the Bleep Do We Know!?: Discovering the Endless Possibilities for Altering Your Everyday Reality,* William Arntz, Health Communications Inc., 2007
- *Awaken the Giant Within: How to Take Immediate Control of Your Mental, Emotional, Physical, and Financial Destiny,* Tony Robbins, Simon & Schuster, 1991
- *The Power of Positive Thinking: A Practical Guide to Mastering the Problems of Everyday Living,* Norman Vincent Peale, Prentice Hall, 1952

### Health and Fitness Books

- *Alternative Medicine, The Definitive Guide,* 2nd edition, John W. Anderson and Larry Trivieri editors, Celestial Arts, 2002
- *The Merck Manual Home Health Handbook,* Robert Porter Editor, 3rd edition, Merck, 2009
- *Prescription for Nutritional Healing: A Practical A-to-Z Reference to Drug-Free Remedies Using Vitamins, Minerals, Herbs, & Food Supplements,* 5th edition, Phyllis A. Balch, CNC, Avery, 2023
- *Fit for Life,* Reprint of the original 1985 edition, Harvy Diamond and Marilyn Diamond, Grand Central Life & Style, 2010
- *Anatomy of an Illness as Perceived by the Patient,* 20th anniversary edition, Norman Cousins, W.W. Norton & Company, 2005

These are among my favorite books. The library of information that sits on my endless bookshelf is a source of inspiration and education. As the DJIA just closed at 44,293.13 (ATH - all time high) Tuesday, November 12, 2024, I'm ever aware that an impending crash is lurking in the shadows.

The DJIA level isn't the only clue to this looming threat; there is the housing bubble, the rapidly rising use of credit card debt and defaults, higher interest rates, and not to mention crippling inflation.

Which brings me to a book listed in in this chapter: *Manias, Panics, and Crashes: A History of Financial Crises,* 8th edition, Robert Z. Aliber and Charles P. Kindleberger, Palgrave Macmillan, 2023. It is worth studying history.

> *Those who do not learn history are doomed to repeat it.*
> —George Santayana, Spanish-American Philosopher

The Great Depression was the most dramatic financial crash of all time, and yet those that did not live through it are unable to benefit from its lessons lest they study history. See Figure R3.2.

**Figure R3.2**   The Great Depression started in 1929 and ended in 1939. This prolonged global economic hardship was characterized by high unemployment rates and widespread business failures. Worldwide gross domestic product (GDP) fell by an estimated 15%. By comparison, worldwide GDP fell by less than 1% from 2008 to 2009 during the Great Recession. In 1929 the value of an automobile was US$800, and yet this man is selling his car for $100 illustrating the dramatic impact of the times.
SOURCE: © Getty Images

# Movies

We are living in an audio visual world, and movies can offer us entertainment, education, and sometimes escape. From 1942 to 1945, during World War II, Hollywood enjoyed its finest hour. Box office revenues and film studio profits hit record levels. That success in Hollywood is no doubt a result of moviegoers wanting a distraction from the global uncertainty from the raging world war.

And if a picture is worth a thousand words, then a moving picture must certainly be worth a million words. Included here are some of my favorite entertainment and educational movies. For me, sometimes a quote or scene from a movie can sum up a core concept that is important to understand.

### Investing and Trading-based Movies

- *Rogue Trader*
  - Miramax, 2000
  - Running Time: 97 minutes
  - Starring: Ewan McGregor
  - Director: James Dearden
  - This is a true story of Nick Leeson, who is infamous for causing the collapse of the Barings Bank in 1995. Barings was the oldest bank in the world (operating for 232 years before the collapse), and Leeson was a trader for the bank. The film does an excellent job of showing how an ordinary young man can allow small losses to spiral into huge $1 billion losses because of his own fear, greed, denial, and lack of risk control. It also shows how an established, reputable bank could be so oblivious as to let it happen. This story illustrates how emotions and psychology can get the better of you in the trading environment if you are not aware that it is possible.
- *Wall Street*
  - 20th Century Fox, 1987
  - Running Time: 126 minutes
  - Starring: Michael Douglas, Charlie Sheen, and Daryl Hannah

- Director: Oliver Stone
- Pure Hollywood, this film is about an ambitious young broker, Bud Fox (Charlie Sheen), who is lured into the illegal, lucrative world of corporate espionage and insider trading when he is seduced by the power, status, and financial wizardry of Wall Street legend Gordon Gekko (Michael Douglas). Fox soon discovers that the pursuit of overnight riches comes at a price that's too high to pay. Many people remember Gordon Gekko's famous "greed is good" line from the movie: "The point is, ladies and gentlemen, that greed, for lack of a better word, is good. Greed is right. Greed works. Greed clarifies, cuts through, and captures the essence of the evolutionary spirit."

- *Boiler Room*
  - New Line Films, 2000
  - Running Time: 120 minutes
  - Starring: Giovanni Ribisi and Ben Affleck
  - Director: Ben Younger
  - This is a fictional story of Seth Davis (Giovanni Ribisi), a college dropout who runs a small-time gambling casino operation out of his apartment. He gets recruited by a Long Island stock brokerage firm, an aggressive, renegade firm far from the traditions of Wall Street. His boss, Jim Young (Ben Affleck), gives a motivational speech at the beginning of the film, but gradually Seth learns that this is a chop shop brokerage firm with a huge team of *pump and dump* high-pressure telemarketing stockbrokers who relentlessly call until they sell whatever the stock du jour for the firm is. The movie is an interesting and disturbing look at what can happen when unethical individuals gain the trust of unsuspecting investors.

- *Trading Places*
  - Paramount Pictures, 1983
  - Running Time: 116 minutes
  - Starring: Dan Aykroyd, Eddie Murphy, Jamie Lee Curtis,
  - Director: John Landis
  - This is a fictional comedy about an upper-class commodities broker, Louis Winthorpe III (Dan Aykroyd), and a poor street

hustler, Billy Ray Valentine (Eddie Murphy), whose lives cross when they are made the subjects of an elaborate bet to test how each man would perform if circumstances of their lives were swapped. Some people speculate that the turtle Trader experiment was inspired by this movie because the brothers Randolph and Mortimer Duke in the movie aim to settle a bet in the same way that Richard Dennis and William Eckhardt did in real life with turtles in late 1983. This entertaining and funny comedy is based on a short story by Mark Twain, *The Million Pound Bank Note*, published in 1893.

- ***The Pursuit of Happyness***
  - Columbia Pictures, 2006
  - Running Time: 117 minutes
  - Starring: Will Smith, Thandiwe Newton, Jaden Smith
  - Director: Gabriele Muccino
  - Based on the true story of salesman Chris Gardner (Will Smith) and his son Christopher Gardner, Jr., (Jaden Smith), this film is based on Gardner's memoir of the same name. The unusual spelling of the film and the memoir's title comes from a mural that Gardner saw on the wall outside of the daycare facility his son attended. The movie is set in San Francisco in 1981 and follows the path of Gardner and his misfortunes leading to him being homeless for a year. He then meets Jay Twistle (Brian Howe), lead manager and partner for Dean Witter Reynolds, and impresses him enough to offer him a position as an intern stockbroker. Spoiler alert, the story has a very happy ending, even after Gardner's many trials and tribulations. An epilogue reveals that Gardener went on to form his own multi-million-dollar brokerage firm in 1987 and sold a minority stake in his brokerage firm in a multi-million-dollar deal in 2006.
- ***The Big Short***
  - Paramount Pictures, 2015
  - Running Time: 130 minutes
  - Starring: Brad Pitt, Ryan Gosling, Steve Carell, Christian Bale
  - Director: Adam McKay

- This is a biographical crime comedy-drama based on the non-fiction 2010 book *The Big Short: Inside the Doomsday Machine* by Michael Lewis. The film shows how the 2007–2008 financial crisis was triggered by the US housing bubble and follows a few savvy traders as they become aware of the impending crisis. Hedge fund manager Michael Burry (Christian Bale) foresees the financial crisis before anyone else and uses his findings to his advantage. Ben Rickert (Brad Pitt) is a retired former trader; his character, based on Ben Hockett, helps two other characters short the housing market. The Epilogue in the film states that the personnel of the banks responsible for the crisis escaped any consequences for their actions, with the single exception of the trader Kareem Serageldin, who was sentenced to 30 months in prison.
- *Too Big to Fail*
  - HBO, 2011
  - Running Time: 98 minutes
  - Starring: Paul Giamatti, William Hurt, Edward Asner, James Woods,
  - Director: Curtis Hanson
  - An American biographical drama television film based on the 2009 nonfiction book *Too Big to Fail* by Andrew Ross Sorkin. In 2008 the mortgage industry crisis and the forced sale of troubled investment bank, Bear Stearns, to commercial banking giant JPMorgan Chase, with federal guarantees was all over the news. Then Lehman Brothers shares began falling rapidly, and Henry Paulson, US Treasury Secretary, was adamant that the government would not subsidize any more acquisitions. With no buyers for Lehman, it is forced into bankruptcy. The resulting collapse of Lehman throws the entire financial system into a freefall. When the insurance firm AIG also began to fail, Paulson and the Treasury rescues AIG with an $85 billion loan, deeming it "too big to let fail." The stock market continued falling until 2009 when it finally stabilized, signaling the end of the crisis.

- *Inside Job*
  - Sony Pictures, 2010
  - Running Time: 108 minutes
  - Starring: Matt Damon, Narrator, Paul Volcker, George Soros, Barney Frank, David McCormick, Eliot Spitzer, Michael Greenberger, Martin Wolf, Kenneth Rogoff, Lawrence McDonald, Harvey Miller, Kristin Davis, William Ackman, Frederic Mishkin
  - Director: Charles Ferguson
  - This finance documentary, about the 2008 financial crisis, won Best Documentary Feature at the 83rd Academy Awards. It was acclaimed by film critics, who praised its pacing, research, and exposition of complex material. It covers the bubble from 2001 to 2007 and walks through the unfolding crisis in 2008. The Great Recession was a global crisis with unemployment rising to 10% in the United States and in Europe. Foreclosures in the United States reached unprecedented levels. Then on October 3, 2008, President George W. Bush signed the $700 billion bill that was called the *Trouble Asset Relief Program* to bail out the banks and failing corporations. Unfortunately, there was little accountability as top executives of the insolvent companies walked away with their personal fortunes intact and avoided prosecution. These executives selected their boards of directors, which handed out billions in bonuses after the government bailout.
- *Margin Call*
  - Lionsgate and Roadside Attractions, 2011
  - Running Time: 109 minutes
  - Starring: Kevin Spacey, Jeremy Irons, Demi Moore, Zachary Quinto
  - Director: J.C. Chandor
  - Many consider this an accurate portrayal of the financial industry. The film takes place over the span of 24 hours in the life of a Wall Street firm on the brink of disaster during the initial stages of the 2008 financial crisis. The firm begins

laying off large numbers of employees, including Eric Dale (Stanly Tucci), head of risk management. Dale attempted to speak about his concerns but was ignored by management, so he hands a flash drive to Peter Sullivan (Zachary Quinto) on his way out. Sullivan discovers that the firm's risk profile is wrong, and it is overleveraged, which will lead to bankruptcy. John Tuld (Jeremy Irons), the firm's CEO, selects Sarah Robertson (Demi Moore) as the scape goat for the company's overleveraged positions. Sam Rogers (Kevin Spacey) as a senior manager reluctantly rallies his traders and informs them of a fire sale to unload their overleveraged positions. They are successful in in selling off most of the bad assets. The movie is fictional and yet illustrates the risks taken by some of the largest banks in the run-up to the 2008 financial crisis.

- *Floored*
  - Documentary, 2009
  - Running Time: 77 minutes
  - Starring: Jon Najarian, Jon Tubbs, Chris Felix, Rick Santelli, Linda Raschke, Pete Najarian, Mike Walsh, Jeff Ward, Greg Riba, Rob Prosniewski, Kenny Ford, Matt Trapani, Jody Michael, Mike Fishbein, Ron Beebe, Jeff Ansani
  - Director: James Allen Smith
  - YouTube link: `https://youtu.be/--H8SY334Zw?si=0uQoNycTI77VPb4o`
  - This documentary provides insight into the changing industry of floor trading and how the old days of trading in the pit are virtually extinct today. In their heyday, floor traders were rock stars in their high stakes and high pressure world. And when they were good at what they did, they made millions. The beginning of the movie states, "In 1997, more than 10,000 people traded on the floors. Later that year, computer trading emerged. Today, 12 years later, only10% remain." Many floor traders that were not able to adapt lost their jobs. Of course, some of the traders began to trade electronically with their own accounts. To that point, toward the end of the film

is a great segment that takes place in Linda Raschke's trading office. She segued from the pit to trading electronically in front of a vast array of monitors and is an example of a floor trader who did adapt. If you are interested in seeing live footage of the open pits in action, and to hear what the old days were like from the actual guys and gals that lived it, this documentary is for you.

- *Enron: The Smartest Guys in the Room*
  - Magnolia Pictures, 2005
  - Running Time: 109 minutes
  - Starring: Peter Coyote (narrator), Bethany McLean, Peter Elkind, Sherron Watkins, Mimi Swartz, Mike Muckleroy, Bill Lerach, Gray Davis, Philip H. Hilder
  - Director: Alex Gibney
  - This documentary is based on the best-selling 2003 book of the same name by *Fortune* reporters Bethany McLean and Peter Elkind. It kicks off with a profile of Kenneth Lay, who founded *Enron*, a US energy company, in 1985. This classic tale of corporate misconduct is a warning to all traders and investors to beware the fundamental reporting data provided by corporations, as they are not always based on reality. In this particular case, Enron's ultimate bankruptcy in 2001 occurred as a result of its accounting scandal that unraveled that same year. At the time it was the biggest bankruptcy in US history with a total of 20,000 employees who lost their jobs. Investors also lost billions of dollars. In 2004, Lay was indicted by a grand jury for his role in the company's failure and was charged with 11 counts of securities fraud, wire fraud, and making false and misleading statements. On May 25, 2006, he was found guilty on six counts of conspiracy and fraud by the jury, and in a separate bench trial, Judge Lake ruled that Lay was guilty of four additional counts of fraud and making false statements. Sentencing was scheduled for October 23, 2006. But, before the sentencing, Kenneth Lay died on July 5, 2006, from an apparent heart attack.

## Entertainment, Inspirational, and Educational, Movies

- *Apollo 13*
  - Universal Pictures, 2005
  - Running Time: 140 minutes
  - Starring: Tom Hanks, Kevin Bacon, Bill Paxton, Gary Sinise, Ed Harris, Kathleen Quinlan
  - Director: Ron Howard
  - An amazing true story of how a routine space flight becomes a desperate battle for survival. This is a triumphant adventure of courage and faith that shows how the NASA team worked together to bring the crew of Apollo 13 safely home. James Lovell (Tom Hanks) was the commander of this now famous failed mission to the moon that he referred to as "the most successful failure in history." One of the most famous lines in the movie is when Lovell says, "Houston we have a problem." Another favorite line is when flight director Gene Krantz (Ed Harris) says, "Failure is not an option." This story is an example of how even when looking into the face of disaster, the NASA team, led by Krantz, was able to use their determined and creative mindset to bring the space ship and crew home when many feared the worst. This is a truly inspiring story.
- *The Right Stuff*
  - Warner Bros., 1983
  - Running Time: 193 minutes
  - Starring: Sam Shepard, Dennis Quaid, Barbara Hershey, Ed Harris, Charles Frank, Scott Glenn
  - Director: Philip Kaufman
  - This movie is based on the history of modern aviation, and the screenplay is an adaptation of the book of the same name by Tom Wolfe. Initially a box-office bomb, grossing about $21 million domestically against a $27 million budget, it turned around after being nominated for eight Oscars at the 56th Academy Awards, four of which it won. The film begins in the desert with the most famous test pilot of all time, Chuck

Yeager (Sam Shepard). You get to see Yeager as the first man on earth to break the sound barrier by going Mach 1. The government demanded secrecy for this groundbreaking development because this was top secret stuff, but any pilot in the United States knew that Yeager was the fastest man on the planet. From Yeager to John Glenn (Ed Harris), the examples in this film exhibit how determination and the passion for pushing the envelope enable us to achieve greatness. The courage to go above and beyond and to risk failure made these men heroes, and much can be learned from them about exploration, fear, failure, and success. The lessons all directly apply to trading and investing in the financial markets.

- *Ford: The Man and the Machine*
  - Filmline International and RHI Entertainment, 1987
  - Running Time: 192 minutes
  - Starring: Cliff Robertson, Hope Lange, Heather Thomas, R.H. Thomson, Chas Lawther, Michael Ironside
  - Director: Allan Eastman
  - YouTube Link: `https://youtu.be/vi17KENM7MQ?si=hS1nqaQg0ZyCG4Gh`
  - This film is based on the true story of Henry Ford (Cliff Robertson), founder of the Ford Motor Company, and the screenplay was inspired by the biography of the same name by Robert Lacey. Set in Ford's era from 1863 to 1947, the movie chronicles his childhood and subsequent rise to fame. Early in his career, Ford worked for Thomas Edison and later founded and incorporated the Ford Motor company in 1903. The film has a number of important lessons, first of which is inspired by Ford's relationship with James Couzens, who was one of the original investors in the company and was also head of the accounting department. Ford was the creative genius behind the development of the motorized vehicle, and yet without Couzens, we would never know of Ford's name or accomplishments. It was Couzens who steered the company's financial direction, sometimes to the dismay of Ford, and kept him out of bankruptcy. Another lesson is the remarkable invention of the assembly line, by Henry Ford in 1913, and round

the clock work schedules that were eight hours in length each, fueling the Industrial Revolution. The efficiency of the work schedule combined with the assembly line enabled Ford to double the minimum daily pay from $2.34 to $5.00. All in all, an outstanding film that illustrates pure entrepreneurial drive and what it can accomplish.

- *Tesla*
  - IFC Films, 2020
  - Running Time: 102 minutes
  - Starring: Ethan Hawke, Eve Hewson, Ebon Moss-Bachrach, Jim Gaffigan, Kyle MacLachlan
  - Director: Michael Almereyda
  - This American biographical drama delves into the life and times of Nicola Tesla (Ethan Hawke), 1856–1943. Born and raised in the Austrian Empire in Croatia, Tesla immigrated to the United States in 1884 where he became a naturalized citizen. Working for a short time at the Edison Machine Works in New York City, he chose to strike out on his own. This may be due to the fact that Thomas Edison (Kyle MacLachlan) disregarded Tesla's suggestions for using *alternating current* (AC) and refused to pay him for his invention. Later, George Westinghouse (Jim Gaffigan), an inventor and businessman of the time, buys Tesla's patents and funds his work, promoting the use of AC current. Tesla's AC current was contrasted with *direct current* (DC) that Edison was a proponent of. The film illustrates the rivalry between Tesla and Edison and how ultimately Edison had more popularity overall. The character Anne Morgan (Eve Hewson), daughter of J.P. Morgan (Donnie Keshawarz), serves as the film's narrator. The film shows the genius of Tesla and how history may have not given him the credit he is due.
- *Maxed Out: Hard Times, Easy Credit and the Era of Predatory Lenders*
  - Magnolia Home Entertainment, 2006
  - Running Time: 87 minutes
  - Starring: Mark Mumma, Ronald Reagan, Elizabeth Warren, Chris Barrett, Dave Ramsey

- Director: James Scurlock
- This documentary about predatory lending is based on the book *Maxed Out* by James Scurlock. It presents numerous stories about easy credit given to students, the poor, the weak and the uninformed, whose lives are ruined by their debt burden, including some cases of suicide. The movie showed examples of high pressure collection agencies that lied and said if the debt wasn't paid the cardholder would be put in jail. While not everyone will agree with Scurlock, this is a valuable perspective and an urgent call to arms in the way we think about debt. He blames financial institutions in our materialistic, debt-ridden society and provides education on an important topic. Scurlock's belief is also that banks and other creditors deliberately market to people who are more likely to have problems paying and that the creditors benefit from connections to government, the debt collection industry, and from lawmaker apathy. Ironically, my daughter's teacher showed this movie in her classroom in high school, to give kids a perspective on how high interest rates and the use of credit cards for luxury items can spell disaster.
- ***The Secret***
  - Prime Time Productions, 2006
  - Running Time: 91 minutes
  - Starring: Bob Proctor, John Assaraf, Jack Canfield, John Hagelin, John Demartini, Joe Vitale
  - Director: Drew Heriot
  - This documentary consists of interviews illustrating the *law of attraction* and is based on the book of the same name by Rhonda Byrne. Considered to be a *New Thought* concept, the *law of attraction* is based on the idea that people and their thoughts are made from energy and that like energy can attract like energy, thereby allowing people to improve their health, wealth, or personal relationships. This approach, sometimes referred to as manifestation, has not been embraced by the

scientific establishment, and yet has many loyal followers including those features in the film.

- ***What the Bleep Do We Know!?***
  - Roadside Attractions and Samuel Goldwyn Films, 2004
  - Running Time: 109 minutes
  - Starring: Marlee Matlin, Elaine Hendrix, Barry Newman, Robert Bailey Jr., John Ross Bowie,
  - Director: William Arntz, Betsy Chasse, and Mark Vicente
  - Here's an interesting film that is part Hollywood and part independent film documentary. It stars Marlee Matlin playing a divorced photographer who tumbles down a metaphysical rabbit hole; her mind-bending voyage through the worlds of science and metaphysical spirituality is mixed with actual interviews with some of the world's leading scientists, doctors, and metaphysical philosophers, including Ramtha (J.Z. Knight). The film will help you think outside the box and possibly see how your thoughts and addictions may very intensely create your reality. It includes lots of scientific data on the brain and how it works, quantum physics, and how these both affect our consciousness and our reality. Some critics claim some of the material is based on pseudoscience. The overriding theme is focused on "we create our own reality" and is considered to be influenced by the New Age world.

Movies are a great way to be educated and entertained. And these days, YouTube offers endless free material for traders and investors. You will notice that a few of the movies listed here have links to YouTube so you can access the content for free.

## Websites

Getting the most current information from a quick search on the internet is a perk of the technological world we live in. Here are some good resources for trading and investing content.

- *TradersCoach.com*
  - https://www.traderscoach.com/
  - Year Founded: 1998
  - Founder: Bennett McDowell
  - Contact: support@traderscoach.com
  - YouTube Channel: https://www.youtube.com/@TradersCoach
  - Description: A robust source for information on a variety of topics including technical analysis, Elliott Wave, trader's psychology, money management, and risk control. Offers a variety of software including the ART, Applied Reality Trading trading software, along with a suite of educational courses and live trading rooms. One-on-one coaching is available upon request. On their YouTube channel, you will find hundreds of educational videos on trading and investing including free weekly livestream events.
- *Wikipedia*
  - https://www.wikipedia.org/
  - Year Founded: 2001
  - Founder: Jimmy Wales and Larry Sanger
  - Description: This online encyclopedia offers free content that is written and maintained by a community of volunteers, known as *Wikipedians*. Surprisingly thorough and accurate, you'll find information on trading, investing, and just about everything. It is ranked fifth most visited website in the world by *Semrush* and is considered to be the largest and most read reference work in history. Available in 331 languages.
- *Investopedia*
  - https://www.investopedia.com/
  - Founded: 1999
  - Founder: Cory Wagner and Cory Janssen
  - Description: An excellent source of quality content on investing and trading, it offers fast answers to questions on everything from fundamental analysis, technical analysis, stocks, bonds, options, commodities, and what's in the current news.
- *Yahoo Finance*
  - https://www.finance.yahoo.com/
  - Founded: 1997

- Founder: David Filo and Jerry Yang
- YouTube Channel: https://www.youtube.com/@YahooFinance
- Description: This is the media property that is part of the Yahoo! Network. It provides financial news, data, and commentary including stock quotes, press releases, financial reports, and original content. You'll find charts on a variety of markets including stocks, ETFs, futures, currencies, bonds, and more.

- *Measuring Worth*
  - https://www.measuringworth.com/
  - Founded: 2006
  - Founder: Lawrence Officer and Samuel Williamson
  - Description: A free online service to calculate relative economic value over time using price indexes. An excellent source of data on everything from the DJIA closing prices from the first day of operation to the price of gold since the year 1257. The calculators on the site can pull up data sets on the DJIA, SP500, NASDAQ, GDP–US, CPI–US, Wages–US, GDP–UK, Interest Rates–US and UK, inflation rates, and more. The site is a wealth of incredibly useful information.

There are many more websites in addition to the ones listed here, and a quick search is sure to turn up sites that will best assist you on your journey.

# Knowledge Is Power

The idea that knowledge is power is not new; the phrase is often attributed to Francis Bacon from his *Meditationes Sacrae,* in 1597. Although, today, I wonder if we may be less and less interested in *true knowledge* (see Figure R3.3) because as a society, our attention span has lessened over time. The media gives us more sound bites than deep information because its focus groups reveal that is the current popular trend.

So we live in the information age, and yet, are we truly seeking to gain more knowledge? In the face of screen time and information overload, often there is a lack of genuine knowledge acquisition. Which brings us to our trading and investing power. Do your best to add *true knowledge* to your mindset and your approach and you are likely to add *human power* to your trading and investing approach.

**Figure R3.3**    MINI POSTER - KNOWLEDGE - Horace Mann, 1796–1859, was an American educational reformer famous for promoting public education. Known as *The Father of American Education,* he argued that universal public education was the best way to turn our children into disciplined and productive citizens. The son of a poor farmer, Mann had little education until he enrolled at Brown University at the age of 20. He inspired the nation to invest in their youth by giving them a path toward true knowledge. Quote from Horace Mann.
SOURCE: © TradersCoach.com

# About the Website: Online Information Portal

Thank you for purchasing this book. I've got so much information to share with you that we couldn't fit it all in the 500+ pages in the printed book. Lucky for you, my fabulous publisher John Wiley & Sons created a companion website that gives you even more valuable content and you can access it by visiting:

`https://www.wiley.com/go/mcdowell/theartoftrading`

Once you visit the website there's lots of material that supplements the printed pages in the book you have in your hands right now. For my loyal software clients, there's updated brand new user's manuals for all of the software you may already have.

And for the folks that are new to `TradersCoach.com` and to me, you'll discover record keeping forms, from Chapter 15, that you can download and start using today. Plus, you'll find my special software settings for the RSI and PPO indicators all located on this special Wiley website portal.

**Here's an outline of what's on the Wiley website:**

- **Website 1:** ART Software Manual

- **Website 2:** OWL, PTF, TLM and ERI Software Manuals

- **Website 3**: Scanning Software Manuals for the Turbo Scanner, Elliott Wave Scanner, Confirmer Scanner, and the Multiple Time Frame Scanner

- **Website 4:** Money Management Software Manuals for the Trader's Assistant Record Keeping software, Trade Size Calculator software, and the Risk Reward Calculator software

- **Website 5:** Record Keeping PDF Forms for the Trader's Assistant Record Keeping ledgers and trade posting cards and much more information on how to develop the best money management approach

- **Website 6:** RSI/PTF Special Software Settings

- **Website 7:** PPO/OWL Special Software Settings

If you have trouble accessing the website, be sure to contact my office at support@traderscoach.com and we'll get you connected.

## It's Time For The Next Step

Congratulations on reaching for your goals in your trading and investing! To keep you up to date with the ever changing developments in this exciting field, we have created a website that will be updated with new information, so that you always have access to what's happening in the current markets. We invite you to visit:

https://www.traderscoach.com/book

**Figure Website**—MINI POSTER—CONGRATULATIONS!—Here at TradersCoach.com we are thrilled to see that you have come this far, congratulations! We are dedicated to helping you reach your trading and investing goals. Which is why we have created a living breathing website portal that will be updated with current information for you to access.

Visit us today at https://www.traderscoach.com/book

# Glossary

There is nothing better than having a thorough dictionary of terms when you are studying an important topic like trading and investing. Which is why I've focused so much effort on making this glossary as complete as possible. The plan is that when you are searching for the meaning of a new subject, word, or acronym, you can go to this glossary and find it alphabetically in a few seconds.

**1B:** See *ART one-bar reversal.*

**2B:** See *ART two-bar reversal.*

**accumulation distribution (A/C):** Momentum indicator that attempts to gauge supply and demand by determining whether there is accumulating (buying) or distributing (selling) of a certain financial instrument by identifying divergences between price and volume.

**annual percentage rate (APR):** The periodic rate times the number of periods in a year. Example: a 5% quarterly return has an APR of 20%.

**Applied Reality Trading® (ART®):**   Applied Reality Trading is a technical analysis system developed by Bennett A. McDowell that focuses on trading the realities of the markets. The primary signals included in this system are the Pyramid Trading Points P-PTP and MP-PTP along with the reversal bars 1B and 2B. Software is available from TradersCoach.com®.

**APR:**   See *annual percentage rate.*

**ART® bear price bar:**   When prices close on the *lower* half of the bar, it is a bearish price bar. The bar is defined by the relation between the *close* and the price bar interval. The bears are in control at the close of the price bar.

**ART® bull price bar:**   When prices close on the *upper* half of the bar, it is bullish. The bar is defined by the relation between the close and the price bar interval. The bulls are in control at the close of the price bar.

**ART® elongated price bar:**   This price bar is at least one-third longer than the previous three to five price bars.

**ART® inside price bar:**   A compressed price bar forming directly after the signal bar in a 2B reversal. It can be used to aggressively enter an ART® reversal trade.

**ART® neutral price bar:**   On this price bar, the open and the close are at the 50% point on the bar when it closes. Both bulls and bears are in stalemate at the close of the price bar.

**ART® one-bar reversal (1B):**   This scalp signal identifies an exact entry and exit. It can also be used for scaling in and scaling out of trends and for counter-trend trading.

**ART® signal price bar:**   The price bar used for a trade entry when using the ART® reversals. It is designated with a 1B or 2B directly above or below the price bar.

**ART® two-bar reversal (2B):**   This scalp signal identifies an exact entry and exit. It can also be used for scaling in and scaling out of trends and for counter-trend trading.

**ask price:**   Also known as the offer. The price a seller is willing to accept.

**ATR:** See *average true range*.

**at-the-money:** An option is at-the-money if the strike price of the option is equal to the market price of the underlying asset.

**average true range (ATR):** Helps determine a market's volatility over a given period. It is calculated by taking an average of the true ranges over a set number of previous periods.

**bar chart:** Consists of multiple price bars, with each bar illustrating how the price of an instrument moved over a specified period. Each bar shows the open, high, low, and close (OHLC) of each price bar.

**basis:** This is your cost of the asset. If you pay $10 per share for a stock and $1 per share for commission, your basis is $11 per share.

**bear:** Someone who believes prices will decline and is pessimistic about future market returns.

**bear market:** A market characterized by prolonged broad declining prices. The downturn in price is in excess of 20%.

**bid–ask spread:** The difference between the bid and ask. The spread narrows or widens according to the supply and demand for the security being traded.

**bid price:** The price a buyer is willing to pay.

**black box system:** This is a 100% mechanical system that requires absolutely NO discretion.

**Black Monday:** Refers to Monday, October 19, 1987, when the DJIA fell 508 points after sharp drops the previous week.

**Black Thursday:** The Wall Street Crash of 1929 began on Thursday October 24, 1929, when the DJIA lost 11% of its value at the opening bell on very heavy trading.

**blue chip company:** A large, nationally recognized, financially sound firm with a long track record. Examples: General Electric and IBM.

**bond market:** Also known as the debt, credit, or fixed income market, is a financial market where participants buy and sell debt securities usually in the form of bonds.

**bracketed market:**   Also known as a consolidating, range-bound, drunk, choppy, sleepy, channeled, sideways, or non-trending market. When a market is bracketed, it is stuck in a price range between an identifiable resistance and support level. About 70% of all markets are bracketed, and 30% are trending.

**breakout:**   A sharp change in price movement after the market has traded sideways for at least 20 price bars. This is beyond a previous high (or low) or outside the boundaries of a preceding price bracket.

**broker:**   An individual or online firm that is paid a commission for executing customer orders; an agent specializing in stocks, futures, forex, ETFs, bonds, commodities, or options and must be registered with the exchange where the securities are traded.

**bull:**   Someone who believes that prices will rise and is optimistic about future market returns.

**bull market:**   A market characterized by prolonged broad rising prices. Over 70% of historic periods have been bull markets.

**call option:**   An options contract with the right to buy a specific number of shares of a stock at a specified price (the strike price) on or before a specific expiration date, regardless of the underlying stock's current market price. A call option writer sells the right to a buyer.

**cancel order:**   An order that cancels an existing order already placed.

**candlestick chart:**   Just like a bar chart that shows the open, high, low and close, OHLC, but is a more visual representation of price movement. The wick is a thin line that shows the price excursion above and below the body.

**cash per share:**   The amount of cash divided by the total number of common stock shares outstanding for a given stock

**CBOE:**   See *Chicago Board of Options Exchange.*

**CBOT:**   See *Chicago Board of Trade.*

**central bank:**   The institution in each country that sets monetary policy, prints money, manages reserves, and attempts to control inflation. In the United States, the central bank is the Federal Reserve System.

**CFTC:**   See *Commodity Futures Trading Commission.*

**channeling market:**   See *bracketed market.*

**chart:**   A graph that depicts the price movement of a given market. The most common type of chart is the bar chart, which denotes each interval's open, high, low, and close (OHLC) for a given market with a single price bar. Other types of charts include candlestick, line, Renko, tick, volume, Heikin Ashi, and point and figure (P&F).

**chart analysis:**   The study of price charts in an effort to find patterns that in the past preceded price advances or declines in a financial market.

**charting platform:**   A computer platform designed to create charts that plot price, volume, and momentum information on a graph.

**Chicago Board of Options Exchange (CBOE):**   Located in Chicago, it is the largest US options exchange and was established by the Chicago Board of Trade in 1973.

**Chicago Board of Trade (CBOT):**   Established in 1848, the CBOT is a leading exchange for futures and options on futures.

**Chicago Mercantile Exchange (CME):**   Founded in 1898 as the Chicago Butter and Egg Board, this is an American financial exchange based in Chicago.

**Chicago Mercantile Group (CME Group):**   The world's largest and most diverse exchange. Formed by the 2007 merger of the Chicago Mercantile Exchange (CME) and the Chicago Board of Trade (CBOT).

**close:**   The period at the end of the trading session.

**CME:**   See *Chicago Mercantile Exchange.*

**CME Group:**   See *Chicago Mercantile Group.*

**commission:**   Fees paid to a brokerage house to execute a transaction.

**commodities:**   Physical goods such as grains, meats, and metals that are traded on a futures exchange.

**Commodity Futures Trading Commission (CFTC):**   The US government agency of the futures industry established in 1974.

**CONF:**   See *Trade Confirmer Scanner.*

**consumer price index (CPI):**   Issued by the Bureau of Labor Statistics, this figure is a measure of inflation and looks at the relative change in prices of a basket of consumer products and services.

**contract:**   A single unit of a commodity or future, which is similar to shares in stocks.

**correction:**   A short reverse in prices during a longer market trend.

**countertrend trade:**   A strategy where a trader attempts to make small gains through a series of trades against the current trend.

**cover:**   To liquidate an existing position (such as sell if one is long; or buy if one is short).

**covered call:**   To sell a call option. At the same time, you own the same number of shares represented by the option in the underlying stock.

**covered put:**   To sell a put option. At the same time, you are holding a short position in the underlying stock.

**CPI:**   See *consumer price index.*

**cryptocurrency:**   Also known as crypto, this is a digital currency that allows people to make payments to each other online without the need for a bank or financial institution.

**data:**   Live streaming price and volume market data provided by data providers either in real time by the minute, or at the end of a trading day.

**day order:**   Order that is in force until the end of the day's trading session.

**day trade:** A trade that is liquidated on the same day it is initiated.

**debt-to-equity ratio:** Ratio demonstrating an institution's debt relative to its equity.

**decimal:** Increment of movement in the stock market.

**deflation:** A drop in average product and services price levels, usually caused by excessive tightening of money supply. Deflation can lead to reduced economic demand and higher unemployment.

**depression:** An economic depression is a sustained period of economic decline that sees a nation's GDP drop at least 10% and is accompanied by a rise in unemployment.

**discretionary trader:** A trader who makes decisions based on his own analysis of the market rather than in response to signals generated by a computerized black box system.

**disinflation:** The slowing growth of average product and services price levels. This can be thought of as the slowing of inflation.

**divergence:** The failure of a market or indicator to follow suit when a related market or indicator sets a new high or low. Some analysts look for divergences as a signal of impending market tops and bottoms.

**diversification:** Trading or investing in a variety of markets and sectors to reduce risk. Don't put all your eggs in one basket!

**dividend:** A payment made to stockholders, usually quarterly, out of a firm's current or retained earnings.

**DJIA:** See *Dow Jones Industrial Average.*

**double witching:** The day when both options and futures expire.

**doubling down:** Adding on to a losing position.

**Dow Jones Industrial Average (DJIA):** A price-weighted index of 30 blue-chip U.S. stocks.

**downtrend:** Declining prices in a given market.

**drawdown:** Decrease in the value of an account due to closed losing trades, or paper losses with a decline in value of open positions.

**earnings per share (EPS):** A firm's total after-tax net earnings divided by the number of common shares outstanding.

**earnings to price ratio (E/P):** Ratio of a company's earnings per share to its share price.

**edge:** See *payoff ratio.*

**Elliott wave analysis:** A method of market analysis based on the theories of Ralph Nelson Elliott. An Elliott wave sequence is made up of five waves in every trend. Waves one, three, and five are impulsive waves that move in the direction of the dominant trend. Waves two and four are corrective waves.

**Elliott Wave Scanner (EW):** Scans for Elliott Wave 3 and Elliott Wave 5. Software is available from TradersCoach.com®.

**elongated price bar:** A price bar that is at least one-third longer than the previous three to five price bards.

**Emotional Reader Index (ERI):** Identifies fear and greed signals in the market that can act as reversals. This software is available from TradersCosch.com®.

**entry:** The point at which you place or open your trade or investment. This is the opposite of your exit.

**E/P:** See *earnings-to-price ratio.*

**EPS:** See *earnings per share.*

**equities markets:** Stock markets.

**equity:** The total dollar value of an account.

**equity curve:** Value of an account over time, illustrated in a graph.

**ERI:** See *Emotional Reader Index.*

**ETF:** See *exchange traded fund.*

**EW:** See *Elliott Wave Scanner.*

**exchange:** A financial exchange is a marketplace where traders can buy and sell financial instruments such as securities, commodities and derivatives. Some well-known exchanges are the NYSE and Nasdaq.

**exchange traded fund (ETF):** A security that tracks a specific index, equity category, or other basket of assets but is traded on an exchange like a single stock.

**exercise an option:** To buy or sell a call or put option by the expiration date on the options contract.

**exit:** The point at which you close your trade or investment. This is the opposite of your entry.

**expiration date:** The last day on which an option may be exercised.

**Fed:** See *Federal Reserve System.*

**Federal Open Market Committee (FOMC):** A 12-member committee responsible for setting credit and interest rate policy for the Federal Reserve System.

**Federal Reserve Board of Governors:** Is the governing arm of the Federal Reserve System, which seeks to regulate the economy through the implementation of monetary policy. The seven members of the board of governors are appointed by US presidents to serve 14-year terms.

**Federal Reserve System (Fed):** The US central banking system, responsible for regulating the flow of money and credit.

**Fibonacci retracement:** The concept that retracements of prior trends will often approximate 38.2% and 61.8%—numbers derived from the Fibonacci sequence.

**Fibonacci sequence:** A sequence of numbers that begins with 1, 1 and progresses to infinity, with each number in the sequence equal to the sum of the preceding two numbers. Thus, the initial numbers in the sequence would be 1, 1, 2, 3, 5, 8, 13, 21, 34, 55, 89, and so on.

**fill:** The price at which an order is executed is considered a fill. For example, if a trade was placed at $32.00 and filled at $32.25 the fill price would be $32.25.

**Financial Industry Regulatory Authority (FINRA):** Agency that oversees US broker dealers. It is the successor to the *National Association of Securities Dealers*, NASD. FINRA was established in 2007.

**financial instrument:** Any form of funding medium.

**FINRA:** See *Financial Industry Regulatory Authority*.

**flat:** When you are not in the market with a live position or when you close out all your positions before the end of the trading day you are considered flat.

**FOMC:** See *Federal Open Market Committee*.

**forecast:** An attempt to predict future market behavior often using ungrounded assessments such as MACD, stochastic, and Elliott waves.

**forex:** See *foreign exchange market*.

**foreign exchange market (forex):** Exists wherever one currency is traded for another.

**fractal:** A geometric figure, each part of which has the same statistical character as the whole.

**fundamental analysis:** The use of economic data and news data to analyze financial markets. For example, fundamental analysis of a currency might focus on such items as relative inflation rates, interest rates, economic growth rates, and political factors. Fundamental analysis is often contrasted with technical analysis, and some investors and traders use a combination of the two.

**futures market:** A financial market where traders buy and sell futures contracts, which are agreements to buy or sell a commodity or security at a specific price and date in the future.

**gap:** A price period in which no trades occur. For example, if a market that has previously traded at a high of $20 per share opens at $22 on the following day. The price zone between $20 and $22 is referred to as a gap-up. If the price zone were to go from $22 to $20 it would be a gap-down.

**GDP:** See *gross domestic product*.

**Globex®:** Today the CME Globex® trading system operates at the heart of CME. Proposed in 1987, it was introduced in 1992 as the first global fully electronic trading platform for futures contracts.

**good till canceled (GTC):** This order remains open with a broker until executed or canceled, regardless of the number of trading days.

**good till date (GTD):** This order remains open with a broker until it gets filled or until the close of the market on the date specified.

**Great Depression:** A severe global economic downturn from 1929 to 1939 that was triggered by the stock market crash on Wall Street, also known as Black Thursday. It is estimated that between 1929 and 1932 the worldwide GDP fell by 15%, which to date is the largest decline in history.

**gross domestic product (GDP):** The monetary value of all products and services produced in a country over a certain period.

**grounded assessments:** Trading and investing rules based on reality, such as price and volume.

**GTC:** See *good till cancelled.*

**GTD:** See *good till date.*

**hedge:** To reduce risk in an investment or trade by offsetting it with another investment or trade.

**hedge fund:** A managed portfolio of investments that is generally unregulated (unlike a mutual fund) and may invest in any highly speculative markets, including options.

**hyperbolic move:** A sharp and significant move to the upside or downside of your position. You might decide to *scale out* of a position to lock in profit if this type of move occurs.

**index:** The weighted average of a number of stocks that are bundled into one index. Examples are the DJIA, and the S&P 500.

**inflation:** Rate of increase in average product and service price levels. Different indexes use different baskets of products and services to compute the average prices. A popular index is the Consumer Price Index.

**instrument:**   See *financial instrument*.

**in-the-money:**   When an option's current market price is above the strike price of a call, or below the strike price of a put. An in-the-money option would produce a profit, if exercised.

**intra-day time frame:**   A shorter time frame ranging from the 1-minute to the 60-minute time frame, used by day traders in making their entry and exit decisions.

**investing:**   The use of financial instruments to invest savings for future gain.

**investor:**   Generally, uses a buy-and-hold approach using weekly and monthly charts to evaluate the market.

**Kelly formula:**   See *optimal f formula*.

**large cap:**   Refers to the size of a firm's market capitalization. Any firm with a market cap greater than $10 billion is referred to as a large cap.

**leverage:**   The ability to control a dollar amount of a financial instrument greater than the amount of personal capital employed. This ability is obtained by using borrowed money.

**limit order:**   This is an order in which you can set the maximum price you want to pay for your purchase, or a minimum price you will accept as a seller.

**liquidity:**   The degree to which a given market is liquid. When volume is high, there is usually a lot of liquidity. Low liquidity in markets can result in poor fills.

**long:**   A position established with a buy order, which profits in a rising price market.

**long call:**   To buy a call option.

**long put:**   To buy a put option.

**MA:**   See *moving average*.

**MACD:**   See *moving average convergence/divergence*.

**margin:** To borrow money from a financial provider (broker or bank) to purchase certain financial instruments.

**margin call:** A Federal Reserve Board and financial service provider requirement that you deposit additional funds or sell some of your holdings to increase the equity in your margin account if it has fallen below the minimum requirement.

**market:** There are many financial markets including the stock, futures, options, forex, and crypto markets, to name a few.

**market capitalization:** Also known as market cap, it is the total value of a publicly traded company's outstanding common shares. It is also used to quantify a financial market exchange's size.

**market cycles:** There are four major market cycles: trending, bracketed, breakout, and corrective.

**market maker:** A broker, bank, or firm such as Goldman Sachs, which buys or sells a security, currency, or futures contract.

**market order:** Order to execute a purchase or sale for the best price available at the time the order is received. This is the simplest and most common order.

**MFI:** See *money flow index.*

**mid cap:** Refers to the size of a firm's market capitalization. Any firm with a market cap between $2 billion and $10 billion is referred to as a mid cap.

**Minor Pyramid Trading Point® (MP-PTP):** An MP directly above or below a Pyramid Trading Point (triangle) indicates a correction in the dominant trend. It can be used for counter trend trading, scaling in and scaling out of a trend, and for scalping.

**momentum:** How fast prices in the markets move over time.

**money flow index (MFI):** A volume-weighted momentum indicator that measures the strength of money flowing in and out of a financial instrument.

**money management:** The use of various methods of risk control in trading and investing. These methods include (1) using proper trade size; (2) not risking more than 2% of your risk account on any one trade; and (3) diversifying your trading or investing account over a number of markets and sectors. Also known as *risk management*.

**moving average (MA):**    An average of data for a certain period. It moves because for each calculation, we use the latest periods' data. By definition, a moving average lags the market.

**moving average convergence/divergence (MACD):**    This is an indicator developed by Gerald Appel. It is calculated by subtracting the 26-period exponential moving average of a given financial instrument from its 12-period exponential moving average.

**MP-PTP:**    See *Minor Pyramid Trading Point*.

**MULTI:**    See *Multiple Time Frame Scanner*.

**multiple time frame analysis:**    Looks at charts of the same financial instrument across multiple time frames to see if the time frames agree or disagree on trend direction.

**Multiple Time Frame Scanner (MULTI):**    Scans to identify financial instruments that have trend alignment on multiple time frames. Software is available from TradersCoach.com®.

**narrowing the spread:**    Reducing the difference between the bid and ask prices of a financial instrument.

**NASD:**    See *National Association of Securities Dealers*.

**NASDAQ:**    See *National Association of Securities Dealers Automated Quotations System*.

**National Association of Securities Dealers (NASD):**    A self-regulatory organization established in 1938 as a result of the Maloney Act. In 1996, the SEC criticized the NASD for putting its interests as the operator of NASDAQ ahead of its responsibilities as the regulator. In 2007 NASD merged with the NYSE, and FINRA was created.

**National Association of Securities Dealers Automated Quotations System (NASDAQ):**    The NASDAQ is an American stock market located in New York City that is heavily focused on technology stocks. It was founded in 1971 by the NASD, who divested themselves of it in a series of sales in 2000 and 2001.

**National Futures Association (NFA):** A self-regulatory organization that works to protect investors and regulates the financial derivatives market in the United States. It was created by the CFTC in 1982.

**New York Mercantile Exchange (NYMEX):** Owned and operated by CME Group, this is the world's largest physical commodity futures exchange, located in New York City. Its two principal divisions are the NYMEX and the New York Commodities Exchange (COMEX), which were once independent companies but are now merged.

**New York Stock Exchange (NYSE):** Known as the *Big Board*, this is a New York City-based stock exchange. It is the largest stock exchange in the world as measured by market capitalization.

**NFA:** See *National Futures Association.*

**NYMEX:** See *New York Mercantile Exchange.*

**NYSE:** See *New York Stock Exchange.*

**OBV:** See *on balance volume.*

**OHLC:** This is an acronym for open, high, low, and close price bar activity.

**on balance volume (OBV):** This method, developed by Joe Granville, is used to detect momentum, the calculation of which relates volume to price change. It attempts to detect when a stock, bond, etc. is being accumulated by a large number of buyers or sold by many sellers.

**open interest:** In futures markets, the total number of open and short positions are equal. This total is called the open interest. When a contract month first begins trading, the open interest is zero. It builds to a peak, and then declines as positions are closed getting closer to expiration.

**open order:** An order to buy or sell a financial instrument that remains in effect until it is either canceled by the customer or executed.

**open outcry pit:** Trade orders are physically communicated with verbal and hand signal communication in stock, option, and futures exchanges by floor traders. Before 2010, open outcry was the primary form of trade execution but has increasingly been replaced by electronic trading, such as the Globex, which was first introduced in 1992.

**optimal *f* formula:** Formula that calculates the optimum fraction of capital, or percent of capital, to risk on any one trade based on win ratio and pay off ratio. It is sometimes referred to as the Kelly formula.

**optimization:** Refers to adjusting trading software parameters with the intention of creating a better outcome with regard to net profit.

**Optimum Wave Locator (OWL):** Identifies either a bullish or bearish trend in the markets and identifies wave 3 in the Elliott Wave pattern. Software is available from TradersCoach.com®.

**option:** The right to buy or sell an underlying asset at a fixed price up to some specified date in the future. The right to buy is a *call option*, and the right to sell is a *put option*.

**options market:** An open market to trade options.

**order flow:** The flow that an order takes from the moment when a trader places the order to when the order is filled and is complete.

**oscillator:** A technical analysis tool that is a trend indicator for discovering short-term overbought and oversold conditions. Most oscillators go from 0 to 100.

**out-of-the-money:** When an option's current market price is below the strike price of a call or above the strike price of a put.

**overbought/oversold indicator:** Attempts to define when prices have risen (or fallen) too far, too fast, and are vulnerable to a reaction in the opposite direction.

**OWL:** See *Optimum Wave Locator*.

**paper gain:** Unrealized capital gain on securities held based on a comparison of the current market price to the original cost.

**paper loss:** Unrealized capital loss on securities held based on a comparison of the current market price to the original cost.

**paper trading:**   Also known as sim, or simulated trading, this is a way to practice buying and selling financial assets like stocks, options, or currencies without using real money.

**Pattern Day Trader Rule (PDT):**   According to FINRA, if you make four or more day-trades over the course of any five business days, and those trades account for more than 6% of your account activity over the period, your margin account will be flagged as a pattern day trader account. Then you will be required to maintain a minimum balance of US$25,000 in the flagged account on a permanent basis.

**pattern recognition:**   Technical analysis that focusses on finding price and volume patterns that signal changes in a trend.

**payoff ratio:**   Average winning trade divided by average losing trade equals the payoff ratio. For example, a 2-to-1 payoff ratio means that you are winning two dollars for every one dollar you lose. Also known as reward-to-risk ratio.

**PDT:**   See *Pattern Day Trader Rule.*

**P/E ratio:**   See *price-to-earnings ratio.*

**percentage in point (PIP):**   The increment of movement in the forex market.

**percentage price oscillator (PPO) histogram:**   This is a technical momentum indicator that shows the relationship between two moving averages in percentage terms. The moving averages are a 26-period and a 12-period exponential moving average (EMA). The plot is presented as a histogram so that centerline crossovers and divergences are easily identifiable

**PIP:**   See *percentage in point.*

**position:**   Your financial stake in a given financial instrument or market.

**position size:**   See *trade size.*

**position trade:**   A trade using daily and weekly charts on which to base decisions which holds positions for days, weeks, or months.

**PPO:**   See *percentage price oscillator histogram.*

**P-PTP:**   See *Primary Pyramid Trading Point.*

**Precision Trend Filter (PTF):**   Determines with a 75% accuracy if there will be higher highs or lower lows for any financial instrument. Software is available from TradersCoach.com®.

**price bar:**   A price bar represents the high, low, open, and close (OHLC) behavior in a measured time interval. Price bars can represent different time frames (intervals) such as 1-minute, 5-minute, daily, weekly, and so on.

**price gap:**   See *gap.*

**price-to-earnings (P/E) ratio:**   The current price of a stock divided by the company's annual earnings.

**Primary Pyramid Trading Point (P-PTP):**   This ART® signal indicates entries and exits into a primary trend trade or investment.

**prop firm:**   Used by day traders enabling them to day trade funded accounts with a value of $25,000 to $300,000 and to receive regular payouts for as much as 90% of their profits.

**psychology:**   The *trader's mindset* is attained when you have mastered your financial psychology. Some challenges in developing this are overcoming fear, greed, ego, and anger when trading and investing.

**PTF:**   See *Precision Trend Filter.*

**PTP:**   See *Pyramid Trading Point.*

**PTP apex:**   The apex points in the direction of the primary trend with a P-PTP pyramid and is at the point of the pyramid. It tells you where to enter. In the case of an MP-PTP pyramid, the apex is pointing in the opposite direction of the dominant trend and signals a correction.

**PTP base leg:**   The base leg is the flat base of a pyramid and tells you where to set a stop-loss exit when looking at a P-PTP pyramid.

**PTP confirmed:**   When the market moves beyond the PTP apex in the direction of the trend on a P-PTP pyramid (triangle), the dominant trend will be confirmed. At that moment, the triangle will turn either *green* or *red* depending on whether it is a bull or bear pyramid. In the case of an MP-PTP pyramid, when the market moves beyond the PTP apex in the direction of the correction, the pyramid will be confirmed and will turn either *green* or *red* depending on whether it is a bull or bear pyramid.

**PTP MinScore:** This adjustable setting on the ART® software determines the number of pyramids you will see on your chart. You can customize the software to give you fewer pyramids that are higher probability or to give you more pyramids that are lower probability.

**PTP potential:** When the pyramid is potential, it will be *yellow.* Once the market moves beyond the apex of the pyramid, it will be confirmed and will turn either *green* or *red,* depending on whether it is a bull or bear. If the market does not confirm the pyramid by exceeding the apex, the yellow pyramid will disappear.

**PTP voided:** If a potential *yellow* pyramid is not confirmed, it will be voided and will disappear.

**put option:** An options contract with the right to sell a security at a specified exercise price, the strike price, on or before a specific expiration date. A put option writer sells the right to a buyer. If the option exercises, the buyer puts the stock to the writer, and the writer must buy it.

**Pyramid Trading Point (PTP):** ART® trend trading signal that identifies exact entries and exits.

**rally:** An upward movement of prices.

**reality-based trading:** When trading and investing in reality, traders focus on the current moment and are free of opinions. Reality-based trading and investing involves looking at what is real in the market, such as *price* and *volume.*

**recession:** A contraction in the business cycle, usually manifesting in slow or negative GDP growth. Two consecutive quarters of negative GDP growth indicate a recession.

**relative strength indicator (RSI):** An indicator developed by J. Wells Wilder, Jr., used to ascertain overbought and oversold conditions.

**resistance level:** In technical analysis, a price area at which a rising market is expected to encounter increased selling pressure sufficient to stall or reverse the advance

**retracement:** A price movement in the opposite direction of the previous price movement. A retracement is usually a price correction.

**reward-to-risk ratio:** See *payoff ratio*.

**risk:** The potential cost of losing money on an investment or trade.

**risk control:** See *money management*.

**risk of ruin:** Is the probability that a trader is likely to lose so much capital that it would be impossible to recover the losses.

**risk-to-reward ratio:** See *payoff ratio*.

**RSI:** See *relative strength indicator*.

**SAR:** See *stop and reverse*.

**scaling in:** Refers to adding onto your current trade position to increase your *trade size*.

**scaling out:** Exiting a portion of your position when your trading rules tell you to. This is a technique that is effective in reducing stress and locking in profit.

**scalper:** A trader who seeks to profit from small price fluctuations.

**scanners:** Software that can quickly search for specific criteria in a variety of markets quickly and effectively. TradersCoach.com® scanners available are the Turbo, Elliott Wave, Trade Confirmer, and Multiple Time Frame scanners.

**seasonality:** Consistent, predictable changes in price during the year due to production cycles or demand cycles for a variety of markets.

**SEC:** See *Securities and Exchange Commission*.

**sector:**   Used to characterize a group of securities that are similar with respect to maturity, type, rating, and/or industry.

**securities:**   See *stock*.

**Securities and Exchange Commission (SEC):**   The US federal agency that is designed to promote full public disclosure and protect the investing public against fraudulent practices in the securities markets. It was established in 1934 as a result of the Securities Exchange Act.

**set-up:**   When your trading rules identify certain criteria that must be present prior to entering the market.

**share:**   A unit of measure for financial instruments in publicly traded companies including stocks, mutual funds, and ETFs.

**shareholder:**   A person or entity that owns shares or equity in a corporation.

**short:**   When you sell before you have bought the item, you are *shorting* the market. This position is implemented with a sale, which profits from a declining price market.

**short call:**   When you sell a *call option* that you don't already own.

**short put:**   To sell a *put option*.

**signal bar:**   A price bar within a pattern that signals a trade entry is setting up. It must complete and closed before it can be called a signal bar.

**simulated trading:**   See *paper trading*.

**slippage:**   The difference in price between what you expect to pay for a trade and what you actually pay. For example, if you attempt to buy at 20 and you end up buying at 20.5, you have a half point of slippage.

**small cap:**   Refers to the relative size of a firm's market capitalization. Any firm with a market cap under $2 billion is referred to as small cap.

**S&P:**   See *Standard & Poor's Corporation*.

**split:**   The division of outstanding shares of a corporation into a larger or smaller number of shares. For example, in a three-for-one split, each holder of 100 shares before would now have 300 shares.

**spread:**   The difference between the bid price and the ask price.

**Standard & Poor's Corporation (S&P):**   A company well known for its rating of stocks and bonds according to investment risk (the Standard & Poor's rating) and for compiling the Standard & Poor's Index.

**stochastic:**   An overbought-oversold indicator, made popular by George Lane, based on the observation that prices close near the high of the day in an uptrend, and in a downtrend, they close near the low of the day.

**stock:**   A financial instrument that signifies an ownership position in a corporation. Stock is the capital raised by a corporation through the issuance of shares.

**stock market:**   This is a market for the trading and investing in company stock that is a security publicly listed on a stock exchange.

**stock symbol:**   Standard abbreviation used to refer to a stock such as AAPL, IBM, or MSFT. Each symbol is unique and is made up of anywhere from one to five letters.

**stop and reverse (SAR):**   Used to close the current trade and immediately open a new trade in the opposite direction.

**stop-loss exit:**   Also referred to as a stop, initial stop, or trailing stop. It is the designated price level where you have determined you must exit the trade if it goes against you.

**stopped out:When a trade or investment goes beyond the stop-loss exit, the trade will be closed.**

**straddle:**   The purchase or sale of an equal number of puts and calls with the same terms at the same time.

**strike price:**   This is the fixed price of an option.

**supply = demand:**   When supply equals demand, both the seller and buyer agree on price but disagree on value.

**support level:**   In technical analysis, a price area at which a falling market is expected to encounter increased buying support sufficient to stall or reverse the decline.

**swing trading:**   Short-term trading approach designed to capture quick moves in the market.

**symbol:**   See *stock symbol.*

**target zone:**   The price level you expect your trade to reach.

**technical analysis:**   The use of price patterns to determine entries and exits with the goal of making a profit. Technical traders and investors use charts to detect these patterns in the market. Technical analysis is often contrasted with fundamental analysis, while some investors and traders use a combination of the two.

**The Trader's Assistant:**   A trade posting and recordkeeping system to keep you organized by recording all trade information on trade posting cards and trade ledgers. Software is available from TradersCoach.com®.

**tick:**   The increment of movement and price fluctuation up or down in a market is called a tick. The value of a tick movement will vary from market to market.

**ticker symbol:**   See *stock symbol.*

**time frame:**   Represented by a price bar interval time such as 2-minute chart, daily chart, and so on.

**TLM:**   See *Trend Line Master.*

**trade:**   When a buyer and seller agree on price but disagree on value a trade occurs. It is the point where one item is traded for another.

**Trade Confirmer Scanner (CONF):**   Scanner that searches for the criteria of the OWL, PTF, and TLM indicators. When these indicators are in alignment, a trade is confirmed. Software is available from TradersCoach.com®.

**trader's mindset:**   See *psychology.*

**trade size:** Also known as *position size*. The size of your trade or investment represented by the number of units (shares, contracts, etc.) of the market you are trading or investing in.

**Trade Size Calculator (TSC):** Risk control software to determine the maximum *trade size* based on variables such as percent risk and equity account size. Software is available from TradersCoach.com®.

**trading:** Opening a position in a financial market, either long or short, with the plan of closing it out at a substantial profit. If the trade goes against you, the plan is to cut losses quickly by using effective risk control.

**trailing stop:** This stop-loss exit moves, as the trade becomes profitable, locking in profit in either a long or short trend.

**trend channel:** Identifies upward or downward sloping trends by placing trend lines on the highs and lows of the channel.

**trend exhaustion:** When a trend ends, it has reached trend exhaustion and is likely to reverse and move in the opposite direction.

**trending market:** Where prices tend to move in a strong direction either up or down. About 70% of all markets are bracketed, and 30% are trending.

**Trend Line Master (TLM):** Identifies bullish and bearish trends and automatically draws trend line on the chart. Software is available from TradersCoach.com®.

**trend trader:** Trades in the direction of the overall trend.

**TSC:** See *Trade Size Calculator.*

**TURBO:** See *Turbo Scanner.*

**Turbo Scanner (TURBO):** Scanner that searches for all of the ART® software criteria including P-PTP, MP-PTP, 1B Reversal, 2B Reversal, Unconfirmed PTPs, plus bracketed markets and breakouts. Software is available from TradersCoach.com®.

**ungrounded assessments:**   Trading and investing rules that try to forecast or predict the market. MACD, stochastic, and Elliott wave are ungrounded assessments.

**uptrend:**   A general tendency for rising prices in a given market.

**VIX:**   See *Volatility Index.*

**volatility:**   Refers to the range of prices in a given period. A highly volatile market has a large range in daily prices, whereas a low-volatility market has a small range of daily prices.

**Volatility Index (VIX):**   The CBOE Volatility Index represents the market's expectations for the relative strength of near-term price changes of the S&P 500 Index. It generates a projection of volatility.

**volume:**   The total number of shares or contracts traded during a given period.

**whipsaw:**   A price pattern characterized by repeated, abrupt reversals in trend. The term is often used to describe losses resulting from a choppy or trendless market.

**win ratio:**   Number of winning trades divided by the total number of trades equals the win ratio. Example a win ratio of 60% means you have 60 winning trades out of 100.

"Are We
Better Off Today
Than We Were
Yesterday?"

**TradersCoach.com** ®
Trade With The Pros !

Quote From: Jean McDowell

**Figure Glossary**   MINI POSTER — BETTER OFF — As you develop your
trading and investing skills, ask yourself "are your skills and profits better off
today than yesterday?" Even if you are a dollar up today over yesterday, that
is a victory. Because steady and consistent small wins and improvements lead to
huge long term wins. Have gratitude for and celebrate every positive step in your
journey. By enjoying the process and repeatedly creating wins you will establish
a winner's mindset. Quote from Jean McDowell.
SOURCE: @ TradersCoach.com, Inc.

# About the Author

**Bennett A. McDowell**, founder of *TradersCoach.com®*, began his financial career on Wall Street and later became a "Registered Securities Broker" and "Financial Advisor" for Prudential Securities and Morgan Stanley. As a financial advisor, Bennett's niche was "Active Trading" and "Investing" for a community of high net worth clients using his own proprietary trading system. This system later became known as the *Applied Reality Trading®*, or the *ART®*, system.

In answer to numerous requests for Bennett to share his successful trading and investing techniques he brought the ART® software to the public in the year 2003. Today the *ART®* system is used in over 85 countries around the world by sophisticated hedge fund managers, individual investors and active traders alike.

An expert in technical analysis and complex trading platforms, Bennett speaks at trade shows including the *Trader's Expo* and writes articles for leading trading publications including *Technical Analysis of Stocks & Commodities* magazine. Internationally recognized as a leader in trading education, Bennett teaches trading to students worldwide through his company *TradersCoach.com®*.

McDowell has written three bestselling books published by John Wiley & Sons, *The ART® of Trading*, *A Trader's Money Management System* and *Survival Guide for Traders*. Plus, his *Elliott Wave Techniques Simplified* book, published by McGraw Hill has helped traders and investors around the world to master this sometimes challenging topic and has become a fan favorite.

Bennett resides in Tucson, Arizona with his wife and two children. He can be reached by E-Mail via Support@TradersCoach.com.

The author Bennett McDowell in his trading office taking a break between trades. SOURCE: @TradersCoach.com.

# Index

Note: Page references with f and t refer to figures and tables.